Ancient Egypt in The Metropolitan Museum Journal

ANCIENT EGYPT IN THE METROPOLITAN MUSEUM JOURNAL

Volumes 1–11 (1968–1976)

Articles by

CYRIL ALDRED
HENRY G. FISCHER
HERMAN DE MEULENAERE
BIRGIT NOLTE
EDNA R. RUSSMANN

The Metropolitan Museum of Art

1977

Composition by The Press of A. Colish
Printed by The Stinehour Press

Third Printing, 1996

Library of Congress Cataloging in Publication Data

Main entry under title:

Ancient Egypt in the Metropolitan Museum journal, volumes 1-11 (1968-1976) articles.

Includes bibliographical references and index.
Egypt.
1. Art, Egyptian—Addresses, essays, lectures.
2. Inscriptions, Hieroglyphic—Addresses, essays, lectures. I. Aldred, Cyril. II. New York (City). Metropolitan Museum of Art. Metropolitan Museum journal.
N5350.A68 709'.32 76-54181
ISBN 0-87099-159-0

Contents

Preface

This series of reprinted articles is offered to scholars whose principal interest is Egyptology, and for whom it may be more convenient to find all the material on their subject within a single volume rather than dispersed among the several volumes in which it first appeared. As formulated by the Museum's Editorial Advisory Committee in February 1967, the articles written by colleagues in other institutions are in every case primarily concerned with the Museum's collections, while those written by members of the Museum staff may deal with subjects of a more general nature. *MMJ* 11 was selected to close the series because it brings the accumulation of Egyptian material to about the same length as one of the larger volumes that have previously been published.

To facilitate the use of references in other works, each page has retained its original pagination, preceded by the appropriate volume number, and each page also shows a new pagination that is consecutive throughout. The consecutive pagination is intended to simplify references in the index, which has been prepared by Edna Russmann, and which is undoubtedly the most useful feature of the book.

Such a project would not be feasible if the original offset negatives were not available for this purpose. For this same reason, it has not been possible to make more than a few very negligible corrections in the text itself, but further alterations would not, in any case, have been desirable. All additional comments have therefore been collected at the end of the series, immediately preceding the index—except, of course, for those addenda that have already appeared at the end of some articles.

Since their names do not appear on the reverse of the title page, a word of thanks must here be given to Helmut Nickel and the other editors of the *MMJ*, past and present, to William Pons, the chief photographer of the Metropolitan Museum, and to Bert Clarke of the Press of A. Colish, who has advised on typography and production.

The greatest share of thanks, however, must go to Lila Acheson Wallace, who has financed this volume as well as much of the research that has gone into it. It is hoped that her generosity will be rewarded by inspiring some of the other curatorial departments of the Museum to produce similar compilations, thereby increasing the value of a journal that has already proved its worth.

H. G. F.

Some Royal Portraits of the Middle Kingdom in Ancient Egypt

CYRIL ALDRED

Keeper of the Department of Art and Archaeology, Royal Scottish Museum, Edinburgh

IN MEMORIAM
William Christopher Hayes,
1903–1963

Among the glories of Egyptian art are the royal sculptures of the Middle Kingdom "that record with searching accuracy not only the facial characteristics of each king, seen at a specific moment of his life's span, but also something of his mood and underlying character."[1] Thanks to the acumen of its curators, the skill and industry of its archaeologists, and the unstinted support of its patrons, The Metropolitan Museum of Art now enjoys the prerogative of housing the finest and most comprehensive collection of these sculptures outside Cairo. Nowhere is it possible to study this particular art in more sympathetic surroundings than in the galleries of the Museum, where a splendid collection of masterpieces ranges over the field of royal portraiture during the greater part of the XIth and XIIth Dynasties.

The astonishing realism of these portraits of Egyptian kings and queens is unique in the art of the ancient world, and was a phenomenon of relatively brief duration. While some eleven hundred years later it provided fresh inspiration and a point of departure for eclectic Egyptian sculptors who sought to recapture an antiquarian remembrance of things past, it remained outside the mainstream of pharaonic art. Some incidental words will be required, therefore, to explain the milieu in which it arose and had meaning.

The royal statues of the Old Kingdom are somewhat rare and mostly fragmentary. With a few exceptions they have been recovered from the great pyramid complexes of the age and reflect an exclusively mortuary art. Only a small number of these sculptures have been found in circumstances which suggest that their purpose was not funerary, such as the ivory statuette of Cheops excavated from the levels of an early temple at Abydos,[2] and the dyad of Saḥu-rēʿ from Koptos, in the Metropolitan Museum;[3] but what has survived is sufficient to suggest that those statues which represented the king as intermediary between gods and men in the shrine of the local deity did not differ in form and feeling from the statues destined for the mortuary chapels. All alike express the character of the ruler as a god incarnate, calm, dignified, aloof from human cares.

Conversely, the statues of Middle Kingdom pharaohs have been found mostly on the sites of temples

1. W. C. Hayes, "Royal Portraits of the Twelfth Dynasty," *BMMA* n.s. 5 (1946–1947) p. 119.
2. W. M. F. Petrie, *Abydos*, II (London, 1903) pls. XIII, XIV.
3. W. C. Hayes, *The Scepter of Egypt*, I (Cambridge, Massachusetts, 1953) p. 71. Also the head from the sun temple of Weser-kaf at Abusir: H. Ricke, "Dritter Grabungsbericht über das Sonnenheiligtum des Königs Userkaf bei Abusir," *ASAE* 55 (1958) pp. 73–75, pl. III.

that were raised to local gods all over Egypt. In such widespread building the pharaohs appear to have been more active than their Old Kingdom predecessors, though the almost complete denudation of the older levels has bequeathed us a very incomplete picture of the true achievement of earlier kings. The relatively few examples of statuary that have been recovered from the pyramid temples of the Middle Kingdom, on the other hand, show that the funerary art of the time differs in mood from the contemporary "official" sculpture and has a character all its own.

Perhaps the uniformity of Old Kingdom sculpture was achieved by strong traditions of craftsmanship handed down by one generation of artists to the next, all working under the auspices of the creator god Ptaḥ of Memphis, whose high priests were the master artists and designers. This religious and court art was penetrated toward the end of the period by new tendencies that find their consummation in the Middle Kingdom. The decay of the central authority and the rapid growth of feudalism in the Vth and VIth Dynasties promoted the rise of a number of provincial towns to greater importance. The regional governors now occupied offices that were hereditary. They no longer sought burial around the pyramid of their lord but hewed their rock tombs in the vicinity of their residence cities. A widespread demand was thus created for the funerary arts, including sculpture, which had developed in Memphis during the early Old Kingdom in the service of the pharaoh and his intimates. It can safely be assumed that the provincial art centers would have been founded or greatly influenced by Memphite craftsmen attracted by the opportunities offered by a new class of patron. They would have trained in their turn local workmen to carry on the traditions they had transplanted, but the chief court artists would hardly have been allowed to relinquish their studios at Memphis, even if they had felt so inclined. Much provincial art in the VIth Dynasty bears the stamp of the uninspired journeyman content to copy old formulae to extinction; and where a piece of more than average quality has survived,[4] it is to be suspected that it is an import from the capital.

These tendencies were intensified during the First Intermediate Period when the Heracleopolitans fell heir to the Memphis workshops and their trained personnel, while rivals such as the princes of Thinis, Dendera, Moalla, Asyut, and Thebes developed their own distinctive versions of the Memphite style in splendid isolation. When, however, the various warring states were pacified under the sovereignty of the Theban Mentu-ḥotpes of the XIth Dynasty, the old influences once more reasserted themselves as the new rulers took over all the traditional trappings of pharaonic power, and their artists refreshed themselves at the fountainhead of pharaonic art—the monuments and traditions of Memphis, the chief cultural and administrative center since the time of the first pharaoh.

We shall have more to say on these stylistic influences later; here we must emphasize the considerable shift in political power that characterized the First Intermediate Period, and the change in outlook that it effected. In place of the lonely god incarnate, there was now a multiplicity of petty monarchs ruling independent districts, who emphasized their divine right to govern less than their ability to keep their provinces orderly and prosperous through their temporal might and public works. This form of benevolent despotism was carried over into the principles of government during the Middle Kingdom when the pharaoh promoted wide-scale economic development by irrigation works, land reclamation, the establishment of trading posts in the Sudan, and the exploitation of mines and quarries for the benefit of the entire nation. The motive force that had built the mighty pyramid complexes of the IIIrd and IVth Dynasties had been the desire of the populace to secure their own welfare by the preservation of their greatest divinity, their pharaoh. In the XIIth Dynasty, however, the wheel had turned a half circle, and it was the concern of the pharaoh to preserve his people by his mighty works. Ammenemes I declared that none was hungry in his time and no one was thirsty; men dwelt in peace through what he said and wrought.[5] His son, Sesostris I, announced that God had made him the Herdsman of the land of Egypt for He knew he would keep it in good order for Him.[6] In such boasts the pharaoh was doing no more than repeating the claims of the many provincial governors during the First Intermediate Period that they had saved their people by

4. E.g., the statues of Nen-khefi-ka (late Vth Dynasty) from Dishasha, and a statue of Ḳar (VIth Dynasty) from Edfu; see also The Metropolitan Museum of Art, acc. no. 62.200, from Gebelaw: *BMMA* n.s. 22 (1963–1964) p. 65.

5. A. Erman, *Literature of the Ancient Egyptians*, trans. A. M. Blackman (London, 1927) p. 74.

6. Erman, *Literature*, p. 50.

their successful armed forays and by their measures against civil disorder and local economic distress caused by famine, the inevitable concomitant of anarchy in Egypt. The pharaohs of the XIIth Dynasty up to the last three kings were little more than first among equals, their founder, Ammenemes I, having apparently usurped supreme power with the support of the feudal nobility, whose former possessions and offices were restored to them.[7] The pharaohs now had to share their authority with provincial governors who dated events to their own years of rule, maintained their own armed forces and fleets of ships, and quarried stone for their own monuments, some of which were of considerable size.[8] Under Sesostris III, however, there was a further change in the political scene. The series of tombs hewn by the provincial lords near their seats of government came to an abrupt halt, and the feudal rule of the great landowners was replaced by a bureaucracy of modest state officials serving in various departments of the central palace administration, a system that was to be developed during the ensuing years of the Second Intermediate Period and the New Kingdom.[9]

These various factors—the changes in political power and ideas of government, as well as the rise and fall of provincial towns as centers of culture—had their impact on the character of the art of the period and determined its distinctive features, as we shall remark in passing.

The last great monument of the Old Kingdom was the pyramid complex of Phiops II at Saqqarah, which seems to have been specially hallowed in afteryears as the final utterance of the legendary pharaohs of a classical age.[10] Not only did Sesostris I in the Middle Kingdom copy its plan and decoration for his mortuary temple at Lisht,[11] but Hatshepsut at Deir el-Baḥri and Amenophis II at Karnak also returned to its reliefs for fresh inspiration in the New Kingdom.[12] The influence of the Phiops monument on Middle Kingdom art was profound, in both an unconscious and a deliberate fashion. By the end of the Old Kingdom a certain style characteristic of Memphite art was disseminated among the other provincial centers of Egypt. Its features can be seen in reliefs from the Phiops monument where a sharp ridge is often used to define the edges of the lips, and the muscles at the wings of the nose are carefully delineated.[13] Such details are particularly evident in the work of lesser sculptors and became exaggerated into a distinctive mannerism by copyists in the provincial centers. The reliefs produced at Thebes, for instance, during the early years of the XIth Dynasty, emphasize not only these idiosyncrasies but also the long lobes of the ears, so characteristic of some of the Phiops reliefs,[14] albeit the attenuated proportions are in the tradition of the First Intermediate Period at Thebes and Asyut.

The contemporary royal statuary of the late Old Kingdom is practically nonexistent, the surviving statuettes of Phiops I and II being on too small a scale to furnish fully reliable data. Nevertheless, the kneeling statuette of Phiops I at Brooklyn[15] and the squatting statuette of Phiops II at Cairo[16] show significant features in the ears placed high, the shallow crown of the head, the large wide eyes with pronounced inner canthi, the eyebrows worked in relief as distinct appliqués, the fleshy lips defined by a sharp line or edge, and the muscles emphasized around the corners of the mouth and nose (Figure 1). These peculiarities, distorted to a formula, are reflected in the contemporary statues of private persons such as that of Idy (Figure 2)[17] in the Metropolitan's collection or those of Nekhebu at Boston.[18] Such a mannerism inspired local schools of artists at Asyut and Thebes, which developed along

7. W. C. Hayes, "The Middle Kingdom in Egypt," *Cambridge Ancient History*, 2nd ed., I, chap. 20 (London, 1961) p. 35.

8. E.g., the alabaster colossus, over 20 feet high, erected by Djeḥuti-ḥotpe in the reign of Sesostris II; P. Newberry, *El Bersheh*, I (London, 1895) pp. 23–24.

9. Hayes, "Middle Kingdom," pp. 44–45.

10. In Middle Kingdom literature the reign of Snefru of the IVth Dynasty was regarded as a golden age; see B. Gunn, "Notes on Two Egyptian Kings," *JEA* 12 (1926) pp. 250–251.

11. Hayes, *Scepter*, I, p. 183.

12. G. Jéquier, *Le Monument Funéraire de Pepi II*, II (Cairo, 1936–1940) pp. 26–27; W. S. Smith, *Art and Architecture of Ancient Egypt* (Harmondsworth, 1958) p. 134.

13. Jéquier, *Monument Funéraire*, II, pl. 40.

14. E.g., Jéquier, *Monument Funéraire*, II, pl. 49; A. M. Blackman, "The Stele of Thethi, Brit. Mus. no. 614," *JEA* 17 (1931) pl. VIII.

15. C. Aldred, *Old Kingdom Art* (London, 1949) nos. 60, 61.

16. G. Jéquier, "Rapport préliminaire sur les Fouilles exécutées en 1925–1926 dans la Partie Méridionale de la Nécropole Memphite," *ASAE* 26 (1926) pl. V.

17. Acc. no. 37.2.2, limestone, height 38 cm., provenance unknown. William C. Hayes, "Two Egyptian Statues," *BMMA* 33 (1938) pp. 107–108.

18. W. S. Smith, *Egyptian Sculpture and Painting* (Cambridge, Massachusetts, 1946) pl. 26a, b.

independent lines during the First Intermediate Period.

The first examples of royal statuary in this provincial version of the late Old Kingdom style are the sandstone statues that Mentu-ḥotpe Neb-ḥepet-rēʿ erected in the forecourt of his mortuary temple at Deir el-Baḥri, a complete seated example of which, carefully bandaged like a corpse, was found by Howard Carter in the Bab el-Ḥosan under its pyramid.[19] These statues are probably little older than the earliest parts of the monument, such as the reliefs from the chapels of the princesses and those from the sides of their sarcophagi.[20] The Museum is fortunate in possessing the head of a standing statue from this group of sculptures found by its Egyptian expedition in 1921–1922 in the forecourt of the king's temple at Deir el-Baḥri (Figures 3, 4).[21] The importance of this head excavated in an unambiguous context hardly needs to be stressed since it is the means of placing in the period of the XIth Dynasty a number of heads that otherwise might have been dated to the latter half of the VIth Dynasty.[22] It infuses the mannerisms of the Phiops II style with a primitive brutal force that in effect creates a new archaism and makes the head a point of departure rather than a late variation on an earlier theme.

The stylistic features are clear for all to see. The wide staring eyes with their long inner canthi and pronounced paint stripe, the eyebrows in relief, the thick lips with their edges defined by ridges and pursed up at the corners into a grimace, and the muscles at the wings of the nose are all present, if less emphasized, in the kneeling statuette of Phiops I at Brooklyn (Figure 1). The same elongated canthi are seen in the reliefs of Neb-ḥepet-rēʿ in the Ḥatḥor shrine from Denderah, where the earlobes are also fleshy and prolonged.[23]

During his reign, Neb-ḥepet-rēʿ overthrew the Her-

19. H. Carter, "Report on the tomb of Mentuhotep Ist, at Deir el-Bahari, Known as Bab el Hoçan," *ASAE* 2 (1901) pp. 201–205; K. Lange and M. Hirmer, *Egypt*, 4th ed. (London, 1968) pls. 80, 81.

20. E. Naville, *The XIth Dynasty Temple at Deir el-Baḥari* (London, 1907–1913) I, pls. XVII–XIX, II, pls. XI–XX. The costume worn by the king in these statues does not necessarily mean that he had already celebrated a jubilee. It is probable, however, that one of the statues was improvised as a substitute for the corpse of the king and buried in the Bab el-Ḥosan as part of the jubilee rites concerning the death and resurrection of the pharaoh.

21. Acc. no. 26.3.29, height 2.03 m.; H. E. Winlock, "Egyptian Expedition, 1925–1927: The Museum's Excavations at Thebes," *BMMA* 23 (1928) part II, p. 24, fig. 25. It should be noted that this head has been joined to a headless statue of the same king, which it happily completes although it evidently came from another statue in the same series.

22. E.g., Louvre, no. E.10299; Vandier, *Manuel*, p. 37, note 1.

23. G. Daressy, "Chapelle de Mentuhotep III à Dendérah," *ASAE* 17 (1917) pp. 226 ff., pl. 3.

FIGURE 1
Head of kneeling statue of Phiops I. The Brooklyn Museum, Charles Edwin Wilbour Fund, 39.121

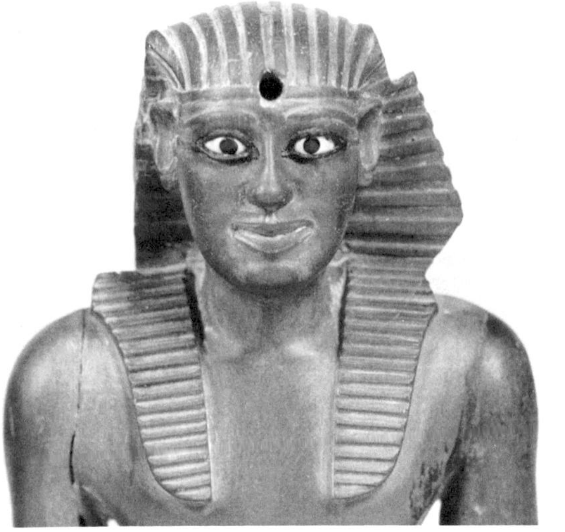

FIGURE 2
Head of seated statue of Idy. The Metropolitan Museum of Art, Rogers Fund, 37.2.2

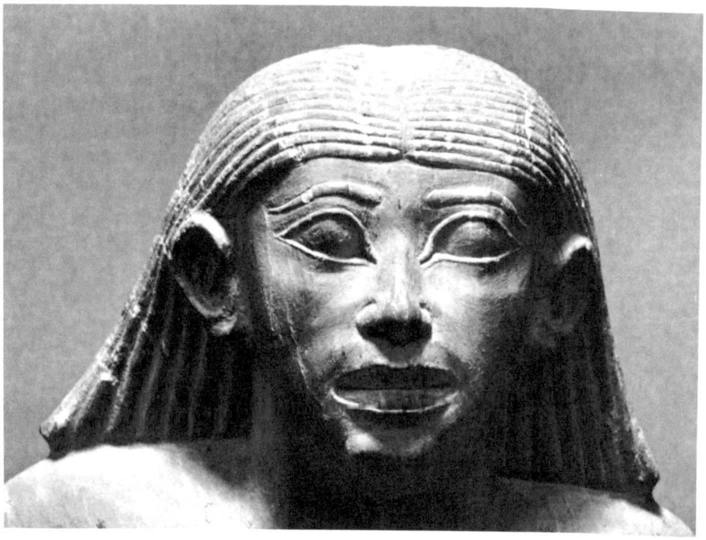

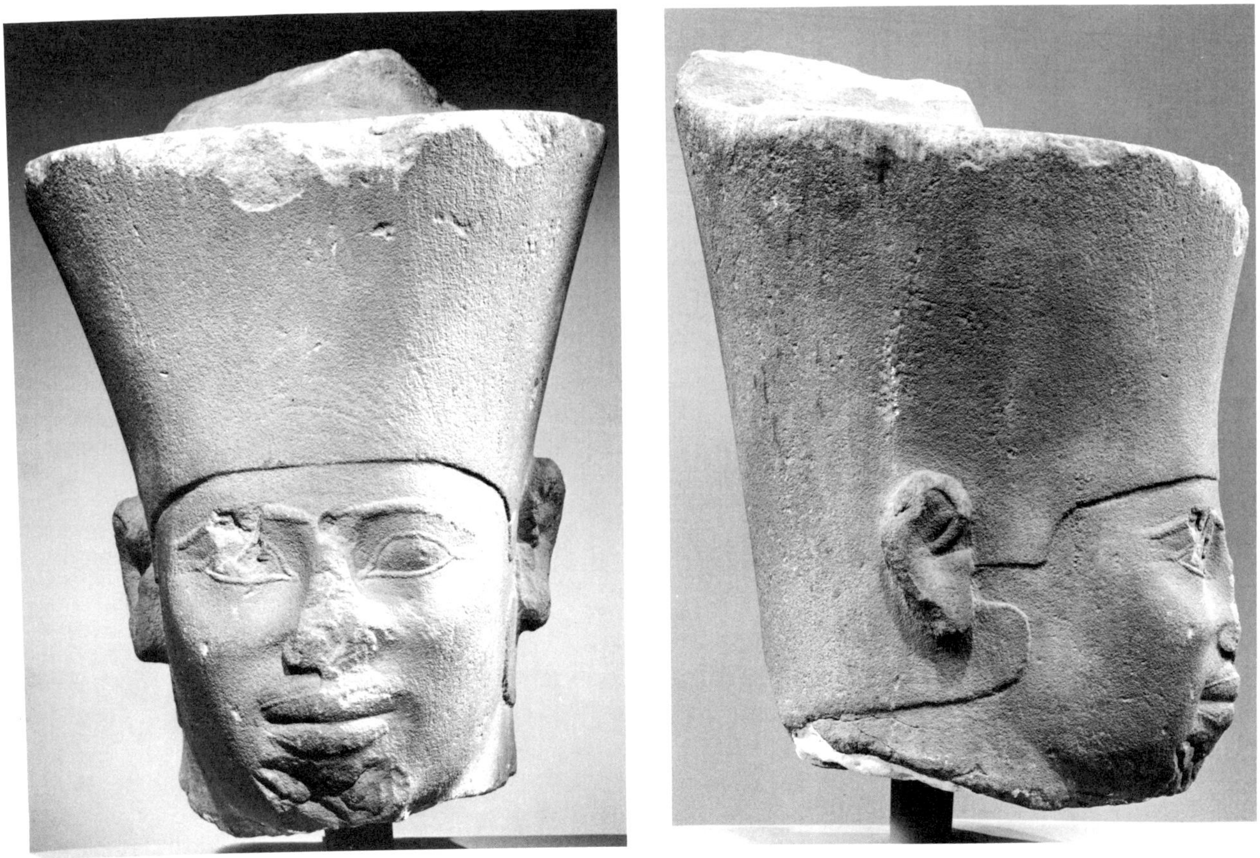

FIGURES 3, 4
Head of Mentu-ḥotpe Neb-ḥepet-rēʿ. The Metropolitan Museum of Art, Museum excavations, 1921–22, 26.3.29

acleopolitan power and united the Two Lands under the rule of a sole pharaoh. It may be surmised that this great victory brought the Thebans into sustained contact with the culture of Memphis and its skilled craftsmen and officials. Indeed, Inyotef-nakhte, the chief sculptor of Neb-ḥepet-rēʿ, had evidently served under the last of the Heracleopolitan kings.[24] A more sophisticated influence is apparent in the later work of the reign, as may be seen in some of the reliefs from Deir el-Baḥri[25] and particularly from Tôd,[26] where an elegance of proportions and a more assured handling of the material reveal that the traditions of pharaonic art were being revived, though infused with a new dynamism.

This progression steadily continued under the successors of Neb-ḥepet-rēʿ, the reliefs of Mentu-ḥotpe Seʿankh-ka-rēʿ from Tôd showing a decided refinement over those of his predecessor, though preserving all their essential features.[27] The influence of the Phiops II monument is seen, for example, in the relief from Armant in Brooklyn,[28] with its return to more classical proportions and elegance in its drawing. Such idiosyncrasies as the *nemes* headcloth with a long, narrow-pleated lappet and the striped wig-cover without a frontlet, as

24. Hayes, "Middle Kingdom," p. 23.

25. E.g., Naville, *XIth Dynasty Temple*, II, pls. v c, vi a, b, d; see also H. G. Fischer, "An Example of Memphite Influence in a Theban Stela of the Eleventh Dynasty," *Artibus Asiae* 22 (1959) pp. 240–252.

26. F. Bisson de la Roque, *Tôd, Fouilles, Institut Français d'Archéologie Orientale* 17 (1934–1936) pl. xviii.

27. Bisson de la Roque, *Tôd*, pl. xxi.

28. R. Mond and O. H. Myers, *Temples of Armant* (London, 1937) pl. xcvi, 1.

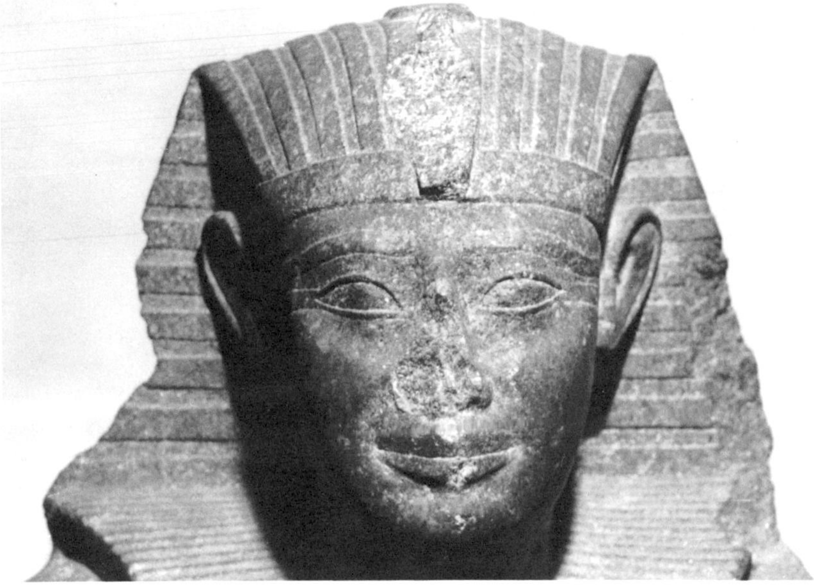

FIGURE 5
Head of Mentu-ḥotpe Seʿankh-ka-rēʿ (?). Cairo Museum, J. d'Entrée 67345

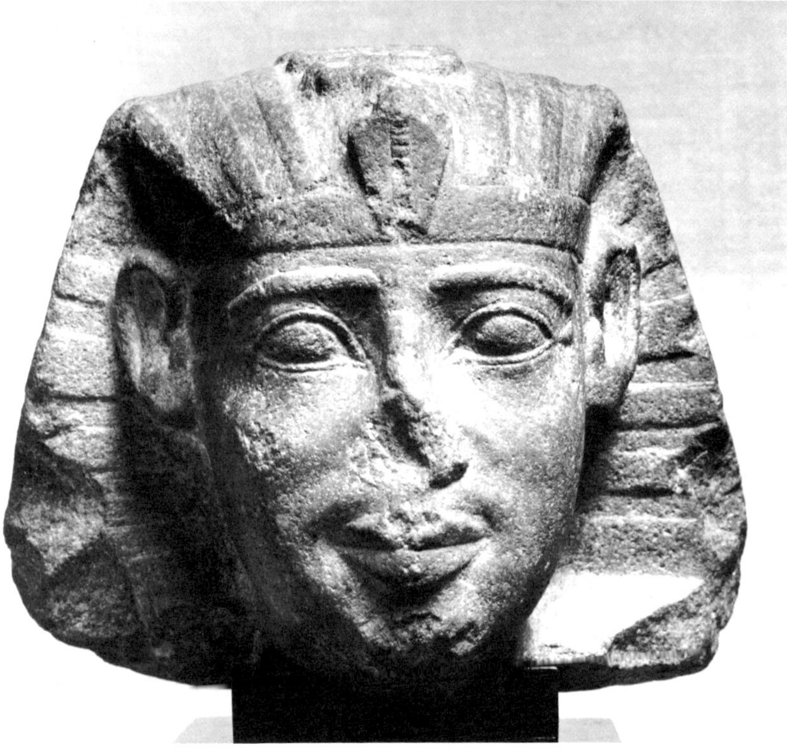

FIGURE 6
Head of Mentu-ḥotpe Neb-ḥepet-rēʿ (?). Edinburgh, Royal Scottish Museum, 1965.2

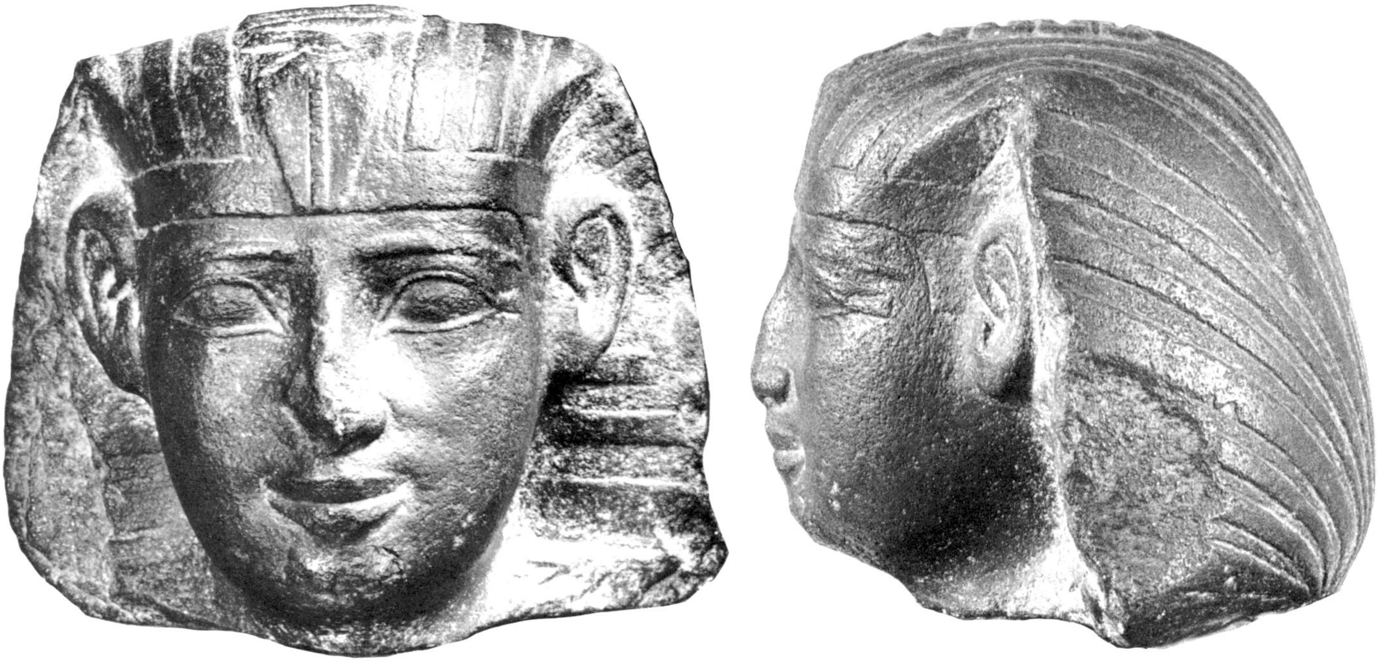

FIGURES 7, 8
Head of Mentu-ḥotpe Neb-ḥepet-rēʿ (?). Bristol Museum, H 5038

well as the loving delineation of the muscles at the wings of the nose, suggest direct copying.[29]

To this period must be dated a number of fragmentary statues that have been considered to represent various kings. The upper part of a gray granite seated statue from Tôd (Figure 5) has been identified as of King Achoris of the XXIXth Dynasty,[30] but obviously belongs to this group. It bears a generic resemblance to the quartzite heads in Bristol and Edinburgh (Figures 6–8)[31] and the gray green arkose head at Basel (Figure 9).[32] All are characterized by their thick everted

29. Jéquier, *Monument Funéraire*, II, pls. 63, 64.

30. Cairo, J. d'Entrée no. 67345, height 65 cm.; *Bulletin de l'Institut Français d'Archéologie Orientale* 50 (1952) pl. II; F. Bisson de la Roque, "Tôd, Fouilles antérieures à 1938," *Revue d'Egyptologie* 4 (1940) p. 73; see note 32 below. Part of a statue of a king seated beside a queen or divinity. I identify the king as Seʿankh-ka-rēʿ, the work appearing a little too sophisticated for the major part of the reign of Neb-ḥepet-rēʿ. The monuments of both kings are common at Tôd. There is no trace of the work of Achoris on the same site.

31. Royal Scottish Museum, acc. no. 1965.2, height 12.5 cm., provenance unknown; Bristol Museum, acc. no. H5038, height 11 cm., provenance unknown. These heads are so alike in material, size, and style that they form a pair, or two in a larger series.

32. Basel, Museum für Völkerkunde, height 15 cm. This head was dated by Ursula Schweitzer, "Ein Spätzeitlicher Königs-

FIGURE 9
Head of Middle Kingdom ruler, XIth or XIIth Dynasty. Basel, Museum für Völkerkunde

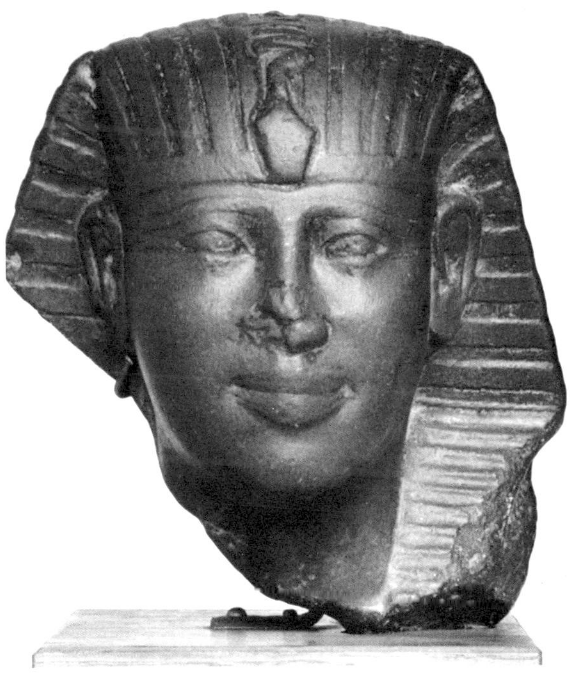

FIGURES 10–12

Head of Ammenemes I (?). The Metropolitan Museum of Art, Fletcher Fund and gift of Dr. and Mrs. Edmundo Lassalle through the Guide Foundation, 66.99.3

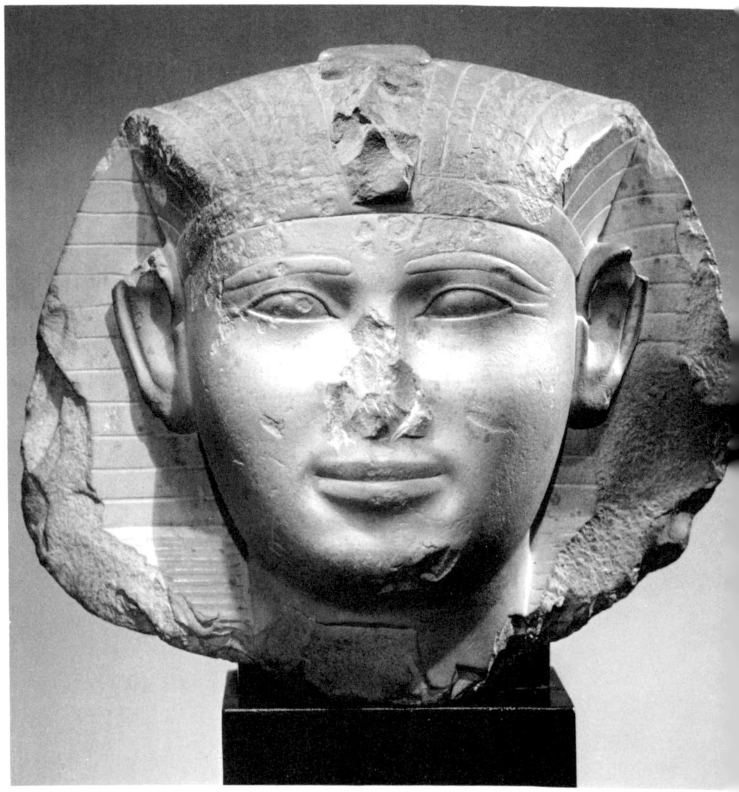

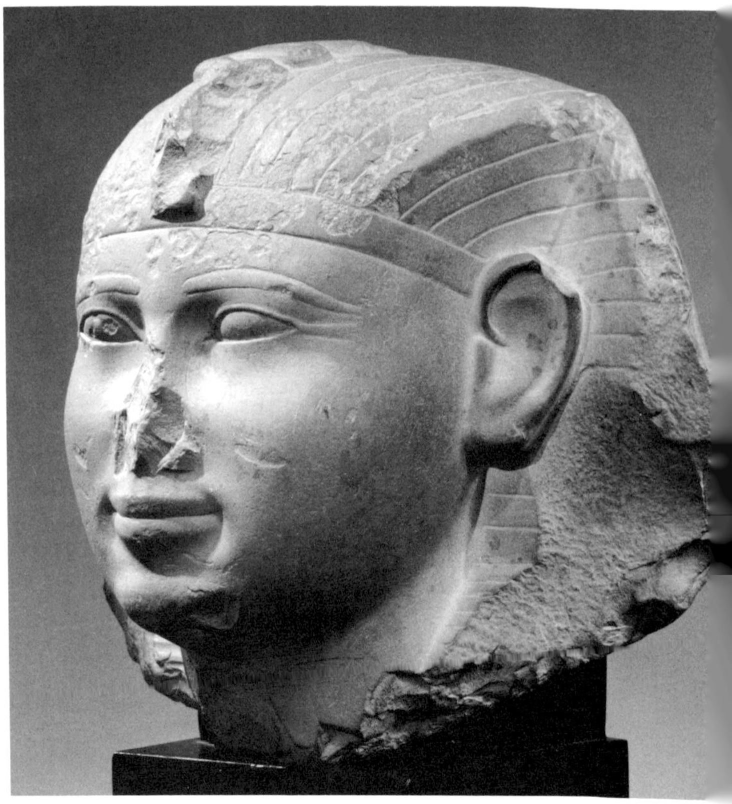

lips, eyebrows in relief, wide staring eyes, fleshy-lobed ears set high, rather flat-topped headcloths with wide single stripes and tall lozenge-shaped uraei-hoods springing from the base of the frontlet with seven or more windings to the body and a tail that extends almost to the back pillar or to the pigtail of the *nemes*. They seem to represent a development in the portrait sculpture of the period, with the Bristol and Edinburgh heads at the beginning and the Basel head at the end of the series.[33] This last specimen marks the transition to the more sophisticated work of the successors of Neb-ḥepet-rēʿ. Related to it is the head in hard yellow limestone from the Gallatin Collection in the Metropolitan Museum (Figures 10–12),[34] which J. D. Cooney has dated to the later years of the XIth Dynasty and has considered most probably to represent Seʿankh-ka-rēʿ.[35] The muscles around the corners of the mouth and nose have the emphatic quality of the work of this period, as Cooney remarks; other features such as the uraeus with its seven loops and the wide-striped headcloth with narrow-pleated lappets are in the style of the dynasty, but the more naturalistic treatment of the eyes and mouth betrays the hand of a craftsman who

kopf in Basel," *Bulletin de l'Institut Français d'Archéologie Orientale* 50 (1952) pp. 119–132, to the Late Period by comparison with royal heads in Turin, Berlin, and Vienna (no. 37: see note 76 below). I am unable to follow her arguments; to my mind her study is a travesty of stylistic analysis. She has failed to appreciate the entirely different handling of the Basel head, the radically different treatment of eyes (with a cosmetic line in the case of the Basel specimen), eyebrows, uraei, mouth, ears, chin, and *nemes*, and the different proportions of the various elements in the heads under discussion. It is equally disturbing to note that she has also lumped Cairo J. d'Entrée 67345 with the Basel head in the work of the Late Period.

33. Probably the Louvre head (E.10299) mentioned in note 22 above should precede the Edinburgh head in this grouping. The eyebrows of this specimen, however, are not in relief but inlaid, though of the same form; the uraeus does not spring from the base of the frontlet but from a little above; the headcloth is not flat-topped in profile but describes a complete arc, as is seen in the wig of Neb-ḥepet-rēʿ on the Denderah shrine.

34. Acc. no. 66.99.3, height 18.1 cm.

35. J. D. Cooney, "Egyptian Art in the Collection of Albert Gallatin," *Journal of Near Eastern Studies* 12 (1953) pp. 3–4, no. 7.

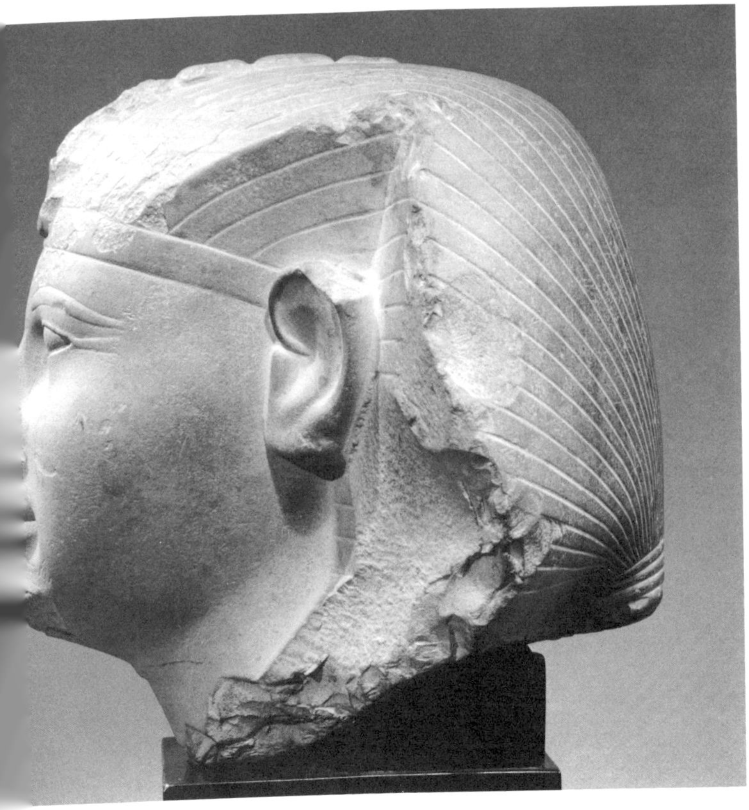

has left behind him the archaisms of an artistic revival. A stylistic feature that relates it to the Basel head and some others of this period (see below) is the lack of tabs on the frontlet before the ears, but it differs from the Basel head in the vertical fall of the wings of the headcloth when seen in a side view.

In the absence of comparable material identified by unimpeachable inscriptions, it would be rash to insist that the king represented in the Gallatin head is Seʿankh-ka-rēʿ in preference to the last Mentu-ḥotpe of the dynasty or to the latter's successor, Ammenemes I. It does bear a resemblance to two of the heads of the Osiride statues excavated by the Egypt Exploration Society at Armant.[36] Though restored by Mineptaḥ, they are generally recognized as originally of a Mentu-ḥotpe of the XIth Dynasty, most probably Seʿankh-ka-rēʿ, who was particularly active at Armant.[37] The specimens at Boston[38] and Cairo[39] show a close likeness in the treatment of the muscles at the corners of the mouth, the slightly smiling lips, the sharp inner canthi of the eyes, and the rather bulbous chin. Seʿankh-ka-rēʿ had a brief reign, and much of his work may have been left unfinished; the Osiride statues, for instance, appear to have lain uninscribed for about six centuries before Mineptaḥ reused them. The summary treatment of the ears of the Gallatin head may therefore be an indication that the statue lacks the final touches, and is a further argument for its identification as Seʿankh-ka-rēʿ.

Whoever it represents, however, the Gallatin head bridges the work of Neb-ḥepet-rēʿ and that of the early XIIth Dynasty. Its stylistic features resemble those of the red granite colossus of Ammenemes I from Tanis,[40]

36. Mond and Myers, *Temples of Armant*, pl. XVI, nos. S.102, S.435.

37. B. Porter and R. Moss, *Topographical Bibliography*, V (Oxford, 1937) pp. 157, 160; Mond and Myers, *Temples of Armant*, pp. 166–168.

38. Museum of Fine Arts, acc. no. 38.1395; W. S. Smith, *Ancient Egypt as Represented in the Museum of Fine Arts*, 3rd ed. (Boston, 1952) p. 79.

39. Cairo Museum, J. d'Entrée no. 67378.

40. Cairo Museum, J. d'Entrée no. 37470; Evers, *Staat*, I, pls. 15–17.

FIGURE 13

Head of seated statue of Ammenemes I. Cairo Museum, J. d'Entrée 60520

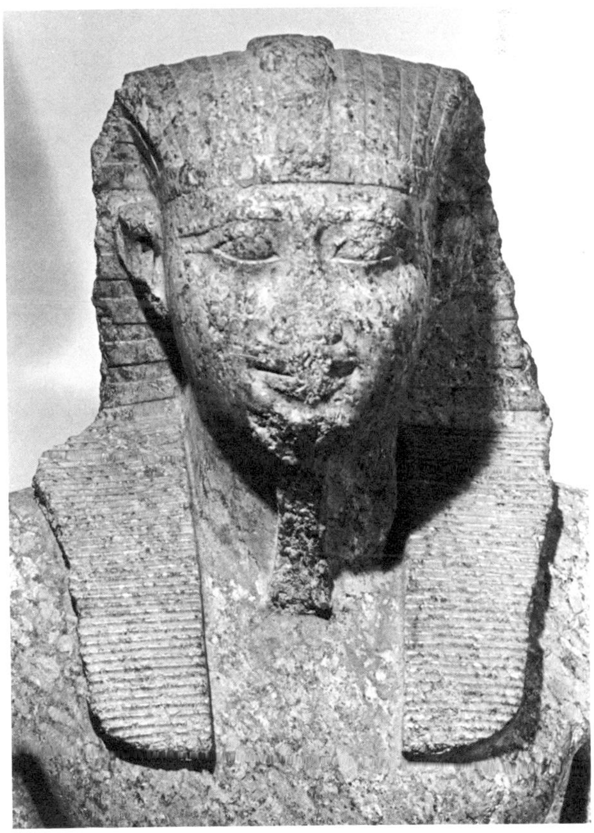

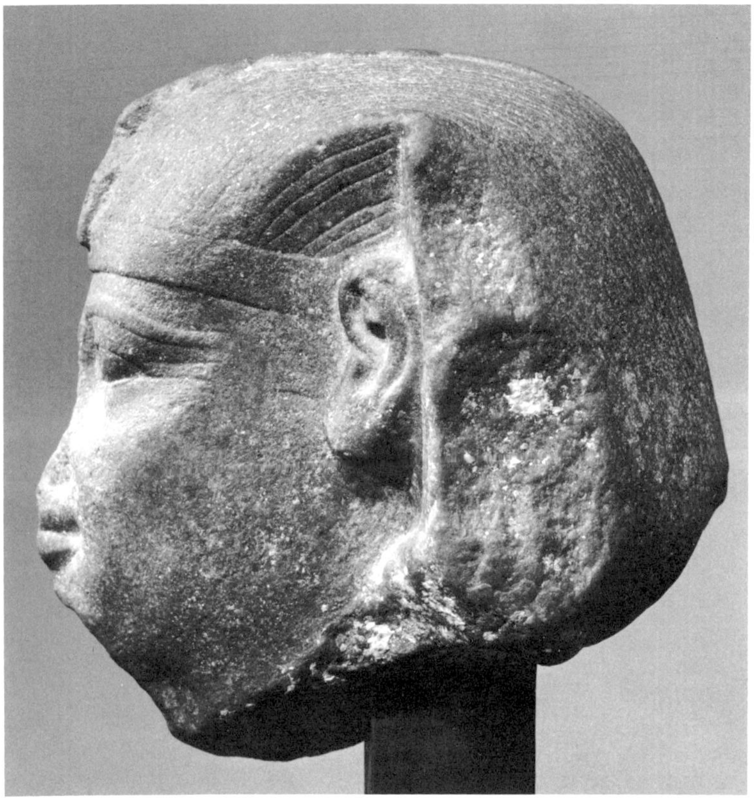

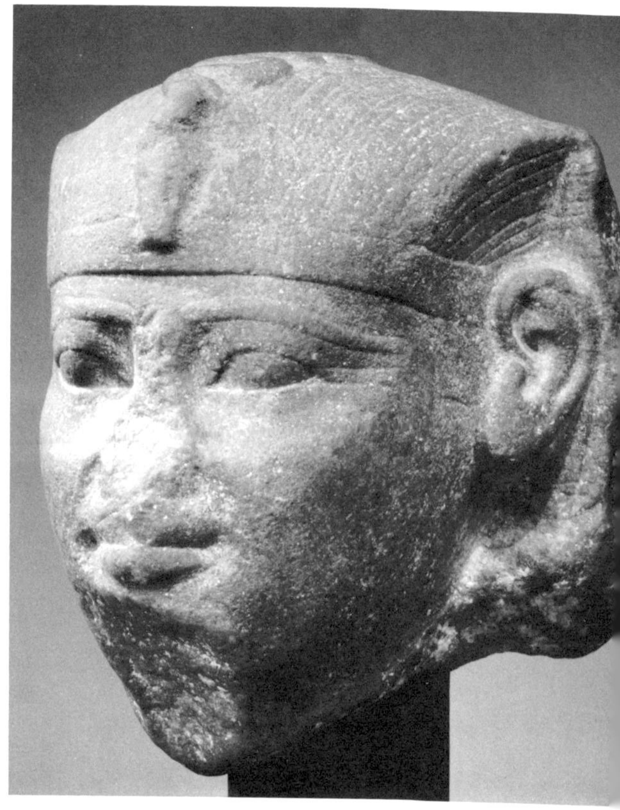

FIGURE 14–16
Head of a sphinx (?), early XIIth Dynasty. The Metropolitan Museum of Art, Fletcher Fund and gift of Dr. and Mrs. Edmundo Lassalle through the Guide Foundation, 66.99.4

with its round face, prominent chin and cheekbones, and faintly smiling lips. The red granite statue of the same king from Faqus (Figure 13)[41] displays a closely similar treatment of the muscles at the corners of the mouth with the same fold of flesh running in an arc toward the chin. The ears, too, lie at the same angle to the cheek; the wig-cover has a closely similar profile, and the root of the pigtail slopes with the same inclination. The frontlet also lacks tabs before the ears and carries its uraeus at the same distance from its lower edge. It differs only in that the frontlet lies directly horizontal above the ears, a reversion to the convention seen in the Brooklyn statue of Phiops I. This anomaly cannot, however, rule out the distinct possibility that the Gallatin statue represents Ammenemes I, whose monuments, though scanty despite his thirty years of rule, may be expected to have survived in greater quantity than those of Seʿankh-ka-rēʿ and the latter's ephemeral successor, Neb-towy-rēʿ.

To this same period is to be attributed another head in the Gallatin Collection (Figures 14–16), which is reputed to have been fished from the seabed off Tyre and is carved from green dolomitic marble, a rare stone for statuary in Egypt, though other examples in marble from the XIIth Dynasty have survived.[42] The great length of the head from back to front, and the high placing of the shoulders, indicated by the springing of the lappets from the side wings of the headcloth, suggest that this fragment may have come from a sphinx. The stylistic features approach those of the larger Gallatin head. The lozenge-shaped uraeus hood with eight

41. H. Gauthier, "Une Nouvelle Statue d'Amen-em-ḥêt Ier," *Mémoires de l'Institut Français d'Archéologie Orientale* 66, part 1 (1934) pp. 43–53.

42. Acc. no. 66.99.4, height 16.4 cm. Other examples in marble in the Metropolitan Museum are acc. no. 29.100.150 (Figure 29 below) and acc. no. 22.1.1638 (H. G. Fischer, "Two Royal Monuments of the Middle Kingdom Restored," *BMMA* n.s. 22 [1963–1964] p. 235).

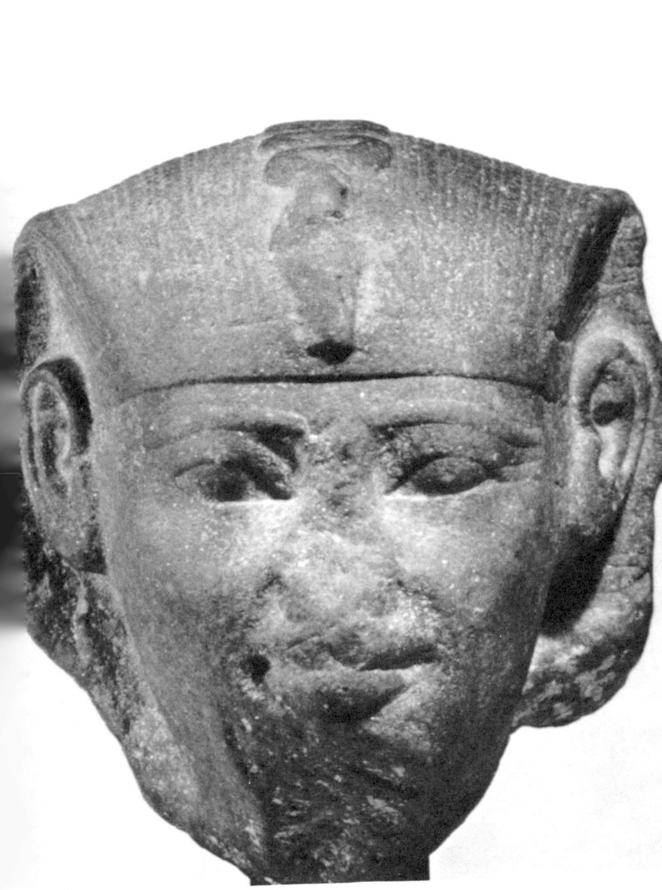

loops to the body emerges from the same point on the frontlet. The wig-cover has a low crown and a similar profile. The eyes are treated as flat planes defined by pronounced paint stripes and inner canthi. The eyebrows are in low relief as appliqués. The ear lies at a similar angle in the corner formed by the cheek and wing of the headcloth and has a thick lobe. The frontlet carries no tabs before the ears. The thick lips are nearer to those of the Bristol, Edinburgh, and Basel heads, but the damage that this head has suffered makes a complete appraisal difficult, nevertheless, the muscles at the wings of the nose are visible. A date in the early XIIth Dynasty, more specifically, in the reign of Ammenemes I, seems probable. It might be objected that the triple-stripe wig-cover is a datum that places this head in the reign of a later king, since such a pattern of *nemes* was not revived before the reign of Ammenemes II.[43] In Egyptian art, however, we must always be prepared for stylistic "sports" that anticipate the conventions of later reigns.[44] The triple-stripe wig-cover already appears on the colossus from Alexandria, identified by H. Evers as of Sesostris I;[45] and since this king had a ten years' co-regency with his father, it is not outside the bounds of possibility that the Alexandrian bust was contemporary with Ammenemes I, if it is not actually of that king. One factor that militates against dating the Gallatin head as late as the reign of Sesostris I is the size, shape, and position of the ear. In the reign of that monarch such features tended to be large and to project from the side of the head in a manner that became a convention for statues of kings wearing the *nemes* during the rest of the XIIth Dynasty.

Large projecting ears resting flat against the wings of the headcloth are seen, for instance, in the head of a gray granite sphinx of Sesostris I excavated by Georges Legrain at Karnak in 1903 (Figure 17).[46] Other features, such as the wide-open eyes with their pronounced inner canthi, the broad, thick mouth, the edges of which are defined by sharp ridges, and the ears placed high, indicate that in a particular regional studio the conventions of the XIth Dynasty style could persist, and raise the vexing question of whether several independent schools of sculptors operated during the Middle Kingdom. Some Egyptologists have sought to define stylistic features which suggest that different traditions were followed by sculptors working at a few main art centers. So acute an observer as J. Vandier,[47] for instance, has claimed to recognize four schools, at Memphis, at Thebes, in the Delta, and in the Faiyum. Such identifications are apparently based upon the finding of statuary on or near different sites—a somewhat arbitrary classification and one that has been properly abandoned in the case of Tanis: no one now speaks of a Tanite school of sculpture since it has become clear that statues of different periods were moved from sites in the Delta to this town in Ramesside or post-Ramesside times.[48]

That there were local groups of sculptors serving the

43. Evers, *Staat*, II, sec. 60.

44. E.g., the statue of Tuthmosis III in the Metropolitan with the seam on the inner edges of the lappets of the *nemes* (Nora Scott, *Egyptian Statuettes* [New York, 1946] no. 17), which anticipated the later XVIIIth Dynasty convention by two or three generations.

45. Evers, *Staat*, I, pl. 36, II, sec. 59.

46. Evers, *Staat*, I, pl. 33.

47. Vandier, *Manuel*, pp. 173–178.

48. W. C. Hayes, "Egypt from the death of Ammenemes III to Seqenenre II," *Cambridge Ancient History*, 2nd ed., II, chap. 2 (London, 1962) p. 11, with note 8; H. Kees, *Ancient Egypt, A Cultural Topography* (London, 1961) pp. 198–199; L. Habachi, "Khatâ'na-Qantîr: Importance," *ASAE* 52 (1952) pp. 443–559.

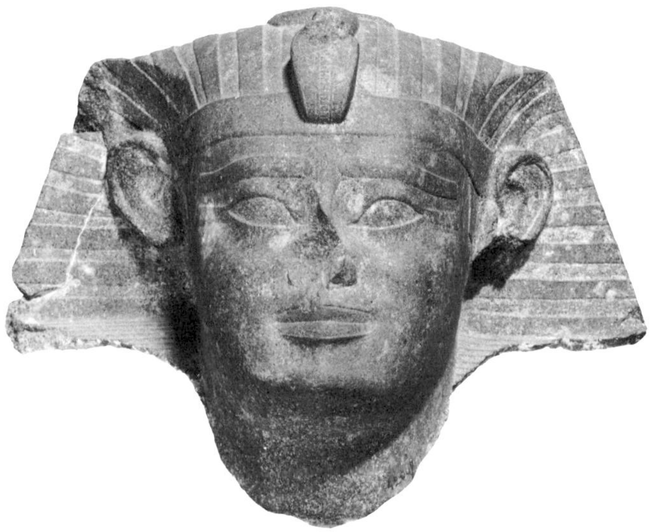

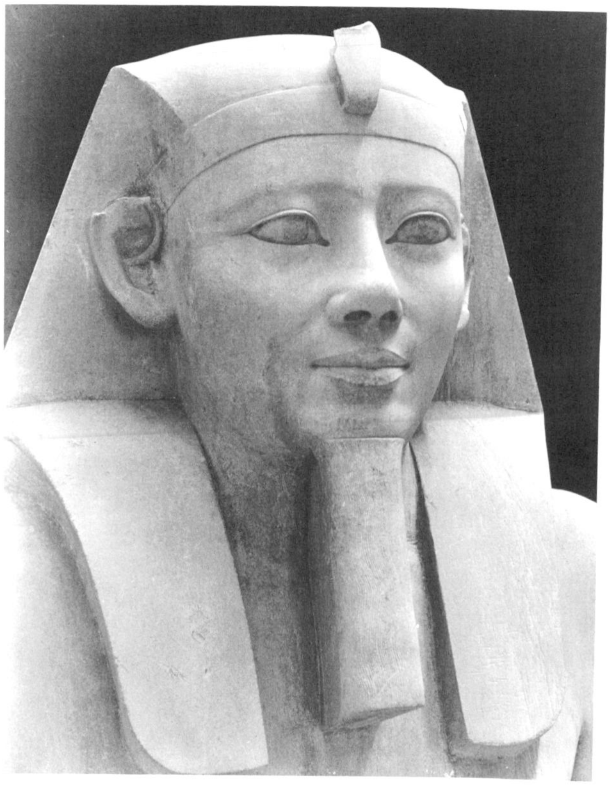

FIGURE 17
Head of a sphinx of Sesostris I. Cairo Museum, Cat. Gén. 42007

FIGURE 18
Head of seated statue of Sesostris I. Cairo Museum, Cat. Gén. 415

needs of such centers as Abydos and Elephantine as well as the residence cities of the feudal governors during the greater part of the Middle Kingdom is reasonably certain; but that there were regional schools of sculpture directly patronized by the court is open to serious doubt. The Mentu-ḥotpes were Upper Egyptian princes, who, even when they had reunited the Two Lands, appear to have retained Thebes as their main residence and the site of their tombs and mortuary temples. The kings of the XIIth Dynasty, however, despite their Southern ancestry, found that a capital city in the North was administratively more convenient. They established their residence near the modern Lisht, not far from Memphis, the traditional pharaonic seat, which also continued in their favor. In this they may have been forestalled by the last king of the XIth Dynasty. They would almost certainly have attracted to their patronage the most skilled sculptors in the land, who would have abandoned local studios, whether at Thebes or elsewhere, to settle at the court. The king's chief sculptor would have been the sole designer of statuary destined for the monuments of the king, whether they were made in soft or hard stones; and if they betray a variety of styles and feeling, this may well be due to factors other than regional art traditions.

In the first place, the earlier kings of the XIIth Dynasty enlisted the aid of publicists to strengthen their claims to the throne vis-à-vis their feudal rivals, and in contemporary literary works they are represented on a heroic scale as powerful terrestrial rulers as well as beneficent gods.[49] It seems to the writer that the skill of the sculptor was also enlisted to serve the same ends of propaganda, so that in the local shrine, the statue of the pharaoh as intermediary between man and the god would express a latent energy and a formidable brooding power that would overawe all who beheld it. The traditions of the Theban sculptors who had infused the earlier statuary of Mentu-ḥotpe Neb-ḥepet-rēʿ with a primitive force were well adapted to serve such needs. The granite statues of Ammenemes I and his son Sesostris I found on Delta sites[50] impress not only by their size but by their brutal appearance, the simplified planes and masses expressing the concept of the king

49. G. Posener, *Littérature et politique dans l'Egypte* (Paris, 1956) esp. pp. 19–20, 60, 86, 115, 140–144.
50. Evers, *Staat*, I, pls. 36–41.

as ruthless overlord. This tendency, springing from the stylistic peculiarities of the Theban style, and carried on by its own momentum once it was established, gave a distinctive realistic character to Middle Kingdom portraiture.

Another factor that has to be considered is the generally long and stable reigns of these XIIth Dynasty monarchs, most of whom celebrated jubilees in their thirtieth regnal years.[51] It is almost certain that they outlived many of their chief craftsmen and that fresh influences were brought to bear on the production of works of art during a long reign. There are also reasons for believing that deliberate changes in portraiture were introduced during the reign of a particular king. The writer has elsewhere[52] sought to show that at a king's advent, a coronation series of statues was produced for him which fixed the official portrait and stylistic features for most of his reign. If, however, he celebrated a jubilee, a new series of statues was produced, often showing changes in his appearance as well as in the contemporary art style. The phenomenon can most readily be demonstrated in the New Kingdom, particularly in the XVIIIth Dynasty, but there is nothing to show that the same practice was not followed in the XIIth Dynasty. Several scholars, for instance, have distinguished portraits of Sesostris III as a youth and as an aged king.[53] For the many temples erected on various sites during this period, both within the borders of Egypt and elsewhere, large quantities of royal statues would have been required for installation in the sanctuaries; and some idea of the activity of the studios can be gleaned from the account of an expedition of over 17,000 men to the Wady Hammamat in the thirty-eighth regnal year of Sesostris I, to cut stone for sixty sphinxes and one hundred twenty statues.[54] More than one master sculptor would be required to carve such a wealth of statuary, and the opportunity for different interpretations and emphases would arise, though all the artists would have to copy more or less faithfully the officially approved portrait modeled by the king's chief sculptor and reproduced by plaster casting, according to a practice that is known for a later period from the studios at Amarna.[55]

Such statuary may be described as "official," and the new uses to which it might be put are seen in the statue that Sesostris III set up on his southern frontier at Semna in the Second Cataract,[56] and also in the seated colossi of Ammenemes III erected on podiums at Biyahmu in the Faiyum.[57] It should be distinguished in purpose and feeling from the sculpture that was produced for the contemporary mortuary temples. When the kings of the XIIth Dynasty abandoned the rock-hewn tomb of their Theban predecessors as the basis for the design of their last resting-places and reverted to the Old Kingdom idea of a royal pyramid built on the desert verges, they also took over the Old Kingdom style of mortuary art. We have already mentioned that Sesostris I copied the plan and decoration of the funerary monument of Phiops II; and the same Memphite tradition is found in the statuary with which these complexes were furnished (Figure 18).[58] The king is represented in the idealistic manner of Old Kingdom art as an immortal. In some statues he is shown as Osiris, the personification of kingship, and two such examples from the covered causeway to the mortuary temple of Sesostris I at Lisht, recovered by the Metropolitan Museum's Egyptian expedition, are exhibited in the galleries. "The faces," wrote William C. Hayes, "though unquestionably inspired by the royal physiognomy, lay no claim to being realistic portraits of the King."[59] All such statues, whether of the ruler in the costume of the living or as Osiris, are carved in limestone, though only examples from the funerary monuments of Sesos-

51. W. K. Simpson, "The Single-Dated Monuments of Sesostris I: An Aspect in the Institution of Coregency in the Twelfth Dynasty," *Journal of Near Eastern Studies* 15 (1956) pp. 214–219; C. Vandersleyen, "Un titre du Viceroi Mérimose à Silsila," *Chronique d'Egypte* 43 (1968) pp. 249–250.

52. C. Aldred, "The 'New Year' Gifts to the Pharaoh," *JEA* 55 (1969) pp. 78–79.

53. E.g., Vandier, *Manuel*, pp. 185, 186.

54. G. Goyon, *Nouvelles Inscriptions Rupestres* (Paris, 1957) no. 61.

55. G. Roeder, "Lebensgrosse Tonmodelle aus einer alt-ägyptischen Bildhauerwerkstatt," *Jahrbuch der Preussischen Kunstsammlungen* 62 (1941) pp. 145–170; I. E. S. Edwards, "An Egyptian Plaster Cast," *British Museum Quarterly* 22 (1960) pp. 27–29.

56. J. M. A. Janssen, "The Stela (Khartoum Museum No. 3) from Uronarti," *Journal of Near Eastern Studies* 12 (1953) pp. 51–55. P. Kaplony, "Das Vorbild des Königs unter Sesostris III," *Orientalia* 35 (1966) pp. 403 ff., challenges the view that the text refers to the erection of a statue, but despite his ingenious arguments, I am not wholly convinced that he has presented a watertight case.

57. W. M. F. Petrie, *Hawara, Biahmu and Arsinoe* (London, 1889) pp. 54–55.

58. Evers, *Staat*, I, pls. 26–29.

59. Hayes, *Scepter*, I, p. 185; for acc. no. 08.200.1 see *BMMA* 3 (1908) p. 171 and fig. 3; for acc. no. 09.180.529 see *BMMA* 4 (1909) p. 120. See also Evers, *Staat*, I, pls. 31–32.

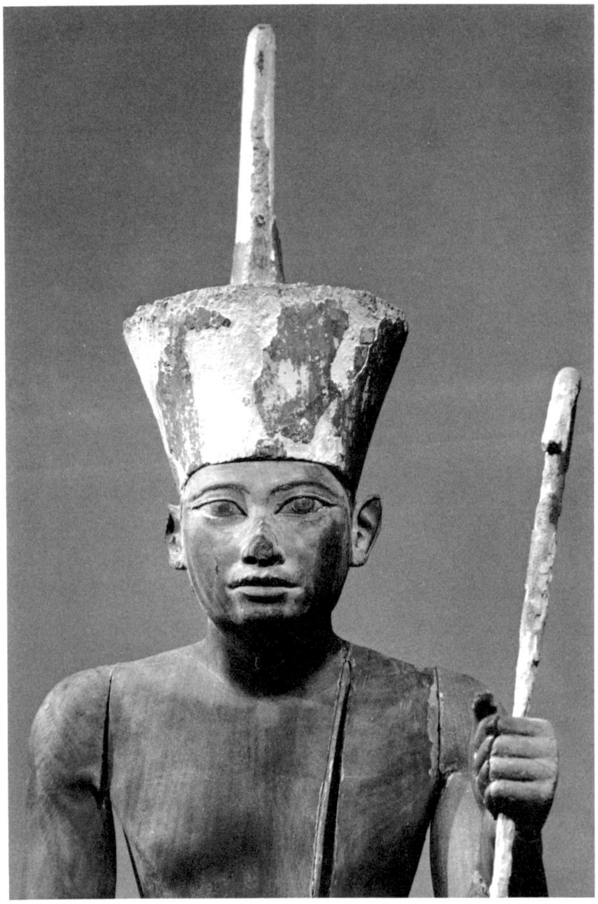

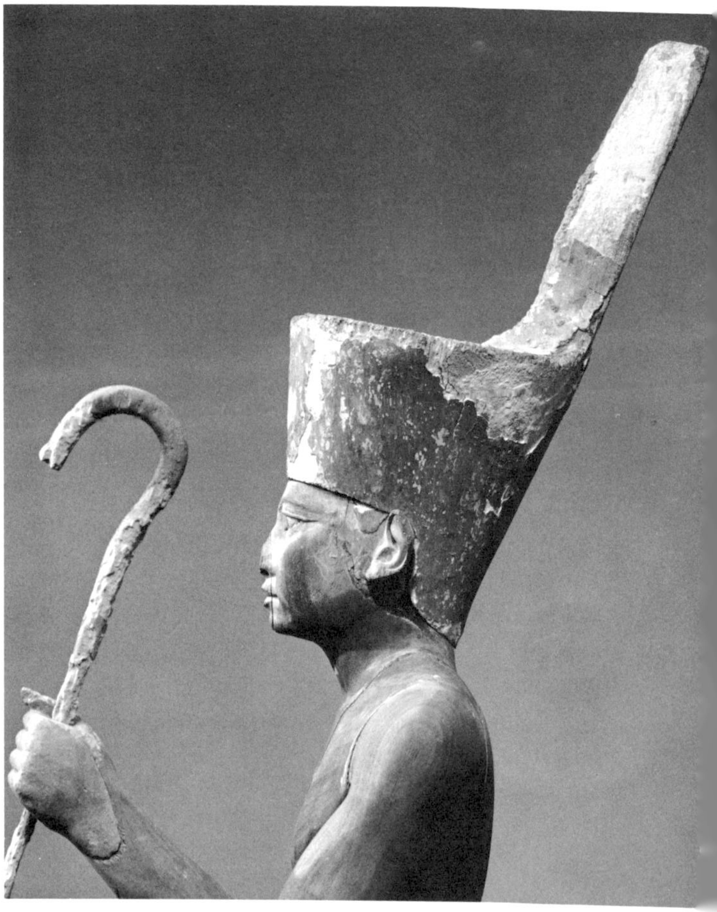

FIGURES 19, 20
Upper part of statuette of Sesostris I. The Metropolitan Museum of Art, Museum excavations, 1913–14, with contribution of Edward S. Harkness, 14.3.17

tris I and Ammenemes III have survived. The softer stone encouraged a less bold handling on the part of the sculptor in order to achieve the required degree of idealization. As far as the portraiture and stylistic details are concerned, these are nearer to the official style than is sometimes recognized.[60] It is due to the accidents of time that hardly any funerary statuary from this period has survived, while statues in the official style from various sites in Egypt are well represented.

A statue that appears to be in the funerary tradition, since its purpose was apparently to serve as a cult object in the burial ceremonies of the high priest Im-ḥotpe, is the painted cedarwood statue of a king wearing the Red Crown of Lower Egypt and carrying a long *ḥeḳat*-scepter (Figures 19, 20).[61] Together with a companion statue wearing the White Crown, now in Cairo, it was found by the Museum's expedition buried in a chamber in the enclosure wall of Im-ḥotpe's mastaba-tomb adjoining the pyramid of Sesostris I at Lisht. For this reason the two statues have generally been identified as representing that king, though they are uninscribed. The modeling of the body is accomplished with a bold assurance, and the articulation of the limbs is far removed from that unhappy paralysis which so often characterizes the wooden sculpture of the First Intermediate Period and sometimes that of the Old Kingdom. While this statue is a masterpiece in the Memphite

60. Evers, *Staat*, I, pls. 29, 44.

61. Acc. no. 14.3.17, wood, traces of pink flesh colors, garments coated with gesso and painted, height 58 cm.; A. M. Lythgoe, "Egyptian Expedition, II: Excavations at the South Pyramid of Lisht, 1914," *BMMA* 10 (1914) supplement, pp. 16–17.

style, the portrait, with its round wide face, prominent cheekbones, large flat eyes with pronounced canthi, and eyebrows in relief, owes much to the Theban traditions of the XIth Dynasty. The docility of the medium has allowed the sculptor to achieve a greater subtlety in the carving of the corners of the mouth and in the convolutions of the ear, which is correctly placed. The ear also attains something of the enlargement that is characteristic of most portraits of the remaining reigns of the XIIth Dynasty, and as in these cases, it also projects sharply outward.

Statues of Ammenemes II and Sesostris II are rare anywhere, and there are no examples in the Museum's collection;[62] but those of their successors are well represented and show the development of the art of royal portraiture during the heyday of the Middle Kingdom. The first in the series is a limestone head found by the Museum's expedition in the filling of a tomb shaft adjacent to the causeway of the pyramid temple of Ammenemes I at Lisht (Figures 21, 22), and as a consequence identified as from a statue of that king.[63] It bears little resemblance either in portraiture or stylistic details to the statues of Ammenemes I, however, and there is little doubt that it represents Sesostris III as a young king. What it was doing at Lisht is something of a mystery, but it may have come from a statue dedicated to Ammenemes I by Sesostris III[64] in the mortuary temple of the earlier king. Its characteristic features are sufficient to distinguish it quite clearly from the work of the first half of the dynasty. The *nemes* wig-cover is of unequivocal triple-stripe pattern, a fashion that became general with Sesostris II,[65] and its frontlet

62. The only example in America known to me is the diorite bust of a king in the Walters Art Gallery, Baltimore (acc. no. 22.351), which I identify as of Sesostris II; see G. Steindorff, *Egyptian Sculpture* (Baltimore, 1946) no. 98, pl. VII.

63. Acc. no. 08.200.2, height 14 cm.; Arthur C. Mace, "Egyptian Expedition: Pyramid of Amenemhet," *BMMA* 3 (1908) pp. 186, 187, 220, fig. 4.

64. Similar statues made in a contemporary style but dedicated to earlier kings are found throughout the dynasty, e.g., Cairo Museum, no. 42.004, in the style of Sesostris I for Saḥu-rēʿ; Royal Scottish Museum, no. 1905.284.2, in the style of Ammenemes III for Snefru. D. Wildung, *Die Rolle Ägyptischer Könige*, Münchner Ägyptologische Studien, no. 17 (Munich, 1969) p. 135.

65. Evers, *Staat*, II, sec. 60.

FIGURES 21, 22
Head of Sesostris III. The Metropolitan Museum of Art, Museum excavations, 1908, 08.200.2

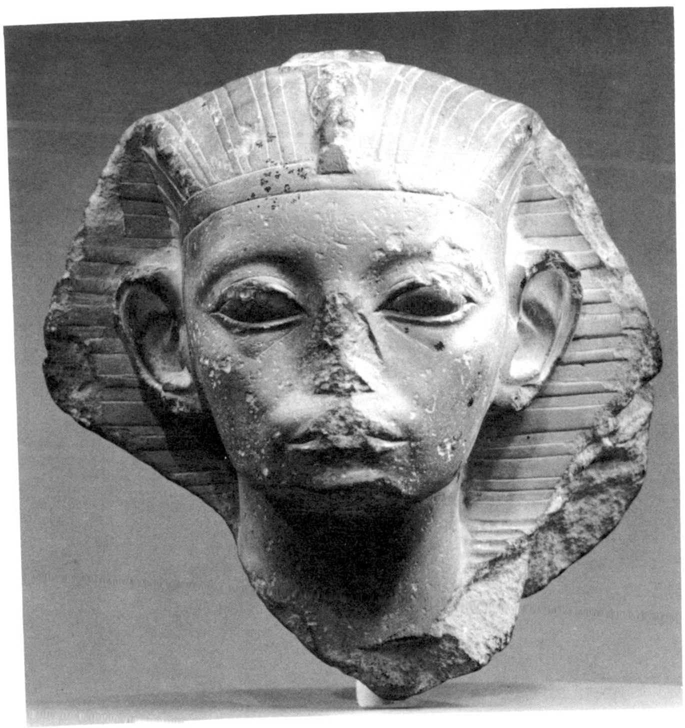

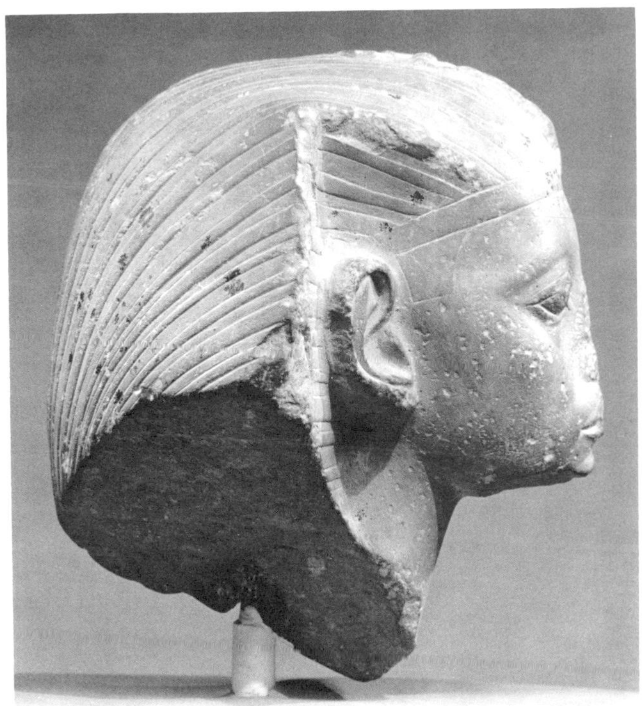

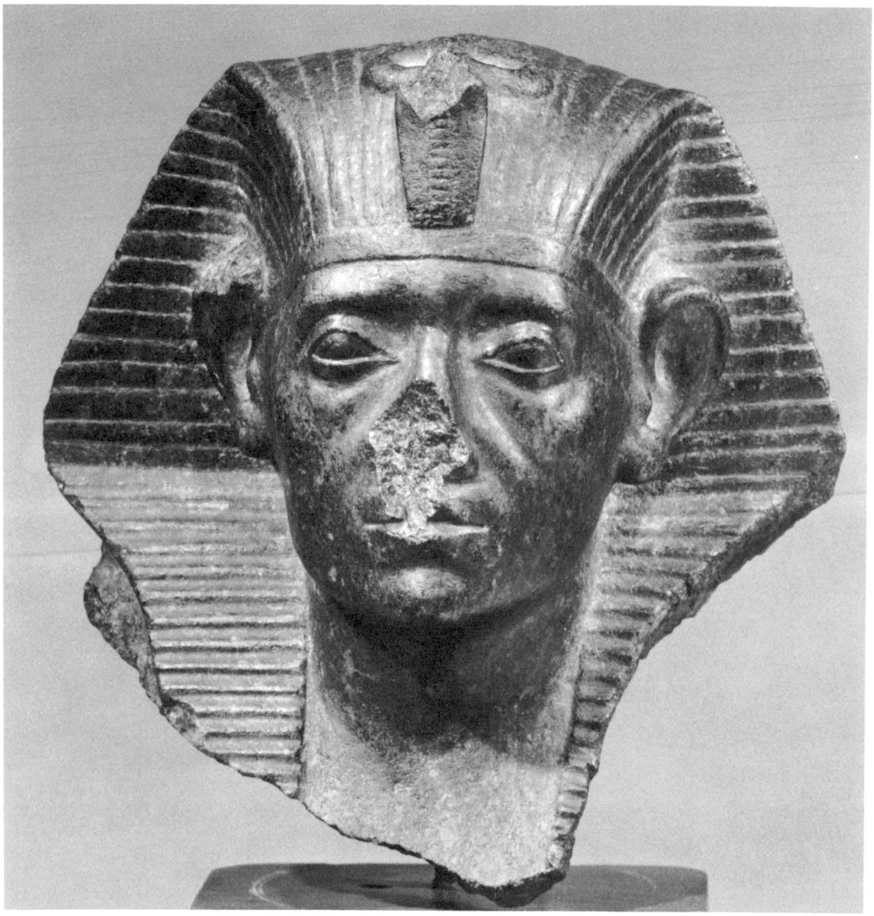

FIGURES 23, 24
Head of Sesostris III. The Metropolitan Museum of Art, Fletcher Fund and gift of Dr. and Mrs. Edmundo Lassalle through the Guide Foundation, 66.99.5

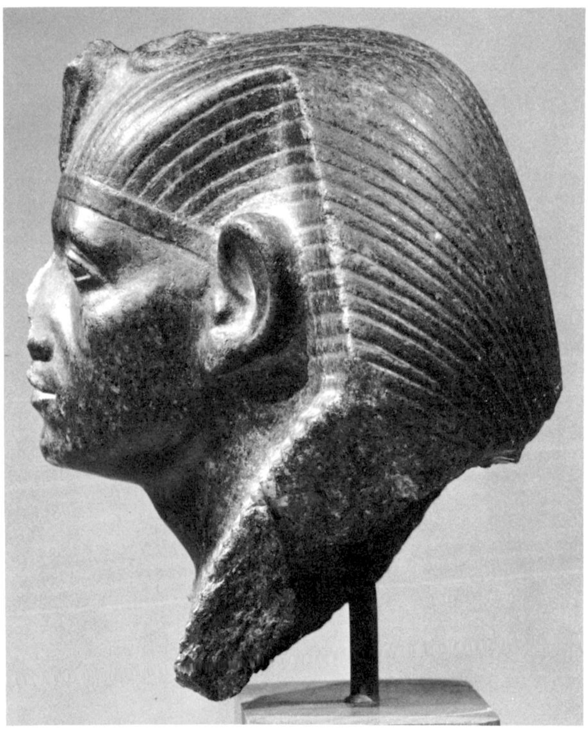

carries tabs before the ears. The uraeus emerges higher up the frontlet, and its body has only three windings. Though the ears have become much larger and project like wings, their lobes are smaller, and they are placed at a natural height. The damage to the chin and the abrasions to mouth and nose have upset the proportions of the face by overemphasizing the muscular nexus around the mouth, which is clearly turned down along its medial line, a characteristic of several portraits of Sesostris III.[66] The eyebrows are no longer defined by arcs carved in raised relief but follow the natural line of the brow. The most striking features, however, are the large, somewhat bulging eyes, with the lids indicated by incised lines, and the inner and outer canthi of similar shape and lacking any exaggeration. These are quite different in their heavy-lidded effect from the flat treatment of the eyes in the portraits of earlier kings. The Lisht head is a somewhat restrained

66. E.g., British Museum, 160 (686); Cairo Museum, no. 42011, 486; Kansas City, William Rockhill Nelson Gallery of Art, 62.11.

version, perhaps because it is carved in the idealistic mortuary tradition, of the characteristic physiognomy of Sesostris III as a young man. As his reign wore on, his portraits developed a realism and an exploration of the underlying structure of the face that can only be the result of the appointment as his master sculptor of an unknown artist of genius.

The evolution of this style can be seen in the black gabbro head in the Gallatin Collection (Figures 23, 24),[67] where the eyes have been treated as orbs lying within their sockets and have lost the last vestiges of the earlier flat treatment. The folds of flesh from the inner corners of the eyes, indicated in the Lisht head by incised lines, hint at the developing pouchiness of the king's later years. The head, however, is in the official style and represents Sesostris III as a man in the full vigor of life. It bears a resemblance to the statue of the same king, said to be from Medamūd, in The Brooklyn Museum,[68] which, however, has been carved with a less adventurous chisel and probably belongs to a "coronation series."[69]

A further stage in the development of the portraiture of the reign is evident in the head of the sphinx (Figures 25, 26),[70] carved in gem-hard gneissic diorite,

67. Acc. no. 66.99.5, height 13.5 cm., provenance unknown; Cooney, "Collection of Albert Gallatin," p. 5, no. 11. Correctly identified by Cooney as of Sesostris III as against my tentative attribution to Ammenemes III (C. Aldred, *Middle Kingdom Art* [London, 1950] no. 70). The form of the loop in the body of the uraeus, however, is not exclusive to Sesostris III, as Cooney maintains, since a statue of Ammenemes III from Karnak in the Cairo Museum has an uraeus with similar convolutions. Enough of the damaged nose remains to suggest that in profile it was probably of aquiline form (cf. the obsidian head in the Gulbenkian Collection), as compared with the more snub shape of Ammenemes III. The *nemes* with its uniform broad bands anticipates the fashion of the succeeding reign.

68. J. D. Cooney, *Five Years of Collecting* (New York, 1956) no. 3.

69. See note 52 above.

70. Acc. no. 17.9.2, height 42.5 cm., provenance unknown; "The Fiftieth Anniversary Exhibition," *BMMA* 15 (1920) p. 129.

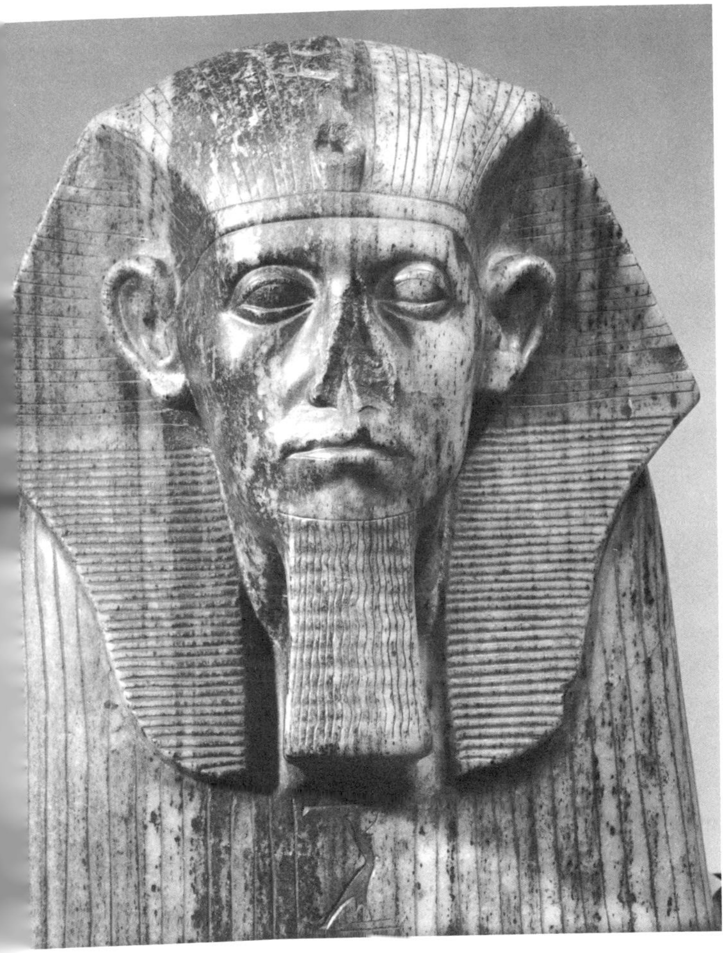

FIGURES 25, 26

Head of sphinx of Sesostris III. The Metropolitan Museum of Art, gift of Edward S. Harkness, 17.9.2

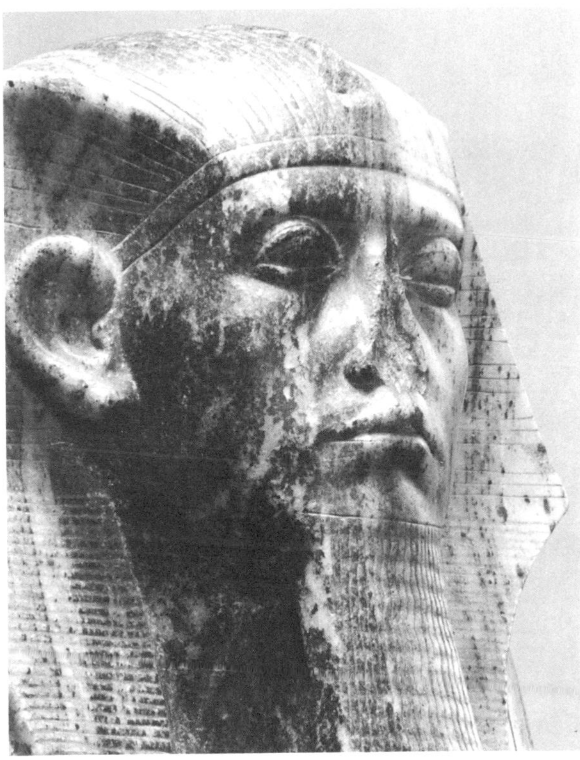

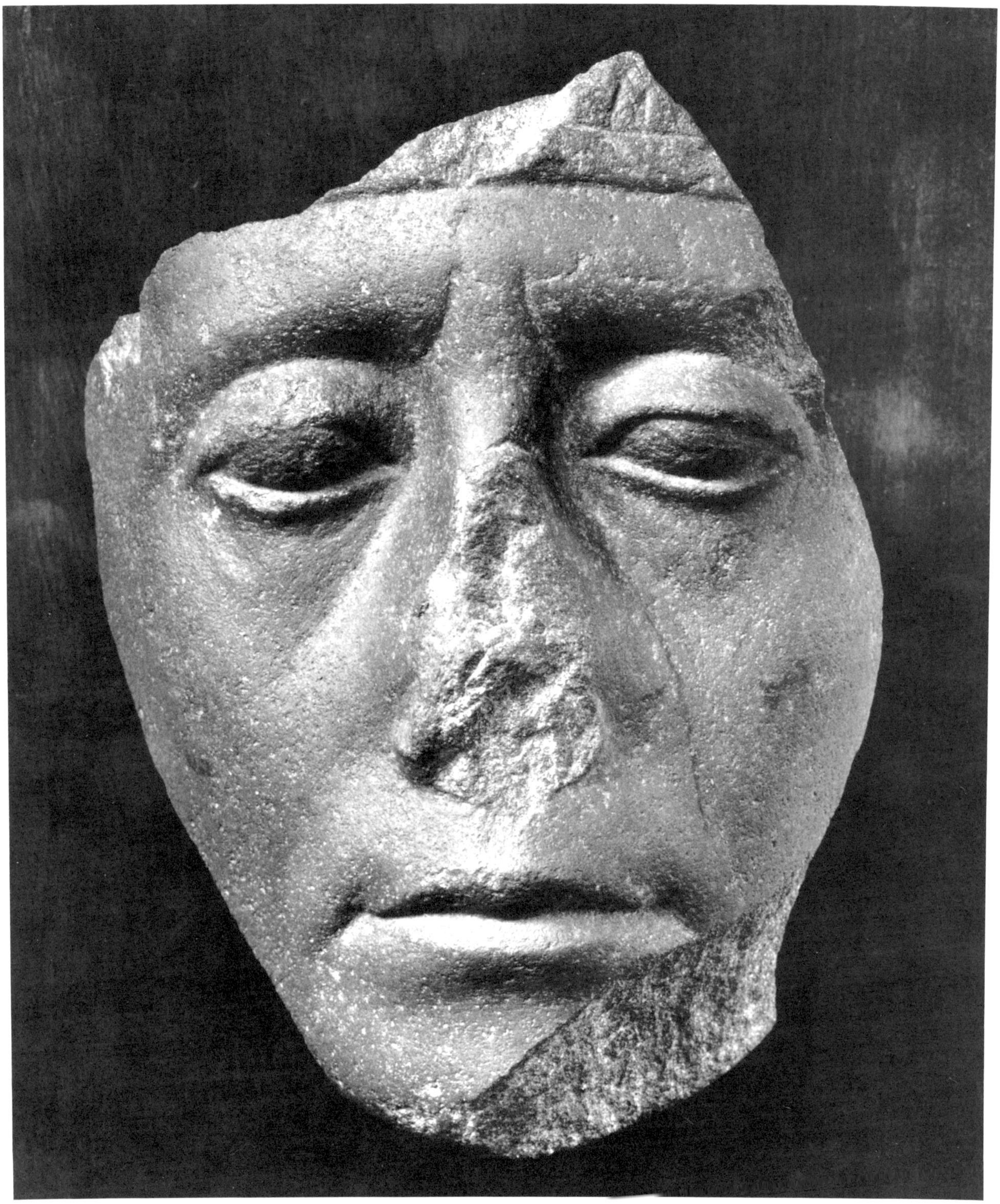

FIGURE 27
Head of Sesostris III. The Metropolitan Museum of Art, Carnarvon Collection, gift of Edward S. Harkness, 1926, 26.7.1394

where the dynamism of the earlier years is replaced by a grimmer expression on the face of a king who not only so reorganized the Egyptian possessions in Nubia and the Sudan that he was afterward worshiped there as a protector of the region, but also broke completely the power of the landed nobility at home, reducing the nomarchs to the status of crown servants. The burden of authority that such measures must have placed upon the pharaoh appears in the brooding latent power of this crouching sphinx with its haunting portrait of an autocrat. With the head shown in Figure 3, it is the only Middle Kingdom royal statue in the Museum's collection that may be identified by an inscription naming the king whom it represents, and therefore making recognition possible on grounds other than those of style and physiognomy. It is one of the few of the reign showing the king wearing the royal beard. The eyeballs within their sockets are carved in the realistic mode of the mature years. The musculature of the face has achieved a little of the flaccidity of advancing years, a transformation that is complete in the magnificent quartzite fragment, one of the world's masterpieces, that was formerly in the Carnarvon Collection and is now in the Metropolitan (Figure 27).[71] Here the grimness of the earlier portraits has been replaced by something less harsh, achieved by the consummate modeling of the very hard stone. The powerful superman, all passion spent, has become the careworn shepherd of his people.

During the long reign of Ammenemes III, the last great king of the XIIth Dynasty, a slight but appreciable modification in the realism of the sculpture of Sesostris III is detectable, and the conventions of the XIIIth Dynasty style are already adumbrated in such features as the summary modeling of the torso with the pectoral muscles joined together, the navel placed at the base of a deep ventral furrow, the disappearance of the sternal notch, and the rise of the corners of the *nemes* headcloth to prominent peaks. Such formulae are a sure indication of the proliferation of lesser studios with sculptors content to copy in isolation. By the reign of Ammenemes III a change had come over the social structure of Egypt, foreshadowing the conditions that were to prevail during the New Kingdom. The pharaoh had secured once more a lonely eminence. The estates of the former provincial barons must have been parceled out among the temples of the chief gods as well as the departments of the palace administration, and their expert staffs, including sculptors, had doubtless been absorbed by the new state machinery. Though the Middle Kingdom temple of Amūn is in too ruined a condition for much evidence to have survived, it was clearly wealthy and patronized extensively by the pharaohs of the Middle Kingdom, particularly by the last two rulers of the XIIth Dynasty. It would appear that the workshops of Amūn would already have been established and accepted responsibility for carving statues of the pharaoh, as was the practice in the New Kingdom. It was such temple ateliers that were called into requisition whenever a massive supply of statuary was suddenly required, as for a new building or at the beginning of a reign or for a jubilee. Such a supplementation of the royal studios in the now centralized state of the late Middle Kingdom probably accounts for the varied styles of portraiture that are characteristic of the period, and makes the identification of statues as representations of Ammenemes III an often hazardous undertaking.[72]

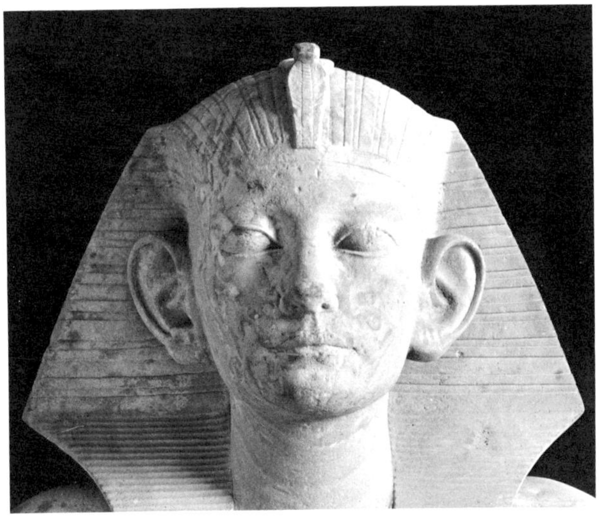

FIGURE 28
Head of seated statue of Ammenemes III. Cairo Museum, Cat. Gén. 385

71. Acc. no. 26.7.1394, height 16.5 cm., provenance unknown; Hayes, "Royal Portraits," pp. 119–124.

72. Hence the sphinxes and twin Niles from Tanis, and the bust from Mit Faris, as well as the Copenhagen head (Evers, *Staat*, I, pls. 111, 112, 120–125, 127–129), have been identified with kings other than Ammenemes III.

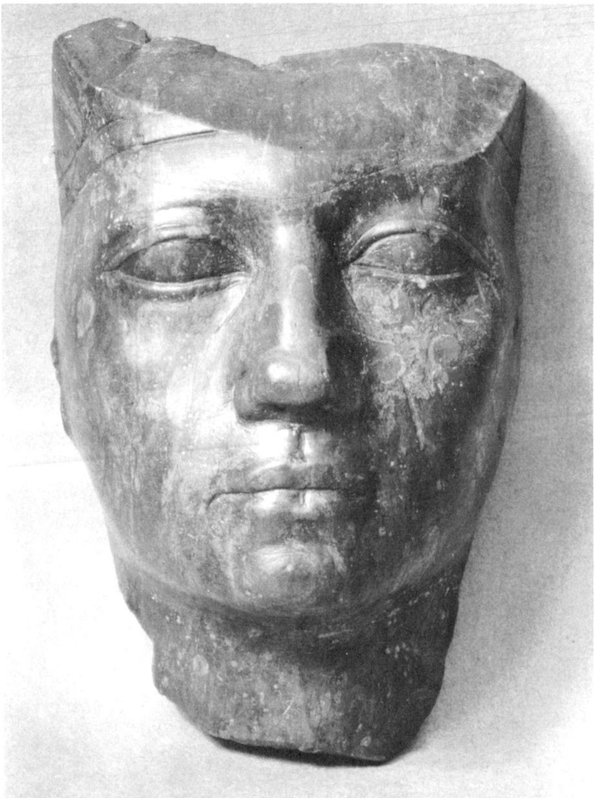

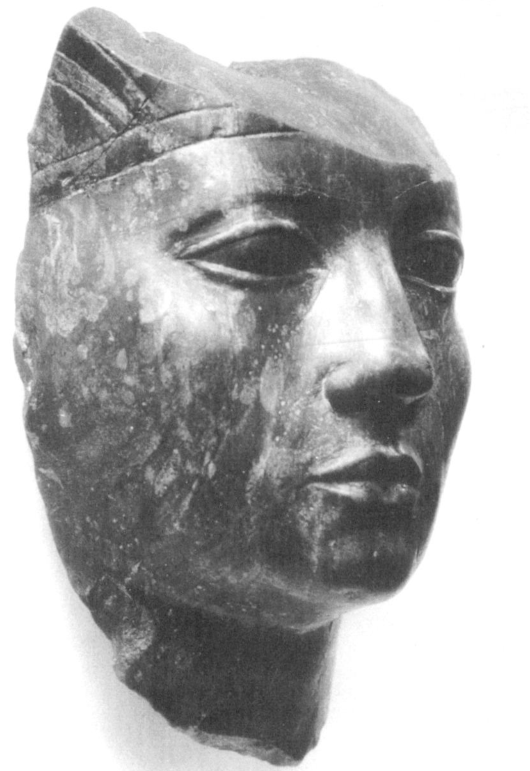

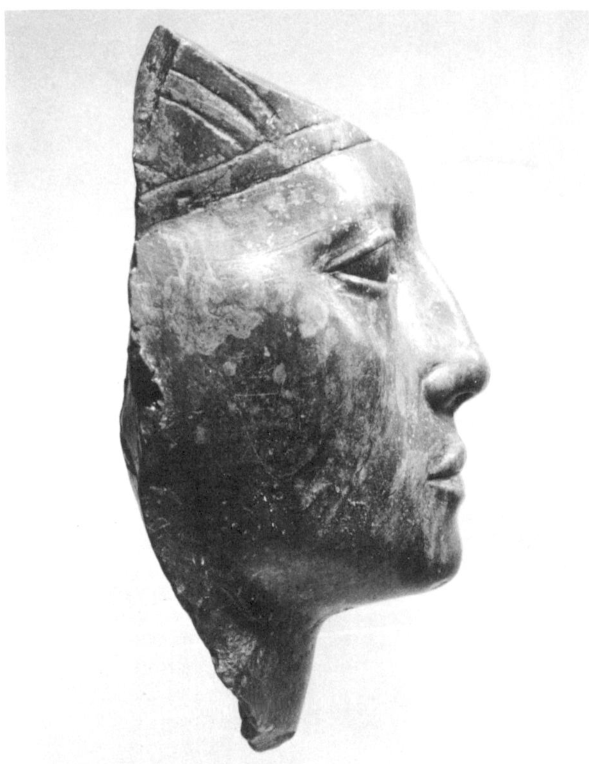

FIGURES 29–31
Head of Ammenemes III, The Metropolitan Museum of Art, The H. O. Havemeyer Collection, bequest of Mrs. H. O. Havemeyer, 29.100.150

A limestone seated statue of the king found near the ruins of the great labyrinthine funerary temple adjoining his pyramid at Hawara (Figure 28)[73] evidently represents the Memphite mortuary style in its latest manifestations. The portrait is idealistically treated, the eyes achieving a flatter effect than was the fashion in his father's reign, and the lips, though unsmiling, having lost the severe cast of the mouth of Sesostris III. Complete monumentality is attained by resting the palms of both hands flat upon the upper thighs, a convention that now entered the repertoire and became almost obligatory for seated pharaohs in this costume.

This idealistic style is seen in a number of portraits

73. Cairo Museum, Cat. Gén. no. 385; Evers, *Staat*, I, pls. 102–104.

of the king, all probably of Memphite inspiration, such as the alabaster head of a sphinx in the Louvre,[74] the head of a king wearing the White Crown in Copenhagen,[75] and possibly the head of an unidentified pharaoh in Vienna.[76] The Metropolitan has an outstanding example in this tradition in the head in mottled gray marble from the Havemeyer Collection (Figures 29–31),[77] which is exceptional for the complete state of the face, the nose having the same slightly arched form with a blunt tip seen in the serpentine head in the Fitzwilliam Museum in Cambridge and in the statues in the Louvre and the State Pushkin Museum of Fine Arts in Moscow,[78] while the eyes are rendered in the characteristic flat relief of the reign. The mouth has that furrow in the middle of its lower lip which is seen in other portraits of the king.[79]

74. Louvre, no. E.10938; P. Kriéger, "Un Portrait d'Amenemhat III, "*Revue d'Egyptologie* 11 (1957) pp. 73–75.

75. Evers, *Staat*, I, pls. 111, 112.

76. Vienna, Kunsthistorisches Museum, no. 37. This head is rather an enigma although B. V. Bothmer is not prepared to date it to the Late Period (cf. Schweitzer, note 32 above). The large ears, lappets without seams, single broad-stripe *nemes* without frontlet (see Louvre sphinx, no. A.23, of Ammenemes II), profile rising to an apogee above the occiput, and uraeus with compressed S-loop high on brow suggest the Middle Kingdom. The portraiture, despite damage, resembles that of Ammenemes III at the Hermitage in Leningrad (no. 729). The natural line of the eyebrows, the flat treatment of the eyes, the profile of the chin, and the pronounced cheeks belong to his reign. Only the mouth worked into an emphatic smile is uncharacteristic of the period, although incipient smiles are found on some statues of the reign (e.g., Leningrad, Hermitage, no. 729, and Cairo Museum, no. 383). There are a sufficient number of individual works from this reign for such an idiosyncrasy to be tolerated. Vienna no. 37 could be an idealistic portrait by the same studio that produced the more realistic or mature version in Copenhagen, no. AEIN 924.

77. Acc. no. 29.100.150, height 9 cm.; "The Exhibition of The H. O. Havemeyer Collection," *BMMA* 25 (1930) p. 75.

78. C. Ricketts, "Head of Amenemmēs III in Obsidian, from the Collection of the Rev. W. Macgregor, Tamworth," *JEA* 4 (1917) pp. 211–212 (Cambridge); Vandier, *Manuel*, p. 202, no. 2 (Louvre and Moscow).

79. E.g., the Fitzwilliam head (see preceding note); the Bubastis Colossus (Evers, *Staat*, I, pl. 114); the Louvre statuette N.465 (O. Rayet, *Monuments de l'Art Antique*, I [Paris, 1884] pl. 9).

FIGURES 32, 33
Bust of Ammenemes III. The Metropolitan Museum of Art, Rogers Fund, 45.2.6

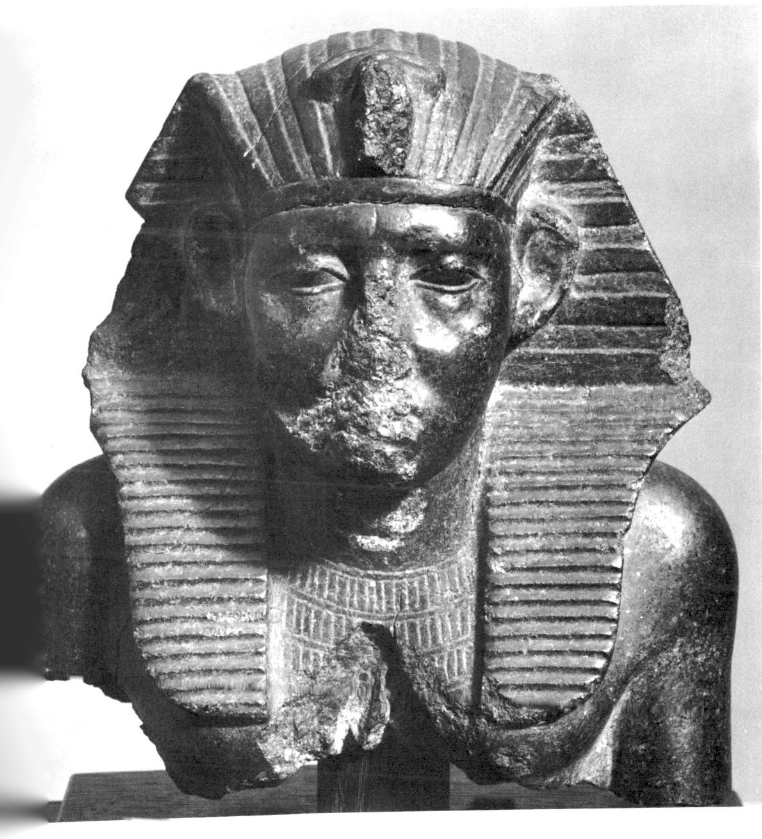

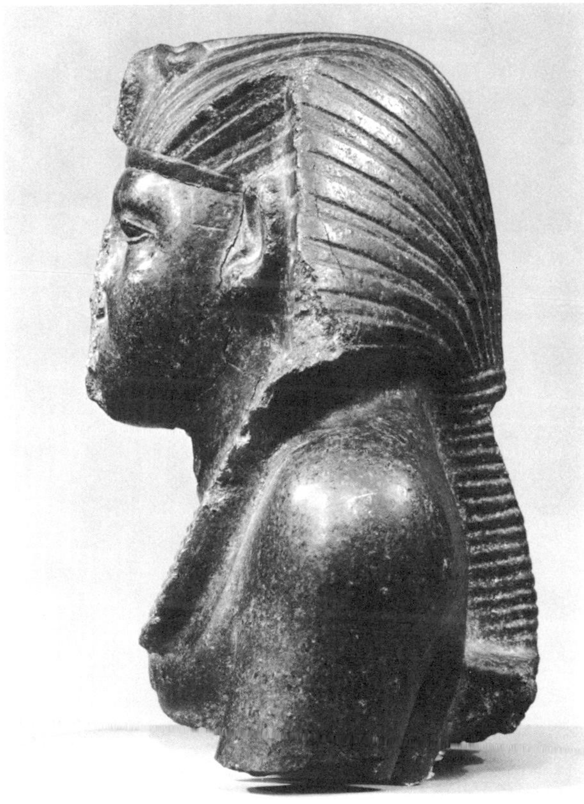

Many of the features of the statuary of Sesostris III, however, were a point of departure for the official style in the reign of Ammenemes III, who was co-regent during his father's last regnal year at least. The two vertical furrows in the brow of the later Sesostris III, for instance, are present in the Louvre statuette,[80] though this represents Ammenemes in his youth, and are also seen in the upper part of a black granite statue in the Metropolitan (Figures 32, 33).[81] Despite the battering that this bust has suffered, the resemblance to a series of granite statues of the king found at Karnak,[82] as well as a head in the Aegyptisches Museum in Berlin,[83] is striking. The wig-cover reverts to the single broad-stripe pattern of the earlier years of the dynasty, but

80. Louvre, no. N.465, see preceding note; cf. Metropolitan Museum, acc. no. 26.7.1394 (Figure 27) and Evers, *Staat*, I, pls. 83, 88.

81. Acc. no. 45.2.6, height 20 cm., provenance unknown; Hayes, "Royal Portraits," p. 122.

82. G. Legrain, *Statues et Statuettes*, I, *Musée du Caire, Catalogue Générale*, XXX (Cairo, 1906) nos. 42014–42016, 42018, 42020.

83. Evers, *Staat*, I, pl. 133.

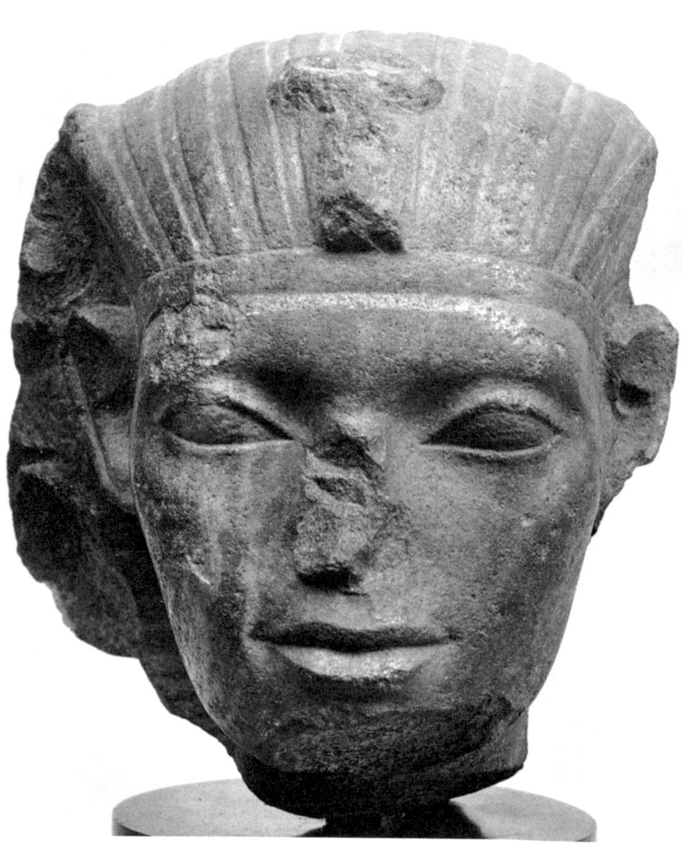

FIGURES 35, 36
Head of Ammenemes III. The Metropolitan Museum of Art, gift of J. Pierpont Morgan, 12.183.6

FIGURE 34
Head of Ammenemes III. The Metropolitan Museum of Art, gift of Dr. and Mrs. Thomas Foulds, 24.7.1

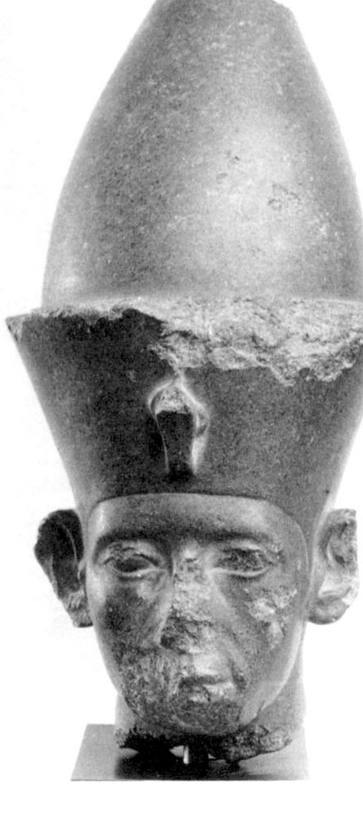

the peaks at the upper corners are more pronounced; at the same time the lappets lack the seam to their inner edges, so common in the work of the succeeding reigns.[84] The bossy cheeks and large ears are characteristic of the portraits of Sesostris III and persisted as a convention, together with a prominent chin, in the work of his son, possibly because both kings inherited a similar physiognomy. The eyes, bulging less from their sockets, and the design of the single compressed S-coil of the uraeus, which now springs from above the frontlet, put this bust firmly in the reign of Ammenemes III. The damage to the face is to be deplored the more because, while this fragment appears to be the work of a Theban studio, presumably sited in the workshops attached to the temple of Amūn, the portrait seems more

84. Evers, *Staat*, II, sec. 70.

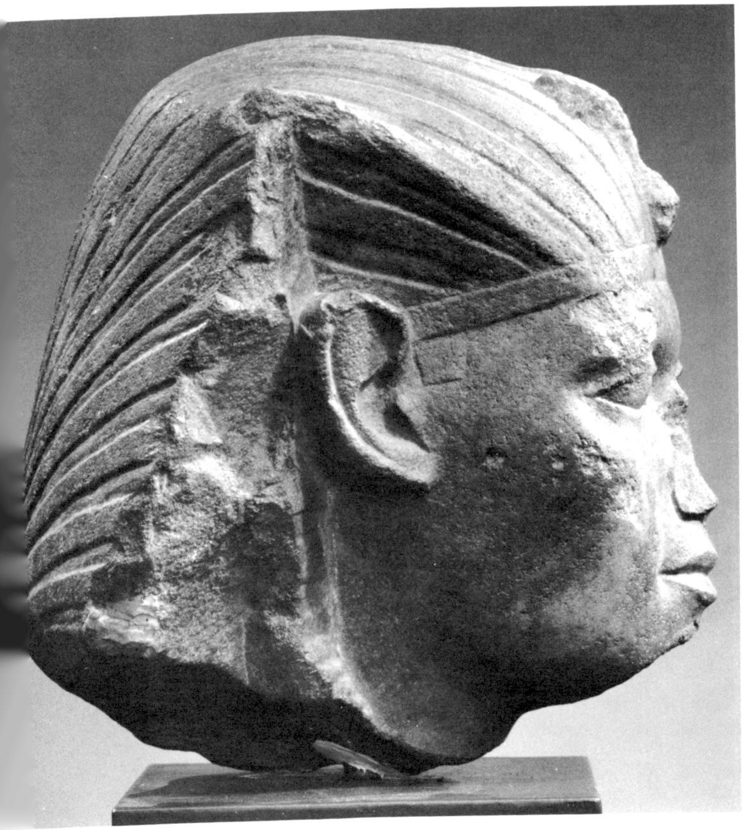

accomplished than that of its congeners in this group.

Another head of official type in the Museum collection shows the king with the marks of old age in the sagging of his facial muscles (Figure 34).[85] Here, although the eyes are sunk more within their sockets, they are not carved as independent orbs. The uraeus, with its single compressed S-coil placed behind the hood, is a critical dating factor. A similar head, also wearing the Double Crown, seen some years ago in the art market, and a head of Amūn with the features of the king, now in Cairo,[86] suggest a Theban provenance for this piece. The expert carving of the eyes and ears and the subtlety of the modeling of the face, which eludes all but the most favorable lighting, show that this is the work of a very accomplished sculptor, whose skill is not entirely obscured by the damage the head has sustained.

The last work to be considered is a quartzite head (Figures 35, 36)[87] that has been accredited to earlier kings, but which in the writer's opinion must be dated to the reign of Ammenemes III. It is in the idealistic style of the studios of Memphis, in the proximity of which its honey brown quartzite was doubtless quarried. The stylistic features are uncompromisingly of the reign of Ammenemes III. The uraeus, springing from above the frontlet, with a compressed S-turn set high on the brow, the upper curve of the *nemes* rising to a peak at each corner, and its crown reaching an apogee near the back of the head before descending rapidly to the root of the pigtail are in the fashion of this period, as is the single-stripe headcloth with its unseamed, narrow-pleated lappets. So are the prominent cheekbones and the everted lips with the double curve on their medial join. The philtrum, however, which is less pronounced than usual, and the relaxed mouth with its incipient smile, are in marked contrast to the tensions represented in the two foregoing heads. Nevertheless, they are found on one of the two colossal heads excavated by E. Naville at Bubastis in Lower Egypt and generally identified as of Ammenemes III on inscrip-

85. Acc. no. 24.7.1, height 42 cm., provenance unknown; Hayes, "Royal Portraits," pp. 123–124.

86. Vandier, *Manuel*, p. 201, pl. LXVII, 2.

87. Acc. no. 12.183.6, height 18.3 cm., provenance unknown; Hayes, "Royal Portraits," pp. 122–123.

FIGURE 37

Head of Ammenemes III. British Museum, 1063

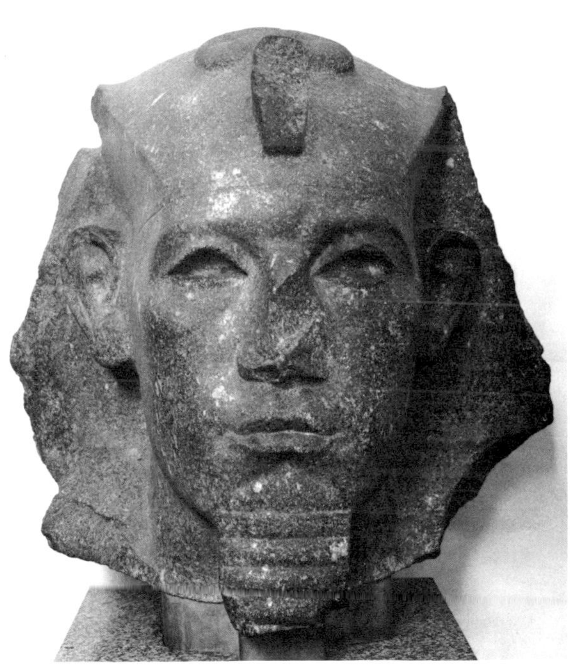

tional grounds (Figure 37).[88] The only exceptional features are the peculiar eyes with their elongation toward the inner canthi. Each is carved, however, in the flattish relief of the reign, and the idiosyncrasy of their unusual shape is not critical enough to deny that they depict Ammenemes III, particularly in view of the variation in the representation of the eye on statues inscribed with his name.[89] Similar eye shapes occur elsewhere on portraits from the dynasty, as on the Gallatin head of Sesostris III (Figure 23). Despite the almost complete loss of the chin and the difference of scale, the quartzite head bears a striking resemblance, particularly in profile, to the colossus from Bubastis in the British Museum.[90]

The portraits we have considered here are not the only examples of royal sculpture of the Middle Kingdom in the Metropolitan Museum, but they form a broad conspectus of the subject, showing the development of an art form that can scarcely be studied more conveniently anywhere else. If, to the eye of the layman, some of the visages may appear brutally shattered, they are still impressive in the melancholy ruin that the hands of time and men have brought upon them. At least half a dozen (Figures 10, 19, 23, 25, 27, 29) are among the supreme masterpieces of their kind, of which any great collection would count itself privileged to display but one example. That the Metropolitan Museum can muster so many among such a comprehensive range of royal portraits must be accounted its good fortune and its sober pride.

88. Evers, *Staat*, I, pl. 115.

89. E.g., Cairo Museum, nos. 385, 42014, 42020; Leningrad, Hermitage, no. 729.

90. Evers, *Staat*, I, pl. 116.

FREQUENTLY CITED SOURCES

ASAE—*Annales du Service des Antiquités de l'Egypte.*
BMMA—*Bulletin of The Metropolitan Museum of Art.*
Evers, *Staat*—H. Evers, *Staat aus dem Stein*, I, II (Munich, 1929).
JEA—*Journal of Egyptian Archaeology.*
Vandier, *Manuel*—J. Vandier, *Manuel d'Archéologie Egyptienne*, III (Paris, 1958).

NOTES

An Egyptian Glass Vessel in The Metropolitan Museum of Art

BIRGIT NOLTE

LOOKING THROUGH the great number of late sand-core vessels in the Greek and Roman Department of The Metropolitan Museum of Art, I came across a sand-core vessel purely Egyptian in character (Figure 1). The pear-shaped vessel is made of translucent, copper blue glass and decorated with white and yellow thread designs. Its height is 8.11 cm., the maximum diameter of the rim 4.0 cm., and the maximum diameter of the body 5.65 cm. A piece including parts of rim, neck, and shoulder was chipped off and has been put back in place. The vessel was bequeathed to the Museum by E. C. Moore in 1891.[1]

Egyptian sand-core vessels are known with certainty to have been produced from the early fifteenth century until the tenth century B.C.[2] Almost four hundred of these glowingly colored and delicately adorned vessels have been preserved as well as innumerable fragments. As far as we know, it was not before the sixth century B.C. that the sand-core technique was revived and a slightly different thread ornamentation became popular in the Mediterranean region.[3] The so-called late

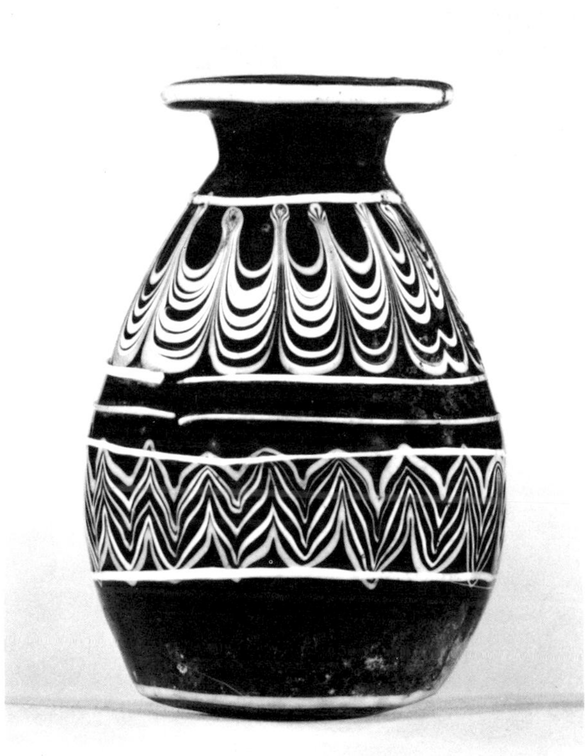

FIGURE 1

Sand-core vessel, Egyptian, mid-XIV century B.C. Height: 8.11 cm. The Metropolitan Museum of Art, bequest of Edward C. Moore, 91.1.1365

1. Acc. no. 91.1.1365; it was recently transferred to the Department of Egyptian Art. I am most grateful to Dr. Henry G. Fischer, Lila Acheson Wallace Curator in Egyptology at The Metropolitan Museum of Art, for his kind permission to publish this vessel.

2. P. E. Newberry, "A Glass Chalice of Tuthmosis III," *Journal of Egyptian Archaeology* 6 (1920) pp. 155–156.

3. P. Fossing, *Glass Vessels before Glass-blowing* (Copenhagen, 1940) p. 42.

sand-core vessels were produced on such a great scale that we still possess thousands of them. The sand-core technique continued to be used until the beginning of the Christian Era, when it was quickly made obsolete by the invention of glassblowing. This revolutionary change turned the manufacture of glass into entirely new channels. Although the Egyptian and the late sand-core vessels were both fashioned around a sandy core,[4] these two types usually differ in quality of glass, in colors, and especially in shapes and ornamental design.

The Egyptian glass vessel from the Greek and Roman Department mentioned above is one of the most interesting specimens. While its shape and even the combination of patterns are almost unique, it can be placed with probability among a series of Egyptian vessels.

To produce this vessel, a pear-shaped sandy core was attached to the end of a metal rod. It was dipped into copper blue, molten glass and turned around until a thick layer covered it. Next the decorations were applied: a white thread of glass was wound in a spiral five times around the upper part of the body and another one six times around the lower part of the body. In both cases a single strand of yellow was added at top and bottom. The ornamentation was pressed into the still soft surface by rolling the vessel on a flat stone slab. Then on the upper part of the body the spirals were dragged upward fifteen times with a bronze pin, so as to obtain the festoons with which Egyptian glass vessels are frequently adorned. They end in loops, where the pin was taken out of the matrix. On the lower part of the body, the spirals were pulled out of place upward and downward to form a featherlike pattern. There are places where the threads are mingled with the matrix, giving the appearance of an additional, translucent, light blue thread design.

The vessel was then rolled again on a flat stone slab. But the material had already annealed too far and had become too stiff to acquire by this procedure a uniform and smooth surface. Next the rim was worked out of the body. The rim still retains traces of the pincers used to shape it. Horizontal threads of glass were then applied to the vessel to complete the decoration. The threads surrounding rim and base are yellow. The one above the festoons is also yellow, while the one below is white. A yellow band divides the upper from the lower part of the ornamentation. The feather pattern is encircled by yellow bands. The horizontal threads surrounding the body partly overlap the festoons and the feather pattern and still protrude in relief. Finally the core with its coating of glass was slipped off the metal rod and probably put between pieces of charcoal for annealing. After the glass cooled, the sandy core was scraped out to obtain a hollow vessel.

Most Egyptian glass vessels are perfectly preserved owing to the dry climate in Egypt. However, Egyptian glass vessels exported to the Mediterranean region[5] and most late sand-core vessels have been damaged by moisture. As the translucent, copper blue vessel in question has hardly suffered from time, I would suggest that this vessel was found in Egypt. The surface retains its polish; there are only a few spots where the glass has turned silver blue through corrosion. Traces of brown earth still adhere to the side of the vessel where it touched the ground.

For several reasons this vessel can only be compared with Egyptian specimens. It is a pear-shaped alabastron. This shape is unknown among late sand-core vessels, which include tall and slender alabastra, amphoriskoi with button-shaped feet, oenochoai, and aryballoi, most of them fitted with different types of handles.[6] Among the various Egyptian glass vessels,[7] however, there are some rare examples in the shape of a pear. Of special interest to us is one in the Museo Egizio, Turin, that is dated to the first years of the reign of Amenhotep III (1403–1365 B.C.). It belongs to the funeral equipment of Cha from tomb no. 8 of Deir el Medineh in Thebes (Figure 2).[8] This vessel, like the one in the Metropolitan Museum, has a protruding rim and a pear-shaped body with a somewhat flattened base, but it is taller, its height being 11.0 cm., and the body is wider, the diameter being 8.0 cm.

4. W. M. F. Petrie, *Tell el Amarna* (London, 1894) p. 27; A. Lucas, *Ancient Egyptian Materials and Industries* (London, 1962) p. 192; B. Nolte, *Die Glasgefässe im alten Ägypten* (Berlin, 1968) p. 29.

5. W. M. F. Petrie, *Ancient Gaza*, II (London, 1932) pp. 10, 48, pl. XXVI, 139, 140; III (London, 1933) pp. 11, 38, sec. 7; IV (London, 1934) p. 11, pl. XXXVI, 1, 2.

6. Fossing, *Glass Vessels*, pp. 43 ff.

7. Nolte, *Die Glasgefässe*, pp. 160 ff.

8. A. Fabretti et al., *Regio Museo di Torino, Antichità Egizie* (Turin, 1882) Suppl. 8480. E. Schiaparelli, *Relazione sui lavori della Missione Archaeologica Italiana in Egitto*, II, *La tomba intatta dell' architetto Cha* (Turin, 1927) pp. 109, 111, fig. 92.

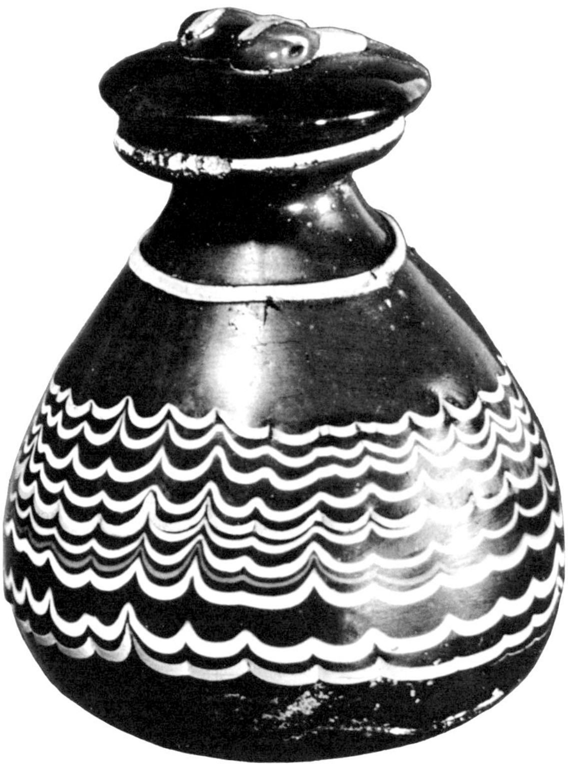

FIGURE 2
Sand-core vessel, Egyptian, early XIV century B.C. Height: 11 cm. Museo Egizio, Turin, no. Suppl. 8480

As this vessel, when excavated, was covered by a glass lid, we can assume there existed a cover of the same kind for the similarly shaped vessel in the Metropolitan Museum, though without such decoration as the little birds on top, which are unique to the cover of Cha's vessel. Such lids were used on Egyptian glass vessels only when they imitated broad-rimmed stone vessels[9] identical in shape to the two vessels under discussion. In contrast, glass vessels copying the shapes of vessels made of materials such as clay and metal seem to have been closed with pieces of linen and wax.[10]

Not only the shapes but also the thread decorations of the two vessels show similarities. The thread designs can easily be distinguished from those copied hundreds of years later in the Mediterranean region to decorate the late sand-core vessels. Apart from differences in the colors (for instance, instead of the Egyptian bright yellow color, there appears an orange; instead of sky blue, a turquoise) there are other differentiating characteristics.

The Egyptian threads are regular in thickness and in distance from one another, whereas the threads of the late sand-core vessels are often surprisingly irregular in spacing and breadth, some of them extremely fine in execution, some rather crude. In the case of an ornamental design with alternating colors, the Egyptian threads were interrupted after each different colored spiral—whether it turned only once or several times around the body. This resulted in a very exact decoration. The ornamentation of the late sand-core vessels, though, was usually built up in another way: A thread of one special color was used once only and was wound without interruption spirally around the body, leaving narrow intervals where ever the color was wanted for the pattern, and broad intervals where ever a thread of another color was to be applied later on. After this procedure, a thread of a second color was coiled on top of the first one to fill in the sparsely decorated areas, crudely crossing places where the first thread had been closely spaced. Up to three different colors were used.

The Egyptian spirals were pulled out of place to form festoons or feather patterns. Any straight bands were applied afterward. A great part of the spirals on the late sand-core vessels, however, often remained untouched to form straight ornamental designs, and usually only the threads of the body's medial areas were dragged into different kinds of festoons and featherlike patterns.

Both of the Egyptian glass vessels referred to above have yellow threads surrounding the rim and the upper part of the body. As the rest of the ornamental design of the vessel in possession of the Metropolitan Museum is much more delicate and reveals a greater technical skill than the simple festoons decorating Cha's vessel, one is inclined to look upon the former vessel as a product of glassmakers who reached a higher degree of craftsmanship. It might therefore be dated to the sec-

9. E.g., British Museum, no. 24391, color pl. in W. Haberey, "Der Werkstoff Glas im Altertum," *Glastechnische Berichte* 30 (1957) fig. 5.

10. G. Daressy, *Fouilles de la Vallée des Rois, Catalogue général* (Cairo, 1902) nos. 24099, 24753, 24769, 24773.

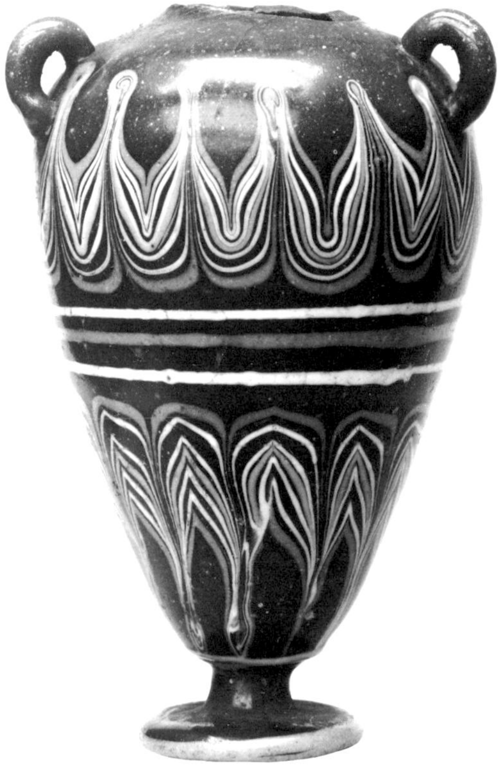

FIGURE 3
Sand-core vessel, Egyptian, first half of the XIV century B.C. Height: 10 cm. Louvre, Paris, no. AF 2622

ond half of the reign of Amenhotep III or to the beginning of the Amarna period. The dating is strengthened by the fact that fragments with similar patterns have been excavated in Malkata[11]—Thebes—as well as in Amarna.[12] However, Cha's vessel was made during the first years of Amenhotep III's reign, when the palace area, Malkata, had not yet been erected. The similarity of a great number of fragments from Malkata and Amarna results from the fact that the same group of manufacturers who worked in Malkata under Amenhotep III followed Amenhotep IV (1365–1347 B.C.), the successor to the throne, to his new capital at Tell el Amarna. As glass had a high trade value, and as the aristocratic class, who were the only ones who could afford these precious objects, had moved, the glassmakers of necessity moved with them from Malkata to Amarna. The decorations on the Metropolitan Museum's vessel can be compared with those on many fragments from these factories, which have the same designs.

As to the regular festoons ending in loops, there is a similar design on a blue fragment from Malkata in the Victoria and Albert Museum, London, no. 421/33-1897, decorated with yellow, white, and light blue, and on a great number of fragments from the South Village and the Magazines in the area of Malkata that are now in the Metropolitan Museum. The same kind of festoon occurs on fragments from Amarna, which are in various other museums, for instance, a very typical one in the Staatliche Museen zu Berlin, Ägyptische Abteilung, no. 131, which shows the same translucent, copper blue matrix adorned with white festoons surrounded by yellow ones, as on the vessel in question.

The same type of feather pattern, though more vivid, appears in the same colors on a fragment from Malkata in the Victoria and Albert Museum, no. 421/48-1897, as well as on many other fragments in similar combinations of colors that were excavated by the Metropolitan Museum in the South Village area and in the Magazines of Malkata. As most of these fragments are very small, they have not been given numbers, and the same is true of many other similar fragments from Amarna in various museums. Many of them are analogous to the fragment in the Staatliche Museen zu Berlin, no. 73. Patterns enclosed by straight horizontal bands occur occasionally in Malkata, but they are much more common in Amarna. Two handled flasks from Amarna show this type of decoration, for instance.[13]

The vessel in the Metropolitan Museum can also be compared with a series of vessels that were previously assigned to a group of manufacturers of the time of Amenhotep III and Amenhotep IV.[14] There are in particular two vessels showing many similar details. One is a glass amphoriskos in the Louvre, no. AF 2622

11. Newberry, "Glass Chalice," p. 156; A. M. Lythgoe, "The Egyptian Expedition 1916–17," supplement to *Bulletin of The Metropolitan Museum of Art* 13 (1918) p. 6; H. E. Winlock "The Work of the Egyptian Expedition," *Bulletin of The Metropolitan Museum of Art* 7 (1912) pp. 187–188.

12. Petrie, *Tell el Amarna*, p. 27; J. D. S. Pendlebury, *Tell el-Amarna* (London, 1935) pp. 95, 142; *Ausgrabung der Deutschen Orientgesellschaft in Amarna* (unpublished).

13. T. E. Peet, "Excavations at Tell el-Amarna," *Journal of Egyptian Archaeology* 7 (1921) p. 175, pl. XXX, top; T. E. Peet et al., *The City of Akhenaten*, I (London, 1923) p. 24, pl. XII, 7.

14. Nolte, *Die Glasgefässe*, no. 11, no. 15, pp. 105 ff.

(Figure 3).[15] This shows two patterns separated by three horizontal bands, a yellow one flanked by white ones, exactly as they occur on the vessel in question. The design consists of festoons and arcades running into feather patterns and ending in loops, again exactly as they decorate the Metropolitan Museum's vessel.

The other vessel of special interest to us is no. 1836 in the Ägyptische Abteilung, Staatliche Museen zu Berlin (Figure 4).[16] It is decorated with a feather pattern encircled by straight bands, as on the Metropolitan Museum's vessel, and adorned with festoons of the same kind as those on Cha's vessel, but in this case bordered by horizontal threads.

Thus it is possible to establish a chronological correlation between the vessel in the Metropolitan Museum and several Egyptian glass vessels and fragments. Certainly the Metropolitan's vessel was produced in Egypt by a group of manufacturers working originally in the palace area of Amenhotep III, Malkata, and later on in the capital of Amenhotep IV, Tell el Amarna. For several reasons I am inclined to date it even more precisely and to ascribe it to the glass factories of Tell el Amarna. There are, for instance, the horizontal bands encircling the patterns as well as the composition of a copper blue matrix decorated with yellow and white threads only. These traits were still rare during the reign of Amenhotep III and became more popular only a little later.

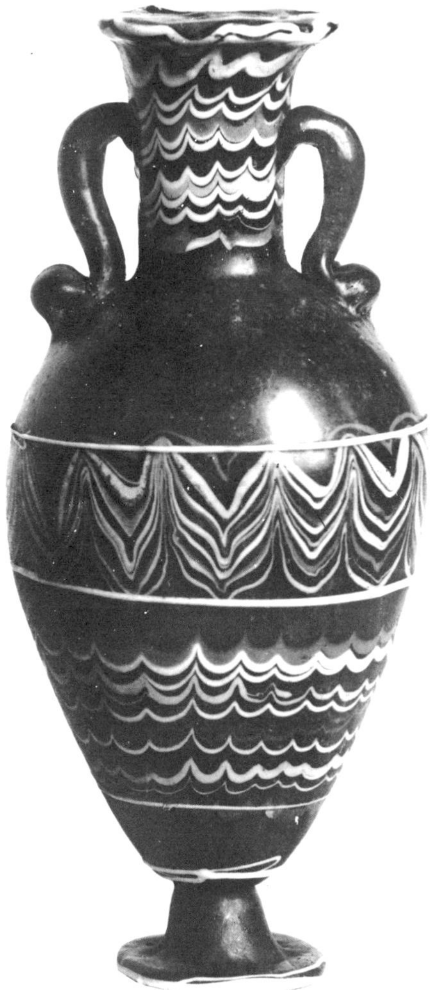

FIGURE 4
Sand-core vessel, Egyptian, first half of the XIV century B.C. Height: 12.5 cm. Staatliche Museen zu Berlin, Ägyptische Abteilung, no. 1836

15. W. Froehner, *Verrerie antique appartenant à M. J. Pierpont Morgan, Collection Julien Gréau*, part I (Paris, 1903) pl. XXIII, 8.

16. R. Lepsius, *Denkmäler aus Aegypten und Aethiopien*, Textband I (Leipzig, 1897) p. 155, fig. 3; *Ars Vitraria, Kunstgewerbemuseum Schloss Koepenick* (Berlin, 1965) p. 31, fig. 4.

Some Emblematic Uses of Hieroglyphs with Particular Reference to an Archaic Ritual Vessel

HENRY G. FISCHER

Lila Acheson Wallace Curator in Egyptology, The Metropolitan Museum of Art

THE SUBJECT OF this brief study is a pair of protodynastic schist dishes that were purchased in Luxor during the winter of 1918–1919, when Ambrose Lansing was conducting the Metropolitan Museum's excavations in the Theban necropolis, across the river. Apart from some astute remarks by William C. Hayes, which will be mentioned presently, little notice has been given to them, and even less notice has been given to an interesting emblematic parallel in the Third Dynasty tomb of Hesi-Re. These three topics will be explored in turn, beginning with the more important of the two dishes.

1. A HIEROGLYPHIC DISH

The elaborate spouted dish illustrated in Figures 1–5 is the most interesting and handsome object in that part of the Museum's Egyptian collection which antedates the Old Kingdom.[1] It is also the most interesting example among a series of schist vessels in which the First Dynasty sculptors exploited their technical mastery to the limit.[2] And, perhaps because the craftsman who created it was more fully aware of the limitations of his material, it is much better preserved than the other examples. The delicate plasticity of the design is securely based upon the solid floor of the dish—a precursor of the "negative space" that is so characteristic a feature of later stone sculpture—and there is an ample, though inconspicuous, amount of reinforcement at particularly vulnerable points, such as the narrow juncture of the spout. Not surprisingly, the functional nature of the piece is combined with an elegance of space, shape, and proportion.

The hollowed outer edge of the dish is enclosed by a pair of arms, the slenderness of which is indicative of their hieroglyphic character, representing the sign 𓂓 (*kꜣ*, "spirit"). They are displayed in low relief on sides and back, with the hands emerging more completely

1. Acc. no. 19.2.16. Length 17.5 cm., width 14.5 cm. Provenance unknown, but in view of the fact that it was purchased in Luxor, Abydos is a possibility. Previously illustrated by N. E. Scott, *The Home Life of the Ancient Egyptians: A Picture Book* (New York, 1944) fig. 25; C. Aldred, *The Egyptians* (London, 1961) pl. 3; W. C. Hayes, *The Scepter of Egypt*, I (New York, 1953) p. 43, fig. 31.

2. W. B. Emery, *Great Tombs of the First Dynasty*, I (Cairo, 1949) p. 101, fig. 58, pl. 40 (A, B) (also W. S. Smith, *Art and Architecture of Ancient Egypt* [London, 1958] pl. 9 [A]); W. B. Emery, *The Tomb of Hemaka* (Cairo, 1938) p. 40, pl. 19 (also W. B. Emery, *Archaic Egypt* [Harmondsworth, 1961] pl. 39 [a]); Emery, *Archaic Egypt*, pl. 38 (a); P. Montet, "Tombeaux des Ire et IVe dynasties à Abou-Roach," *Kêmi* 8 (1946) pp. 176–177, pl. 5. Cf. J.-Ph. Lauer, *La Pyramide à Degrés: Compléments*, III (Cairo, 1939) pp. 10–11, fig. 16. A First Dynasty example in limestone is shown by Emery, *Archaic Egypt*, pl. 35 (a); those of the following dynasty, made of schist and other stones, are heavier and less refined, as illustrated by Emery's pls. 35 (b) and 39 (b).

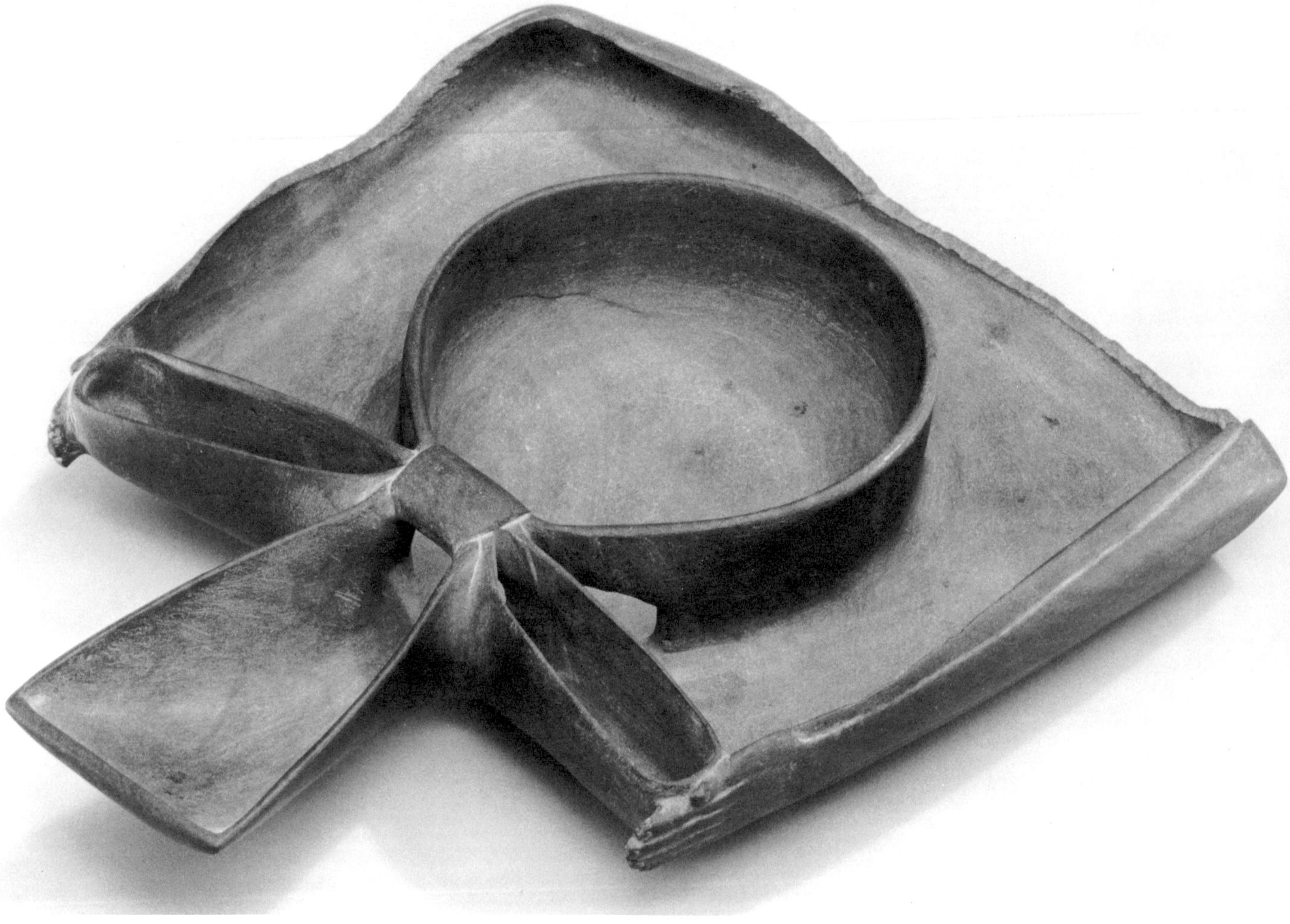

FIGURE I
Ritual vessel. The Metropolitan Museum of Art, Rogers Fund, 19.2.16

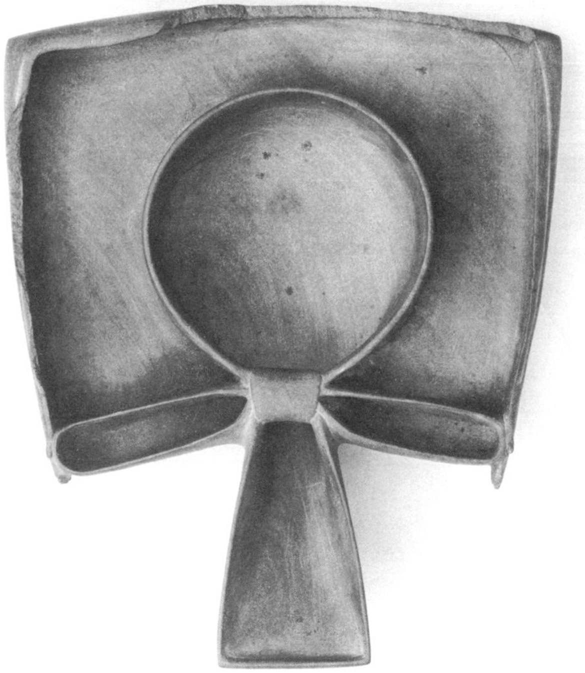

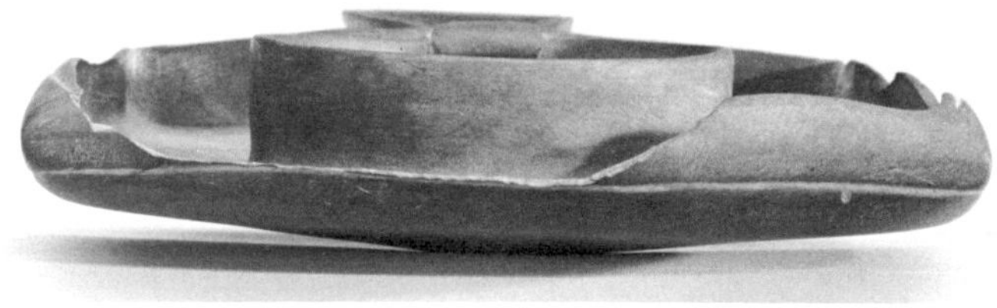

FIGURES 2–4
Top, rear, and side views of the Metropolitan Museum's ritual vessel

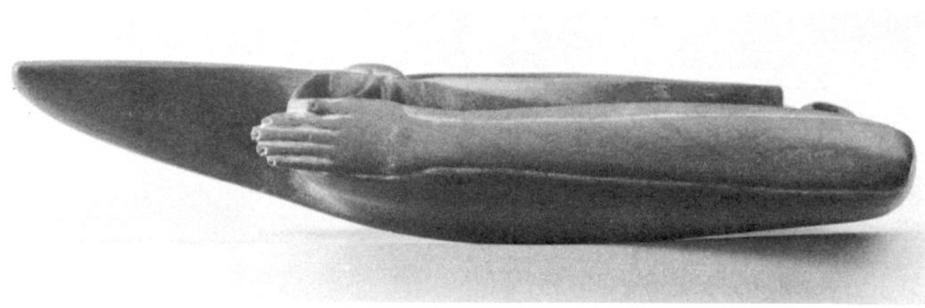

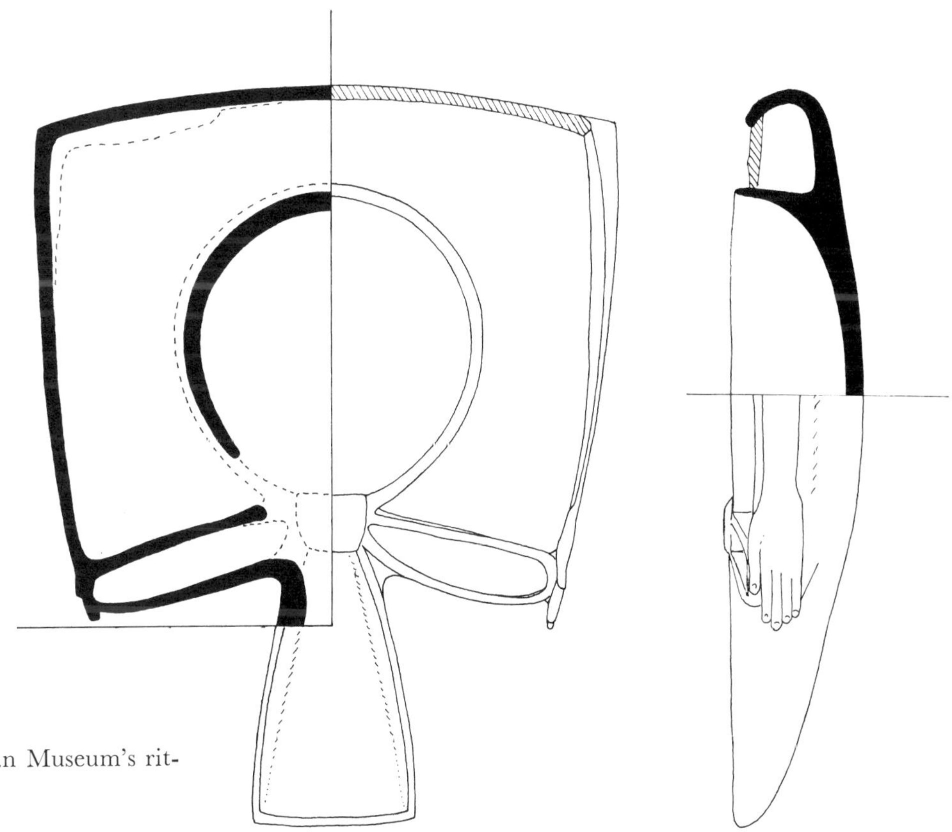

FIGURE 5
Structure of the Metropolitan Museum's ritual vessel

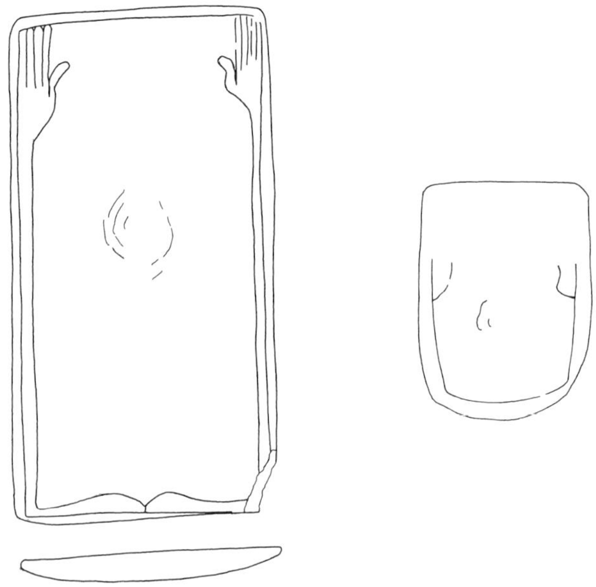

FIGURE 6
Protodynastic cosmetic palettes. After Quibell

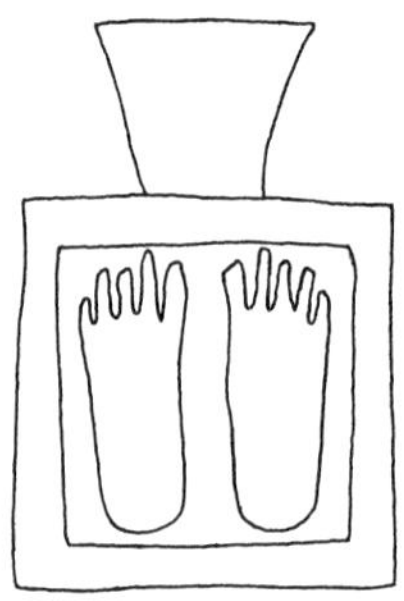

FIGURE 7
Old Kingdom footbath. After James

in the round. This device similarly frames at least two protodynastic schist cosmetic palettes (Figure 6),[3] but in the present case its meaning is more explicit, for the arms present an emblem that is evidently to be interpreted as an archaic form of the hieroglyph ☥ (*‘nḫ*, "life"). The lower part of the sign serves as a spout, and the three loops of the upper part are inconspicuously pierced with apertures of diminishing width so that water could flow throughout the emblem and become imbued with its potency. This idea is akin to that of the much later "cippi of Horus," such as the Metternich stela (The Metropolitan Museum of Art, acc. no. 50.85), over which water was poured so that the virtue of the stela's magical spells could be tapped for the relief of stings and bites.[4] In the present case, however, the water was almost certainly intended for lustration or libation, and a similar combination of rectangle and projecting spout is echoed in a receptacle used for bathing, as represented at the beginning of the Fourth Dynasty (Figure 7).[5]

The lustration ritual of ancient Egypt, whether it was performed for the living or for the dead, was intended as much more than a purification. As evidenced by the Old Kingdom Pyramid Texts, as well as later scenes from tombs and temples, it also provided the recipient with life. In New Kingdom depictions of lustrations the stream of water takes the form of a series of ☥-signs, sometimes alternating with 𓌀, emblematic of "power" (Figure 8).[6] One unusual example shows water poured over a god from a vessel that is held by

3. J. E. Quibell, *Archaic Objects, Catalogue général du Musée du Caire* (Cairo, 1904–1905) nos. 14234, 14235. In neither case is the provenance known; but both show signs of wear at the center, as well as traces of green eye-paint. I am not altogether certain about the authenticity of a third example, which is illustrated in Henri Asselberghs, *Chaos en Beheersing* (Leiden, 1961) no. 107, pl. 59.

4. N. E. Scott, "The Metternich Stela," *BMMA* n. s. 9 (1950–1951) pp. 201–217. The use of these objects is discussed by P. Lacau, "Les statues 'guérisseuses,' " *Académie des Inscriptions et Belles-lettres, Monuments et Mémoires* 25 (1921–1922) pp. 189–209; K. Seele, "Horus on the Crocodiles," *Journal of Near Eastern Studies* 6 (1947) p. 48.

5. W. M. F. Petrie, *Medum* (London, 1872) pl. 13; T. G. H. James, *British Museum, Hieroglyphic Texts*, 2nd ed., I (London, 1961) pl. 2 (3).

6. For the complete papyrus see E. L. B. Terrace and H. G. Fischer, *Treasures of Egyptian Art from the Cairo Museum* (London, 1970) pp. 153–156. The scene illustrated is discussed by A. Blackman, "Sacramental Ideas and Usages in Ancient Egypt," in *PSBA* 40 (1918) pp. 86 ff., and in *Recueil de travaux relatifs à la philologie et à l'archéologie égyptiennes et assyriennes* 39 (1920) pp. 53–55. During the New Kingdom the stream of ☥-signs was confined to the lustration of the king (for further examples see A. Calverley, *The Temple of King Sethos I at Abydos*, III [London and Chicago, 1938] pl. 35; IV [London and Chicago, 1958] pl. 43; and Oriental Institute, *Medinet Habu*, V [Chicago, 1957] pls. 296, 309), but Blackman (*Rec. trav.* 39, p. 54) shows a scene from a private tomb of the early Eighteenth Dynasty (N. Davies, *Five Theban Tombs* [London, 1913] pl. 21) in which each of the streams of water falls upon a large ☥-sign. The Eleventh Dynasty representation illustrated by Blackman, p. 53 (cf. E. Drioton, "Une figuration cryptographique sur une stèle du Moyen Empire," *Revue d'Egyptologie* 1 [1933] pp. 217–218, fig. 7) may express the same idea.

FIGURE 8
Detail of a Twenty-first Dynasty funerary papyrus. Cairo Museum, T. 14/7/35/6 (photo: Archives photographiques, Paris)

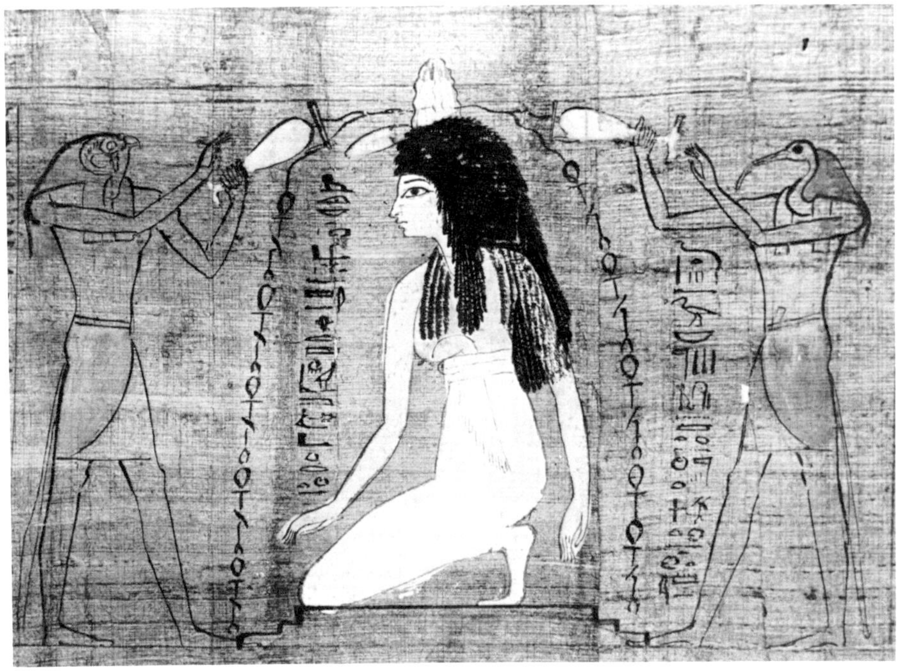

the ☥-sign (Figure 9),[7] and in other cases the lustration of the king is poured from a jar in the form of 𓏁☥, combining 𓏁 and ☥.[8] This type of vessel more commonly served for libations to the gods, and, in a funerary context, the Pyramid Texts speak of the quickening and rejuvenating effects of cold water offered to the deceased, for example, "A libation is poured! Wake up O sleepers!"[9] In both cases, for purification as well as libation, these texts refer to the water as an exudation that has come forth from Osiris, or "the water which is in thee."[10] It accordingly seems appropriate that it be dispensed by one's own ka, but it should be noted that the ka shares the same benefit; one spell says: "Purify thyself. Thy ka purifies himself. He sits and he eats with thee."[11] If, as these texts suggest, the spouted dish was employed to confer some benefit upon its owner after his death, with the help of his ka, the distinction between lustration and libation becomes difficult, for there was

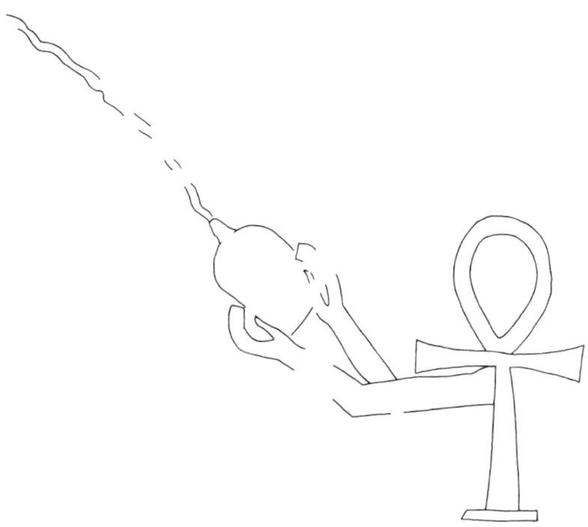

FIGURE 9
Drawing on an erased relief of Queen Hatshepsut, Karnak

7. H. Nelson, "Certain Reliefs at Karnak and Medinet Habu," *Journal of Near Eastern Studies* 8 (1949) pl. 23. Here the ☥-sign replaces the erased figure of Queen Hatshepsut, but the same idea is depicted in other cases, e.g., the ☥-sign with arms enclosing offerings: Oriental Institute, *Medinet Habu*, VII (Chicago, 1964) pl. 512.

8. Discussed by G. Jéquier, "Materiaux pour servir à l'établissement d'un dictionnaire d'archéologie égyptienne," *BIFAO* 19 (1922) pp. 137–139.

9. Pyr. 1010–1011. Pyr. 1878 has "Arise ye who are in your tombs, cast off your bindings."

10. A. Blackman, "The Significance of Incense and Libations," *ÄZ* 50 (1912) pp. 69–75.

11. Pyr. 789, 1357. Cf. Pyr. 683: "N. is pure and his ka is pure."

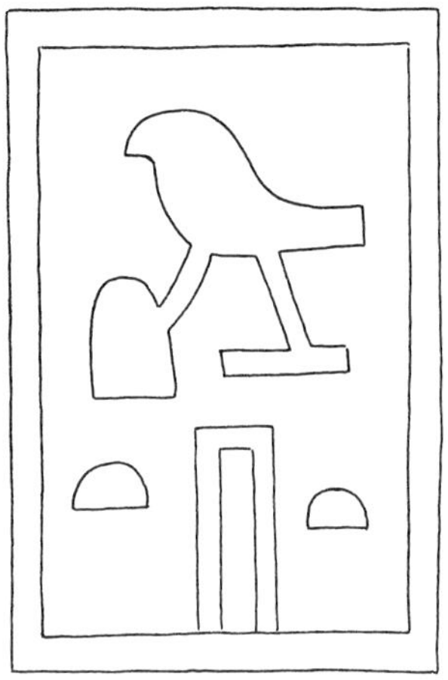

FIGURE 10
Name of the Horus Aha. After Emery

FIGURE 11
Panel from the mastaba of Hesi-Re. After Quibell

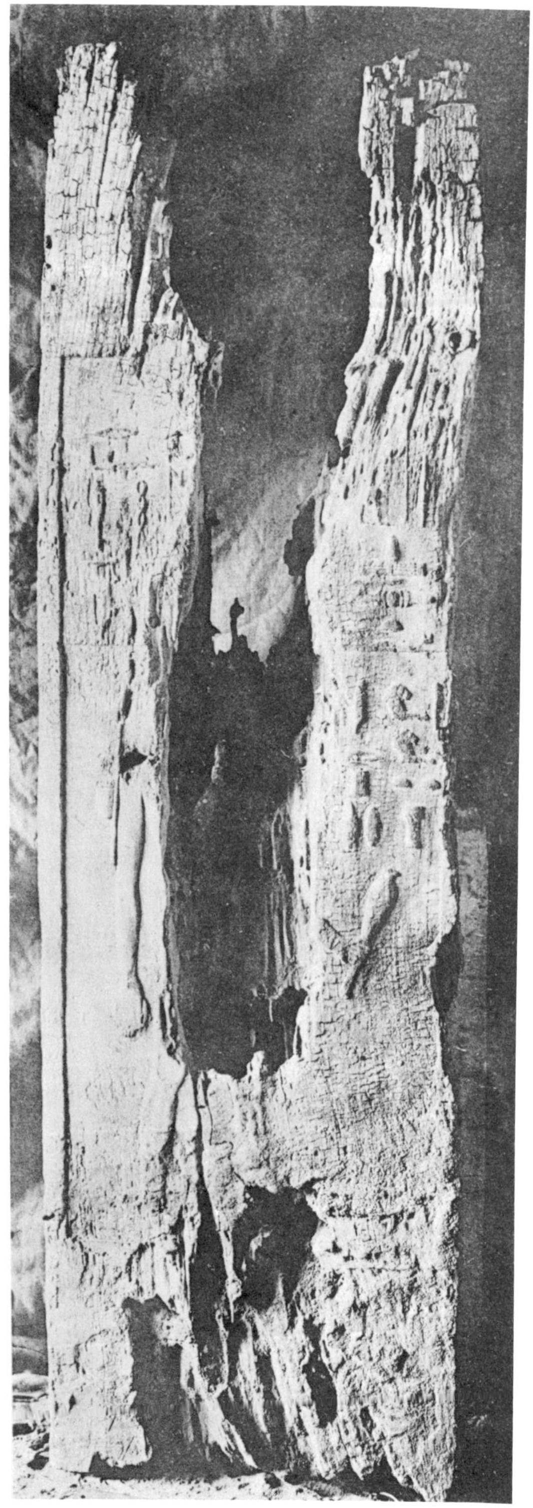

a tendency to regard them as one and the same when the object of the ritual was not immediately at hand.[12]

While there is no question that its principal function was to "present life" by means of the water poured out of it, the dish may also embody a second idea; as William C. Hayes has suggested,[13] it may spell out the name of an official called 𓋹𓂓 (ꜥnḫ-kꜣ[.ỉ?]), who is well known from sealings on wine jars of the reign of Den, the fifth king of the First Dynasty.[14] As will presently be seen, the form of the ☥-emblem would suit that date, as would the workmanship of the dish; nearly all of the protodynastic schist vessels that show the greatest degree of virtuosity derive from tombs dated to the same reign.[15]

12. Cf. H. Bonnet, *Reallexikon der ägyptischen Religionsgeschichte* (Berlin, 1952) p. 425.

13. Hayes, *Scepter*, I, p. 42.

14. Perhaps to be read *Kꜣ*[.*i*]-ꜥ*nḫ*[*w*], "my spirit lives." For references (all on jar sealings) see A. Klasens, "Een Grafsteen uit de eerste dynastie," *Oudheidkundige Mededelingen uit het Rijksmuseum van Oudheden te Leiden* N. R. 37 (1956) p. 20 (20). Klasens, "The Excavations of the Leiden Museum of Antiquities of Abu-Roash," *Oudheidkundige Mededelingen* . . . N. R. 42 (1961) p. 125, and Emery, *Great Tombs*, III (London, 1958) pls. 79 (16), 80 (26–29), 81 (30–32). One example (W. M. F. Petrie, *Tombs of the Courtiers* [London, 1925] pl. 3 [5]) is as early as Djer; the rest are dated to Den and his queen Merneith. Cf. also P. Kaplony, *Die Inschriften der ägyptischen Frühzeit*, I (Wiesbaden, 1963) p. 455, where the suggested reading is ꜥ*nḫ*-*kꜣ*, "he whose ka lives." Kaplony thinks that there were two officials bearing this name in the reign of Den.

15. The first of the examples cited above, in note 2, comes from the tomb of an official who served under Den and his successor. The second example, from the so-called tomb of Hemaka, and the one published by Montet are linked to no other king than Den. The one first illustrated in Emery's *Archaic Egypt* is similarly "dated to the middle First Dynasty."

Emblematic combinations of hieroglyphs are not uncommon in hieroglyphic writing, the best-known example being the use of 𓁒 in place of 𓁒 in the writing of *mśi*, "give birth," where the emerging child is replaced by the phonetic sign for *mśi* (𓄟).[16] A First Dynasty example of such a combination in a personal name is provided by the customary writing of the Horus Aha (Figure 10), in which the falcon holds the hieroglyph 𓂚 (*ꜥḥꜣ*).[17] An even closer parallel seems to occur on one of the wooden niche panels from the Third Dynasty mastaba of Hesi-Re, also known as 𓄣𓏏𓇋𓇋 (*Ḥsy*), where he holds a large 𓏁-jar, the type of jar generally used for libations (Figure 11).[18] This example will be discussed at greater length in Part 3 of this article.

There is some question, however, whether the ☥-sign would be symbolically presented to a nonroyal person even if he possessed so appropriate a name.[19] If the vessel did belong to Ankh-ka, we must assume that this emblem was used more freely at the beginning of the Dynastic Period than it was thereafter. There is no direct evidence to this effect,[20] but the 𓍶-emblem, which is closely related to ☥ and is interchanged with it in various contexts,[21] encircles the necks of two officials on reliefs dating to the early Old Kingdom,[22] after which it disappeared as a necklace, but is sometimes held in the hand, precisely like the ☥-sign, by divinities in Old Kingdom statuary.[23]

Here it should be noted that, of the various readings that have been proposed for 𓈗, the name conventionally read as "Den," one alternative neatly fits the possibility that the libation vessel was made for the king himself; according to Kurt Sethe the pair of hieroglyphs should be transliterated *wdi-mw*, "he who gives water."[24] But his interpretation remains uncertain, and even if it could be confirmed, it would have no specific application to the form of the lustral vessel beyond the probability that a king of such a name may well have possessed one of exceptional quality. And in such a case one might perhaps expect a costlier material than schist. It remains possible, of course, that the king "who gives water" had such a vessel specially made for his courtier named Ankh-ka, but that possibility is, to say the least, as remote as it is tempting.

Regardless of the question of royal or nonroyal ownership, there can be little doubt that the central emblem of the dish is, in fact, the sign of life. That point seems established by the later connection between life and lustration as well as by the fact that the emblem is held in the hands of the 𓂓-sign. The only other emblem with which it might be identified—the so-called Isis knot (𓎬)—is as closely associated with ☥ as 𓍶 is;[25]

16. This and other "ideographische Verbindungen" are dealt with by E. Edel, *Altägyptische Grammatik*, I (Rome, 1955) par. 62; for a further example see H. G. Fischer, "An Early Occurrence of *ḥm* 'servant,'" *MDIK* 16 (1958) pp. 135–137. Similar writings were more commonly adopted in the later periods, as cryptographic alternatives to the usual orthography; for example, the monogram for *ḥtp-di-nśwt* discussed by J. Clère in *Studi in memoria di I. Rosellini*, II (Pisa, 1955) pp. 35–42; cf. E. Drioton, "Recueil de cryptographie monumentale," *ASAE* 40 (1940) pp. 305–429.

17. The example in Figure 10 is taken from W. B. Emery, *Ḥor-Aḥa* (Cairo, 1939) p. 20, fig. 13; cf. W. M. F. Petrie, *Royal Tombs*, II (London, 1901) pl. 3; similarly for (Petrie, *Royal Tombs*, II, pl. 2 [12]); for (Petrie, *Royal Tombs*, II, pl. 13); occasional writings of the name of the Horus Djer with perched on the sign (Petrie, *Royal Tombs*, II, pl. 15 [105, 106]) and the stela of this king, H. G. Fischer, "An Egyptian Royal Stela of the Second Dynasty," *Artibus Asiae* 24 (1961) fig. 6 facing p. 53 (the drawing of P. Newberry in *PSBA* 36 [1914] pl. III, 1, is not accurate in this respect). Also the combination , surmounted by a panther, for in *nb[t] ḥwt ꜥnḫ*, the epithet of Mafdet (Petrie, *Royal Tombs*, II, pl. 7 [10] and I [London, 1900] pl. 7 [4]; cf. W. K. Simpson in *American Journal of Archaeology* 67 [1963] p. 86).

18. J. E. Quibell, *Excavations at Saqqara (1911–12): The Tomb of Hesy* (Cairo, 1913) pl. 7 (3).

19. I discuss the later history of this question in a forthcoming issue of *ÄZ*, vol. 100 (1973), 23–27.

20. The predynastic example cited by G. Jéquier, "The Most Ancient Representation of the Sign ☥," *PSBA* 39 (1917) pp. 87–88, is invalidated by the remarks of F. W. von Bissing, "Die angebliche älteste Darstellung der 'Lebensbinde,'" *ÄZ* 57 (1922) p. 137.

21. G. Jéquier, "Les talismans ☥ et 𓍶," *BIFAO* 11 (1914) pp. 142–143; also P. Lacau and H. Chevrier, *Une Chapelle de Sésostris I à Karnak* (Cairo, 1956) p. 143.

22. Louvre, A 39 (R. Weill, *Des Monuments et de l'Histoire des IIe et IIIe Dynasties* [Paris, 1908] pl. II) and Cairo Museum, Cat. gén. 57121, the reliefs of *ꜥIy-nfr* (E. Staehelin, *Untersuchungen zur ägyptischen Tracht im Alten Reich* [Berlin, 1966] p. 105, Abb. 10, 23).

23. Mycerinus triad, Cairo J. d'Entrée 40679 (G. Reisner, *Mycerinus* [Cambridge, Massachusetts, 1931] pl. 43 [b, d]); Sahure dyad, The Metropolitan Museum of Art, acc. no. 18.2.4 (Hayes, *Scepter*, I, fig. 46 on p. 70).

24. K. Sethe, *Beiträge zur ältesten Geschichte Ägyptens* (Leipzig, 1905) pp. 39–41. The other suggestions are conveniently listed by I. E. S. Edwards, "The Early Dynastic Period in Egypt," chap. XI in *Cambridge Ancient History*, rev. ed., I (Cambridge, 1964) p. 21, note 2.

25. H. Schäfer, "Djed-Pfeiler, Lebenszeichen, Osiris, Isis," *Studies Presented to F. Ll. Griffith* (London, 1932) p. 430.

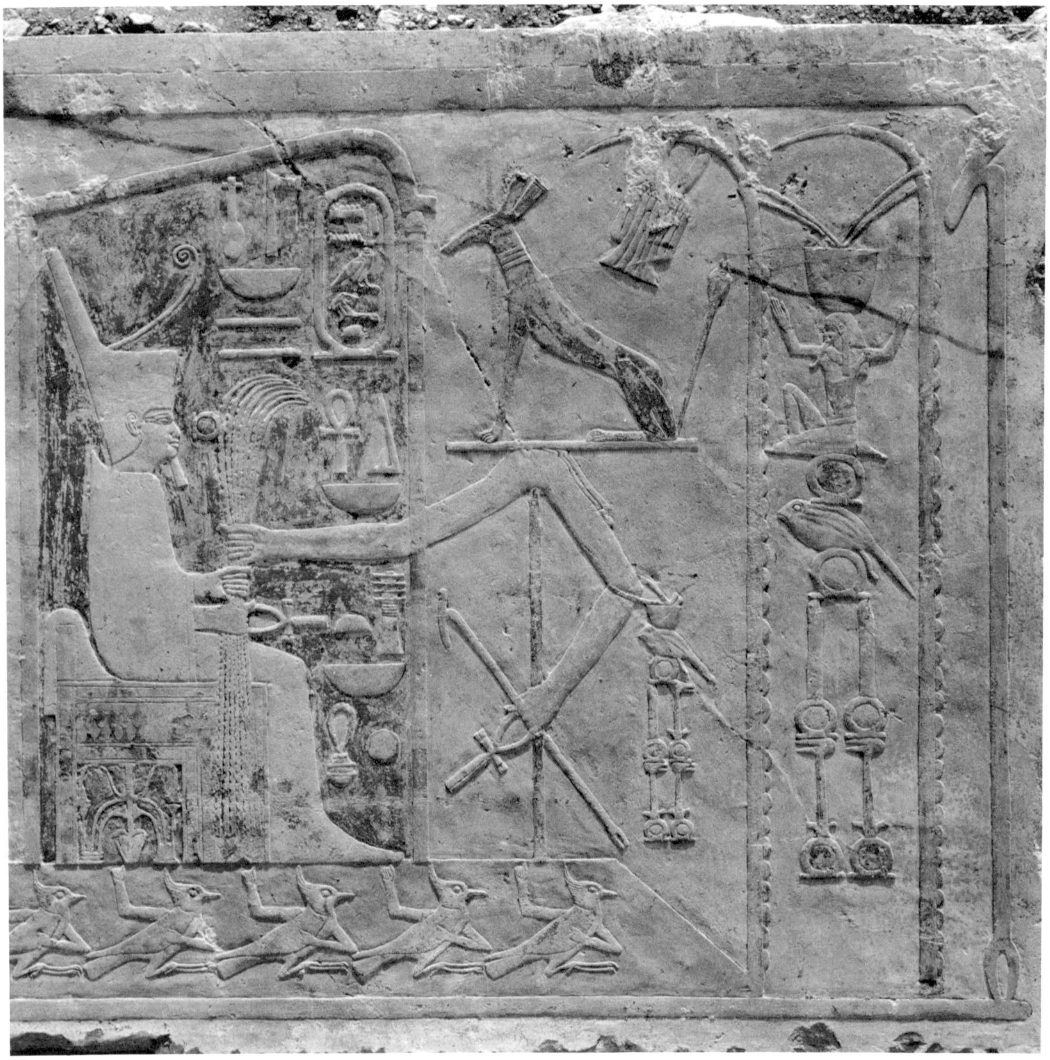

FIGURE 12

Right half of a lintel of Amenemhet I, from Lisht. Cairo Museum (Metropolitan Museum expedition photograph)

unlike these two emblems, however, it was not held in the hands before the Eighteenth Dynasty,[26] but was characteristically suspended. The difference in usage may be seen in a Twelfth Dynasty relief that has been cited as a parallel presentation of ☥ and 𓎬 (Figure 12).[27] The ☥-sign was regularly held by anthropomorphic gods, using the loop as a handle, from the Second Dynasty onward;[28] it seems to have been extended in the same manner from the claws of the Horus falcon at the very beginning of the First Dynasty.[29]

26. As pointed out in the forthcoming article mentioned in note 19.

27. Cf. Schäfer, "Djed-Pfeiler," *Griffith Studies*, p. 428, fig. 7. A more complete view of the stone, which was uncovered during the Metropolitan Museum's 1906–1907 season of excavation at Lisht, has been published by W. K. Simpson, "Studies in the Twelfth Egyptian Dynasty," *Journal of the American Research Center in Egypt* 2 (1963) p. 61 and pl. 8.

28. Petrie, *Royal Tombs*, II, pls. 21–23.

29. Kaplony, *Inschriften*, III, pl. 5 (5); cf. P. Newberry's drawing in W. Brunton et al., *Great Ones of Ancient Egypt* (New York, 1930) fig. 6, p. 45. The falcon presenting the ☥-sign is not otherwise attested before the Third Dynasty (Djoser).

Two comparable emblems, both on ivory fragments dating to the reign of Den or earlier (Figure 13),[30] appear in segments of friezes, alternating with the emblem 𓌀. As far as the later evidence is concerned, this context would suit either 𓋹 or 𓎬. However that may be, the emblem in question represents a three-looped bow that differs in only one particular from the form of 𓋹 that is known from inscriptions. In the first case, all the elements are presented edgewise (Figure 14, left), while in the second case the lateral elements are turned ninety degrees so that only one side of the loop is visible (Figure 14, right). In both cases the lower ends may also be flattened out and brought together, as was usual from the Second Dynasty onward.[31] I believe that the first of these alternatives, showing all the elements in profile, was adopted for the libation dish primarily because this provided a system of walls for the compartments and spout, and not because an emblem other than 𓋹 was intended.

The explanation that has just been suggested strongly supports Heinrich Schäfer's conclusion that 𓋹 and 𓎬 originally had the same meaning, for their structure is even more closely identical than he supposed.[32] A further confirmation is provided by an early Second Dynasty combination of 𓋹 and 𓊽 (Figure 15), which later became a combination of 𓎬 and 𓊽 (Figure 16),[33] as it remained in the dynasty following.[34]

The form 𓋹 was evidently adopted as a hieroglyph because of its simplicity and clarity. As a hieroglyph it acquired the more explicit meaning of a sign that,

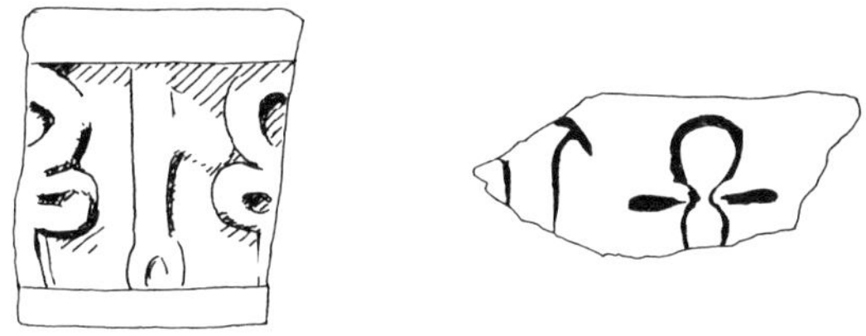

FIGURE 13
First Dynasty ivory fragments from Abydos

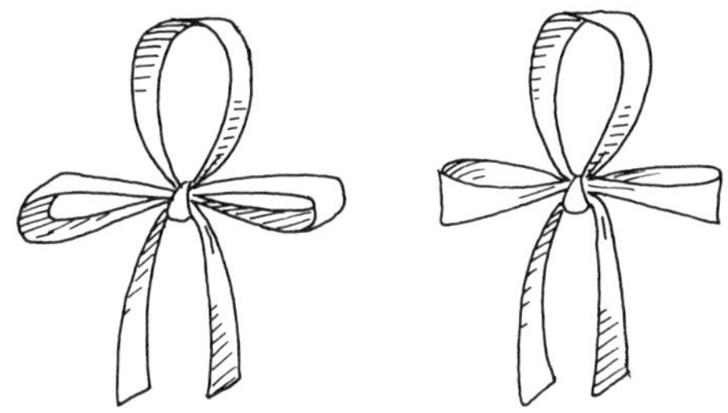

FIGURE 14
Structure of 𓎬 and 𓋹

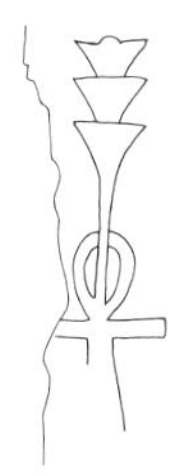

FIGURE 15
Combination of 𓋹 and 𓊽. After Petrie

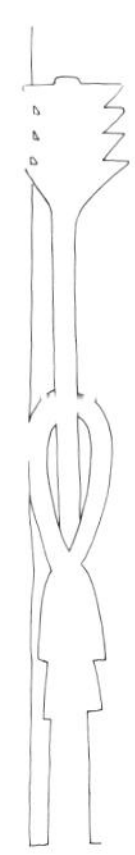

FIGURE 16
Combination of 𓎬 and 𓊽

30. The first (Petrie, *Royal Tombs*, II, pl. 6 [1]) is from the tomb or cenotaph of Djer, the second (Petrie, *Royal Tombs*, II, pl. 39 [34] is from that of Queen Merneith.

31. For a hieroglyphic example from the tomb of Semerkhet see Petrie, *Royal Tombs*, I, pl. 7 (4).

32. Schäfer, "Djed-Pfeiler," *Griffith Studies*, p. 429. On p. 426 he defines the difference between the two emblems in terms of a division in the lateral elements of 𓋹, which, as will be pointed out presently, does not seem to have occurred until the Fourth Dynasty.

33. The first combination is from the reign of Ni-netjer: W. M. F. Petrie, *Gizeh and Rifeh* (London, 1907) pl. 5 E (bottom left); cf. Kaplony, *Inschriften*, III, fig. 746. The second is from the reign of Kha-sekhemwy: J. E. Quibell, *Hierakonpolis*, I (London, 1900) pl. 2. Cf. H. Schäfer, "Der Reliefschmuck der Berliner Tür," *MDIK* 4 (1933) p. 3, fig. 2 (d, g), where combinations of 𓋹 and 𓌀, and 𓎬 and 𓌀, are also exhibited (a, b).

34. Schäfer, "Der Reliefschmuck," *MDIK* 4, fig. 2 (c, e) (cf. C. M. Firth and J. E. Quibell, *The Step Pyramid* [Cairo, 1935] pl. 43) and (f) (Quibell, *Tomb of Hesy*, pl. 17).

FIGURE 17
Early Fourth Dynasty example of ☥. After Fakhry

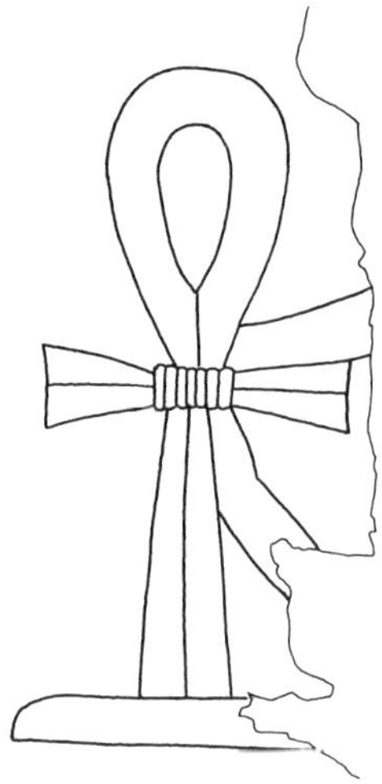

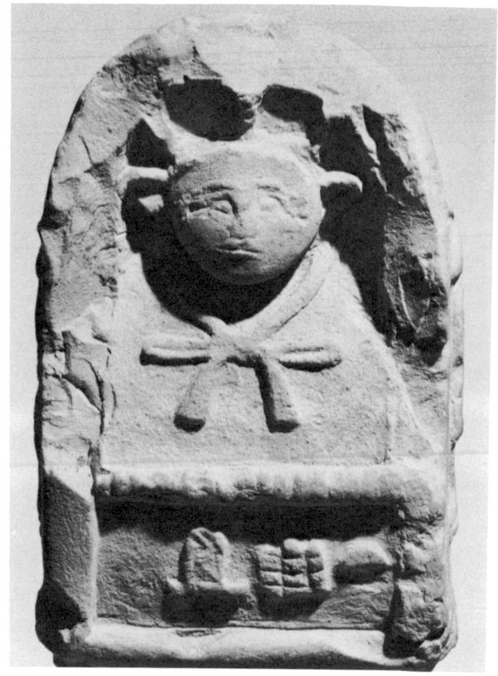

FIGURE 20
Front of an archaic limestone image of Triphis in the form of a *b3t* emblem (photo: courtesy of Ernst Kofler)

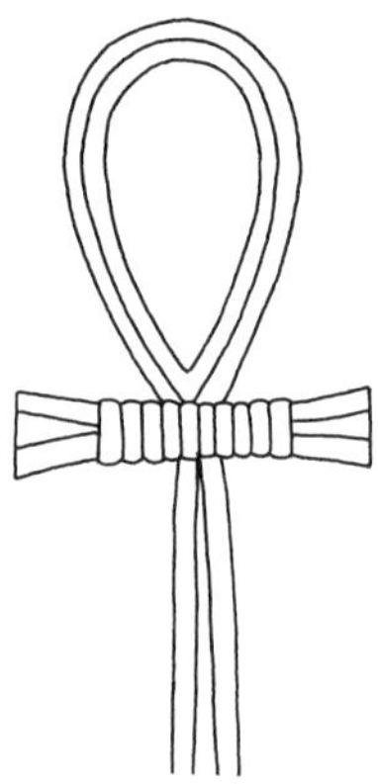

FIGURE 18
Twelfth Dynasty example of ☥. After Bisson de la Roque and Clère

being held, indicates divinity, the power to bestow life. In the more ornamental variation, 𓎬, the lateral loops have gradually drooped downward, whereas in the ☥-hieroglyph they maintain their horizontal position.

By the beginning of the Fourth Dynasty the conventionalized knot at the center of ☥[35] had become elongated and was sometimes vertically divided (Figure 17), as though it represented a superimposed binding,[36] and the horizontal projections fairly consistently showed

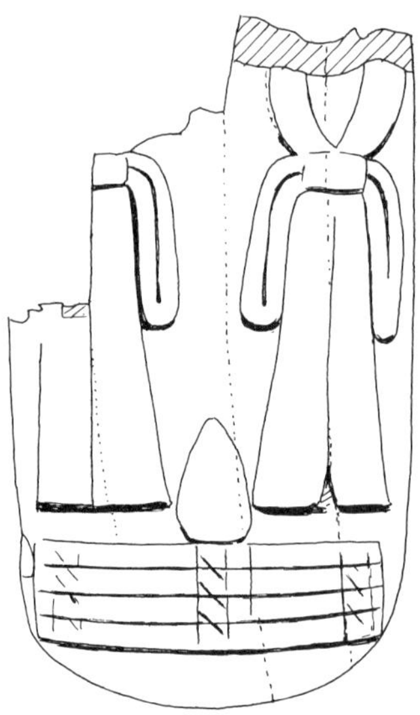

FIGURE 19
Lid of an archaic ivory box from Helwan

35. As Margaret Murray points out in "Knots," *Ancient Egypt* 1922 (London) pp. 14–19, there was a reluctance to represent knots very realistically prior to the Middle Kingdom. A reef knot was shown as early as the Sixth Dynasty, but this is evidently an exception (A. Mariette, *Les Mastabas de l'Ancien Empire* [Paris, 1889] p. 240).

36. Figure 17 is taken from A. Fakhry, *The Monuments of Sneferu at Dahshur*, II, part 1 (Cairo, 1961) fig. 44 (cf. fig. 43, with restoration of the two arms attached to ☥). Figure 18 is from F. Bisson de la Roque and J. J. Clère, *Rapport sur les Fouilles de Médamoud (1927)*, *Fouilles de l'Institut Français d'Archéologie Orientale du Caire* 5 (Cairo, 1928) pl. 7. The vertical divisions also appear in the knot of 𓎬 : Schäfer, "Der Reliefschmuck," *MDIK* 4, fig. 2 (c), and Firth and Quibell, *Step Pyramid*, pl. 58, both Third Dynasty (Djoser).

a longitudinal division that extended to the very end. This detail was probably assimilated from the vertical division of the lower part, as in the case of a Twelfth Dynasty example in which a further division was added throughout (Figure 18). In any case the subdivision of the horizontal projections is not an original feature of the sign, although it conceivably was intended to suggest the presence of the two sides of the original loops.[37]

In view of the identity of ☥ and [hieroglyph] in the Archaic Period, it is possible that the ornamental inscription shown in Figure 19, which is carved on the lid of a Second or Third Dynasty ivory box from Helwan, is to be read *ʿnḫ-ḥtp*, "The Living One is Content" (with [hieroglyph] repeated for the sake of symmetry).[38] Similarly the bow at the neck of the *bꜣt*-emblem in the Kofler collection (Figure 20) might be regarded as an ☥-sign, worn in the same manner as the [hieroglyph]-necklace mentioned earlier, but it may be inadvisable to refer to subsequent examples of [hieroglyph] in the same way, since this form gradually acquired a distinct identity as an ornamental bow.[39] Even as late as the Eighteenth Dynasty, however, it remained strongly associated with ☥, being employed as a permissible substitute for this in the hands of nonroyal anthropoid coffins and shawabty figurines.[40]

2. A DISH IN THE FORM OF A LOTUS LEAF

In view of the fact that it was purchased with the libation dish, the schist object shown in Figures 21–23 must also be given some notice, with attention to the possibility that these two pieces may have been associated.[41] Unfortunately, it seems likely that the curved edge of the leaflike form was trimmed down in ancient or more recent times in order to eliminate some chipping that made the implement less serviceable or attractive.[42] If the edge has been reworked, the end of the stem may also have been trimmed for the same reason. But it is difficult to conceive of the stem as a link to a larger composition, fashioned from one and the same piece of stone; and if the end of the stem is intact, its widening diameter could not have enabled it to be securely mortised to a second piece.

Regardless of these considerations, the object certainly represents a lotus leaf, as may be seen from the notch at the bottom, and the attachment of the stem.[43]

37. Until and unless there is earlier evidence for the division that extends to the outer edges, Schäfer's distinction between this and the lateral loops of [hieroglyph] ("Djed-Pfeiler," *Griffith Studies*, p. 426) does not seem valid. For the same reason G. Jéquier, "Les talismans," *BIFAO* 11 (1914) p. 135, thinks that the lateral elements are "une autre tige plus courte ou un faisceau de petites brindilles posées horizontalement." W. Westendorf ("Beiträge aus und zu den medizinischen Texten," *ÄZ* 92 [1966] p. 152) also takes them to be a separate element, viz, the hieroglyph [hieroglyph]; this comparison again supposes that the horizontal division is original, for [hieroglyph] has four ends; cf. the examples given by Murray, "Knots," *Ancient Egypt* 1922, pp. 17–18, figs. 34–37.

38. Figure 19 is drawn from a photograph in Zaki Saad, *Royal Excavations at Saqqara and Helwan (1941–1945)* (Cairo, 1947) pl. 15 (B). For the name *ʿnḫ-ḥtp* (or *Ḥtp-ʿnḫ*) see H. Ranke, *Die Ägyptischen Personennamen*, I (Glückstadt, 1935) pp. 66 (6), 258 (2); all the references are Middle Kingdom (with the exception of a possible example of later date, note 69 below), but there is no reason to think the name may not have occurred earlier; cf. H. Junker, "'Der Lebendige' als Gottesbeiname," *Anzeiger der phil.-hist. Klasse der Österreichischen Akademie der Wissenschaften* 1954, no. 12, p. 180. For a later parallel for the symmetrical repetition of *ʿnḫ*, see the center of the false door in P. A. A. Boeser, *Beschreibung der aegyptischen Sammlung des niederländischen Reichsmuseums der Altertümer in Leiden*, II (The Hague, 1909) pl. 7 (8).

39. Contrary to the view I expressed in *Journal of the American Research Center in Egypt* 1 (1962) p. 12. For the same archaic example of the *bꜣt*-emblem shown in Figure 20, see also H. W. Müller, *Ägyptische Kunstwerke, Kleinfunde und Glas in der Sammlung E. und M. Kofler-Truniger Luzern* (Berlin, 1964) no. A 31. For the later associations see G. Jéquier, *Les Frises d'Objets des sarcophages du Moyen Empire* (Cairo, 1921) pp. 335–336, and W. Westendorf, "Beiträge," *ÄZ* 92 (1966) pp. 144–151.

40. As pointed out in the forthcoming article mentioned in note 19 above.

41. Acc. no. 19.2.17. Maximum length 18.1 cm., width 11.4 cm. It has not been illustrated previously, but is mentioned as a "slate dish of intricate design . . . carved in the shape of a leaf" by Hayes, *Scepter*, I, p. 42.

42. The rather crudely beveled edge of the leaf probably accounts for the lack of symmetry, as well as the fact that only the very beginning of the uppermost veining is to be seen on the underside. Traces of a sandy accretion seem to be visible in a pitted portion of the beveled edge, and I am inclined to think the reshaping is ancient, but cannot be certain that it is not quite recent, as stated on the Museum's catalogue entry, and on at least one exhibition label.

43. Since some of the outer edge has evidently been lost, it remains uncertain which of the two types of lotus known to the most ancient Egyptians it represents—the white (Nymphaea lotus Sav.) or the blue (Nymphaea caerulea L.). As L. Keimer points out, the dentelated edge of the white variety is rarely represented in Egyptian art ("Note sur la représentation exacte d'une feuille de *Nymphaea Lotus* L.," *ASAE* 28 [1928] pp. 38–42; "Nouvelles recherches au sujet du *Potamogeton Lucens* L.," *Revue de L'Égypte Ancienne* 2 [1929] pp. 232–235]). The leaf-shaped vessel cited in the next note does have such an edge, but its convoluted form and fragmentary state leave its identification somewhat in doubt.

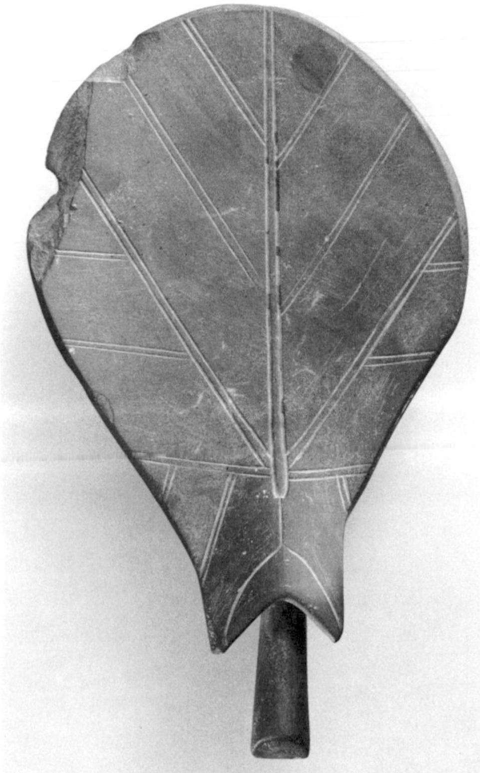

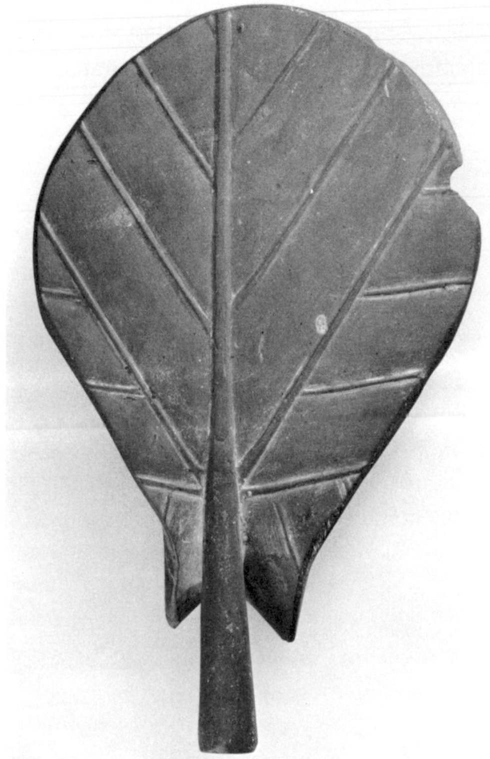

FIGURE 21
Dish in the form of a lotus leaf, upper side. The Metropolitan Museum of Art, Rogers Fund, 19.2.17

FIGURE 22
Underside of the dish shown in Figure 21

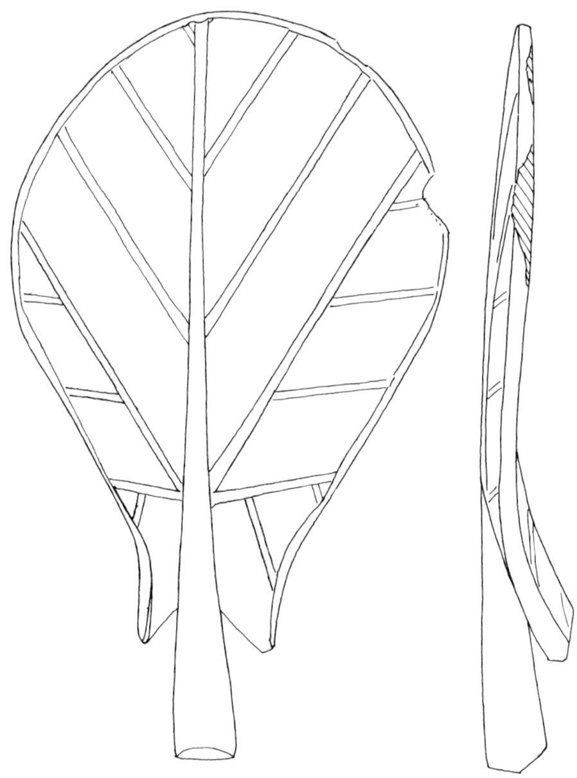

FIGURE 23
Drawings of the underside and profile of the dish shown in Figure 22

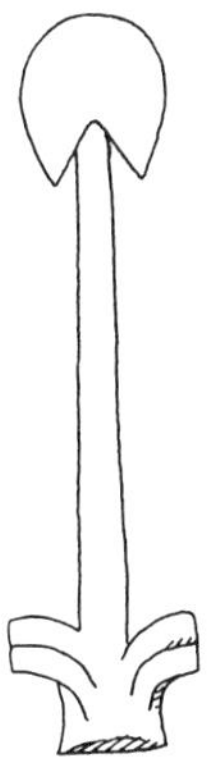

FIGURE 24
Hieroglyph from a panel of Hesi-Re

The pattern of veining is schematic but is realistically differentiated on the two sides, carved in relief on the underside and incised on top. Similar relief veining appears on the bottom of a fragmentary bowl dating to the reign of Den.[44]

Assuming that its present form reflects no more than marginal modification, and that the stem served as a handle, this projection would have been held between the thumb and index finger, or more probably between the thumb and middle finger with the index extended along the underside of the leaf for support. Manipulated in this way, it might have been utilized as a serving dish.

The possible association of the lotus dish and libation dish is suggested not only by their origin, but by the similarity of scale and material. The schist of the lotus dish is bluish gray rather than dark green, however, and the workmanship is somewhat inferior. Although it is undoubtedly protodynastic, there is less certainty that it belongs precisely to the middle of the First Dynasty. And while libation vessels—albeit of quite different form—were used in later periods, there is, to my knowledge, no evidence for a food server of this kind in the presentation of offerings.

It might further be considered that the lotus leaf, equated with the upper part of the hieroglyph [hieroglyph] (Figure 24),[45] might effect a symbolic multiplication of offerings placed upon it. But, unlike the ☥-sign on the libation vessel, the hieroglyph is not otherwise known to have been associated symbolically with any implement used in the offering rituals.[46] In the face of so many uncertainties, it seems best to draw no conclusions from the fact that the two schist pieces were acquired together.

3. PERSONAL NAMES: EMBLEMATIC ALLUSIONS AND IDEOGRAPHIC COMBINATIONS

The panel of Hesi-Re, which has been mentioned earlier in connection with the emblematic aspects of the schist libation dish, is very fragmentary and, perhaps for that reason, has received scarcely any of the attention that has been given to its more complete counterparts from the same Third Dynasty mastaba. Enough is preserved, however, to show that one hand grasps a [hieroglyph]-jar, while the other holds a round object between the thumb and flattened palm (Figure 25). It might be considered that these appurtenances represent the priestly side of Hesi-Re's activities, just as, on the other panels as well as this one, the scribal kit betokens his administrative functions.[47] Yet it seems unlikely, to judge from royal statuary of the Sixth Dynasty and later,[48] that anyone but the king would be shown handling ritual vessels intended for the service of the gods.

The true explanation is to be found in the context of the panels, or, to put the matter more precisely, in their lack of context. Neither the scribal kit nor the jar is to be found in other two-dimensional representations of the tomb owner dating to the Old Kingdom, but in these cases the tomb owner is commonly surrounded by attendants who keep accounts for him and perform

44. W. B. Emery, *Hemaka*, pl. 19c and (more clearly) *Archaic Egypt*, pl. 39 (a); see note 2 above.

45. Figure 24 is from one of the Third Dynasty panels of Hesi-Re, Cairo Museum Cat. gén. 1428. The leaf was arranged similarly in the preceding dynasty on the base of the statue of Khasekhem (Quibell, *Hierakonpolis*, I, pl. 40), but was turned sideways, with the notch outward, during the first half of the First Dynasty (Narmer; Quibell, *Hierakonpolis*, I, pl. 26 B; Den, Petrie, *Royal Tombs*, I, pl. 15 [16, 18]).

46. A mirror of much later date has the form of a lotus leaf, complete with stalk and bulb, but this is a naturalistic representation and probably has no reference to the hieroglyph (L. Keimer, "La signification de l'hiéroglyphe *rd*," *ASAE* 48 (1948) pp. 97–100, figs. 10, 11).

47. The titles are conveniently listed by Kaplony, *Inschriften*, I, pp. 581–584.

48. First attested in royal statuary by the schist statuette in the Brooklyn Museum (acc. no. 39.121); good photographs in Cyril Aldred, *Old Kingdom Art in Ancient Egypt* (London, 1949) pls. 60–61.

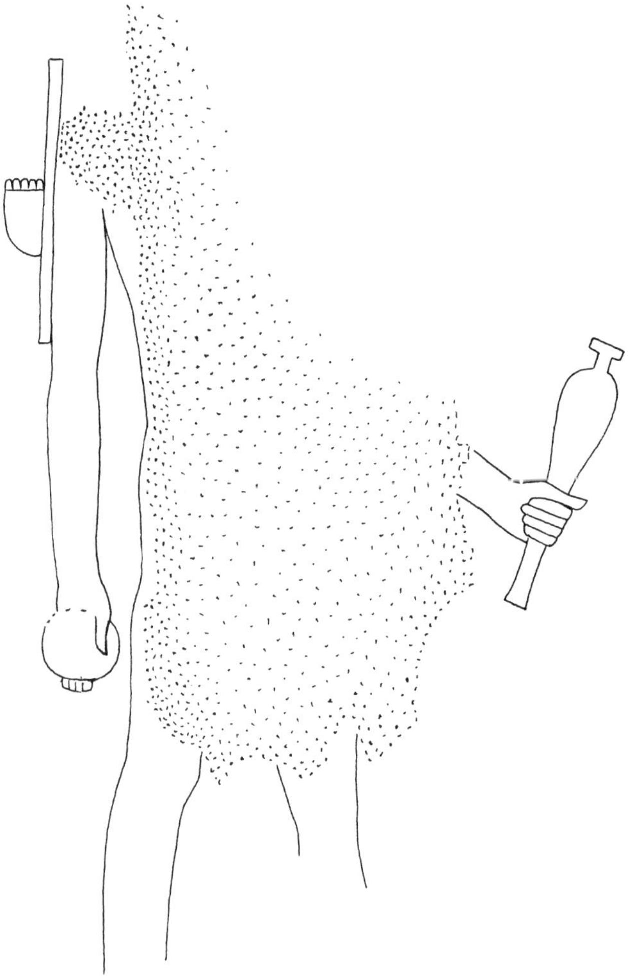

FIGURE 25
Lower part of the panel of Hesi-Re illustrated in Figure 11

Even if the -jar was placed in Hesi-Re's hand for some such reason as this, it is difficult to believe that it did not, at the same time, allude to his name, and that it would not have been recognized as such by anyone who knew him by the shorter version of his name, Hesy. A rather similar emblematic allusion to the most distinctive element of a name occurred in at least one other instance during the Old Kingdom; the false door of a man named *Nḫt-sȝ.ś*, "Her protection is mighty," shows a large *sȝ*-sign ( ) superimposed on a miniature replica of a false door behind the owner (Figure 26).[54]

The round object in Hesi-Re's other hand may be a flat loaf of bread ( )[55] or a lump of natron. The position of the hand favors the first alternative, but does not rule out the second. The second alternative is favored by the size of the object, but this does not rule out the first. Perhaps the lump of natron is the more likely alternative, since it is known to accompany the funerary ritual of libation/lustration.[56] In either case one might expect the fingertips to be curled upward; it would seem that they were extended in order to reveal the object's round contour as clearly as possi-

other services, including the presentation of the -jar.[49] Hesi-Re's reliefs and paintings are remarkable for the absence of such a retinue,[50] and it is doubtless for that reason that he himself carries the items in question. This reasoning is supported by the existence of statues, dating from the Fourth Dynasty onward, that represent the tomb owner as a scribe, for the statue is an isolated monument, lacking the context with which the reliefs were so frequently supplied.[51]

There is no parallel in statuary for the -jar from before the Twelfth Dynasty, but the single example that is known suggests a very similar conclusion. It belonged to a simple steward who is not given any priestly titles either on the statuette or on the coffin in which it was found;[52] thus isolated with the deceased, it provided, as an intermediary identified with himself, a benefit borrowed from the statuettes of two female offering-bearers stationed outside the coffin, each of whom carries a -jar as well as a basket of offerings.[53]

49. For an example of both see H. Junker, *Gîza*, II (Vienna and Leipzig, 1934) figs. 18, 19.

50. Cf. Quibell, *Tomb of Hesy*, pp. 17–18.

51. For the earliest examples, belonging to Ka-wab, the son of Cheops, see W. S. Smith, *A History of Egyptian Sculpture and Painting in the Old Kingdom* (London, 1946) pp. 30–31. The generic scribal statue should be distinguished from other cases where an implement is more specifically emblematic; as far as I know, the only example of this kind that antedates the New Kingdom is the Second or Third Dynasty statue of a shipbuilder ( ) who has an adze over his left shoulder (British Museum, no. 70: *Hieroglyphic Texts*, VI [London, 1922] pl. 19; E. A. W. Budge, *Egyptian Sculptures in the British Museum* [London, 1914] pl. 1).

52. G. Steindorff, *Grabfunde des Mittleren Reichs in den Königlichen Museen zu Berlin*, I, *Das Grab des Mentuhotep* (Berlin, 1896) pl. 7. The statuette is Berlin, 4650.

53. Steindorff, *Mentuhotep*, pl. 11.

54. A. Mariette, *Les Mastabas*, p. 366.

55. For the writing and meaning see K. Sethe, *Übersetzung und Kommentar zu den altägyptischen Pyramidentexten*, II (Glückstadt-Hamburg and New York) p. 236. Also A. Weigall, "Upper Egyptian Notes," *ASAE* 9 (1908) p. 111.

56. Cf. H. Junker, *Gîza*, III (Vienna and Leipzig, 1938) p. 104, fig. 10a on p. 106.

FIGURE 26
Detail of the false door of Nḫt-s3.s. After Mariette

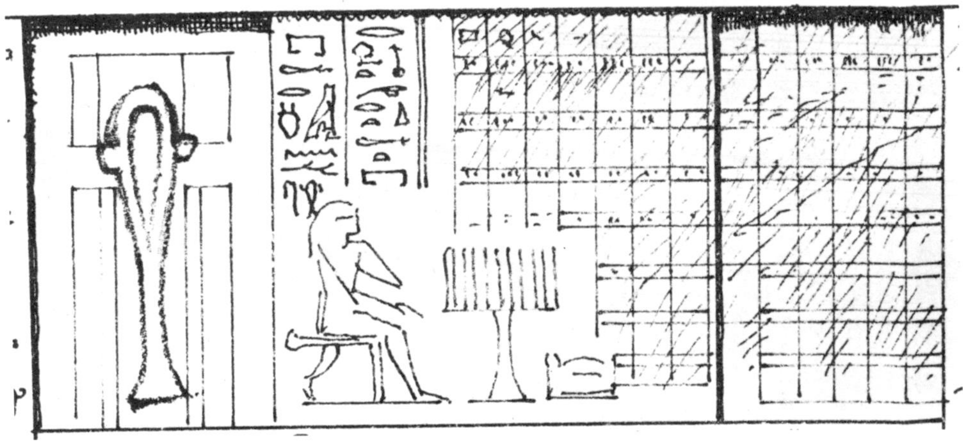

ble.[57] I feel somewhat doubtful, however, that the object has an emblematic meaning in its own right, as a graphic allusion to ⊙, referring to the second element in the name Hesi-Re. It is true that in the reign of Djoser, when Hesi-Re made his tomb, the sun disk was represented in a curious context, attached to the upper edge of broad collars worn by divinities.[58] But the disk would hardly be expected to appear in the hand of an individual, even if it were suggested by an object of similar shape; and the indirectness of such an allusion seems contrary to the rather literal mentality of the Egyptians. Furthermore, nonroyal names of the Old Kingdom, such as [hieroglyphs], consistently use a phonetic writing in referring to the name of Re, in contrast to royal names, which employ the ideographic ⊙.[59]

I do not know of further emblematic writings of names prior to the New Kingdom, but a Twelfth Dynasty stela in the Louvre shows an analogous presentation of the epithet *nb im3ḫ*, "possessor of reverence," which, by this period, was often reduced to [hieroglyphs], as it is here, so that it was possible to convey the meaning by putting a large [hieroglyph]-hieroglyph in the hand of the individual who "possesses" it (Figure 27).[60]

From the mid-Eighteenth Dynasty onward, devices of this kind became increasingly popular, and it may be no coincidence that there was, at the same time, an increasing tendency to place inscriptions on the body of a statue, as had been done in the Archaic Period. The interrelationship of the inscriptional and representational aspects of Egyptian monuments is evident throughout pharaonic history, but these aspects complemented each other more discretely in the Old, Middle, and early New Kingdom. To illustrate how completely amalgamated they sometimes became in the later periods, three categories of examples may be cited.

57. Thanks to the kindness of Labib Habachi and Henry Riad, I have been able, at the last minute, to check this detail on a photograph that was taken under different lighting. It should also be noted that the hand is represented, for the sake of clarity, as though viewed from the other side. This peculiarity does not occur on the other surviving panels of Hesi-Re, but is known from a Third Dynasty relief of only slightly later date (A. H. Gardiner, T. E. Peet, and J. Černý, *The Inscriptions of Sinai*, 2nd ed. [London, 1952, 1955] pl. 1 [1 a] and p. 53, where it is recognized that the king in question is Sekhemkhet, the successor of Djoser). For this last example, cf. W. S. Smith, *A History of Egyptian Sculpture and Painting in the Old Kingdom*, 2nd ed. (Oxford, 1949) p. 273, fig. 32. Dr. Habachi assures me that no detail is to be seen within the disk.

58. H. Schäfer, "Reliefschmuck," *MDIK* 4, p. 14, pl. II (a). Also note the hieroglyphic monogram [hieroglyph] (*ḥ3t hrw*, "the course of the day," e.g., N. de G. Davies, *Mastaba of Ptahhetep and Akhethetep*, II [London, 1901] pl. 17), where the sun disk rests on a butcher's block.

59. Cf. A. Erman and H. Grapow, *Wörterbuch der Aegyptischen Sprache*, II (Leipzig, 1928) p. 401. This distinction was not made in the Archaic Period, to judge from an unpublished stela uncovered by the excavations of the Egyptian Department of Antiquities at Saqqara, which names a "scribe of the document house," [hieroglyphs], *Ḥwi-R'*. Cf. Kaplony, *Inschriften*, III, pl. 139 (834).

60. Louvre, C 85; C. Boreux, Musée National du Louvre, Département des antiquités égyptiennes: *Guide-catalogue sommaire* (Paris, 1932) p. 146; P. Pierret, *Recueil d'inscriptions inédits du Musée Égyptien du Louvre*, II (Paris, 1878) p. 6.

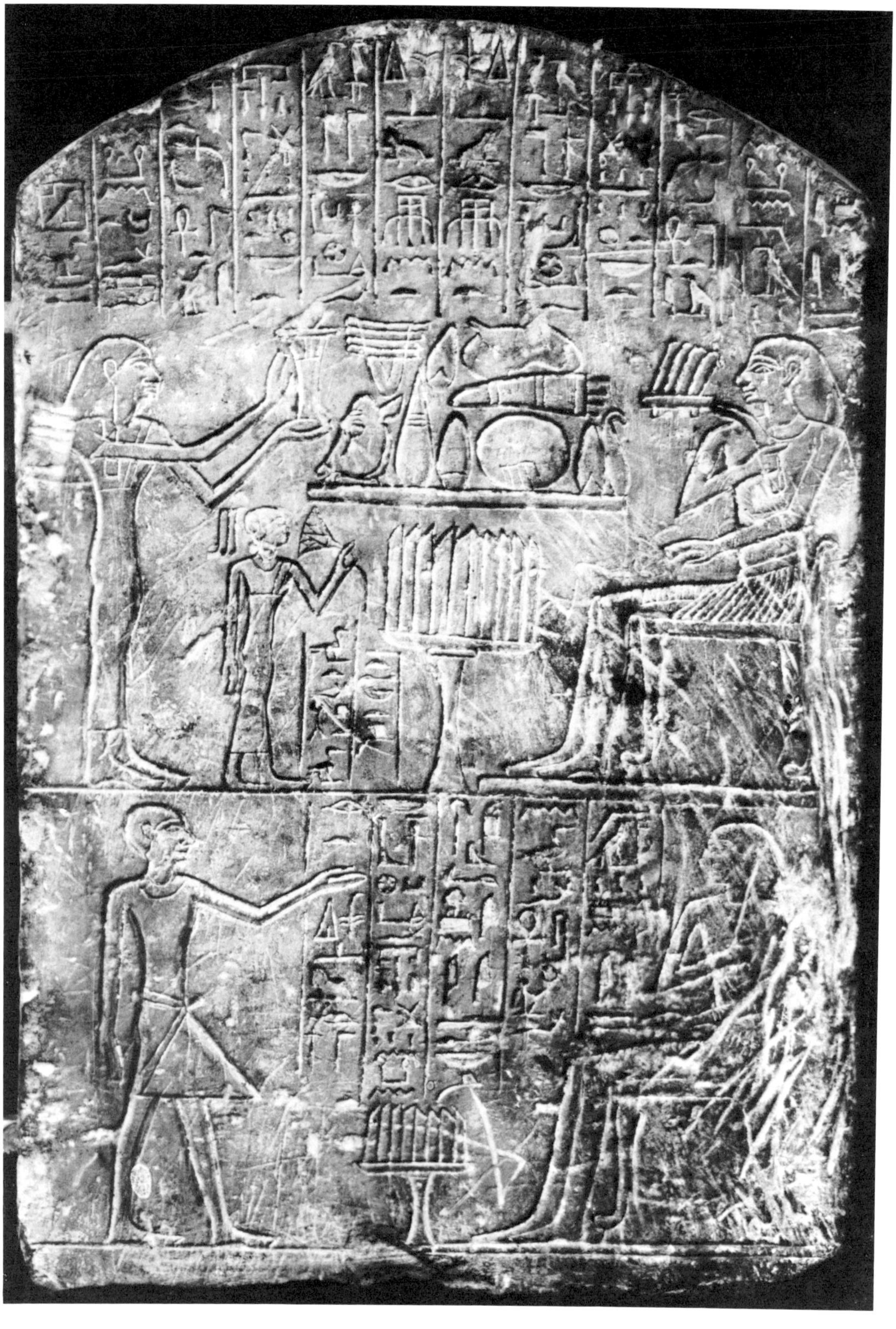

FIGURE 27
Verso of late Middle Kingdom stela. Louvre, C 85 (photo: Archives photographiques, Paris)

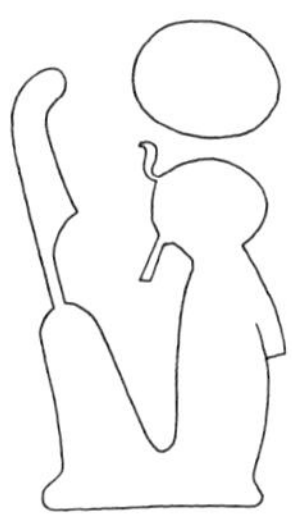

FIGURE 28
Emblematic writing of *Nb-mꜣʿt-Rʿ*, Amenophis III. After Hayes

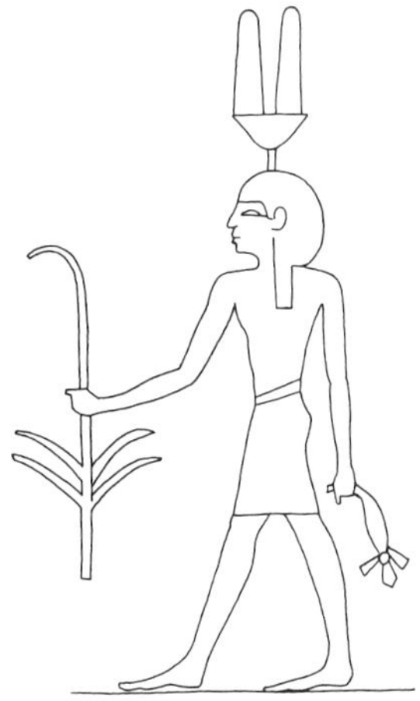

FIGURE 31
Emblematic writing of the name *Šd-św-Nfrtm*. After Drioton

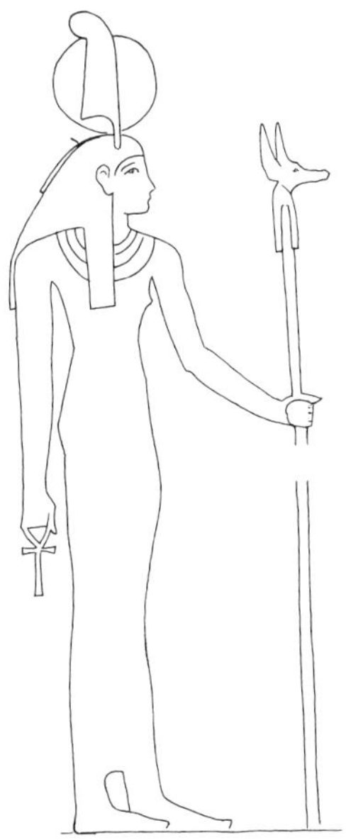

FIGURE 29
Emblematic writing of *Wśr-mꜣʿt-Rʿ*, Ramesses II

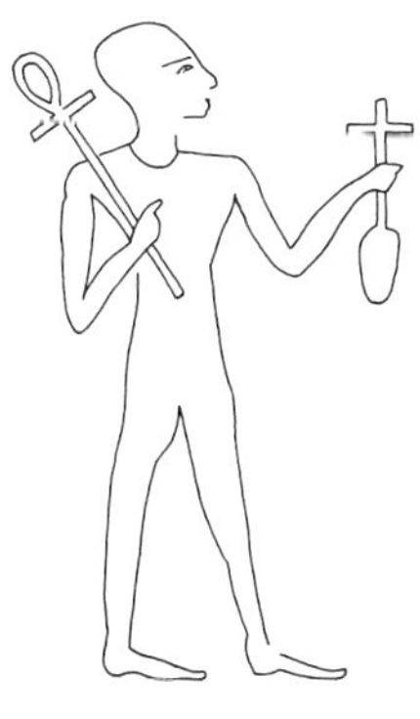

FIGURE 30
Emblematic writing of the name *ʿnḫ-ẖrd-nfr*. After Naville

1. The praenomen of Amenophis III, *Nb-mꜣʿt-Rʿ* (Figure 28),[61] and that of Ramesses II, *Wśr-mꜣʿt-Rʿ* (Figure 29),[62] provide the most familiar ideographic combinations of the kind that is first attested from the First Dynasty. In the first case the king (*nb*, "lord"). holds or "possesses" the feather representing *mꜣʿt*, and his head is surmounted by a sun disk (*Rʿ*). In the second case a personification of *mꜣʿt*, with the sun disk on her head, holds the hieroglyph *wśr* as though it were a staff. The names of nonroyal individuals are similarly represented by monograms on two statues dating to the Twenty-second Dynasty (Figures 30, 31);[63] one is 𓋹𓀔𓄤, presumably meaning "May the beautiful child live!", while the other is [hieroglyphs], "May (the god) Nefertem save him!"

2. Such abbreviations are also to be found in three-dimensional sculpture of the New Kingdom and later,

61. See W. C. Hayes, "Inscriptions from the Palace of Amenhotep III," *Journal of Near Eastern Studies* 10 (1951) p. 158, figs. 30–33. The drawing is taken from his S 33 in fig. 31.

62. This example is taken from the north wall of the chapel to the south of the great temple of Abu Simbel.

63. Figure 30 is from E. Naville, *The Store City of Pithom* (London, 1888) pl. 4; this is British Museum, no. 1007. Figure 31 is from Drioton, "Recueil de cryptographie monumentale," *ASAE* 40, p. 318 (also L. Borchardt, *Statuen und Statuetten von Königen und Privatleuten im Museum von Kairo*, III [Berlin, 1930] no. 741, p. 68). These writings may well have been inspired by royal examples such as that of Ramesses III in Oriental Institute, *Medinet Habu*, VIII (Chicago, 1970), pl. 643.

for example, the seated figure of a queen in a boat in the British Museum, representing the name *Mwt-m-wiꜣ*, "Mut is in (her) divine bark";[64] a contemporary statue in Berlin that presents the praenomen of Mutemweya's royal son, Amenophis III, as described earlier;[65] the well-known statue in the Cairo Museum embodying the name *Rꜥ-mś-św*, Ramesses (II), in the form of a child (*mś*) who holds (*św*) and wears the sun disk on his head;[66] the statue group representing this king's praenomen (*Wśr-mꜣꜥt-Rꜥ*) over the door of his larger temple at Abu Simbel;[67] and the falcon group in the Metropolitan Museum representing *Nekht-Hor-heb* (Nektanebo II of the Thirtieth Dynasty).[68] In the last case the falcon (Hor) stands behind a smaller figure of the king, who holds a scimitar (for *nḫt*, "mighty") in one hand and the hieroglyph (*ḥb*, "festival") in the other; taken together, these elements spell out the name meaning "Horus is mighty in jubilees."

3. Even more remarkable are the rarer cases where an emblem is either supplemented by a hieroglyph or is used as part of a following inscription. One example, dating to the mid-Eighteenth Dynasty, is the fragmentary statue of a man from whose neck a large ☥-pendant is suspended; the hieroglyph is added below this, and the whole probably represents the owner's name: *ꜥnḫ-ḥtp*.[69] In another case a block statue of the Twenty-third Dynasty has a pendant in the form of , and the column of inscription below it begins with the

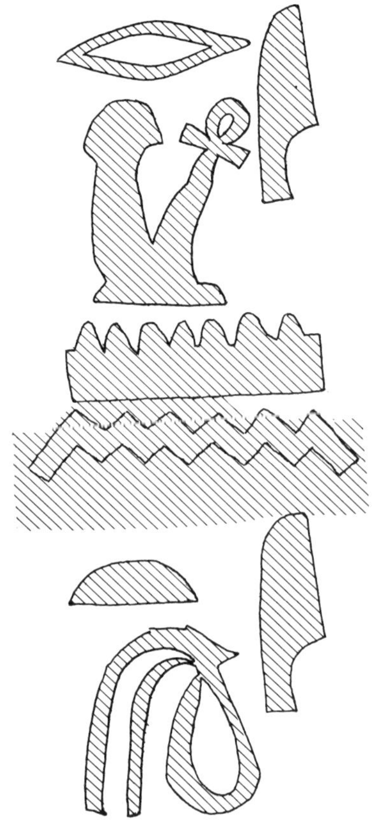

FIGURE 32
Detail of a late Twelfth Dynasty inscription. Museum of Fine Arts, Boston, acc. no. 1971.403

64. British Museum 43: *Hieroglyphic Texts* VII, pl. 6; Budge, *Guide to the Egyptian Galleries (Sculpture)* (London, 1909) pp. 110–111.

65. Berlin, 2293: A. Erman, "Königsnamen durch Skulpturen ausgedrückt," *ÄZ* 29 (1891) pp. 124–125, and J. Vandier, *Manuel d'archéologie égyptienne*, III: *La Statuaire* (Paris, 1958) pl. 155 (4).

66. Cairo J. d'Entrée 64735; P. Montet, "Les statues de Ramsès II à Tanis," *Mélanges Maspero*, I, 2e fasc., *Mémoires publiés par les membres de l'Institut Français d'Archéologie Orientale du Caire* 66 (Cairo, 1935–1938) p. 501, pl. 2; also Vandier, *Manuel*, pl. 133 (2). Cf. the cryptographic equivalents discussed by Drioton, "Recueil de cryptographie monumentale," *ASAE* 40, pp. 318, 322–323 (18).

67. Most clearly illustrated on the title page of David Roberts, *Egypt and Nubia* (London, 1846) and in the photograph shown by Labib Habachi, *Features of the Deification of Ramesses II, Abhandlungen des Deutschen Archäologischen Instituts Kairo, Ägyptologische Reihe* 5 (Glückstadt, 1969) pl. 5 (a); cf. Habachi's pp. 9–10 as well as the other rebus writings in statuary of the same king, pp. 37–39, figs. 24–29. His fig. 29 (Cairo CG 1235) is also discussed by V. Wessetzky, "Königsname und Titel Ramses' II. in doppelter rundplastischer Darstellung," *ÄZ* 97 (1971) pp. 140–142. It may be added that the statue group over the entrance at Abu Simbel is paralleled by the writing of the king's name within the same temple: .

68. H. E. Winlock, "Recent Purchases of Egyptian Sculpture," *BMMA* 29 (1934) fig. 2, p. 187; cf. J. Yoyotte, "Nectanébo II comme faucon divin?," *Kêmi* 15 (1959) pp. 70–74.

69. E. Naville, *The XIth Dynasty Temple at Deir el-Bahari*, part III (London, 1913) p. 22 and pl. 5 (3). Since the principal inscription is lost, it cannot be proven that the combination of hieroglyphs represents the name. The alternative is to interpret both signs as a "motto," like those of the small Middle Kingdom clasps shown in H. E. Winlock, *The Treasure of El Lāhūn* (New York, 1934) pl. 13. These two hieroglyphs are actually combined in one of the elements of a Middle Kingdom necklace (J. de Morgan, *Fouilles à Dahchour en 1894–1895* [Vienna, 1903] pl. 5 [47]), but it seems likely that this was the central element of a continuous inscription. In the case of the statue the pendant itself is probably simply ☥, like the one worn by the Twenty-fifth Dynasty statue of Hor-em-akhet, Cairo Museum, Cat. gén. 42204 (G. Legrain, *Statues et Statuettes de Rois et de Particuliers*, III [Cairo, 1914] pp. 12–13, pl. 11).

title [hieroglyphs].[70] No such title is to be expected, however, and it is perfectly clear that this belongs to the pendant, above it, representing the familiar office of [hieroglyphs], as elsewhere in the inscriptions of the same statue.

Considering the ease with which hieroglyphs could be used for emblematic purposes, one can hardly find it surprising that this possibility was promptly recognized, and that—in the case of royal monuments at least—it was eventually exploited to the full. If, furthermore, one considers that rebus allusions are also attested on Greek monuments, where the link between writing and representation was far less evident,[71] the paucity of such allusions in the classical periods of Egypt—the Old, Middle, and early New Kingdoms—becomes even more significant. It emphasizes the degree to which, in these periods, the artist-scribe respected the complementary relationship of inscriptions and larger-scale representations; the phonetic aspect of this combination was properly confined to the hieroglyphs, while the larger representations remained purely ideographic.

Postscript: An indirect allusion to a personal name is possibly to be recognized in a late Twelfth Dynasty inscription recently purchased by the Boston Museum of Fine Arts (acc. no. 1971.403);[72] the owner's name is [hieroglyphs], "He who lives," and in one of his titles (Figure 32), *iry mnit*, "keeper of the *mnit*-necklace," the hieroglyph [hieroglyph] (or [hieroglyph]) clearly, and most exceptionally, holds the [hieroglyph]-sign in place of the knife (?) or the stick and cord.

The ritual vessel Metropolitan Museum 19.2.16 is also mentioned and illustrated by Ursula Schweitzer, *Das Wesen des Ka* (Glückstadt, 1956) p. 21 and pl. 1a; she reports that Hermann Kees saw a similar piece in the Desert Institute at Esbet Walda in Egypt.

PERIODICALS ABBREVIATED

ASAE—Annales du Service des Antiquités d'Égypte.
ÄZ—Zeitschrift für ägyptische Sprache und Altertumskunde.
BIFAO—Bulletin de l'Institut Français d'Archéologie Orientale du Caire.
BMMA—The Metropolitan Museum of Art Bulletin.
MDIK—Mitteilungen des Deutschen Archäologischen Instituts Abteilung Kairo.
PSBA—Proceedings of the Society of Biblical Archaeology.

70. Cairo Museum, Cat. gén. 42211; Legrain, *Statues et Statuettes*, III, p. 29, pl. 20.

71. See Brigitte Freyer-Schauenburg, "ΚΥΩΝ ΛΑΚΩΝΟΣ-ΚΥΩΝ ΛΑΚΑΙΝΑ," *Antike Kunst* 13 (1970) pp. 98–99.

72. To be published in a forthcoming article by William K. Simpson in *Chronique d'Égypte*. Dr. Simpson has kindly supplied me with a photograph of this piece and has given permission to cite the detail in question.

Old Kingdom Cylinder Seals for the Lower Classes

HENRY G. FISCHER

Lila Acheson Wallace Curator in Egyptology, The Metropolitan Museum of Art

It has long been apparent that, in addition to the usual type of Old Kingdom cylinder seal, the surface of which was completely covered with hieroglyphic inscriptions, a second type of cylinder seal came into use before the end of the Sixth Dynasty.[1] This type shows figures that may, in some cases, resemble hieroglyphs but are employed decoratively; they are often combined in pairs that more usually face inward than outward, and in such cases may be either partly fused (*trompe l'oeil*) or else reversed head to foot (*tête bêche*).

The clearest evidence for the dating of the Old Kingdom examples is the presence of a royal name accompanying the design. Since only two examples, both naming Pepy I, have heretofore been published, one of which presents some problems, it seems worthwhile to exhibit three more that have come to light—especially since they extend the chronological range. The total of five examples will be presented chronologically.

1. The earliest and most interesting of these royal seals (Figures 1, 2) is from the collection of Georges Michailides, who has kindly permitted me to include it.[2] Its material appears to be a reddish crystalline limestone; the height is 5 cm., the width 2.3 cm., and the hole measures 1.7–1.8 cm. in diameter. The surface of the seal is slightly concave. It is said to have been found at Abusir. Beside the Horus name of Djedkare (Isesy), and separated from it by a pair of vertical notched dividers, two dogs and two crocodiles are symmetrically arranged in tête-bêche pairs. The decoration bears a close resemblance to that of a limestone cylinder seal excavated below the floor level of the Old Kingdom temple at Abydos (Figure 3), which not only has a

1. The principal discussions are: P. Newberry, *Scarabs* (London, 1906) pp. 49–50; H. Frankfort, *Studies in Early Pottery of the Near East*, I, *Mesopotamia, Syria, and Egypt and Their Earliest Interrelations* (London, 1924) pp. 132–135; H. Frankfort, "Egypt and Syria in the First Intermediate Period," *JEA* 12 (1926) p. 88; H. Frankfort, *Cylinder Seals* (London, 1939) pp. 296–297; A. Scharff, "Über einige fremdartige Darstellungen auf Siegelbildern aus dem späten Alten Reich und der ersten Zwischenzeit," *ÄZ* 67 (1931) pp. 95–102; H. Junker, "Zwei Schein-Rollsiegel aus dem Alten Reich," *Mélanges Maspero*, I, fasc. 1, *Mémoires publiés par les membres de l'Institut Français d'Archéologie Orientale du Caire*, no. 66 (Cairo, 1935–1938) pp. 267–271; P. Kaplony, *Die Inschriften der ägyptischen Frühzeit* (Wiesbaden, 1963) I, p. 45, II, pp. 677–678.

2. I am also indebted to him and to Edward Wente for the impression shown in Figure 2. After this article was submitted, I was informed by Peter Kaplony that he plans to include the Michailides cylinder in a forthcoming monograph on Old Kingdom seals, to be published by the Fondation Égyptologique Reine Elisabeth in Brussels.

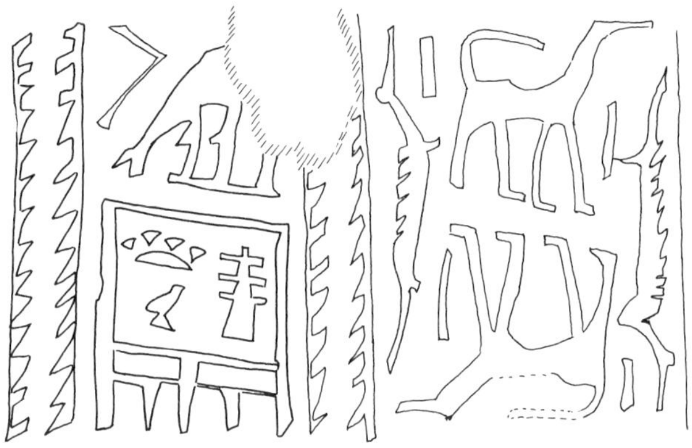

FIGURE I

Cylinder seal (example 1). Michailides Collection, Cairo. This and subsequent reproductions of cylinder seals are approximately the same size as the originals

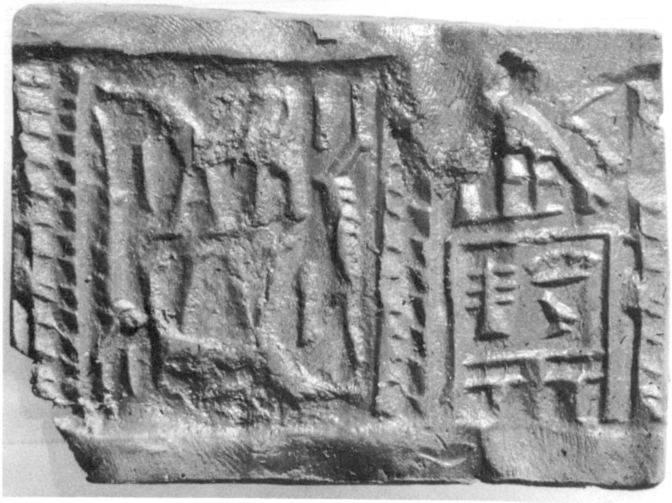

FIGURE 2

Impression of the seal shown in Figure 1

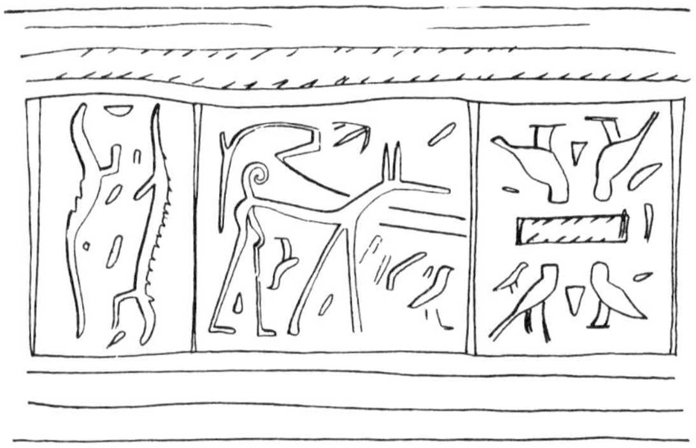

FIGURE 3

Cylinder seal from Abydos. After Petrie

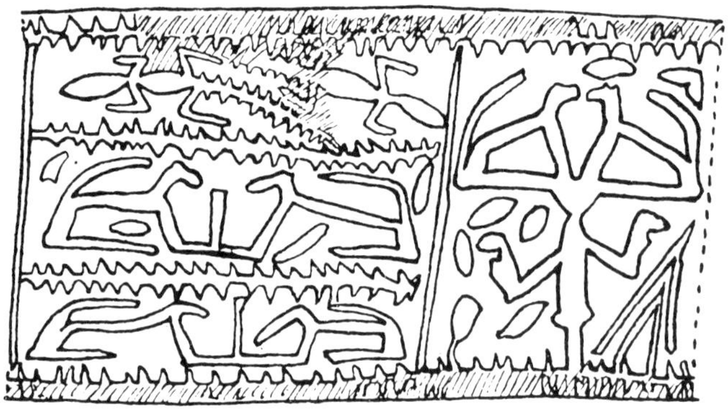

FIGURE 4

Seal from Abusir. Staatliche Museen, Berlin, 15600. After Scharff

similar dog and a tête-bêche pair of crocodiles, but also shows notched borders at the top and bottom.[3] A wooden seal from Abusir, excavated at the pyramid temple of Neferir-kare, the third king of the Fifth Dynasty (Figure 4), also shows some similarities; it has tête-bêche crocodiles and recumbent animals, with notched horizontal dividers and borders.[4]

2. Alexander Scharff has published a limestone cylinder seal (Figure 5) on which the Horus name of

3. W. M. F. Petrie, *Abydos*, II (London, 1903) p. 29, pls. 12 (276), 16 (12). Kaplony, *Inschriften*, II, p. 678, implies that this is protodynastic since it was found at a First Dynasty level, and he compares a steatite seal in Z. Saad, *Royal Excavations at Saqqara and Helwan (1941–1945)* (Cairo, 1947) p. 166; the latter is different in material, however, and does not show a tête-bêche arrangement or any other detail that specifically relates it to the series under discussion. On the other hand the Abydos seal has some details in common (material, figures of owls and crocodiles) with W. M. F. Petrie, *Scarabs and Cylinders* (London, 1917) pl. 7 (163), which Kaplony (*Inschriften*, I, p. 44, III, fig. 634) assigns to the Old Kingdom prior to the end of the Fifth Dynasty.

4. Berlin 15600; Scharff, "Über einige fremdartige Darstellungen," *ÄZ* 67 (1931) pp. 96–97, fig. b.

Pepy I is preceded (or followed) by figures representing cattle, cuts of meat, fish, and a bee.[5] The bee might be thought to signify "honey," in an enumeration of offerings, but other seals (e.g., Figure 7) display the same sign in contexts that cannot be explained in this manner.[6] Furthermore, as Scharff notes, the bee appears as an isolated motif on a number of button seals.

3. A second seal of Pepy I, formerly in the Spencer Churchill Collection, has twice been illustrated by Henri Frankfort on the basis of a drawing by Percy Newberry (Figure 6).[7] It is now in the British Museum (66808), and thanks to the kindness of T. G. H. James, the following data may be supplied: Its material is steatite and it measures 7.5 cm. in height, 1.9 cm. in diameter. The Horus name *Mry-tꜣwy*, followed by *Mry-Rʿ*, is flanked by two columns of inscription, which give the titles and epithets of an official: "Liegeman of the Great House, who does what his lord orders," and "Noble of the King, Companion of the House, who does what his lord orders." Beside this is a much longer column of signs representing pairs of opposed apes and men with staves, along with groups of curved and straight lines that apparently serve only to fill space. Frankfort concluded that the apes, and so on, were added subsequently to the rest. James has written me that he does not believe that this part of the decoration was cut at the same time, but would not suggest priority. If Frankfort is right, it is curious that the inscription referring to the king is so much shorter than the full height of the cylinder; from this circumstance one might argue that the column with the apes was earlier, and that the other columns were reduced in scale so as to adapt the inscriptions to the remaining space. As will be pointed out later, however, the choice of material favors the priority of the inscription, as does the selection of titles. While the amount of margin at the top and bottom is unparalleled, other cases may be cited in which the inscription does not fill the entire circumference of the seal.[8]

4. The upper part of a brown limestone seal from the Nash Collection, bearing the Horus name of the same king, is published here with the further assistance

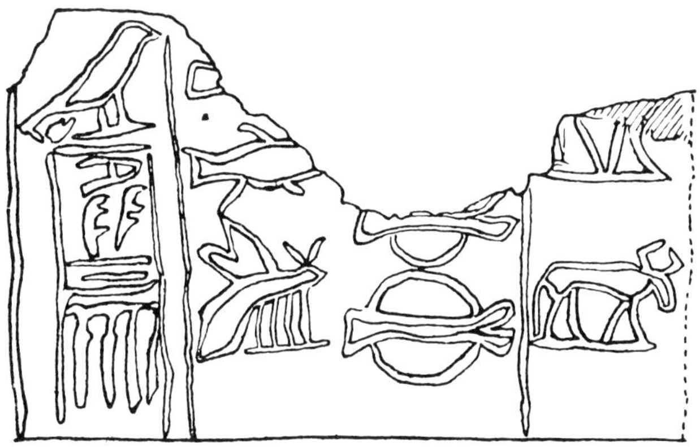

FIGURE 5
Cylinder seal (example 2). Staatliche Museen, Berlin, 16431. After Scharff

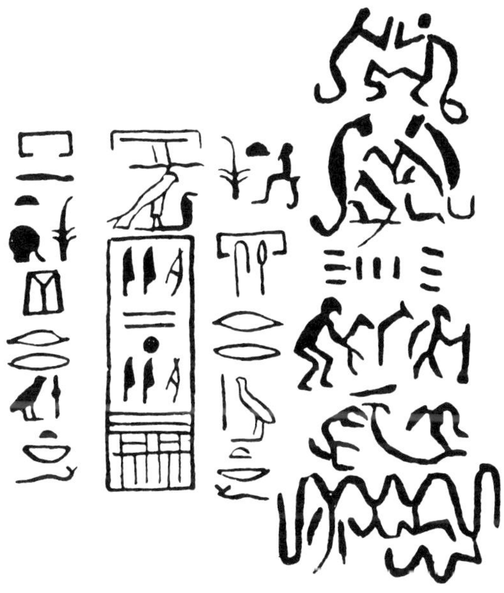

FIGURE 6
Cylinder seal (example 3). British Museum, 66808. After Newberry

5. Berlin 16431; Scharff, "Über einige fremdartige Darstellungen," *ÄZ* 67 (1931) p. 99, fig. e; Scharff notes that the cuts of meat might possibly represent a bird net. The height is 5 cm.

6. For cylinder seals see also Scharff's fig. c ("Über einige fremdartige Darstellungen," *ÄZ* 67 [1931] p. 97) and Cairo Cat. 14518 (J. E. Quibell, *Archaic Objects, Catalogue général des antiquités égyptiennes du Musée du Caire* [Cairo, 1905] pl. 59).

7. Frankfort, "Egypt and Syria," *JEA* 12 (1926) p. 88; Frankfort, *Cylinder Seals*, pp. 296–297.

8. E. g., H. R. Hall, *Catalogue of Egyptian Scarabs, etc., in the British Museum* (London, 1913) no. 2602 (British Museum 25422). Cf. also the next example (no. 4).

of T. G. H. James, who has supplied a vinagel impression and the essential data (Figures 7, 8).[9] The surviving portion is 2.8 cm. high and 2.6 cm. in diameter, and the diameter of the hole is 1.4 cm. The titles "King of Upper and Lower Egypt" and "Two Ladies" are followed by a column containing the title and epithet of an official who is a funerary priest and "one who does [what is praised]" or "who does [what his lord commands]."[10] Between this and the Horus name *Mry-t3wy*, which brings up the rear, there is a column of emblematic or decorative figures: a bee, an ape, and a space filler that resembles a branch. In view of the position of the ape, this figure may have been complemented by a tête bêche companion, but the traces do not confirm this possibility with any certainty. The sequence of columns is suggested by the fact that a half column's width of space has been left between the apparent beginning and end. The amount of the seal that is lost is at least half the original height, to judge from the fact that most variants of the epithets beginning with require scarcely more than two quadrants of space (Figure 9).[11] If so, the "Two Ladies" title may

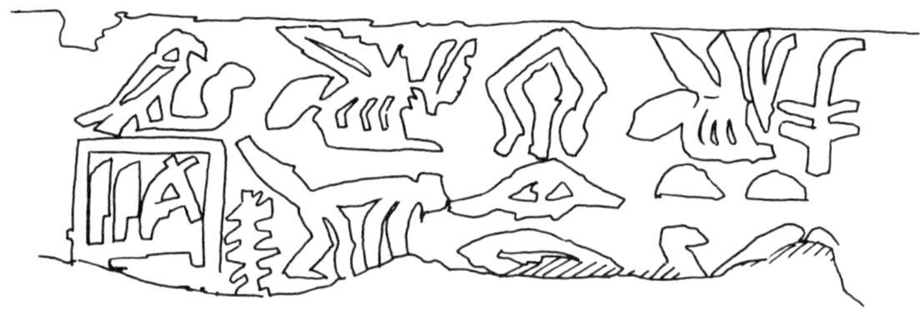

FIGURE 7
Cylinder seal (example 4). British Museum, 65855

FIGURE 8
Impression of the seal shown in Figure 7

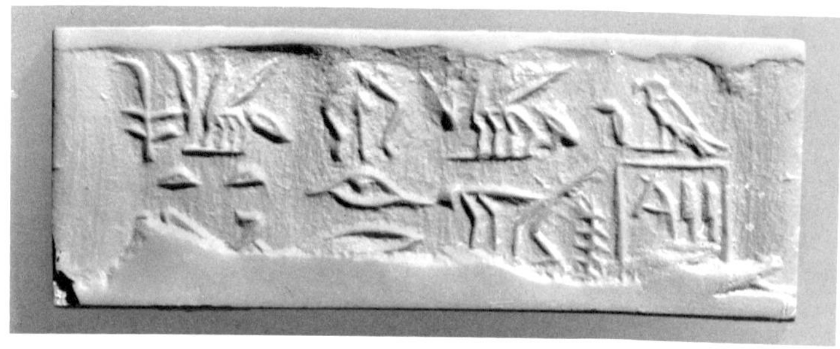

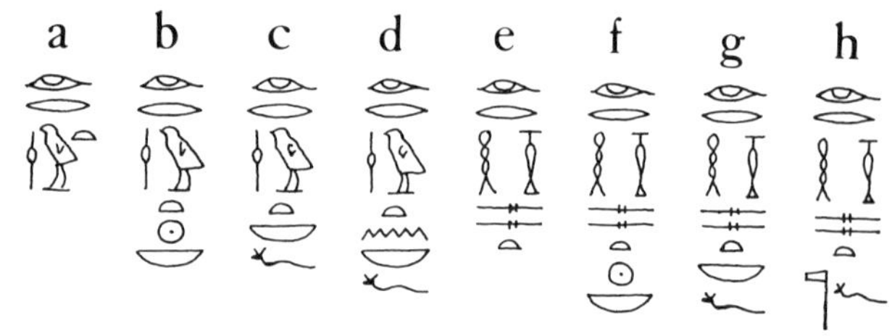

FIGURE 9
Epithets on cylinder seals (see note 11)

9. British Museum 65855. Mentioned by Kaplony, *Inschriften*, II, bottom of p. 677. The material has previously been catalogued as "brown quartzite," but James agrees that it is a softer material, and that limestone is probably the correct designation.

10. For the title, cf. the accompanying bone seal, Cairo Journal d'Entrée 72625 (height 4.7 cm., diameter 2.4 cm.). This is apparently the one indistinctly reproduced by J. E. Quibell and A. G. K. Hayter, *Teti Pyramid, North Side* (Cairo, 1927) p. 19, which was found in the tomb of *K3.ỉ-m-ḥst*. The title *ḥm-k3* also occurs on a bronze seal of Shepsekare, Cairo J. d'E. 45041 (height 5 cm.), G. Daressy, "Cylindre en bronze," *ASAE* 15 (1915) p. 94.

1/2

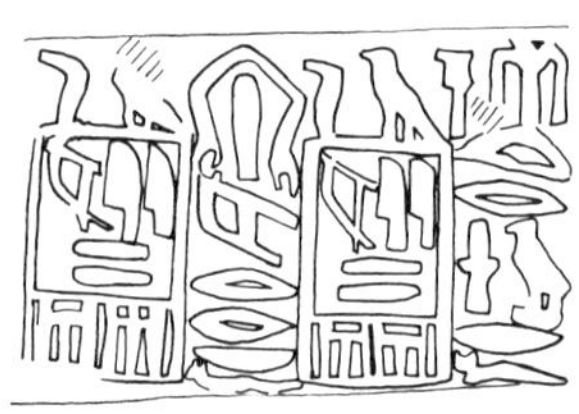

11. The sources of the epithets in Figure 9 are as follows:
   a. Pepy I: British Museum 5495 (Hall, *Scarabs*, p. 264, no. 2605); Metropolitan 35.9.6 (different grouping of signs).
   b. Pepy I: Metropolitan 07.228.95; cf. H. Schäfer, *Ägyptische Goldschmiedearbeiten* (Berlin, 1910) p. 15 (7) (different grouping, name of Mycerinus).
   c. Pepy I: Figure 6; *PSBA* 21 (1899) p. 170; Newberry, *Scarabs*, p. 55, fig. 31; Petrie, *Scarabs*, pl. 10 (4); Brussels E 7311 (*Chronique d'Égypte* 31 [1956] p. 89); Cairo J. d'E. 72625 (Quibell and Hayter, *Teti Pyramid, North Side*, p. 19, feminine ⌓ lacking); Brooklyn 44.123.32; probably Metropolitan 17.5 (with restored); also horizontally: British Museum 51083 (Hall, *Scarabs*, p. 301, no. 2865, with restored). Earlier (Sahure): Junker, *Gîza*, VII (Leipzig and Vienna, 1944) fig. 96b, p. 235. Later (Pepy II): Brooklyn 49.50.
   d. Pepy I: British Museum 29061 (Hall, *Scarabs*, p. 264, no. 2604; cf. (a son of Neferirkare, Junker, *Gîza*, VII, fig. 97, p. 237).
   e. Pepy I: British Museum 29061 (Hall, *Scarabs*, p. 264, no. 2604); British Museum 5495 (Hall, *Scarabs*, p. 264, no. 2605); Metropolitan 07.228.95; Metropolitan 26.7.10 (P. Newberry, *The Timins Collection* [London, 1907] pl. 21 [15]). Later (Pepy II): Brooklyn 49.50.
   f. Pepy I: only attested in a horizontal line: Metropolitan 07.228.95.
   g. Pepy I: British Museum 51083 (Hall, *Scarabs*, p. 301,

FIGURE 10 Cylinder seal (example 5). University Museum, Philadelphia, E 621

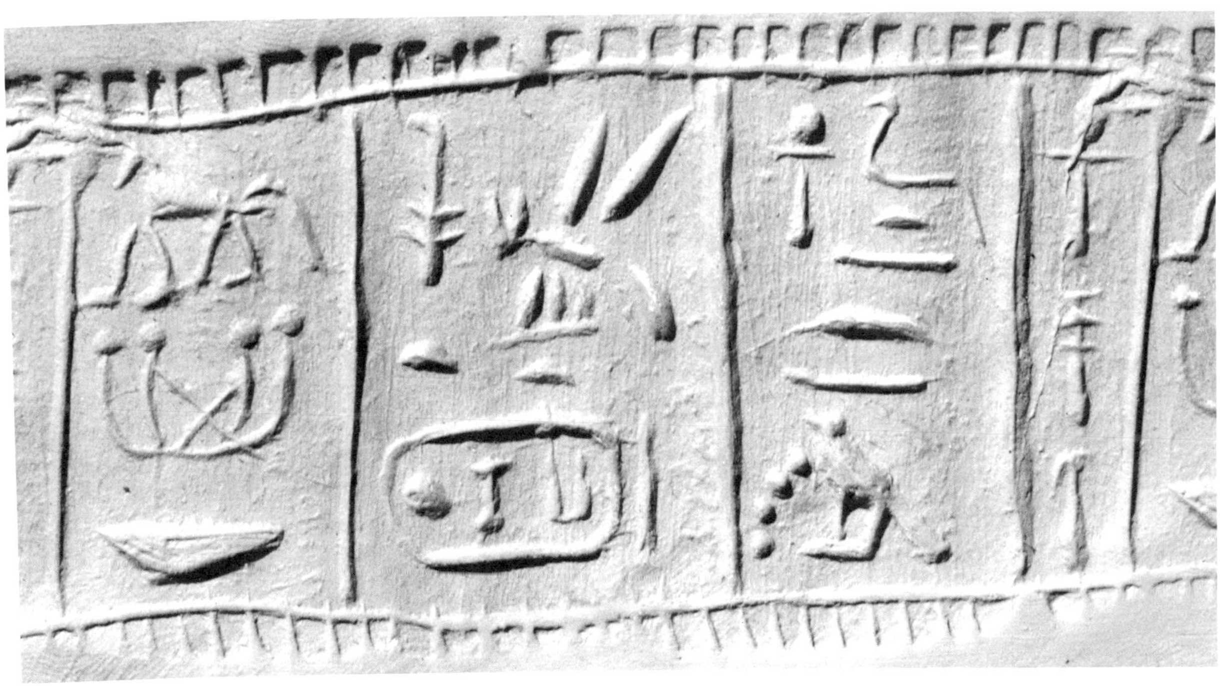

FIGURE 11 Impression of the seal shown in Figure 10

no. 2865); Petrie, *Scarabs*, pl. 10 [5]; Brooklyn 44.123.32. Earlier (Weserkare): Cairo J. d'E. 45041/45495 (*ASAE* 15 [1915] p. 94, lacks feminine 𓏏). Later (Merenre and Pepy II): *Rec. trav.* 32 (1910) p. 41, fig. 2 (the sign [sign] is to be restored).

h. Pepy I: British Museum 25422 (Hall, *Scarabs*, p. 263, no. 2602; also arranged horizontally: Petrie, *Scarabs*, pl. 10 [5]; Louvre 13441 (*ÄZ* 86 [1961] 23).

For similar epithets from other sources see J. Janssen, *De Traditioneele Egyptische Autobiografie*, I (Leiden, 1946) pp. 46–47, nos. 120, 123, 141, 142, 144–146.

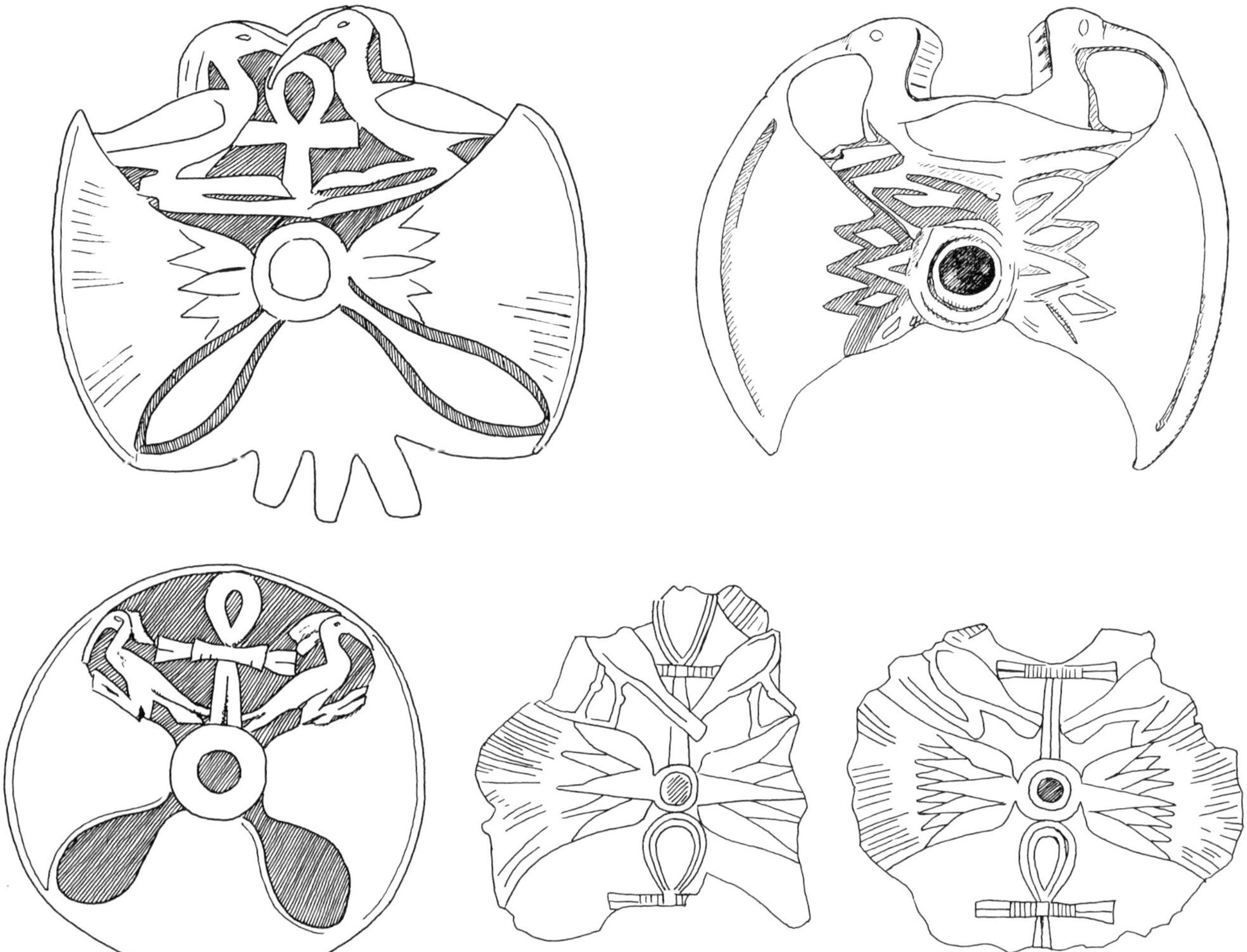

FIGURES 12–15 Old Kingdom diadems

be completed by the name *Mry-ẖt*. The omission of a cartouche after is unusual, although the same situation occurs on a cylinder seal of Mycerinus, where *Nśwt-bỉty Nbty* is again followed by the *Nbty*-name alone.[12] The Horus name *Mry-tꜣwy* might well have been followed by the missing praenomen *Mry-Rʿ* or the nomen *Ppy*, both of which are attested as the second element within the *śrẖ*-enclosure.[13] This would provide one of the two names that customarily appear in a cartouche, but hardly compensates for the aforementioned omission.

5. The latest of the series (Figures 10, 11) is a cylinder seal of Pepy II that was bought in 1891 by Mrs. John Harrison on the advice of Emil Brugsch and was subsequently donated to the University Museum, Phila-

12. Cairo J. d'E. 36262, G. Legrain, "Achats à Louqsor," *ASAE* 4 (1903) p. 134. Cf. also J. Černý et al., *The Inscriptions of Sinai*, part II (London, 1955) inscription 16, where these two titles are followed by the *Nbty*-name *Mry-ẖt* and the cartouche *Mry-Rʿ*, in that order.

13. Addition of *Mry-Rʿ*: Figure 6 above; also Metropolitan 26.7.10 (Timins Coll.); Metropolitan 17.5; Brooklyn 44.123.32; Newberry, *Scarabs*, figs. 21, 31; Petrie, *Scarabs*, pl. 10 (4); Hall, *Scarabs*, no. 2602 (British Museum 25422). Addition of *Ppy*: Hall, *Scarabs*, no. 2603 (British Museum 47460), 2865 (British Museum 51083, followed by or); Louvre 13441, H. G. Fischer, "Three Old Kingdom Palimpsests," *ÄZ* 86 (1961) p. 23; W. L. Nash, "Cylinder of Pepi 1st," *PSBA* 21 (1899) p. 170. At least nine examples can be cited where these additions do not occur.

delphia.[14] It is made of limestone and measures 7.8 cm. in height and 5.3 cm. in diameter, with a hole that varies from 0.7 to 0.8 cm. in maximum width. A toothed border somewhat like that of example 1 appears at the top and bottom, and plain vertical lines divide the field into three wide compartments. A narrower compartment, containing the signs 𓋹𓊽𓌀, "life, stability, and prosperity," may represent leftover space, as in the case of example 4. The name of "the King of Upper and Lower Egypt," *Nfr-k3-Rʿ*, appears at the center and continues with "living forever and ever." The remaining compartment contains a baboon and, above the sign 𓎟, a figure that is difficult to identify. Possibly this represents an extremely stylized pair of monkeys facing one another, i.e., (). An almost equally schematic tête-bêche group appears on a cylinder in University College, London: .[15]

Thus the curious type of seal decoration is not only attested throughout the Sixth Dynasty, but as early as the penultimate reign of the preceding dynasty, at which time it already shows the tête-bêche arrangement of confronted pairs. Even the simpler type of confronted pair does not otherwise seem to have been popular in the Old Kingdom, although it must be admitted that there is very little evidence on which to base a comparison. Three out of four examples of Old Kingdom diadems with the crested ibis motif show the outward orientation as opposed to one that has the birds facing inward (Figures 12–15).[16] In one of the three cases the pair is overlapped; a seal impression shows lions arranged in the same manner (Figure 16).[17] And while pairs of serpo-felines on protodynastic palettes address each other, those that appear in the Old Kingdom emblem of Cusae are again turned outward (Figure 17).[18] The same outward orientation is displayed by a pair of seated lions on the painted pectoral of an Old Kingdom statue.[19] The greater popularity of

14. E 621. I am indebted to David O'Connor for assistance in making the impression illustrated here, as well as for his permission to publish it.

15. Petrie, *Scarabs*, pl. VI (147). The drawing is taken from A. Evans, *Scripta Minoa*, I (Oxford, 1909) fig. 55, p. 122.

FIGURE 16
Seal impression. After Jéquier

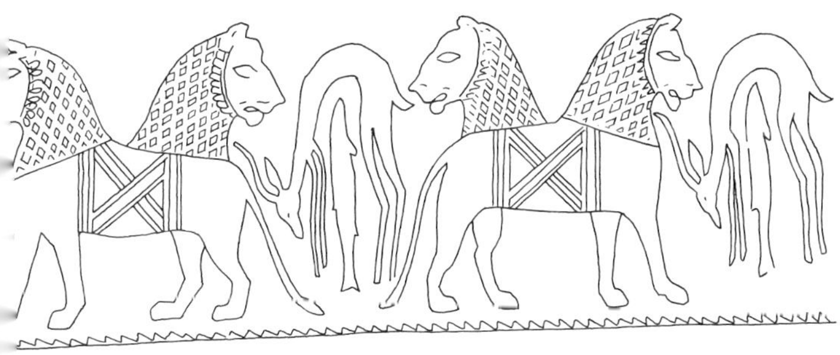

FIGURE 17
Emblem of Cusae. After Blackman

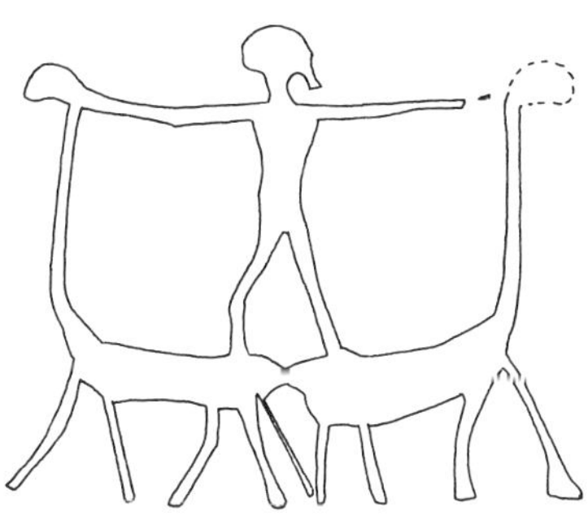

16. D. Dunham, "An Egyptian Diadem of the Old Kingdom," *Bulletin of the Museum of Fine Arts* (Boston) 44 (1946) pp. 24–25, figs. 1–4, and A. Abu-Bakr, *Excavations at Giza 1949–1950* (Cairo, 1953) fig. 69, p. 84 (Figure 15 above). The exception, Boston 37.606A (Figure 12), is the principal subject of Dunham's article. Figure 13 is drawn from Dunham's fig. 7 (Leipzig), Figure 14 from photographs corresponding to his fig. 8 (Cairo).

17. G. Jéquier, *Le monument funéraire de Pepi II*, III (Cairo, 1940) fig. 68, p. 67; for the halters, cf. G. Jéquier, *Les pyramides des reines Neit et Apouit* (Cairo, 1933) pl. 5. As these examples show, crossed animals are not so rare in ancient Egyptian art as Frankfort indicates in his *Studies*, p. 121; he cites the cranes of *M3-nfr* (H. Fechheimer, *Die Plastik der Ägypter* [Berlin, 1923] p. 129) as an exception, but they occur in other cases: e.g., H. Junker, *Gîza*, VI (Vienna and Leipzig, 1943) figs. 14, 16; Metropolitan 08.201.1; R. F. E. Paget and A. A. Pirie, *The Tomb of Ptah-hetep* (London, 1898) pl. 31. Cf. also the caged birds, Paget and Pirie, *Ptah-hetep*, pl. 32; J. Capart, *Une rue de tombeaux à Saqqarah*, II (Brussels, 1907) pl. 84, among other examples; and the hieroglyph for 𓅬𓅬𓅬 in Jéquier, *Monument funéraire Pepi II*, III, pl. 4.

18. See W. S. Smith, *History of Egyptian Sculpture and Painting in the Old Kingdom* (London, 1946) fig. 33, p. 118, and for the emblem of Cusae in the Old Kingdom, cf. Jéquier, *Monument funéraire Pepi II*, III, pl. 21, A. M. Blackman, *Rock Tombs of Meir*, IV (London, 1924) pls. 4, 4A, 6, 11. The reorientation of the motif is a further indication of its Mesopotamian origin, which was independently recognized by L. Heuzey, "Égypte ou Chaldée?", *Comptes rendus de l'Académie des Inscriptions et Belles-Lettres* 27 (1899) p. 66, and A. E. P. Weigall citing P. Newberry in "Miscellaneous Notes," *ASAE* 11 (1910) pp. 170–171, and further discussed by G. A. Wainwright, "El Hibah and Esh Shurafa," *ASAE* 27 (1927) pp. 97–101, and by Frankfort, *Studies*, pp. 119–121, where there are some further comments on the "antithetical group."

19. L. Borchardt, *Statuen und Statuetten*, I, *Catalogue général des antiquités du Musée du Caire* (Berlin, 1911) p. 103 (Cairo Cat. 139).

the confronted pair during the Middle Kingdom, as evidenced by Twelfth Dynasty pectorals,[20] may be the result of the same influence that favored this orientation on the cylinder seals. But cylinder seals and button seals are the only vehicle for the more extreme form of confrontation—the tête-bêche arrangement. This is not attested in the protodynastic period either,[21] and Scharff and Frankfort are probably correct in attributing it to foreign influence from the East.

Another feature that merits further consideration is the choice of material. Like many inscribed Old Kingdom cylinder seals of the normal variety, a few of the type under consideration are made of wood (Figure 4) or steatite (Figure 6).[22] Limestone is much more usual, however, and its use is almost entirely confined to this class of cylinders.[23] In addition to the four with royal names (examples 1, 2, 4, 5; Figures 1, 5, 7, 10) and the one from Abydos (Figure 3), there are several other limestone examples that clearly belong to the Old Kingdom: the two seals published by H. Junker in *Mélanges Maspero*, I (Figures 19, 20),[24] Berlin 16433

FIGURE 18

Cylinder seal. Cairo Museum, Journal d'Entrée 72610

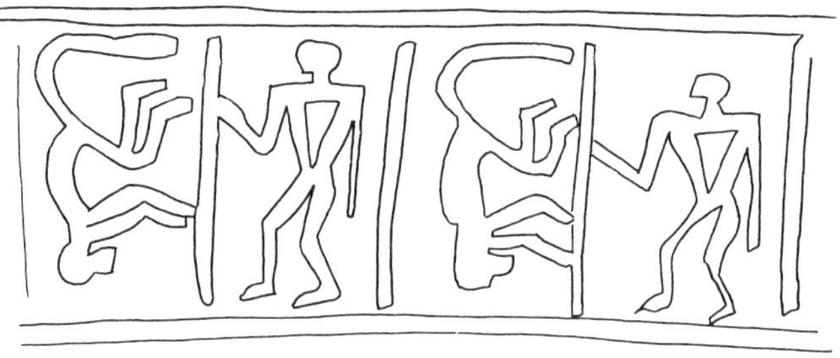

20. Borchardt, *Statuen und Statuetten*, II (Berlin, 1925) p. 2 (Cairo Cat. 381, 382); R. Engelbach, *Riqqeh* and *Memphis*, VI (London, 1915) pl. 1; J. De Morgan, *Fouilles à Dahchour Mars–Juin 1894* (Vienna, 1895) pls. 15–16 and cf. 19–20; H. E. Winlock, *Treasure of El Lāhūn* (New York, 1934) pls. 5–6; Burlington Fine Arts Club, *Catalogue of an Exhibition of Ancient Egyptian Art* (London, 1922) pl. 50 (no. 10). Similarly the axe blade of *Ḥwnś* (*sic*) in William C. Hayes, *The Scepter of Egypt*, II (New York, 1959) fig. 126, p. 213 (Metropolitan 26.7.834), as opposed to another Middle Kingdom axe blade (H. Ranke, "The Egyptian Collections," *University Museum Bulletin* [University of Pennsylvania, Philadelphia] 15, nos. 2–3 [November 1950] p. 74), which shows apes turned inward, but with heads looking outward; cf. E. Kühnert-Eggebrecht, *Die Axt als Waffe und Werkzeug im alten Ägypten* (Berlin, 1969) pls. 20 (1 [outward], 2 [inward]), 22 (outward), 24 (1 [reverse of above-mentioned University Museum example, which is also shown here, 3], 2 [inward]).

21. William Ward sees a late predynastic antecedent in a ring that "has four falcons arranged in such a manner that opposite pairs are tête-bêche" ("The Origin of Egyptian Design-Amulets ['Button Seals']," *JEA* 56 [1970] p. 73, fig. 3 [c] on p. 72). But it is difficult to believe that the artist intended a diagonal comparison of this kind. In connection with the point made above, in note 18, it is also significant that the disk with confronted birds that Ward exhibits as another antecedent (his fig. 3 [d]) shows a thoroughly Mesopotamian style and technique of inlay; the border of white alabaster diamonds set in black paste (W. B. Emery, *The Tomb of Hemaka* [Cairo, 1938] p. 29 [no. 309]) reduplicates Sumerian inlays of shell and bitumen, and the inlays of two other disks (Emery's pl. 12 [D, E]) display the same influence. For the similar use of channels for inlay see, for example, E. Heinrich, *Kleinfunde aus den archaischen Tempelschichten in Uruk* (Berlin and Leipzig, 1936) p. 27, pl. 26; P. Delougaz et al., *Pre-Sargonid Temples in the Diyala Region*, Oriental Institute Publications, no. 58 (Chicago, 1942) fig. 26.

Ward's attempt to find an example of "linear fusion" in an Old Kingdom headrest (his fig. 6) is even less convincing. In this headrest a pair of arms replaces the usual central column, with the hands cupped to support the head. Ward's drawing fails to indicate the division of the arms (cf. R. Engelbach and B. Gunn, *Harageh* [London, 1923] pl. 9 [7–8]), which appears in all the other examples mentioned in his note 1, p. 76, and my own note 20 in "Varia Aegyptiaca," *Journal of the American Research Center in Egypt* 2 (1963) p. 33, as well as *Illustrated London News*, June 4, 1938, p. 1001 (nos. 1, 3). None of the other five headrests (including Cairo J. d'E. 43059) shows the fluting that, in the Harageh example, is assimilated from the more customary upright in the form of a column. As illustrated in *Journal of the American Research Center* 2 (1963) p. 32, fig. 8, brachiomorphic implements are well known from the Archaic Period through the Old Kingdom and later, and in every case the hand is an ideographic addition, one that has a meaningful connection with the use of the object in question. It is difficult to see how this very concrete sort of hieroglyphic allusion is directly related to patterns in which quite disparate elements are fused so that, for example, the horns of the *bꜣt*-emblem coincide with the forelegs of a pair of lions, as in the case of Figure 4 above.

22. G. A. Reisner, *Mycerinus* (Cambridge, Massachusetts, 1931) p. 234 (and pl. 64j); Cairo J. d'E. 72610 (Figure 18; height 3.4 cm., width, 2.3 cm.); G. Brunton, *Mostagedda* (London, 1937) pl. 60 (2, blue glazed); Brooklyn 44.123.33 (brown steatite); Petrie, *Scarabs*, pl. 7 (157) ("hard green stone" according to the Sotheby catalogue of the Macgregor Collection, June 26–July 6, 1922, p. 61 [488]). The "pierre grise" of G. Jéquier, *Tombeaux de particuliers* (Cairo, 1929) p. 52, might be limestone; cf. note 29 below.

23. The only exceptions known to me are a Fifth Dynasty seal, Brooklyn 44.123.30, which will be described presently, and Berlin 16432 (Scharff, "Über einige fremdartige Darstellungen," *ÄZ* 67 [1931] fig. f, p. 99).

24. Junker, "Zwei Schein-Rollsiegel," *Mélanges Maspero*, I, fasc. 1, pp. 267–271; cf. his *Gîza*, VII, p. 90. Also reproduced by Kaplony, *Inschriften*, III, fig. 634. According to Junker, the seals name two "sealbearers" called *Wḏꜣw* and *Mrì-św-ʿnḫ* who were in the service of a certain *Ṯntì*. If so, the sequence of names is exceptional; one would expect "*Ṯnti* [estate], sealbearer *Wḏꜣw*." Cf. Junker, *Gîza*, III (Vienna and Leipzig, 1938) p. 159, and the statues of various retainers of *Wr-ìr.n.ì*, Cairo Cat. 110, 114, 118,

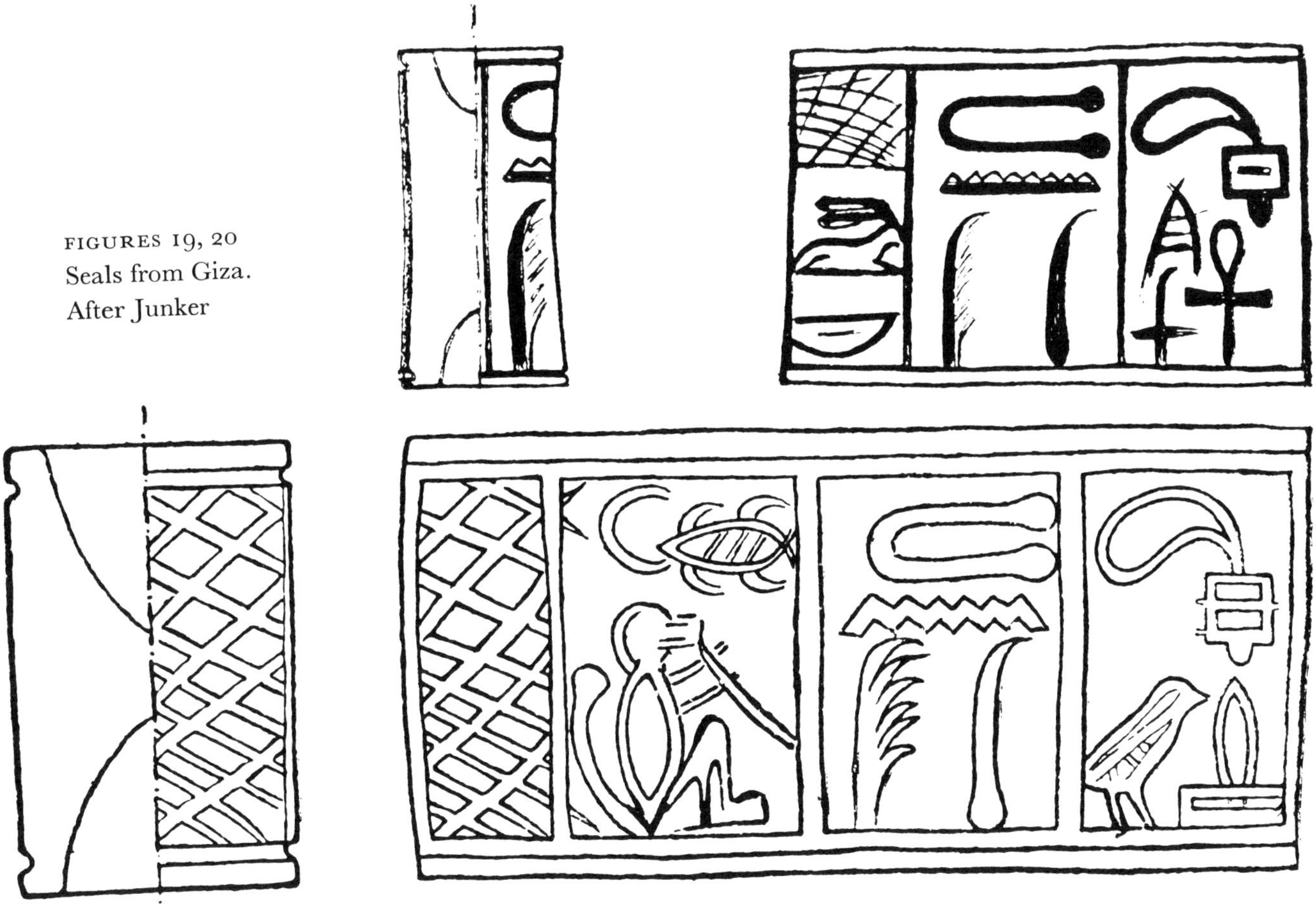

FIGURES 19, 20
Seals from Giza.
After Junker

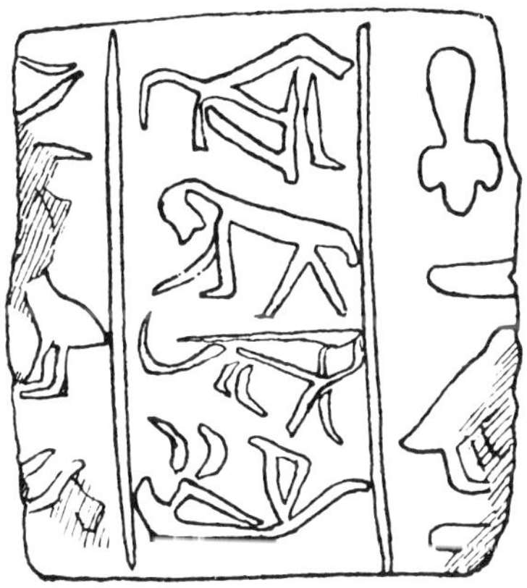

FIGURE 21
Cylinder seal.
Staatliche
Museen, Berlin,
16433. After
Scharff

(Figure 21),[25] Berlin 15399,[26] Berlin 18170,[27] University College 11090,[28] Brooklyn 44.123.29 (similar to the

FIGURE 22 Titles mentioning *ḏ3w* (see note 25)

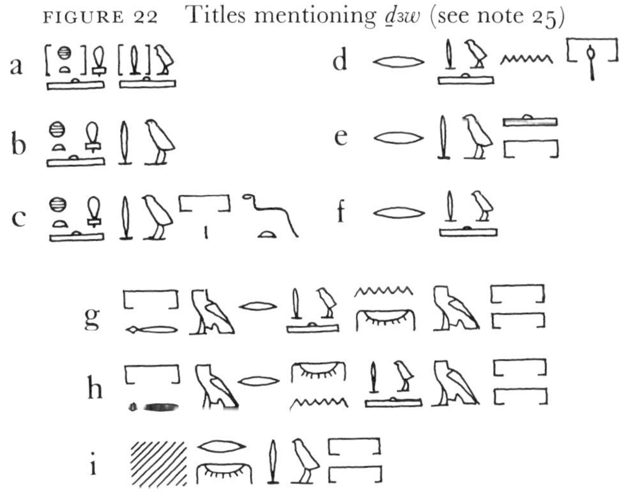

119. It is also possible that one of the seals names the "Sealbearer of the stores [*ḏ3w*—see next note] *Ṯnty*" and the "Sealbearer of *Mr-św-ʿnḫ Ṯntì*." For the name *Mr-św-ʿnḫ*, cf. S. Hassan, *Excavations at Gîza*, I (Oxford, 1932) pp. 104 ff. Kaplony, *Inschriften*, I, p. 453 (5) reads this *ʿnḫ-mrj-nyśwt*.

25. Scharff, "Über einige fremdartige Darstellungen," *ÄZ* 67 (1931) fig. g, p. 98; my information concerning the material derives from the notes of Rudolf Anthes, who gives the height as 5.1 cm. and the diameter as 2.7 cm. The restoration of the hieroglyphs at the left edge remains uncertain. The column at the right is to be read *ḫtm ḏ3w* (Figure 22 a), for which cf. Figure 22 b (Cairo J. d'E. 36262; Legrain, "Achats à Louqsor," *ASAE* 4 [1903] p. 134) and Figure 22 c (note 28). The word *ḏ3w* also occurs in the titles *ìry ḏ3w n pr-ḥḏ*, "keeper of stores of the treasury" (Figure 22 d: Louvre 251); *ìry ḏ3w pr*, "keeper of stores of the domain" (Figure

foregoing),[29] and Cairo Cat. 14518.[30] Besides these, W. M. F. Petrie's *Scarabs and Cylinders* contains at least five other limestone cylinders (the material is often unspecified in this and other publications). One of them (his pl. 7 [156]) shows a sketchy *serekh*, which, as Petrie points out, might possibly contain the Horus name *Mry-tȝwy*, i.e., Pepy I; another (his pl. 6 [143]) has a complex scroll design that links it with Middle Kingdom scarabs; the rest are of uncertain date.[31]

Limestone is also the material of a crudely inscribed seal that apparently bears the Horus name [hieroglyphs], i.e., the mid-Fifth Dynasty ruler Re-neferef (Figure 23).[32] As in the case of a few other limestone seals, the rest of the inscription is probably meaningless.[33] If so, this seal provides an early example of the sort represented by no. 2 above (Figure 5).

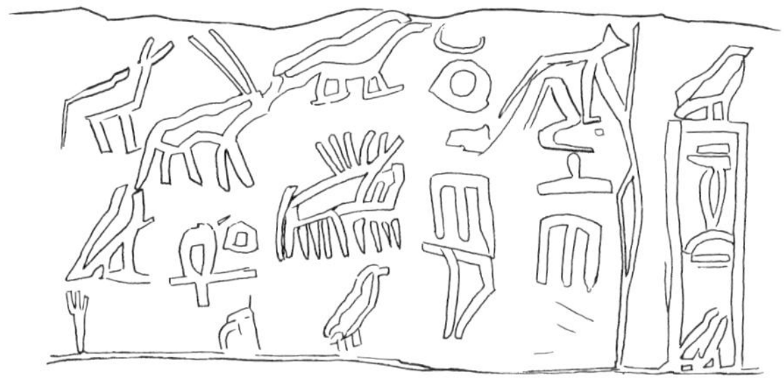

FIGURE 23

Cylinder seal, Cairo Museum, Journal d'Entrée 72209

Junker has described his pair of limestone seals as "Schein-Rollziegel," not intended for actual use, on the grounds that they were made of a softer stone than was generally utilized for cylinders, that they were incompletely pierced and could not accommodate a pin or cord, and that the carved detail of the smaller seal was filled with black pigment, which would have been lost if the surface had been rolled on damp mud or clay. His reasoning is persuasive, and it is supported by two exceptions that seemingly prove his conclusion to be the rule: the two limestone cylinder seals that have completely normal inscriptions, consisting of non-royal titles and the Horus names of kings, also show an incomplete perforation or the absence of any hole whatever, the first mentioning Isesy,[34] the second Neferirkare and Neuserre.[35] In the latter instance the complete

22 e: E. Drioton and J.-Ph. Lauer, "Un groupe de tombes à Saqqarah," *ASAE* 55 [1958] p. 234, pl. 20 d); *iry ḏȝw* (Figure 22 f: unpublished false door of *Ḥtpì*, Saqqara); *ìmy-r ḏȝw n nbw m prwy pr-ʿȝ*, "overseer of the stores of gold in the two domains of the palace" (Figure 22 g: doorway of *Ḫʿ-ʾInpw*; Chicago, Field Mus. of Natural Hist. 31690); *ìmy-r nbw n ḏȝw m prwy pr ʿȝ*, "overseer of gold of the stores of the two domains of the palace" (Figure 22 h: T. G. H. James, *Hieroglyphic Texts from Egyptian Stelae*, I, 2nd ed. [London, 1961] pl. 26 [2]); and [*ìmy?*]*-r nbw ḏȝw prwy*, "[over]seer (?) of gold of the two storehouses" (Figure 22 i: James, *Hieroglyphic Texts*, I, pl. 26 [2], and A. Mariette, *Les Mastabas de l'ancien Empire* [Paris, 1889] p. 431. The term [hieroglyphs] is used in much the same way as [hieroglyphs], another word for "storehouse," but is differentiated from the latter, P. Posener-Kriéger and J. L. De Cenival, *Hieratic Papyri in the British Museum*, 5th ser., *The Abu Sir Papyri* (London, 1968) pls. 62 (47) and 63 (c), respectively.

26. Newberry, *Scarabs*, p. 49, fig. 25; A. Scharff, *Altertümer der Vor- und Frühzeit Ägyptens*, II (Berlin, 1929) p. 95, fig. 62.

27. Berlin 18170; Scharff, *Altertümer*, II, p. 97, fig. 64 c.

28. Petrie, *Scarabs*, pl. 7 (163), and Kaplony, *Inschriften*, III, fig. 634. The entire inscription reads "Sealer of the treasure of the estate, (and specifically) the granary of barley." The other titles of the Keeper of the Treasure *Ḥtpì* (preceding note) similarly refer to the granary, as also in Drioton and Lauer, "Un groupe de tombes," *ASAE* 55 (1958) p. 234.

29. Drawing, from Newberry, in Kaplony, *Inschriften*, III, fig. 635. I owe further information to the kindness of Richard Fazzini, who informs me that the dark gray color of the surface is due to patination, with darker areas caused by mold.

30. Quibell, *Archaic Objects*, p. 279, pl. 59. Quibell describes the material as "soft white limestone," rather than "terre-cuite" or "clay" as stated in J. De Morgan, *Recherches sur les origines de l'Égypte*, II (Paris, 1897) p. 257, fig. 857; Evans, *Scripta Minoa*, I, p. 122, fig. 57.

31. Petrie, *Scarabs*, pl. 6 (140, 142, 144). Other limestone seals: W. M. F. Petrie, *Koptos* (London, 1896) pl. 24 (42), p. 24; and perhaps Bibliothèque Nationale 515 (Scharff, "Über einige fremdartige Darstellungen," *ÄZ* 67 [1931] p. 97, fig. c; L. Delaporte, *Catalogue des Cylindres Orientaux . . . de la Bibliothèque Nationale* (Paris, 1910) p. 290, states that no. 515 is "jaspe brun," but the execution of the design shows that it is carved in a much softer material; Edna Russmann, who has examined the seal on my behalf, confirms this point (cf. note 29 above).

32. Cairo J. d'E. 72209. Height 3.5 cm. From Saqqara, near the tomb of *Ptḥ-ḥtp*. Just possibly the name begins with [hieroglyphs], in which case it belongs to Isesy, as in the case of no. 1 above (Figure 1). But [hieroglyphs] is much more probable, and this is definitely to be read in the case of Univ. Coll. 11106 (Petrie, *Scarabs*, pl. 9 [5.8, 1]), which I hope to discuss elsewhere.

33. Among the other examples are Petrie, *Scarabs*, pl. 7 (161); Reisner, *Mycerinus*, p. 234, pl. 64 k; Cairo J. d'E. 37094, 37096 (from excavations of Barsanti at Zawiyet el Aryan); Berlin 18168, 18169 (Scharff, *Altertümer*, II, pp. 96–97). In the present case one might recognize the unusual title [hieroglyphs] (cf. H. G. Fischer, "The Butcher *Pḥ-r-nfr*," *Orientalia* 29 [1960] pp. 169 [d], 178), but the rest is uncertain and so, therefore, is this.

34. Berlin 16432; Scharff, "Über einige fremdartige Darstellungen," *ÄZ* 67 (1931) p. 99, fig. f. This mentions the sun temple of Neuserre, but the Horus name is evidently [hieroglyphs]. The height is 4 cm. In Charlottenburg.

35. Brooklyn 44.123.30. Height 7.5, diameter 3.5 cm.

omission of perforation may, however, be explained by the fact that the seal was not finished; there is space for three horizontal lines at the bottom, as in the case of a sealing of Neferirkare shown in Junker, *Gîza*, VII, fig. 197, but the first line is incomplete and the space below it is blank. Another unfinished seal, displaying the Horus name of the Fifth Dynasty ruler Men-kau-Hor, and made of "black granite," has only the beginning of a perforation.[36] But it is difficult to explain why the hole is also lacking in the case of two other seals of Neuserre—one described as "terre emaillée,"[37] the other, "grey stone."[38] It may or may not be coincidental that this king is associated with all three of the seals of the normal variety that lack any perforation whatever.

While the presence of a hole cannot be confirmed in every case, this detail having been overlooked in most publications, it does in fact appear in most of the limestone cylinder seals under discussion,[39] and I know of only four other cases in which it does not occur. One, bearing illegible inscriptions, is a seal the ends of which are similarly inscribed.[40] In this respect it is comparable to a second example, which has decorative motifs and, in addition, a floral design on either end;[41] Frankfort has cited Asiatic parallels for this usage.[42] The third unperforated seal is the one in Petrie's *Scarabs* (pl. 6 [143]) that has a Middle Kingdom scroll design. The fourth is a seal with illegible inscription that derives from Barsanti's excavations at Zawiyet el Aryan (Cairo J. d'E. 37094).

It is true that no mud or clay sealings have survived to confirm the functional use of seals of the type that were usually made of limestone,[43] but the surviving number of Old Kingdom sealings is in any case very limited. I know, from personal experience, that it is quite possible to make clear impressions of limestone seals without injuring the surface. Depending on the quality of the limestone, some of these would, of course, more readily show signs of wear than those made of steatite, and at least two limestone cylinder seals do in fact show evidence of use; one is described as "worn,"[44] the other, "badly worn."[45]

To my mind the material and general character of the limestone seals suggest that they were made for persons of relatively lowly station. These individuals, if they had any title at all, were merely funerary attendants and "sealers."[46] Unable to afford costly workmanship[47] and probably, in many cases, incapable of reading an inscription, they were often satisfied with illegible assemblages of signs and motifs.

Conversely, it is difficult to imagine that a thoroughly literate Old Kingdom official would have had much regard for devices on the order of the tête-bêche composition or trompe-l'oeil fusions, such as a *b3t*-emblem the horns of which simultaneously represent the forelegs of two lions (Figure 4). Devices of this sort evidently

36. British Museum 48989: Hall, *Scarabs*, p. 263, no. 2601.

37. Cairo J. d'E. 44200. Height 5.2 cm., diameter 2.5 cm. According to the Journal d'Entrée the seal was found by Borchardt at Abusir in 1913, by which time, however, he had concluded his excavations at that site and was excavating at Tell El Amarna. One of the more conspicuous titles is apparently to be read 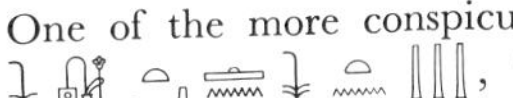, "Scribe of royal documents of the king's words," but the group  is uncertain. Another is  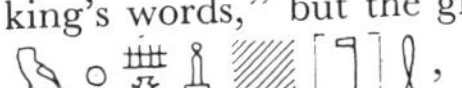, which is the first explicit evidence for the cult of Hathor as well as Re in this particular sun temple. As these remarks indicate, the inscription is only partly legible and the signs are extremely rudimentary and peculiar. My interpretation of them is based on photographs kindly supplied by Henry Riad. According to Christine Lilyquist, the surface is not glazed, as the Journal d'Entrée states, but the material is uncertain.

38. British Museum 48988: Hall, *Scarabs*, p. 262, no. 2600.

39. Nos. 1 (Figure 1), 2 (Figure 5), 4 (Figure 7), 5 (Figure 10); Cairo Cat. 14518 (Quibell, *Archaic Objects*, pl. 59); Cairo J. d'E. 37096, Reisner, *Mycerinus*, p. 234, pl. 64 k; Brooklyn 44.123.29; Berlin 15399 (Scharff, *Altertümer*, II, p. 95, fig. 62); Berlin 16431, 16433 (Scharff, "Über einige fremdartige Darstellungen," *ÄZ* 67 [1931] p. 99, fig. e, and p. 98, fig. g, respectively); Berlin 18168–18170 (Scharff, *Altertümer*, II, pp. 96–97, fig. 64 a–c). Barbara Adams informs me that a hole is also present in all but one of the eight cylinder seals in University College, London: Petrie, *Scarabs*, pls. VI (140, 142, 144), VII (156, 161, 162, 163).

40. British Museum 48987: Hall, *Scarabs*, p. 261, no. 2596.

41. Bibliothèque Nationale 515 (see above, note 31).

42. Frankfort, *Cylinder Seals*, p. 298.

43. The impression shown in Figure 16 consists of noninscriptional motifs (cf. note 17 above), but there is otherwise little resemblance to the limestone seals that are under discussion.

44. Petrie, *Abydos*, II, p. 29 (no. 276).

45. Reisner, *Mycerinus*, p. 234, pl. 64 k.

46. For "funerary priest" (*ḥm-k3*) see Figure 7 above; titles of "sealers" are represented by Figure 20 above, Petrie, *Scarabs*, pl. 7 (163), and Brooklyn 44.123.29 (cf. notes 28–29). Berlin 15399 (Newberry, *Scarabs*, p. 49, fig. 25) has the titles 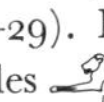 and 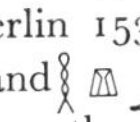; the first of these is oriented outward in both directions, as though it were a decorative motif; the second is upside-down in relation to the first; and both are interspersed among noninscriptional motifs, including trompe l'oeil emblems. It does not seem possible that either of these titles is to be taken at face value.

47. The relationship between cheapness of material, poor workmanship, and unintelligibility is further demonstrated by a cylinder seal described as "clay incised wet," Petrie, *Scarabs*, pl. 7 (162).

express a popular taste that is at variance with the scribal sobriety of Egyptian art, in which representations are generally well grounded on a base line, and all the elements are discrete and well defined. An analogous contrast is presented by the household gods eventually known as Toueris and Bes, hybrid fusions of man and beast, as opposed to the hieroglyphic assemblages of forms that constitute the so-called animal-headed gods.[48]

It was only after this article was virtually completed that I read William A. Ward's "The Origin of Egyptian Design-Amulets ('Button Seals')" in *JEA* 56 (1970) pp. 65–80. While I cannot agree with Ward's denial that any foreign influence is to be seen in the Egyptian use of the tête-bêche and trompe-l'oeil devices (cf. note 21 above), my conclusions are otherwise very much in agreement with his views concerning the button seals that continue to display such devices. He emphasizes that what he calls "the design-amulet tradition" belonged primarily to the lower classes and that "the popular art of the masses was more readily susceptible to change and could deviate more easily from a classical norm than the more formal art of the conservative upper classes."

PERIODICALS ABBREVIATED

ASAE—Annales du Service des Antiquités d'Égypte.
ÄZ—Zeitschrift für ägyptische Sprache und Altertumskunde.
JEA—The Journal of Egyptian Archaeology.
PSBA—Proceedings of the Society of Biblical Archaeology.

ACKNOWLEDGMENTS

In addition to the more specific acknowledgments in the preceding pages, I want to thank Steffen Wenig and Joachim Karig for additional data concerning cylinder seals in East Berlin (15399) and Charlottenburg (Berlin 16431–16433, 18168–18170).

48. Cf. H. Frankfort, *Ancient Egyptian Religion* (New York, 1948) p. 12, who calls them "pictographs, not portraits," and "ideograms."

NOTES

Sunshades of the Marketplace*

HENRY G. FISCHER

Lila Acheson Wallace Curator in Egyptology, The Metropolitan Museum of Art

IN HER *Fellahin of Upper Egypt* (London, 1927) p. 168, Winifred Blackman writes: "When the warmer weather begins the traders erect rough booths looking like primitive umbrellas, under which they can take shelter from the heat." I noticed dozens of these umbrellas during a drive through the eastern Delta in the summer of 1968, and was struck by the fact that they are identical in construction to a type of sunshade that was represented in ancient Egyptian reliefs and paintings over a period of five centuries, from the early Fifth Dynasty down to the beginning of the Twelfth (c. 2450–1950 B.C.). The only significant difference is that the present-day sunshades are planted firmly in the ground (Figure 1), whereas those shown in the ancient scenes are always portable.

At least twenty-seven sources may be cited for the ancient use of such shades; nearly all of them, like the one illustrated, show a cloth stretched over a pair of sticks that are crisscrossed diagonally, these in turn being supported by a pole that is attached at the point of intersection; and nearly all show the end of the cloth

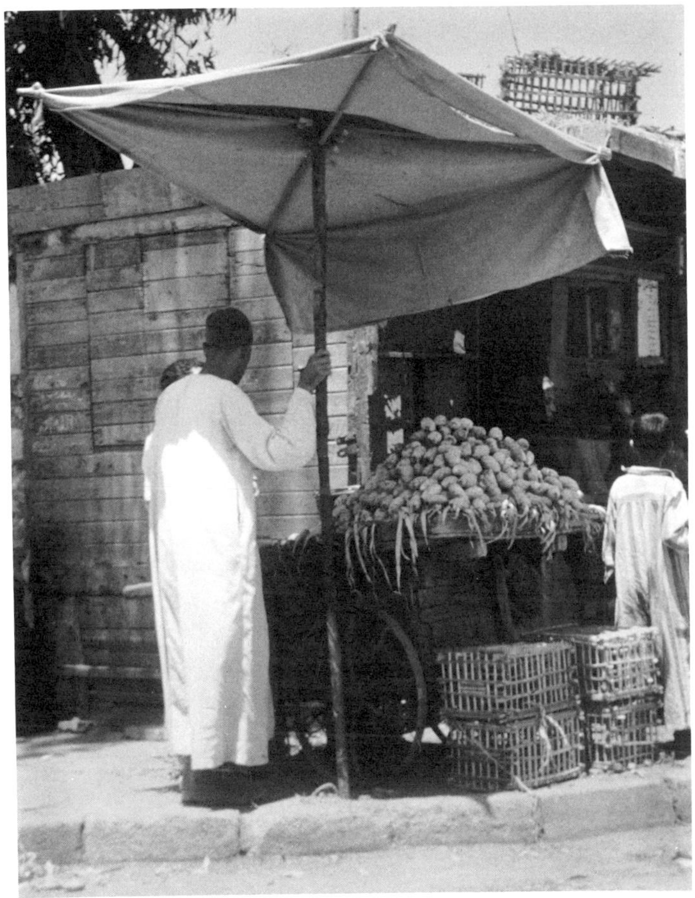

FIGURE 1
Country market vendor in the Egyptian Delta

*Were this note of sufficient length to warrant a dedication, it might be offered to the memory of Victor Baltard's iron parasols of Paris, which sheltered Les Halles from 1859 to 1969; it seems doubly ironic that these seemingly impervious descendants of the ancient sunshades should have survived no longer than the ideal life-span of the ancient Egyptians—110 years.

hanging freely on one side. The sources, listed in approximately chronological order, are as follows:[1]

Dyn. V

1. C. R. Lepsius, *Denkmaeler aus Aegypten und Aethiopien*, II (Berlin, n.d.) pl. 9 (also A. Mariette, *Les Mastabas de l'Ancien Empire* [Paris, 1889] p. 570).
2. H. T. Mohr, *The Mastaba of Hetep-her-akhti* (Leiden, 1943) fig. 44, p. 79.
3. S. Hassan, *Excavations at Gîza*, II (Cairo, 1936) fig. 240, opposite p. 220.
4. N. de. G. Davies, *The Rock Tombs of Sheikh Saïd* (London, 1901) pl. 5.
5. Lepsius, *Denkmaeler*, II, pl. 78b.
6. H. Wild, *Le tombeau de Ti*, fasc. 3, *Mémoires de l'Institut Français d'Archéologie Orientale du Caire*, no. 65 (Cairo, 1966) pl. 150 (also G. Steindorff, *Das Grab des Ti* [Leipzig, 1913] pl. 122).[2]

Dyn. VI

7. F. W. von Bissing, *Die Mastaba des Gem-ni-kai*, I (Leipzig, n. d.) pl. 22 (also W. Wreszinski, *Atlas zur altägyptischen Kulturgeschichte*, III [Leipzig, 1936] pl. 9).

8a. *Mrr-w(ỉ)-k3(.ỉ)*, Oriental Institute Sakkarah Expedition, *The Mastaba of Mereruka*, II (Chicago, 1938) pls. 167–168.

8b. Wife of *Mrr-w(ỉ)-k3(.ỉ)*, Wreszinski, *Atlas*, III, pl. 11.

9. *Nḫbw* (records of Museum of Fine Arts, Boston, G 2381).
10. A. M. Blackman and M. R. Apted, *The Rock Tombs of Meir*, V (London, 1953) pl. 31.
11. N. de G. Davies, *The Rock Tombs of Deir el Gebrâwi*, II (London, 1902) pl. 8.
12. Davies, *Deir el Gebrâwi*, I (London, 1902) pls. 8, 9.
13. *Śnfrw-ḥr-ỉšt.f*, H. de Morgan, *Fouilles à Dahchour en 1894–1895* (Vienna, 1903) pl. 20.
14. H. Junker, *Gîza*, V (Vienna and Leipzig, 1941) fig. 20, p. 84.
15. L. Borchardt, *Denkmäler des alten Reiches*, *Catalogue général du Musée du Caire* (Berlin, 1937) no. 1536B.

Dyn. VIII

16. Davies, *Deir el Gebrâwi*, II, pl. 18.

Dyns. IX–X

17. J. Vandier, *Mo'alla* (Cairo, 1950) fig. 4, p. 53.
18. Tomb of *Śt-k3* (Aswan).

Dyn. XI

19. Dendera shrine of *Nb-ḥpt-R'* Mentuhotep (L. Habachi, "King Nebhepetre Menthuhotp," *Mitteilungen des Deutschen Archäologischen Instituts Abteilung Kairo* 19 [1963] fig. 7, p. 24, pl. 6).
20. Tomb of Queen *Nfrw* (e.g., G. Steindorff, *Catalogue of the Egyptian Sculpture in the Walters Art Gallery* [Baltimore, 1946] no. 239; H. G. Fischer, "Eleventh Dynasty Relief Fragments from Deir el Bahri," *Yale University Art Gallery Bulletin* 24, no. 2 [October, 1958] fig. 1, p. 28).
21. Tomb of Queen *Nfrw*, burial chamber (Figure 5 below; H. E. Winlock, *Excavations at Deir el Bahri 1911–1931* [New York, 1942] pl. 13).
22. Wooden coffin of *'3šyt* (Cairo Journal d'Entrée 47355).
23. Louvre stela C15 (E. Drioton, "Une figuration cryptographique sur une stèle du Moyen Empire," *Revue d'Égyptologie* 1 [1933] pl. 9).
24. Tomb of *Sbk-ḥtp* (Kom Ombo; S. Wenig, "Eine Grabkammer des mittleren Reiches aus Kom Ombo," *Staatliche Museen zu Berlin: Forschungen und Berichte* 10 [1968] pl. IV [at end of volume] and color pl. 6).
25. P. E. Newberry, *Beni Hasan*, II (London, 1893) pl. 31.[3]

Dyn. XII

26. Newberry, *Beni Hasan*, II, pl. 16.
27. N. de G. Davies, *The Tomb of Antefoker* (London, 1920) pl. 3

In six of these occurrences (7, 8a and b, 13, 19, 25) the shade itself is missing, but its former existence can be determined from the way the support is held, as well as by the general context. In three other cases a portion of the shade is missing: 4 (supporting structure), 9 (flap at side), 27 (top).

1. Several of these are also cited and illustrated by J. Vandier, *Manuel d'archéologie égyptienne*, IV (Paris, 1964) especially pp. 337–339, in connection with scenes showing carrying-chairs.

2. This closely resembles a further example on an unpublished block of relief in the Cairo Museum, Journal d'Entrée 39864, which was noticed too late to include in the present list. The sunshade is similarly carried horizontally in a procession of offering bearers and the crosspieces show the same attachments, but no flap is visible.

3. For the date of this (tomb 29) and the following example from Beni Hasan (tomb 17) see W. Schenkel, *Frühmittelägyptische Studien* (Bonn, 1962) pp. 83 (j) and 81.

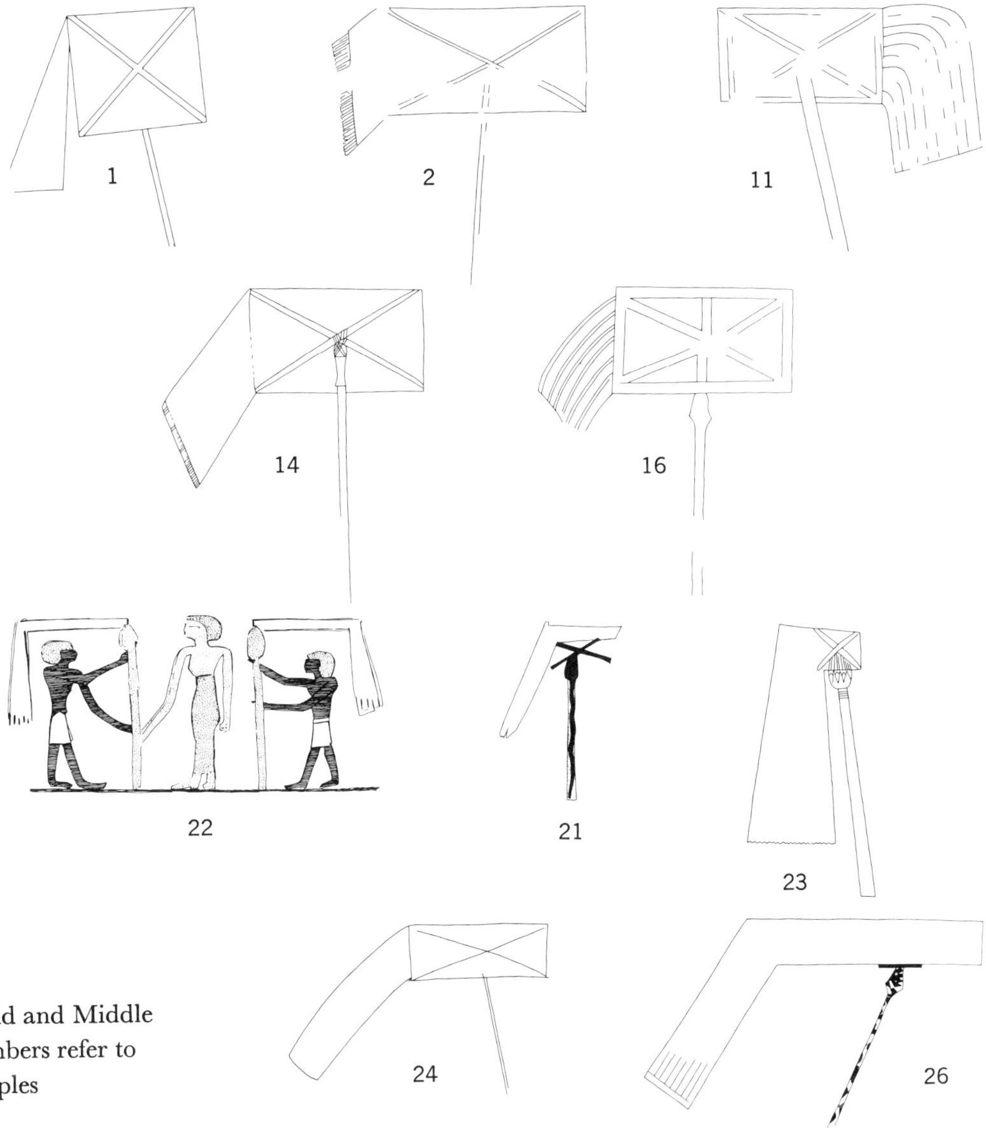

FIGURE 2
Sunshades of the Old and Middle Kingdom. The numbers refer to the tabulated examples

Some of the variations may be explained on stylistic grounds: after the Old Kingdom the crisscrossed sticks are much less frequently displayed (they appear in 21, 23, and 24 only) and the pole is generally terminated at the lower edge of the cloth. This is also true of the earliest and latest Old Kingdom examples (1 and 16). One Eleventh Dynasty example (23) shows the pole joined to the crosspieces, as does another (21) of the same period, but in the last case the entire supporting structure is placed below the cloth.

Other variations are more difficult to interpret. In no. 16, for example, there are three crosspieces; but the third is vertical, continuing the line of the pole beneath it, and it may have been added because the top of the pole terminates at the edge of the shade, as has just been described. Three examples—two at Deir el Gebrawi (11, 16) and one from Giza (5)—show a frame or border around the crosspieces; this might be taken to represent the edges of the cloth, these having been rolled inward when the four corners were tied, as shown by the present-day example. There is no reason, however, to assume that the ancient sunshades were so crudely assembled, and in at least one case (no. 6; Figure 3) it is clear that the cloth was attached by eight bands—four at the ends of the crosspieces and four more midway between the ends and intersections.

The other variations primarily concern the pendant flaps. The flap is omitted in one case only (10); it is generally longer than that of the modern example, but no. 2 is quite comparable in this respect. Sometimes the flap shows a series of parallel lines that may represent reinforcement, or the seams of strips sewn together; in the case of nos. 11 and 15 the lines more probably indicate divisions, i.e., a long fringe, but this explanation does not seem to fit no. 16, where double lines run down to a continuous edge, or no. 26, where evenly spaced lines run down to a continuous plain border. Other examples (2, 6, 14, 22) show a fringe at the very edge of the flap. The most exceptional case is that of no. 1, in which a cloth hangs down from a single corner rather than from the length of one side of the sunshade. This may represent the usual flap, as seen from a different point of view, but it is reminiscent of the pennant that is carried in the early Fourth Dynasty tomb paintings of Nefer-Maat.[4] An even closer resemblance to a pennant occurs in the case of nos. 20 and 27; while these seem to bear at least some kinship to the type of sunshade that is under discussion, there is no indication of the flat portion that is the essential element in most of the other examples, and the implements are carried over the shoulder. The flat portion, complete with supporting structure, is reduced to negligible proportions in the case of a contemporary Eleventh Dynasty example (23), however, and there is no reason, in principle, why a sunshade should not be carried over one shoulder (as it is in no. 6). But it is nonetheless true that most of the later examples where the shade is held by women seem more hieratic than functional (17, 18, 20, 22, 23, 24, 27).

In all of these cases, as noted earlier, the sunshade is portable. In the examples from the Fifth Dynasty (1–4) and one from the beginning of the Sixth Dynasty (8a), it is held beside, or over, a standing person, and this usage is more common in the examples of later date (Eighth–Twelfth Dynasties, nos. 16, 19, 25, 26, 27). During the intervening period the sunshades accompanied a man (or woman) in a carrying chair: once at the end of the Fifth Dynasty (5) and more commonly during the Sixth Dynasty (7, 8b, 9–15). Again at the end of the Fifth Dynasty (6) and more frequently in examples later than the Old Kingdom (17, 18, 20, 24, 27) the object is simply carried, and in such cases it seems to be presented to the tomb owner as a piece of equipment; that is certainly true of nos. 6 and 24, as also no. 23, where the pole is not carried but is steadied, with the butt placed on the ground. Similarly no. 21 shows the pole on the ground without any figure whatever, since it belongs to a frieze of offerings. Sometimes the bearer holds the shade over himself (or more properly herself: 17, 18, 22, 24). An Eleventh Dynasty example (22) shows a pair of attendants steadying sunshades as described above, while the pole of one of the shades is also held by a woman who stands between them, and for whom the shade is intended.

The more usual type of portable sunshade, throughout the Pharaonic Period, was the lighter and far more manageable implement that is represented by the

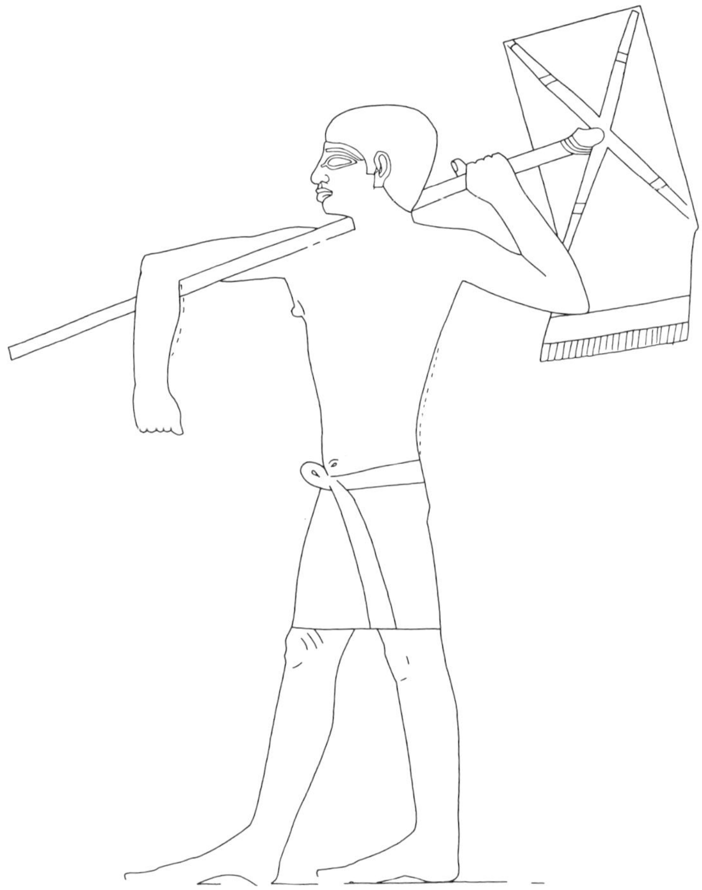

FIGURE 3
Example 6. After Wild

4. W. M. F. Petrie, *Medum* (London, 1892) pl. 28.

hieroglyph.[5] It seems probable that its more unwieldy counterpart was most frequently used as a fixed awning even during the five hundred years when it was shown in the hands of attendants. The markets that are pictured in Old Kingdom scenes of daily life must have been provided with some sort of shade, as are the present ones. A fixed awning is not likely, however, to have been represented in such cases, and the Old Kingdom scenes showing barter are as devoid of any local setting as are most representations of other occupations;[6] the same is true of the very meager evidence of this subject in later tombs.[7] Nor is the textual evidence of much help. If any credence could be given the proposal by Montet that , for which he claims an Old Kingdom occurrence, is the same as the New Kingdom term , "merchant,"[8] one might interpret the latter as a *nisba*-formation based on (later), "shade." But the reading of the crucial initial sign of Montet's Old Kingdom example is no more than a guess, and there does not seem to be any other occurrence of *šwyty* that antedates the New Kingdom. Moreover a caption in the burial chamber of Queen Neferu (no. 21; Figures 2, 5) clearly indicates that the type of sunshade under discussion was called ★, "star,"[9] and this in turn provides the meaning of a hitherto unexplained caption above the head of the missing attendant who held the sunshade in no. 3 (Figure 4); he is ★, "the parasol bearer.'

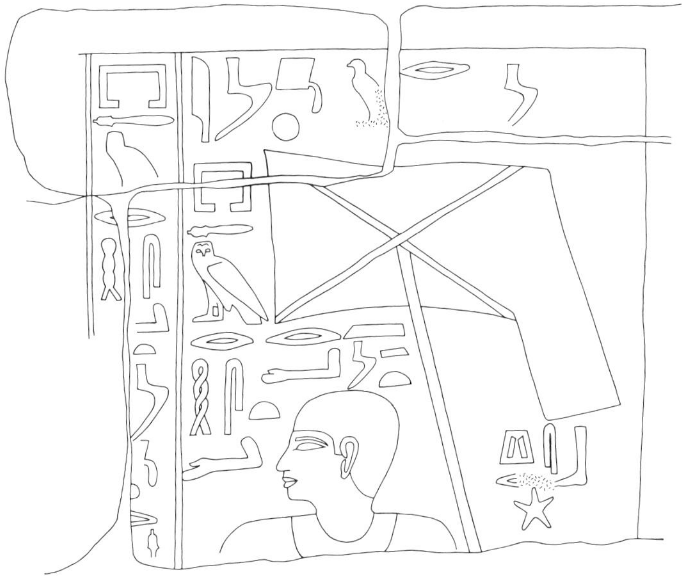

FIGURE 4
Example 3. After Hassan

The name of the parasol is readily explained by the crisscrossed supports beneath the cloth, which, in combination with the support on which they rest, resembles the tapering points of the five-pointed star (★) as represented by the ancient Egyptians.[10]

5. G. Jéquier, *Les frises d'objets, Mémoires de l'Institut Français d'Archéologie Orientale du Caire*, no. 47 (Cairo, 1921) pp. 254–255; W. Needler, "Three Relief Sculptures of the Early Pyramid Age from Lisht," *Royal Ontario Museum Annual* 1959, pp. 35–36.

6. For the Old Kingdom scenes see L. Klebs, *Die Reliefs des alten Reiches* (Heidelberg, 1915) p. 116; also *Ptḥ-špśś* (B. Porter and R. L. B. Moss, *Topographical Bibliography*, III [Oxford, 1931] p. 79 [8]) and reliefs from the Unis causeway (S. Hassan, "Excavations at Saqqara 1937–1938," *Annales du Service des Antiquités de l'Égypte* 38 [1938] p. 520, pl. 96; S. Hassan, "The Causeway of *Wnìs* at Sakkara," *Zeitschrift für ägyptische Sprache* 80 [1955] pl. 13 [fig. 2]). For the "scanty treatment of architectural forms" in such scenes, cf. W. S. Smith, *History of Egyptian Sculpture and Painting in the Old Kingdom* (London, 1946) p. 349.

7. N. de G. Davies, *Two Ramesside Tombs at Thebes* (New York, 1927) p. 57, pl. 30.

8. P. Montet, *Scènes de la vie privée dans les tombeaux égyptiens de l'Ancien Empire* (Strasbourg, 1925) p. 320; cf. M. Megally, *Études sur le Papyrus E 3226 du Louvre*, II (Paris, 1969) p. 368.

9. The following objects are represented on the block that is illustrated in Figure 5:

, *ḥ'(ḳ)*, "razor" (cf. Jéquier, *Frises d'objets*, p. 126).

, *ḫry-'*, "holder" (cf. Jéquier, *Frises d'objets*, p. 128; for the determinative, cf. Posener-Kriéger and Cenival, *Abusir Papyri* (London, 1958) pal. pl. 12).

, *ìkmw*, "shields" (the half-effaced sign following this word cannot be related to the puzzling addition cited by Jéquier, *Frises d'objets*, p. 231; it looks like ?).

★, *śb3*, "sunshade."

, *ḫt 'n(y)*, "writing tablet of wood" (cf. Jéquier, *Frises d'objets*, p. 266. The tablet bears the epistolary formula , "Thy condition is like (that of) one who lives a million times"; cf. T. G. H. James, *Heḳanakhte Papers*, [New York, 1962] pp. 120–122).

, *ḫt gśtì*, "scribe's palette of wood" (cf. Jéquier, *Frises d'objets*, p. 266).

, *nfyt*, "fan" (for fire; cf. Jéquier, *Frises d'objets*, p. 297).

, "*ḥs*-jars."

10. There does not appear to be any indication that this image was considered less literally, and that the night sky was regarded as a sunshade supported by stars. Nor does such an idea suit the hieroglyph for night ( ) as explained by M. Chatelet, "Une des causes de l'obscurité nocturne," *Bulletin de l'Institut Français d'Archéologie Orientale* 18 (1921) p. 21.

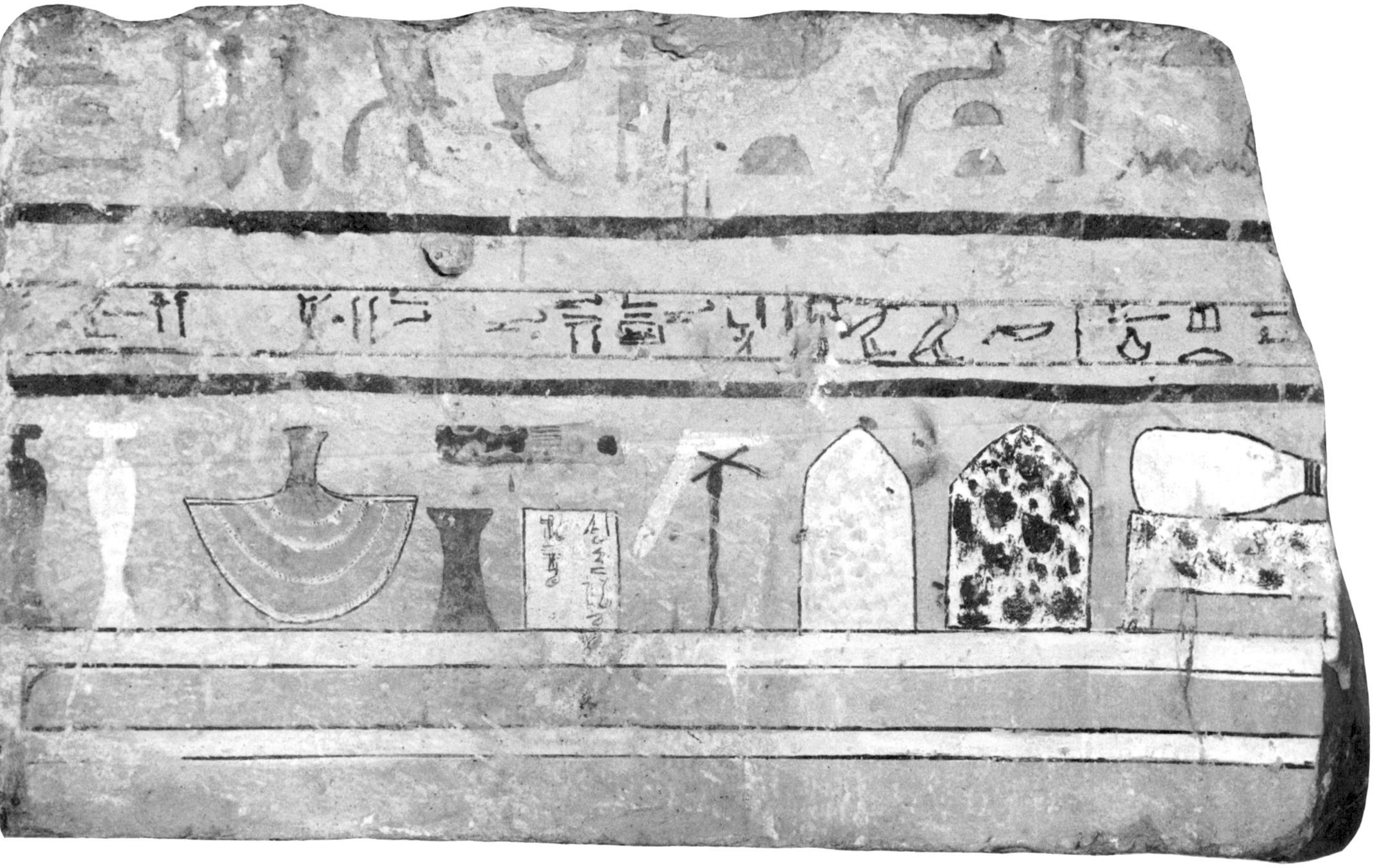

FIGURE 5
Section of frieze of offerings, burial chamber of Queen *Nfrw*: Example 21

In short, despite the absence of any evidence for it much beyond 2000 B.C., the rectangular sunshade in its contemporary form is nonetheless so similar to its ancient counterpart that it probably represents the continuation of an uninterrupted tradition.[11] Furthermore its present use—though totally unattested from ancient times—may very well be the one for which it was originally contrived. One must conclude on a final note of caution, however, for it is just possible that so simple a device might have been reinvented, or that it might have been used beyond the borders of Egypt and have been reintroduced from a neighboring area after its use had been discontinued in the Nile Valley. Although I know of no evidence for this type of sunshade in the ancient Orient, it has been observed in Jordan and Mecca,[12] and a more rudimentary version, lacking the pendant flap, is currently used in regions as far afield as Colombia and Ecuador.[13]

11. One may compare the evidence for the revolving fan, which is only occasionally attested in the Old and Middle Kingdom (e.g., the Fourth Dynasty chapel of Meresankh III at Giza; also C. M. Firth and B. Gunn, *Teti Pyramid Cemeteries* [Cairo, 1926] fig. 99, p. 260) but continues in use in various parts of the Middle East, and is known from some actual examples of Egyptian origin dating to the Roman period (Jéquier, *Frises d'objets*, pp. 253–254, referring to H. Schäfer, *Priestergräber vom Totentempel des Ne-user-Rê* [Leipzig, 1908] p. 51).

12. By Yehya Aboubakr, the Egyptian director of the Arab Information Agency in Canada.

13. As reported by M. L. Bristol, of Sherman, Connecticut.

NOTES

Offering Stands from the Pyramid of Amenemhet I

HENRY G. FISCHER

Lila Acheson Wallace Curator in Egyptology, The Metropolitan Museum of Art

IN AN ARTICLE entitled "Two Royal Monuments of the Middle Kingdom Restored" (*The Metropolitan Museum of Art Bulletin* 22 [1963–64] pp. 235–245) I concluded that the upper portion of a red granite offering stand donated by Dulaney Logan (63.46) derived from the North Pyramid at Lisht and that it was one of a pair that stood in front of our offering table from that pyramid (09.180.526). Further evidence for this conclusion has subsequently come to light among notes that were made by William C. Hayes in the winter of 1933–34, recording miscellaneous material that had been excavated at the North Pyramid during previous seasons. These notes show a fragment of an offering stand (apparently left at the site) that was identical in material, scale, and design (Figures 1, 2).[1] Since it shows the tops of the heraldic plants of Upper and Lower Egypt, as in the case of the more complete stand (Figure 3), this fragment confirms the existence of the pair as well as the correctness of the provenance.

As the late Dr. T. George Allen pointed out (by letter to Eric Young), the phrase on the top of the more complete stand (Figure 4) poses a difficulty. To him the lack of the indirect genitive after (*tpt*) suggested that the signs in question may actually be (*wḥmt*), which would yield the meaning: "mansion which repeats offerings." This may in fact be the right solution, despite the apparent lack of any parallel for such a designation, and despite the likelihood that such a designation would more probably employ the infinitive of *wḥm* ("mansion of repeating offerings") rather than a participle.[2]

On the other hand the alternatives and were both carefully considered when my drawing was made, and *ḥwt tpyt* actually occurs in the following statements referring to a temple of Amenemhet I's grandson, Amenemhet II, presumably located at Abydos:[3]

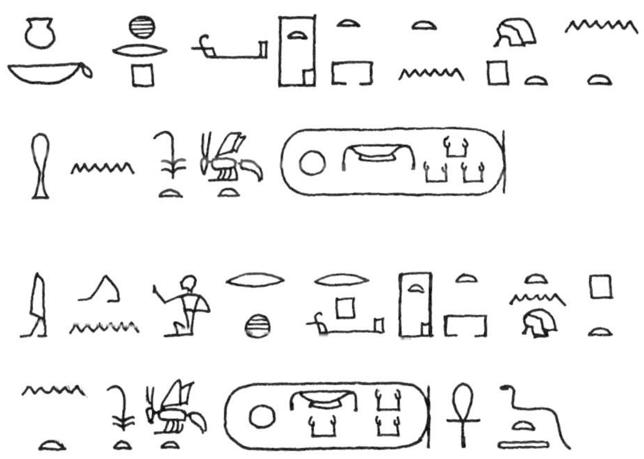

1. Described thus: "Fragment of a red granite column-like object, circular in plan, with a minimum diameter of 17 cm., but flaring out toward the top at a rate of 1.5 cm. in 8 cm. Maximum height of fragment 13 cm. over all. (Breaks of fragment, top and bottom, are sloping and uneven.) Around the "column" runs the design shown in the drawing below (projection) carved in relief 8 mm. high: 2 *sma* signs with upright papyrus clump and looped-over lotus (?) . . . All extant surfaces polished."

2. Theoretically one might interpret the phrase as a passive construction (the mansion "offerings are repeated"), but in this case the passive *śdm.f* might be expected rather than the *śdm.tw.f* form.

3. *Hieroglyphic Texts in the British Museum* II (London, 1912) pl. 10 (BM 576); III, pl. 38 (BM 256). In both cases the speaker is "revered with Khentamentiu Lord of Abydos" and has the title *ỉmy-r ʿḥnwty*. But they do not appear to be related by kinship.

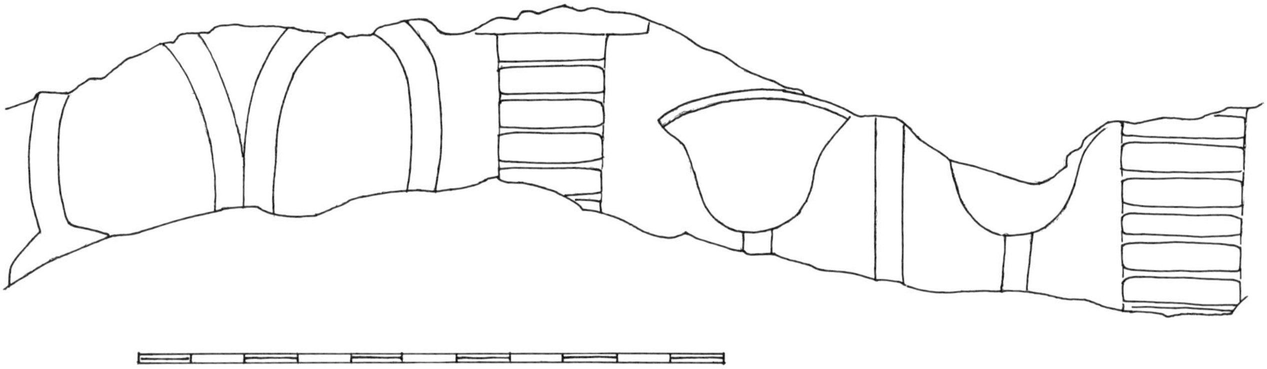

FIGURE 1
Design on fragment of red granite offering stand found at Lisht

FIGURE 3
Design of offering stand from Lisht, accession number 63.46, front and back, lower two-thirds restored

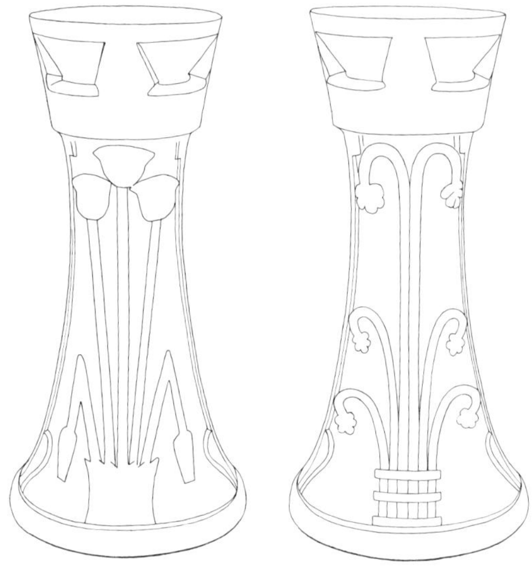

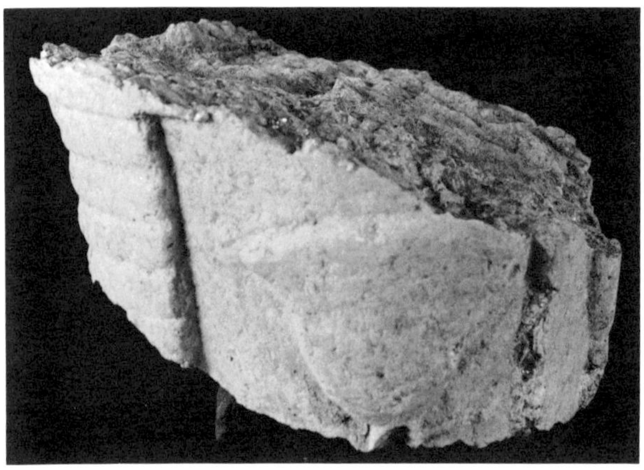

FIGURE 2
Fragment of offering stand found at Lisht

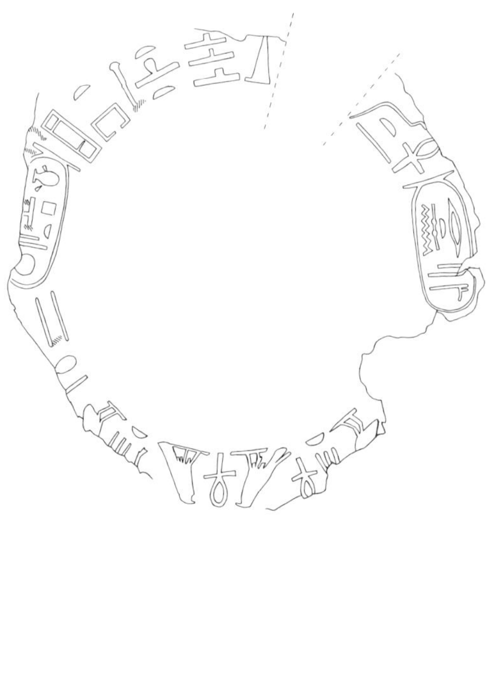

FIGURE 4
Inscription in basin of offering stand 63.46

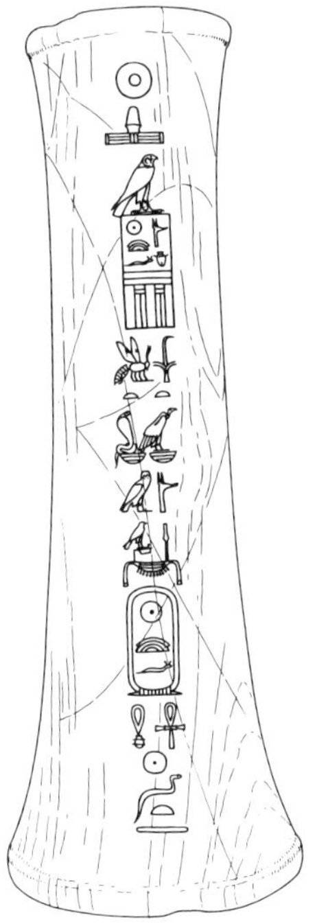

FIGURE 5
Drawing of diorite offering stand, The Metropolitan Museum of Art, Rogers Fund, 07.228.24

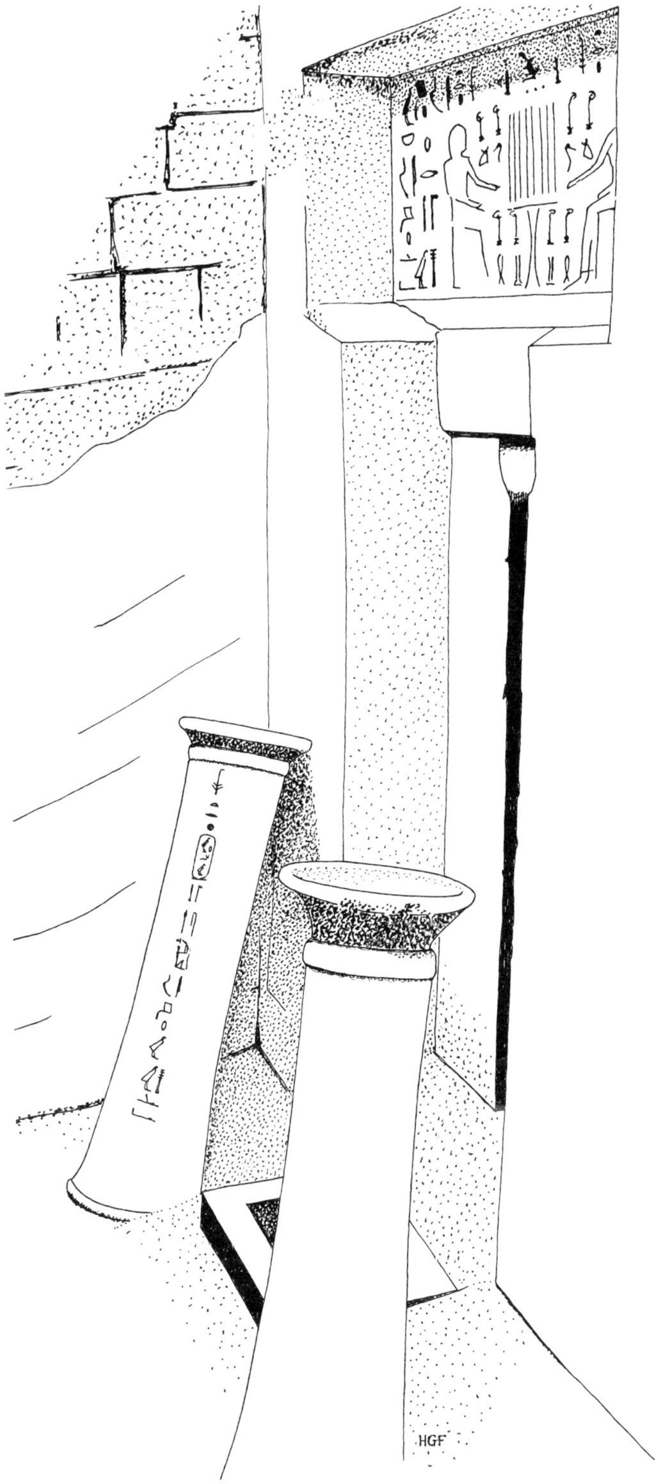

FIGURE 6
Offering niche of Giza tomb 1453

The first says: "I was one who directed this first mansion of the majesty of the King of Upper and Lower Egypt *Nbw-k3w-Rʿ*." The second says: "I came to direct this first mansion of the King of Upper and Lower Egypt *Nbw-k3w-Rʿ*, may he live forever!"

Probably the problem is to be resolved by interpreting the phrase in question as a case of graphic transposition: "offerings of the first mansion of *Śḥtp-ib-Rʿ*."[4]

The revised translation suggests a new and more concrete explanation for the inscription of an earlier

4. The use of as the determinative of "offerings," rather than a more current form, showing one or both ends of the string on either side of the papyrus sealing ( ), might suggest that the three signs are actually and that the correct reading is *ḥtp ḥtpt* "altar of offerings" (is not unusual as a writing of *ḥtp*; compare A. Erman, "Defective Schreibungen," *Zeitschrift für ägyptische Sprache* 29 [1891] p. 37). But recurs more clearly on the sides of the more intact stand (*The Metropolitan Museum of Art Bulletin* 22 [1963–64] p. 239), where it alternates with in the common expression *ḥtpt ḏf3w* "offerings/food."

offering stand in the Metropolitan Museum (Figure 5).[5] This has been taken to mean: "Rēʿ is content [with] the Horus Woser-yeb Chephren. . . ," but more likely refers to "the offering of Re" or "the altar of Re" [provided by] "the Horus Woser-yeb Chephren. . ." In the second case the word 𓊵 would designate the flat offering stone beside which the stand was placed,[6] as in the Old Kingdom tomb chapel shown in Figure 6.[7]

5. Acc. no. 07.228.24. Said to come from a site near Bubastis, specifically Horbeit; this provenance offers a further indication for the northeastern extension of the Heliopolitan Nome in the Old Kingdom, which I have discussed in *Journal of Near Eastern Studies* 18 (1959), pp. 133–134. The drawing derives from William C. Hayes, *Scepter of Egypt*, I, p. 64, as does the following quotation. The initial publication of the stand was by Ambrose Lansing, *The Metropolitan Museum of Art Bulletin* 2 (1907) pp. 180–181. For a similar stand of Chephren, bearing a quite different inscription, see H. G. Fischer, "Old Kingdom Inscriptions in the Yale Gallery," *Mitteilungen des Instituts für Orientforschung* 7 (1960) pp. 306–307.

6. As it is designated in the biography of *Wnỉ*, K. Sethe, *Urkunden des Alten Reiches* (Leipzig, 1933) p. 107, line 17. There is little Old Kingdom evidence among which to look for a parallel for 𓊵 in either sense, but one might compare the sign [hieroglyph] that appears on some calcite canopic jars of the Sixth Dynasty, opposite the column of inscription that identifies the deceased; the addition of this hieroglyph "evidently marked them as destined for the Necropolis" (C. Firth and B. Gunn, *Teti Pyramid Cemeteries* (Cairo, 1926) p. 126, pl. 12 A, B.

7. After a photograph in the records of Albert Lythgoe, now in the Boston Museum of Fine Arts, representing the offering niche of Giza tomb 1453. The limestone stand on the left is in Berkeley, as is the offering basin (H. F. Lutz, *Egyptian Tomb Steles and Offering Stones of the Museum of Anthropology and Ethnology of the University of California* [Leipzig, 1927] pls. 4 [6] and 3 [5]). For examples of pottery stands *in situ* see G. A. Reisner, *Bulletin of the Museum of Fine Arts* 33 (1935) p. 71; Abdel-Moneim Abu-Bakr, *Excavations at Giza 1949–1950* (Cairo, 1953) pl. 63 B; H. Junker, *Gîza* I (Vienna, 1929) pp. 199–200, fig. 40, pl. 8 b. These stands are also represented on the jambs flanking offering niches (Junker, *Gîza* III [1938] fig. 31, p. 171), where it is seen that they serve for all categories of offerings. Other representations (e.g., Junker, *Gîza* III, fig. 35, p. 191) show that the tall stands supported relatively small bowls and dishes.

Redundant Determinatives in the Old Kingdom

HENRY G. FISCHER

Lila Acheson Wallace Curator in Egyptology, The Metropolitan Museum of Art

Battiscombe Gunn has long since made the observation that hieroglyphic inscriptions of the Old Kingdom characteristically omit determinatives if these ideographs are supplied by the accompanying representations.[1] Thus, on a stela or architrave, the two-dimensional figure of the owner may itself be regarded as an enlarged determinative, supplementing the phonetic writing of the name that precedes it. And a statue may similarly be regarded as a three-dimensional enlargement of the determinative belonging to the name inscribed on its base.

It is therefore appropriate, as far as the monuments of this period are concerned, to speak of "redundant determinatives" in describing those exceptional cases where a hieroglyphic determinative is added to a personal name even though the name is directly connected with a representation that performs the same function. As might be expected, a certain number of exceptions do in fact exist. But a rather more surprising feature emerges when the exceptions are tabulated in which men and women are associated. In such cases—and they constitute the majority of the total—the feminine names tend to show the determinative while the masculine names do not. The first and most important category to be considered is statuary, either pairs of statues or group statues, representing the tomb owner and the members of his household.

1. STATUARY

	OWNER	WIFE	SON(S)	DAUGHTER
(1) Figure 1 (two statues)	— (A)	 (B)	 (B)	
(2) Figure 2[2]	—		—	
(3) Figure 3[3]	—			
(4) Figure 4[4]			—	
(5) Abubakr, *Giza*, pls. 20, 21 (two statues)[5]	—			
(6) Figure 5[6]	—			

1. Cecil M. Firth and Battiscombe Gunn, *Teti Pyramid Cemeteries* (Cairo, 1926) p. 171, n. 2. Compare also *PN* II, p. 18, n. 19.

2. A granite statue of the owner (Junker, *Gîza* V, fig. 29 B) likewise shows his name without determinative.

3. The correction of the owner's title is presented in Henry G. Fischer, "An Old Kingdom Monogram," *Zeitschrift für Ägyptische Sprache und Altertumskunde* 93 (1966) p. 62.

4. For the identification of the two figures see below, pp. 14–15. A statue of the tomb owner and two daughters (Hassan, *Gîza* I, p. 116, pl. 74) shows no determinatives.

5. A second statue of the owner's wife (pl. 22) lacks the determinative.

6. Limestone statuette of seated couple from tomb G 2231X = G 2178 (Smith, *History of Sculpture and Painting*, p. 74). I am indebted to Dr. William K. Simpson for helping me to locate and copy this

	OWNER	WIFE	SON(S)	DAUGHTER
(7) Figure 7[7]	—	[hieroglyph]		
(8) M. G. Fraser, "The Early Tombs at Tehneh," *ASAE* 3 (1902) pp. 123–124 (second example)	—		—	[hieroglyph]
(9) Figure 8	—	[hieroglyph]		
(10) CG 55	—	[hieroglyph]	——	
(11) CG 100	—	[hieroglyph]	—	
(12) CG 376	—	[hieroglyph]	—	—
(13) Figure 9[8]	—	[hieroglyph]	—	
(14) Berlin 8801, Berlin Museum, *Ägyptische Inschriften aus den Königlichen Museen* I (Leipzig, 1913) pp. 71, 267	—	[hieroglyph]	—(?)	
(15) B. A. Turayev, *Statui i Statuetki* (Petrograd, 1917) p. 6 and pl. 2 (2)	—(?)	[hieroglyph]	—	

To this list one may also add (16) the female servant statues CG 110, 114 (Figure 10), 118, all from [hieroglyphs] "the funerary estate of the Overseer of the Treasury *Wr-ir.n(.i)*," and more specifically from his tomb. In each case this designation of the tomb owner, without determinative, is followed by the name of the servant, which has the determinative [hieroglyph].[9]

Most of the 16 examples are from the Memphite cemeteries, either Giza (1–6), Saqqara (10–12, 16, and probably 13), or Medum (9); two are known from Tehna, in Middle Egypt (7–8). The earliest of them is no. 9, dating to the beginning of the Fourth Dynasty; the next earliest are 1, 7, 8 (beginning of the Fifth Dynasty); most of the others also belong to the same dynasty, but no. 2 is as late as the Sixth, and nos. 4 and 5 cannot be much earlier. It will be noted that the determinative [hieroglyph] follows the names of women throughout the Old Kingdom, but [hieroglyph] does not appear in this context before some point well within the Fifth Dynasty.[10]

I have found only four group statues that show the determinative after the name of the principal male figure and, with a single exception, the woman's name shows the same feature. In one case (CG 62) the determinative [hieroglyph] is given to a man—presumably the

example. The woman, presumably the wife of the man beside whom she is seated, is named *Ḫwit-Rʿ* (not to be found in *PN*, but compare masc. *Ḫwi-Rʿ*, in *PN* II, p. 309 [26]). The man's principal title is evidently to be read *śḥḏ iḳd(w) ḥwsi(w)* "Inspector of builders and constructors" and his name is *'Iti*. I do not know of any other occurrence of a title mentioning *ḥwsi*, but it does not seem possible to read [hieroglyphs], which would represent a very abnormal writing of *iḳdw*. For the combined use of the two virtually synonymous terms for building one may compare a passage in the biography of *Nḫbw* (Figure 6), which comes from a nearby tomb (G 2381–2382): "I [founded?] the *ka*-mansions there, they being built and constructed" (Dows Dunham, "The Biographical Inscriptions of Nekhebu in Boston and Cairo," *JEA* 24 [1938] pl. 2 foll. p. 2). It will be noted that *ḳd* and *ḥwsi* are presented in the same sequence and have a common determinative that could be interpreted as either [hieroglyph] or [hieroglyph] (Alan Gardiner, *Egyptian Grammar*, 3rd ed. [Oxford, 1957] Sign List A 35, 34); in Gustave Jéquier, *La pyramide d'Oudjebten* (Cairo, 1928) fig. 16, p. 18, the latter has the form [hieroglyph], while another late Old Kingdom inscription shows [hieroglyph] (George A. Reisner, "The Dog Which Was Honored by the King of Upper and Lower Egypt," *BMFA* 34 [1936] p. 96).

7. One might compare this and the following example with architraves like those considered below, in section 3. A masculine name-determinative appears in a somewhat similar context, Hassan, *Gîza* III, fig. 127, p. 151, but here the name is preceded by an offering formula, so that this inscription is a much more independent entity than in the case of examples 7 and 8.

8. John D. Cooney, "Three Egyptian Families of the Old Kingdom," *Bulletin Brooklyn Museum* 13/3 (Spring, 1952) p. 6. The drawing is based on a rubbing made by Edna Russmann. On another family group of the same person (Metropolitan Museum of Art 52.19) the name of the daughter lacks a determinative, as does that of the owner; the wife's name has not survived.

9. Determinatives are also absent from the names on a statue of a male funerary priest belonging to the same group (CG 119) and on one of the statues representing the owner (CG 272), but another statue of his does show a determinative (CG 211).

10. Note also the example of [hieroglyphs], Junker, *Gîza* I, fig. 63, p. 252. It may also be noted that the wife who has the determinative [hieroglyph] in example 1 is given the determinative [hieroglyph] on the false door of her son (BM 1223: T. G. H. James, *Hieroglyphic Texts from Egyptian Stelae, etc.*, 2nd ed. [London, 1961] pl. 8, p. 8): for this distinction see Henry G. Fischer, "Four Provincial Administrators at the Memphite Cemeteries," *Journal of the American Oriental Society* 74 (1954) p. 28. The early Fourth Dynasty use of the determinative [hieroglyph] after the name of Queen *Ḥtp-ḥr.ś* (Reisner and Smith, *Hist. Gîza Necrop.* II, fig. 40, pl. 29) may similarly be explained by her status; *Ḥtp-ḥr.ś* II has the same determinative on the coffin of her daughter *Mr-śy-ʿnḫ* III (J. d'E 54935).

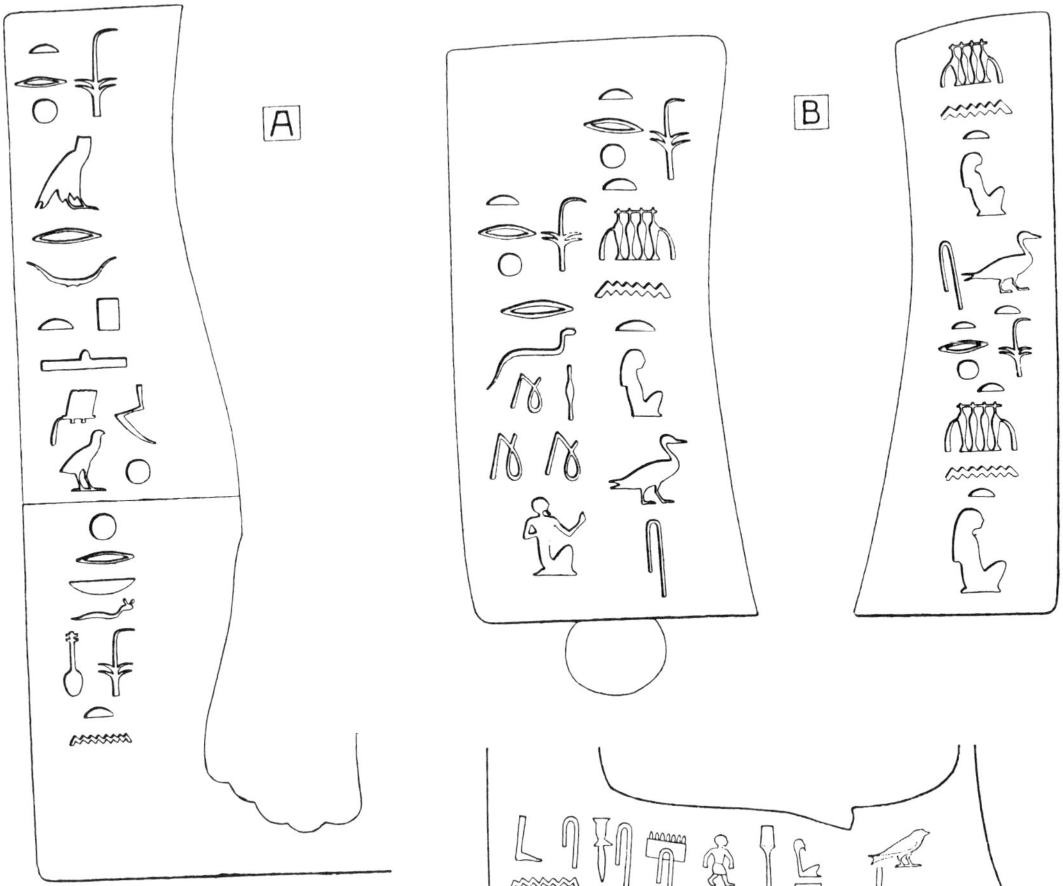

FIGURE 1
Example 1. From Junker, *Gîza* III, fig. 32, p. 186

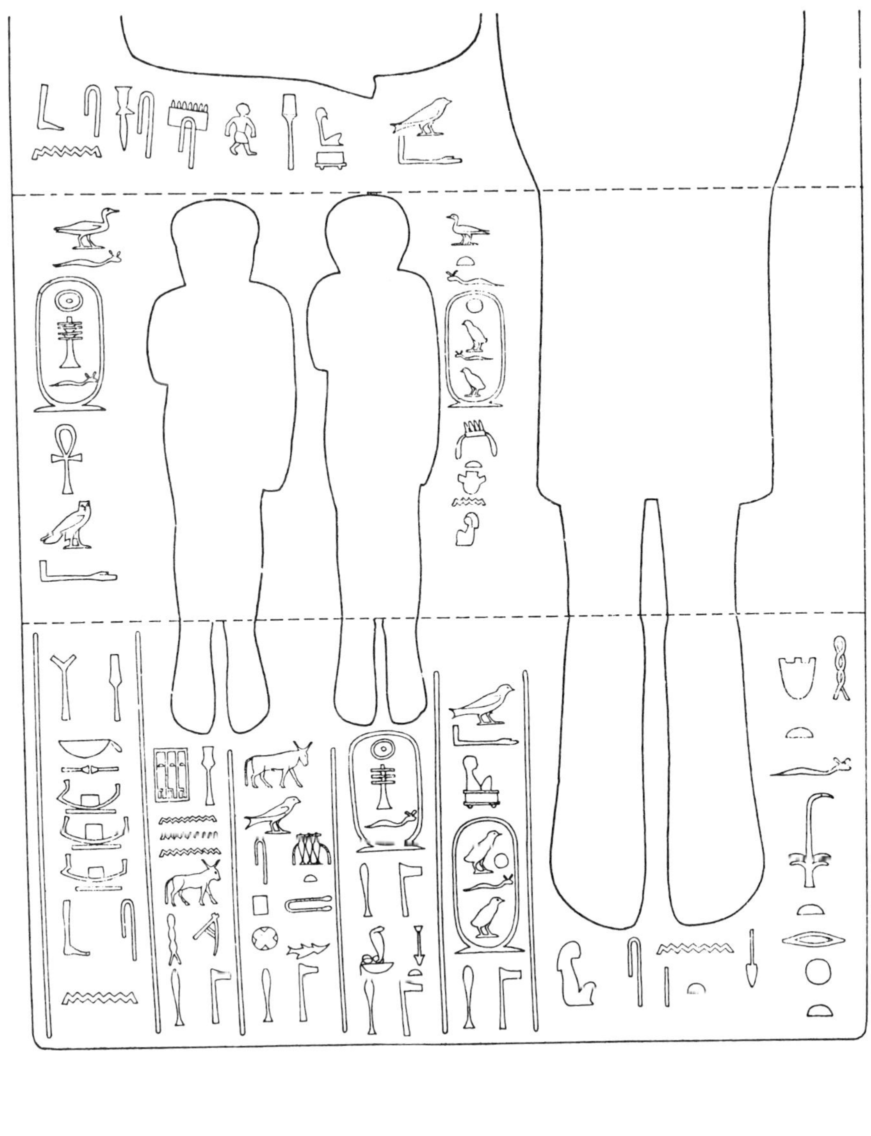

FIGURE 2
Example 2. From Junker, *Gîza* V fig. 29A, p. 109

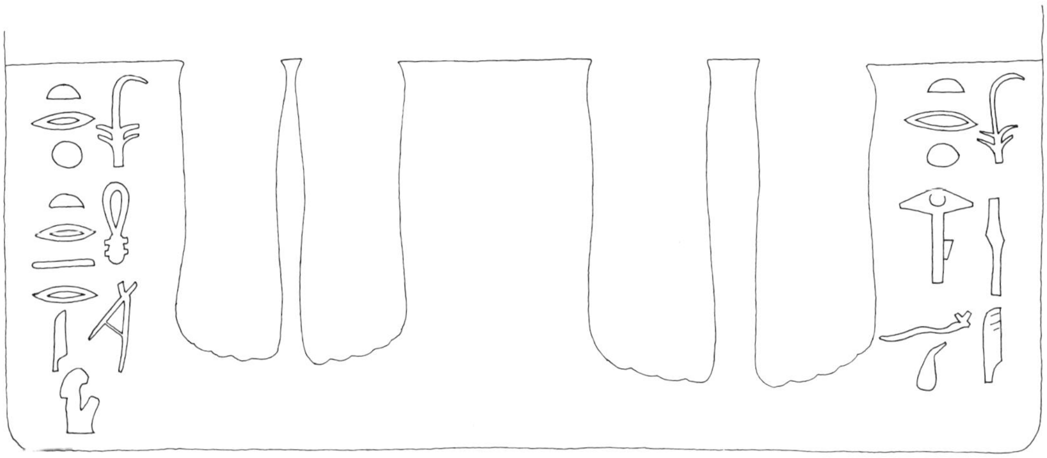

FIGURE 3
Example 3. From Junker, *Gîza* IX, fig. 27, p. 68 (corrected)

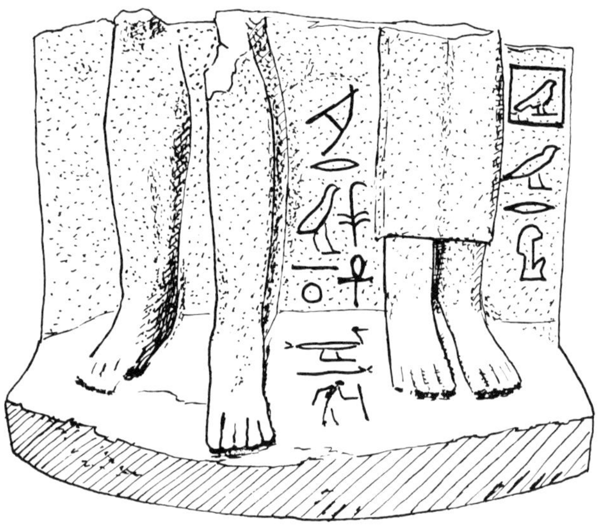

FIGURE 4
Example 4. Drawn from photograph, Hassan, *Gîza* I, pl. 75

FIGURE 5
Example 6. Museum of Fine Arts, Boston, 12.1485

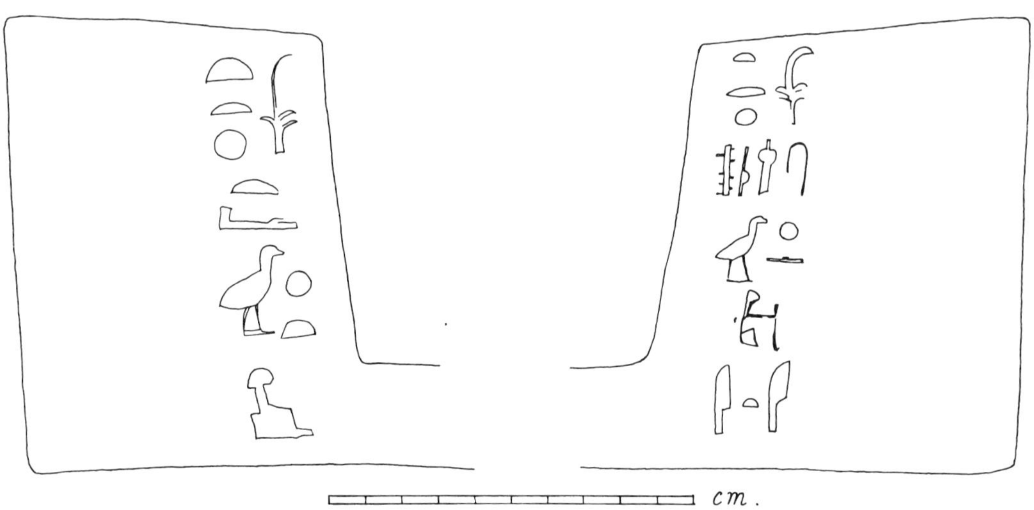

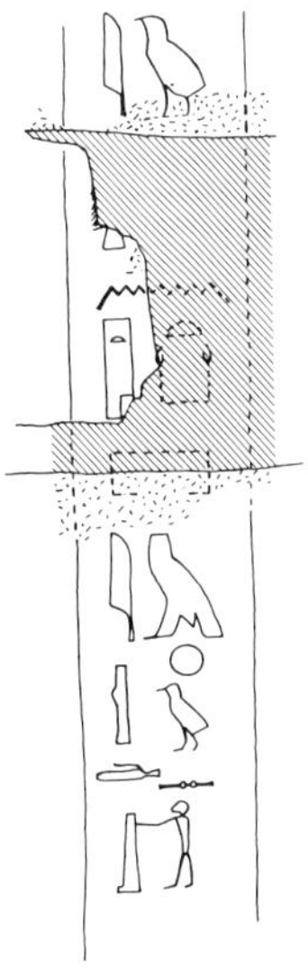

FIGURE 6
Portion of inscription of *Nḫbw*. After Dunham

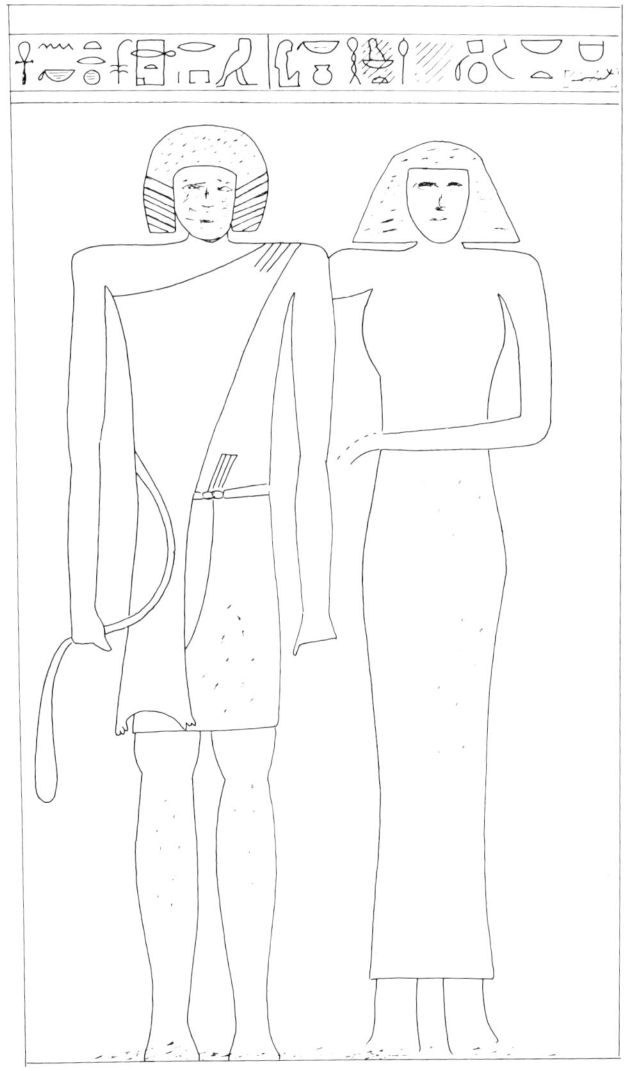

FIGURE 7
Example 7. From Fraser, *ASAE* 3 (1903) pl. 3

FIGURE 8
Example 9. Cairo Museum, CG 3, 4

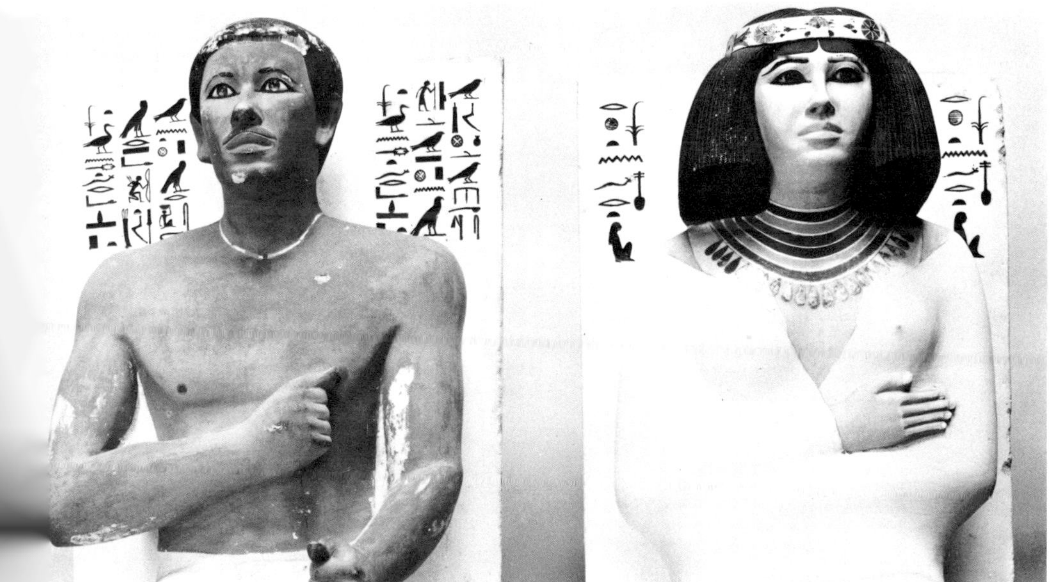

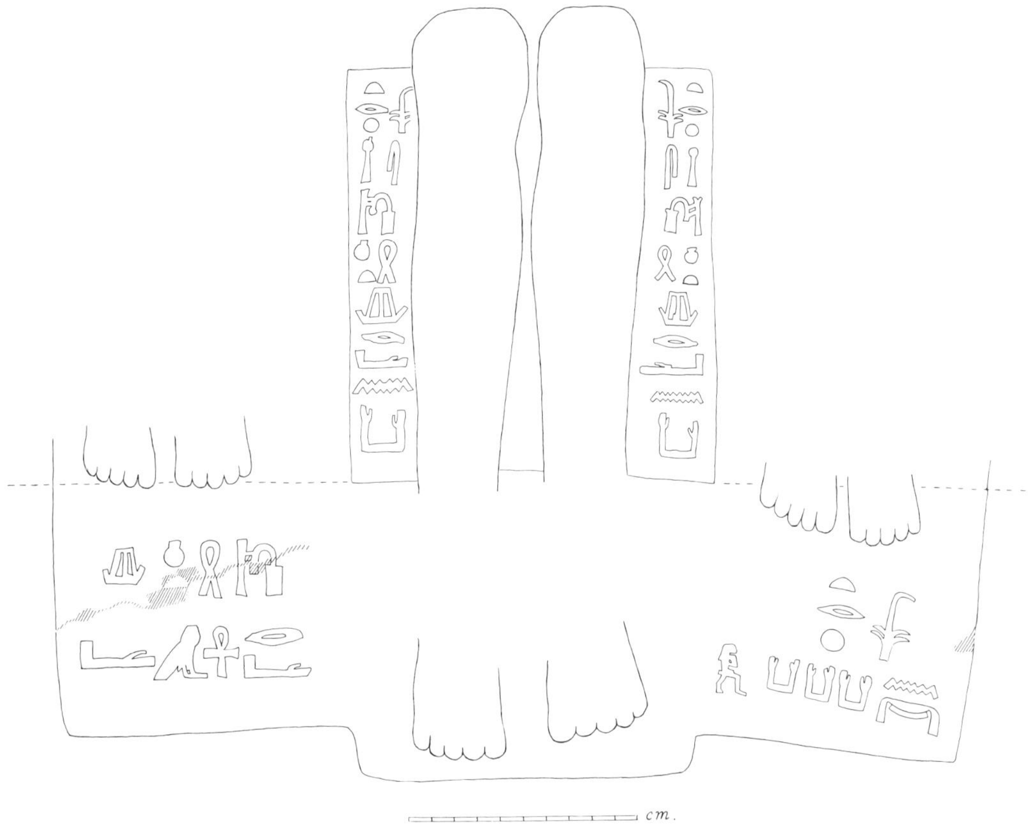

FIGURE 9
Example 13. Brooklyn Museum, 49.215

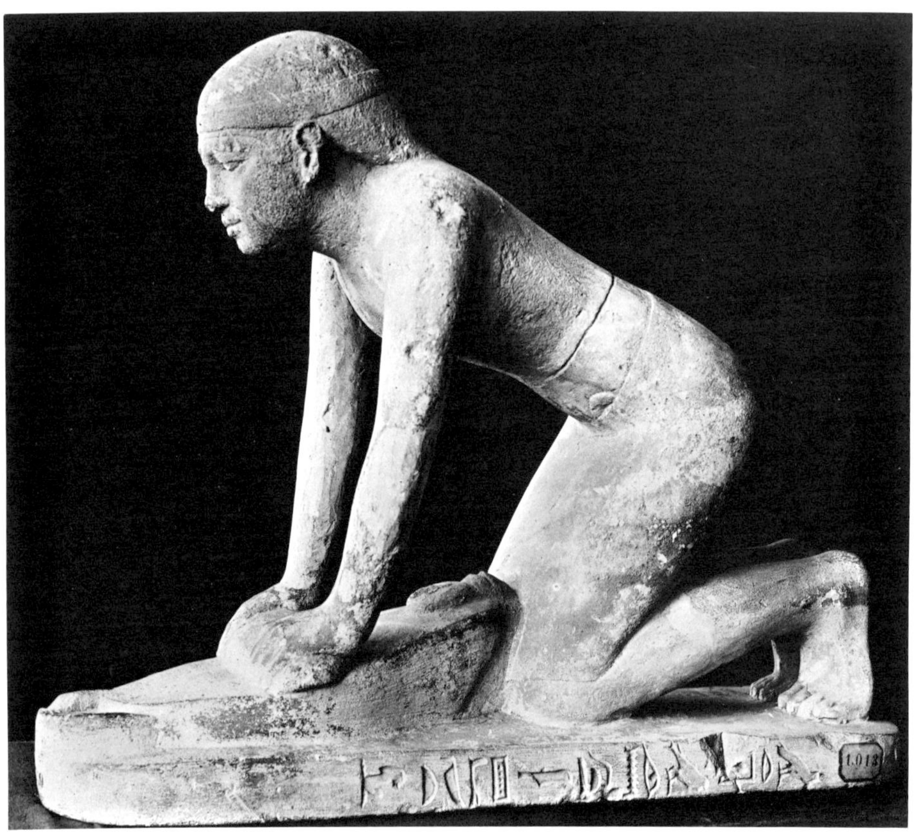

FIGURE 10
Example 16. Cairo Museum, CG 114

tomb owner—as well as to a woman who is presumably his wife, but is absent from the name of the son that is adjacent to his father's.[11] In the second case (Junker, *Gîza* V, fig. 42, p. 149), the names of a man and woman have the determinative and , respectively. It is probably significant that they do not represent the tomb owner and his wife, but their relationship to him, and to each other, is unspecified. The third statue shows, on the rearward surface of the backpillar, an incised inscription (Figure 11) identifying a man named *Kꜣp* (determinative) and a woman whose relationship was specified but is now obliterated; her name is *Ḥy* (determinative).[12] Since a fragment of a second, seated statue of *Kꜣp* was found near this one, it seems likely that both represent the tomb owner.[13] The fourth case (CG 44) is the only one that gives the man a determinative (again) while the name of the woman, his daughter, lacks it. In this case, however, the name of a second female figure, designated "wife,"[14] was never added to her titles, and so it seems possible that the omission of a determinative after the daughter's name was unintentional. It is also possible that addition of a determinative after the man's names may have been fostered by the somewhat complex manner in which they are presented: "*‘ꜣḫi*, who is called *‘Ip*." The form of the determinative, as in the two preceding cases, is most unusual; the other male statues that have a name-determinative (nine examples noted, including the aforementioned CG 62)[15] all have the more honorific rather than the commonplace

FIGURE 11
Museum of Fine Arts, Boston, 21.2602

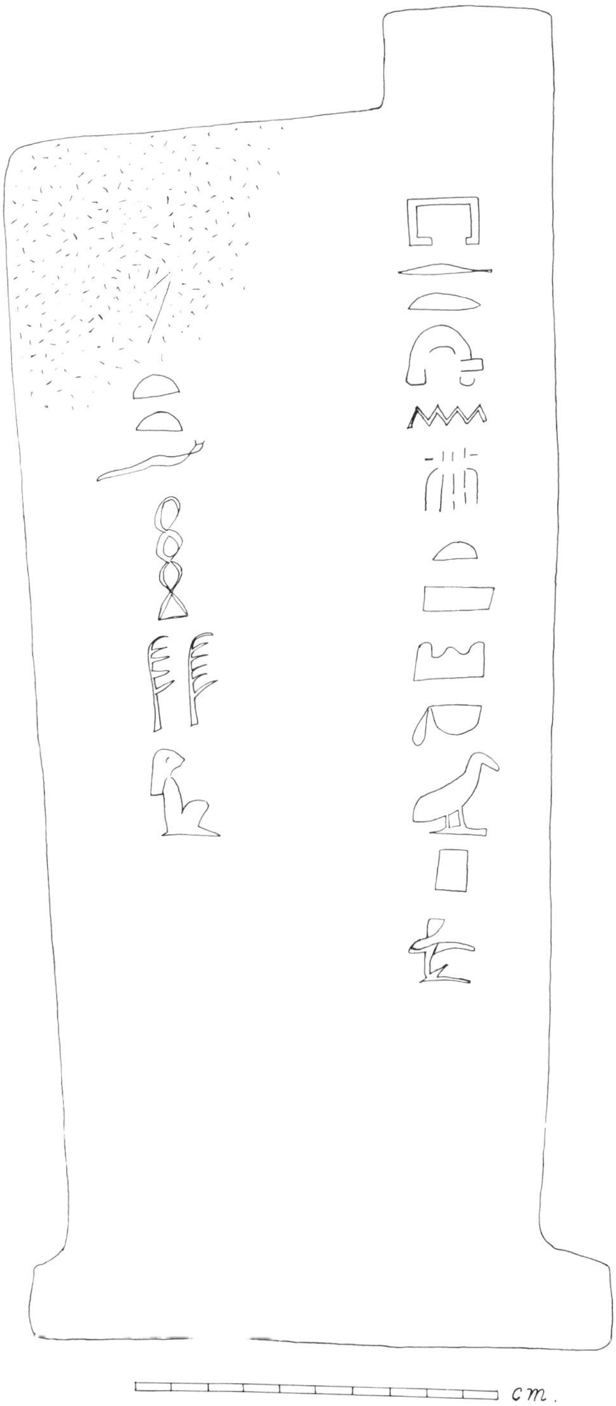

11. The name of the son in Borchardt's copy is to be corrected to compare *PN* I, p. 263 [10].

12. Mentioned by Smith, *History of Sculpture and Painting*, p. 72, and Reisner, *Hist. Giza Necrop.* I, pl. 67 [d]. I am obliged to Dr. Simpson for enabling me to copy the inscription. The man's titles are evidently to be read *iry sḏꜣwt n pr ‘ꜣ* (compare Junker, *Gîza* VI, fig. 83, p. 215, and VII, fig. 50, p. 135) and *ḫnty š*. In the wife's inscription Smith reads as in [*ḥmt.f m*]*rt.f*, and that may be the most plausible interpretation, especially since the preceding traces on the much eroded surface suggest the form of .

13. Smith (see preceding note) thinks that this and the first statue, found in the debris of a street, came from the serdab of G 4522, whereas Reisner assumed that they belonged to G 4520, the mastaba of *Ḫwfw-‘nḫ*, along with a statue of *Ḫwfw-‘nḫ* that was found with them.

14. For this designation, instead of the usual *ḥmt.f*, see also Junker, *Gîza* III, figs. 14, 15, pp. 129, 131.

15. Junker, *Gîza* VIII, fig. 4, p. 17 (two other statues lack determinatives); XI, fig. 11, p. 17, fig. 51a, p. 109; Hassan, *Gîza* I, p. 115, pl. 70 (no determinative on other statues pls. 72, 74); S. Hassan, "Excavations at Saqqara 1937–1938," *ASAE* 38 (1938) p. 506; Abd el Hamid Zayed, *Trois études d'égyptologie* (Cairo, 1956) p. 16; CG 67, 211 (no determinative on other statues of the latter, as noted in note 9, above), CG 377 (no determinative on other statues, CG 61, 65, 66, 181).

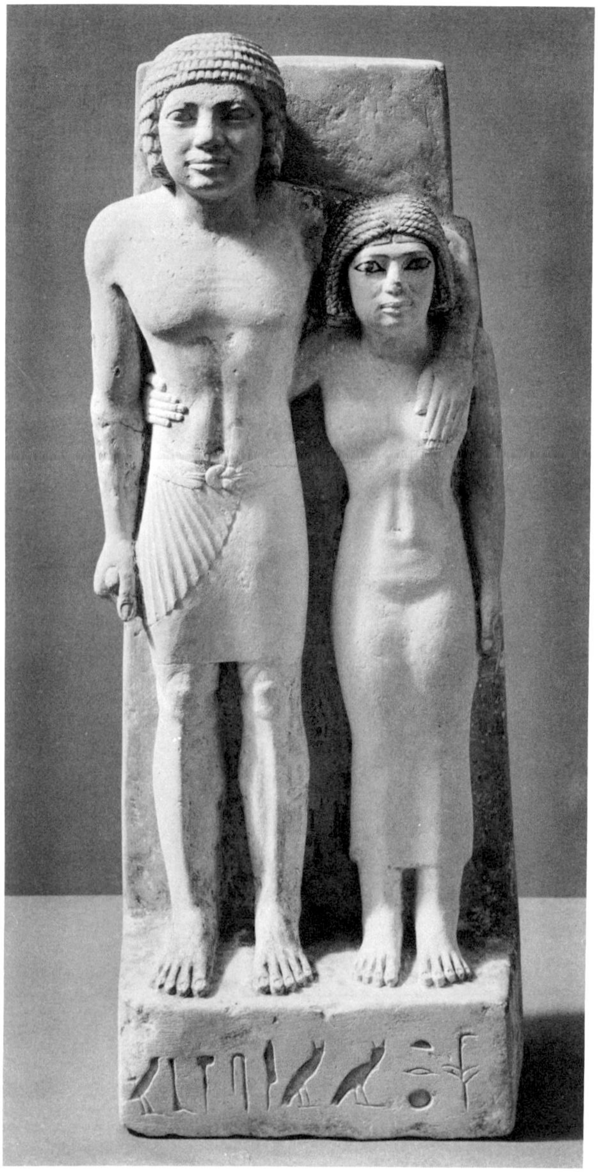

FIGURE 12

The Metropolitan Museum of Art, Rogers Fund, 48.111

if the tomb owner is represented, in contrast to the use of with the name of a son in example 1.[16]

The majority of group statues, like Old Kingdom statuary in general, show no determinatives whatever; I know of about forty such groups. And a surprising number of statues were evidently not inscribed at all, as though the context of the tomb provided sufficient identification. In the case of a well-preserved polychrome statue such as that of *ꜣḫw* (Abubakr, *Giza*, pls. 50–51, pp. 89–90) the omission of an inscription hardly seems fortuitous, and the presence of his wife's name on her own statue (Abubakr, *Giza*, pl. 52, p. 90), although lacking a determinative, may be analogous to the use of the determinative after the wife's name in contrast to its absence after the name of the husband. In another case the statues of the tomb owner and his wife lack inscriptions (Hassan, *Giza* II, pls. 18, 19), whereas the statue of an estate manager named *Pr-nb(.i)* is identified by title and name (Hassan, *Gîza* II, pl. 20, p. 61).

A group statue in the Metropolitan Museum inscribed with the names *Mmi* and *Śꜣbw* (Figure 12)[17] would seem to contradict the evidence of the preceding examples, since both names evidently belong to the man, leaving the woman (presumably his wife) unnamed.[18] But the fact that he has his arm around her, reversing the usual procedure, suggests that this statue belongs to her burial rather than his; a close analogy is provided by the group statue of Queen Hetep-heres II with her arm around her daughter Meresankh III, from the tomb of the latter.[19] This conclusion is confirmed by a second statue that represents the wife alone, yet again bears her husband's name: .[20]

Similar considerations are also to be recognized in the case of example 4, which has inaccurately been described as a standing couple representing the tomb owner *Mr-św-ꜥnḫ* and his wife.[21] The sole inscription

16. One further example shows the determinative following the name *ꜥnḫ(.i)-m-ꜥ-Rꜥ*, Turayev, *Statui i Statuetki*, p. 5 and pl. 3 (4), but the inscription is only given in typescript, and not altogether accurately.

17. MMA 48.111: Nora E. Scott, "Memy-Sabu and his Wife," *Bulletin of The Metropolitan Museum of Art* 7 (1948–49) pp. 95–100.

18. Theoretically might designate the woman, since the writing of the title might apply to either sex and the second name is written in signs of lesser height. But *Mmi* does not seem to be attested as a feminine name before the Middle Kingdom (*PN* I, p. 149 [18]) while both *Mmi* and *Śꜣbw* are well known for men; the feminine counterparts of these names in Old Kingdom inscriptions are *Mmit* (CG 1586, wife of *Mmi*) and *Śꜣbt*/*Śꜣbwt* (*PN* I, p. 299 [20–21]).

19. Boston MFA 30.1456: Dows Dunham, "A Statuette of Two Egyptian Queens," *BMFA* 34 (1936) pp. 3–5.

20. As seen from the photograph published in the article cited above, note 17, and the accompanying text. The owner of the statue died in 1962, and I have not been able to trace its present location.

21. Hassan, *Gîza* I, caption to pl. 75.

identifying the man is a vertical column of hieroglyphs between the two figures: [hieroglyphs]. One might expect another name to follow, i.e., "*Mr-św-ʿnḫ*'s eldest son NN," but there is no trace of any hieroglyphs on the sole remaining space that might have been used for this purpose, beside the right leg of the figure. A second *Mr-św-ʿnḫ*, who is evidently a son, is shown on the owner's false door (Hassan, *Gîza* I, fig. 182, p. 109), and it seems likely that he is "the eldest" son who is represented in the statue. The unusual inscription is perhaps to be explained by comparison with a stela in the Cairo Museum, CG 1394 (Figure 13), the top half of which is occupied by the dedication of a grandson. It reads: "The overseer of the treasury and scribe of royal archives, *'Isi*, the son of her daughter; it is he who made this for her." In this case the terminal position of the filiation formula is intended to point downward, as it were, to the grandmother who is represented beneath—*Nfrt-wnn.ś*. In the case of *Mr-św-ʿnḫ's* statue, the formula "his eldest son" may similarly refer to his father's burial beneath the serdab, rather than to one of the representations of the latter with which this statue was placed.

The woman who stands beside *Mr-św-ʿnḫ* is identified as the owner's daughter on another statue group (Hassan, *Gîza* I, pl. 74, p. 116). The beginning of her inscription is lost, but traces of the sign [hieroglyph] can be detected, and this must apply to a term of relationship that—since it is placed in its normal position, before her name—presumably refers to the adjacent figure. The restoration that is indicated is accordingly [[hieroglyphs]][hieroglyph] "his sister."

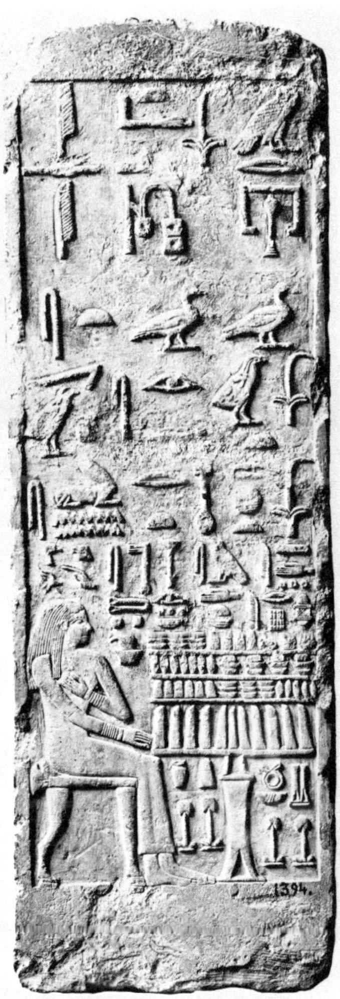

FIGURE 13
Cairo Museum, CG 1394

2. TWO-DIMENSIONAL REPRESENTATIONS

Old Kingdom representations in relief are, as one might anticipate, even more rarely accompanied by redundant name-determinatives than statues are; if both the determinative and representation are on the same plane, the redundancy is much more apparent. A few examples may nonetheless be cited, and in every case the presence and absence of determinatives conforms to the same pattern as the 16 examples in statuary:

(17) Fourth Dynasty slab stela of [hieroglyphs] (*Nfrt*) (Figure 14).[22] Of all the Fourth Dynasty slab stelae this is the only one that shows a determinative at the end of the owner's identification. Inasmuch as the early Fourth Dynasty example in statuary (example 9) involves virtually the same name, it may be considered whether the determinative has not been suggested by the meaning, "One who is beautiful."[23] But in that case one would expect to find the same writing on the

22. Lowie Museum of Anthropology, University of California, Berkeley, 6–19801. See Reisner, *Hist. Giza Necrop.* I, pl. 18b, p. 190 (G 1207).

23. For ideographs of this sort compare [hieroglyphs] (Junker, *Gîza* VI, fig. 32, p. 110; XII, p. 122; CG 57123, etc.); [hieroglyphs] (CG 110; compare *PN* I, p. 49 [24]); [hieroglyphs] (CG 1454, 1466); [hieroglyphs] (E. Drioton and J.-Ph. Lauer, "Un groupe de tombes à Saqqarah," *ASAE* 55 [1958] p. 229); [hieroglyphs] (Gustave Jéquier, *Le monument funéraire de Pepi II* III [Cairo, 1940] fig. 22, p. 37).

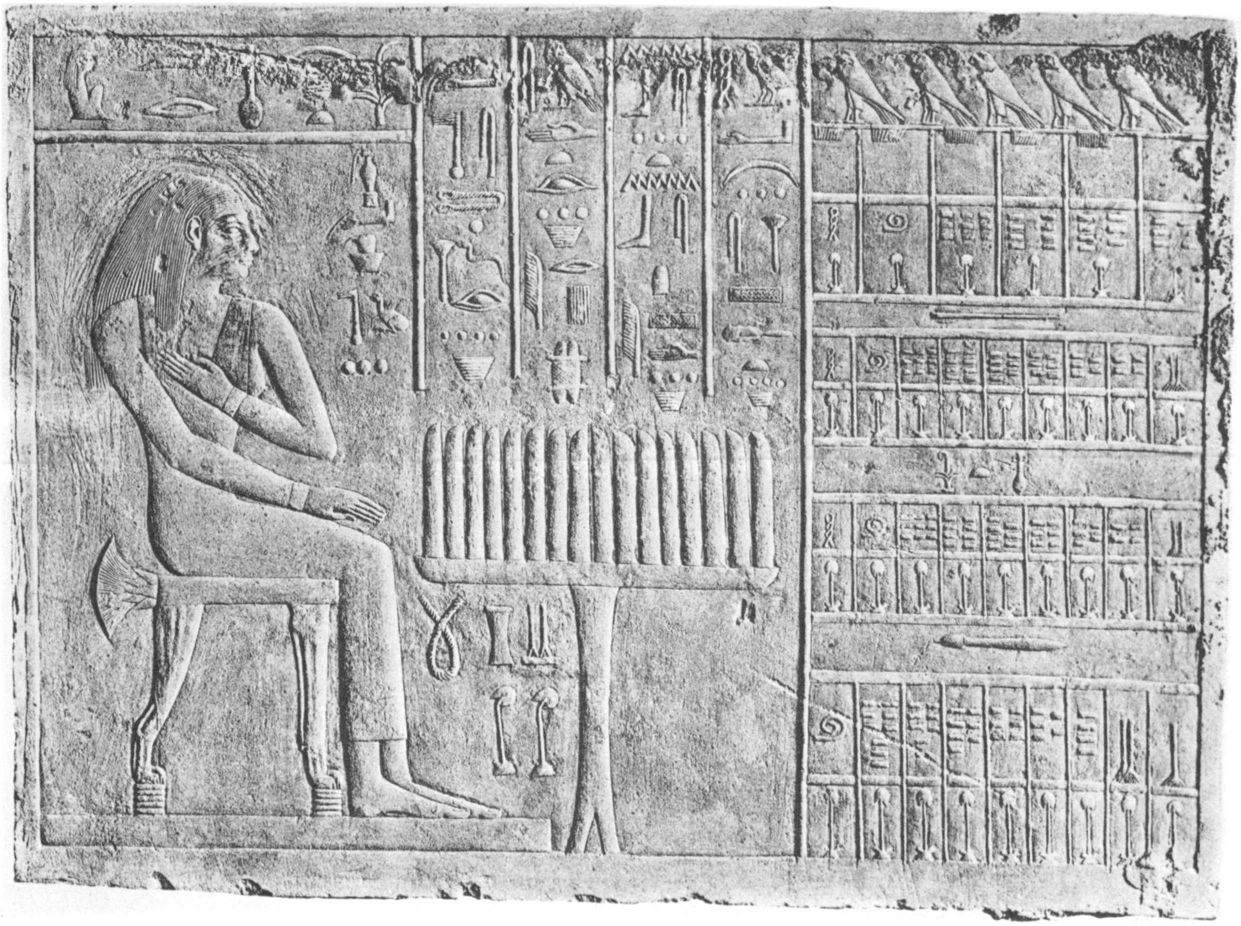

FIGURE 14
Example 17. From H. F. Lutz, *Egyptian Tomb Steles* (Leipzig, 1927) pl. 2 (2)

stela of *Rʿ-ḥtp* and *Nfrt*, in the tomb from which CG 3 and 4 derive, and there the determinative [hieroglyph] is lacking (W. M. F. Petrie, *Medum* [London, 1892] pl. 15). Nor do I know of any other evidence for an ideographic connection between [hieroglyph] and *nfrt* in Old Kingdom personal names.[24] Example 23, below, also involves a woman named [hieroglyphs], but this again occurs in the context of masculine names that lack determinatives. It therefore seems reasonable to conclude that [hieroglyph] is, in fact, simply a name-determinative.

(18) The false door of *Nfr-k³* and *Ṯtt* (Figure 15)[25] is not easy to date; it can hardly be as early as the beginning of the Fourth Dynasty, as Curto states (*Gli Scavi*, p. 33), and judging from the form of the determinatives, it would seem to be later than the beginning of Dynasty V. The offering niche may well belong to

24. Compare, for example, Abubakr, *Giza*, fig. 74, pp. 88, 90 (the latter a statue); Hilda F. Petrie and Margaret A. Murray, *Seven Memphite Tomb Chapels* (London, 1952) pl. 2; Junker, *Gîza* IX, fig. 15, p. 41. The sign [hieroglyph] does occur as a determinative of the name itself in some Middle Kingdom examples, but all of these cases involve a plural: [hieroglyphs] (CG 20219h) *Nfrwt* (? *PN* I, p. 202 [18] suggests *Nfrt-rḫwt* [?]); [hieroglyphs], [hieroglyphs] (CG 20086k, 20540f), variant writings of *Ḥ³t-šps̀wt* and [hieroglyphs] (CG 20057h), evidently *Śnwt*. Note also the Middle Kingdom title of a priest of Hathor who was [hieroglyphs] (G. Maspero, *Le Musée Égyptien* III [Cairo, 1915] p. 56).

25. Curto, *Gli Scavi*, fig. 22, pl. 2. I am indebted to Professor Curto for providing me with the photograph on which my drawing is based, and to William Pons for rephotographing to correct distortion.

the woman who is seated at the left of the offering table, opposite her husband.[26] Her name, *Ṯtt*, has the determinative while his lacks it,[27] and their names are written together on the crossbar and drum lintel beneath this scene, "*Nfr-k*ꜣ and *Ṯtt*," again with a

26. As suggested by the reiteration of her name on the crossbar and drum-lintel, and by the prominence of female offering bearers (as well as men). Her position on the dominant left side of the offering scene also fits this conclusion, although this point in itself is not conclusive; compare Abubakr, *Giza*, fig. 95A, p. 109, and the other examples cited in Henry G. Fischer, "A Scribe of the Army in a Saqqara Mastaba," *Journal of Near Eastern Studies* 18 (1959) p. 272. In the present case, however, it is confirmed by the fact that her figure is somewhat larger than that of her husband.

27. The presence of after the epithet *im*ꜣ*ḫ(t)* is remarkable, although sometimes occurs as a determinative after *im*ꜣ*ḫw* in other contexts (for example, *Urk.* I, p. 217, line 15; p. 252, line 13; *LD* II, 110[k]). Curto is probably right in taking the next group of signs as a feminine name (pp. 21–22), but the name may be *Ḥnwt.śn*, and not *Ḥnwt.s*; compare the writing Junker, *Gîza* VI, fig. 29, p. 106, and compare *PN* I, p. 243 [29], 244 [1] and II, p. 337. Possibly one might read *im*ꜣ*ḫ(t) nt ḥnwt.ś*. For *im*ꜣ*ḫw* + the genitive see *Wb.* I, 82 [7], and for the epithet "revered with her (or his) mistress" see Henry G. Fischer, *Dendera in the Third Millennium B.C.* (Locust Valley, New York, 1968) p. 211, note 820; Norman de G. Davies, *The Rock Tombs of Sheikh Saïd* (London, 1901) pl. 25; Clarence S. Fisher, *The Minor Cemetery at Giza* (Philadelphia, 1924) p. 143, pl. 48 (1); and the unpublished drum-lintel of , Toledo (Ohio) 06.24. In most of these examples, however, the identity of *ḥnwt* is indicated by the context, and no such indication is provided in the present case.

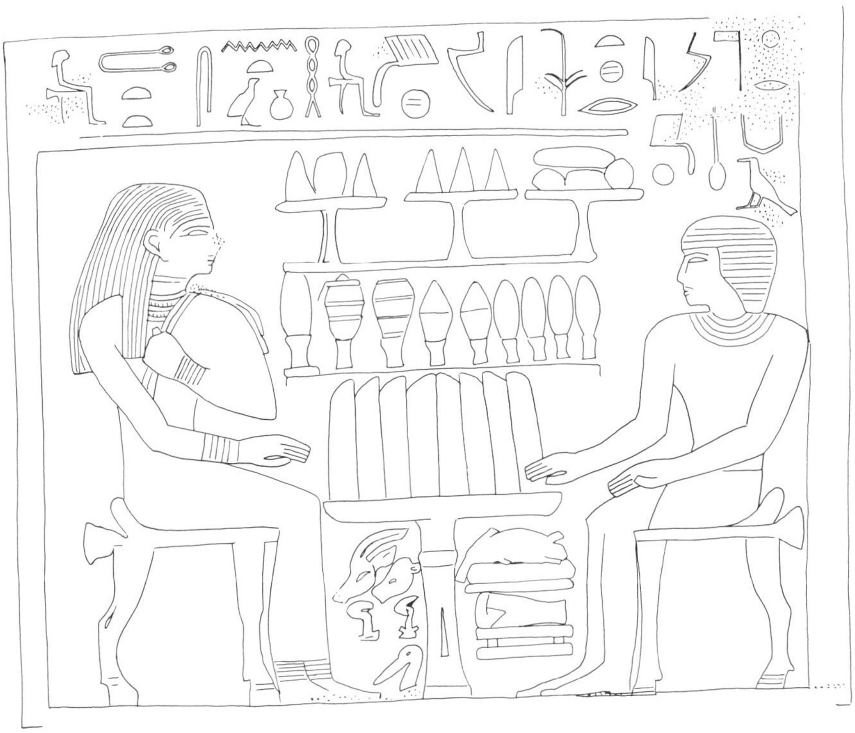

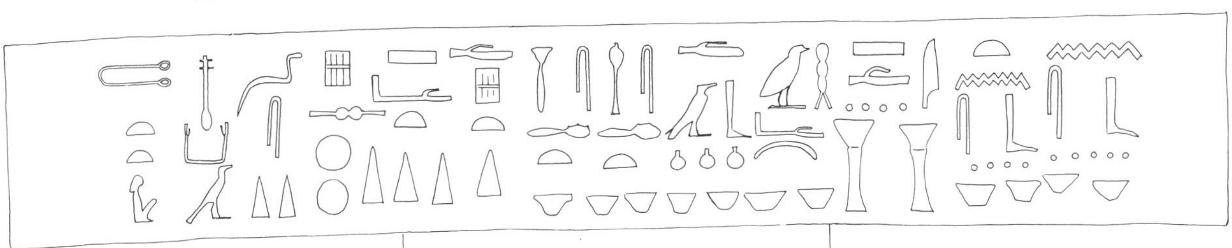

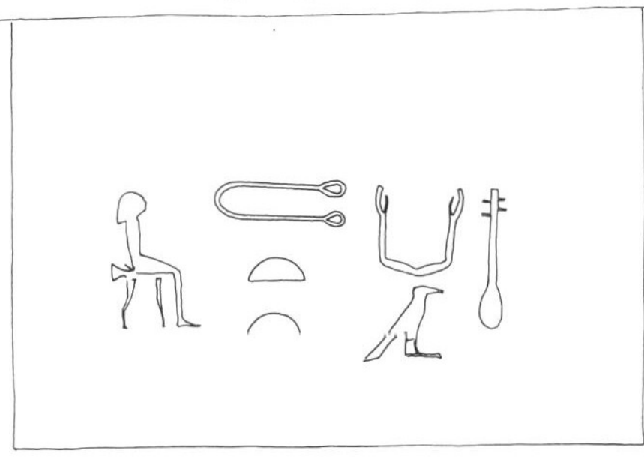

FIGURE 15
Example 18. Drawn from photograph, courtesy Turin Museum

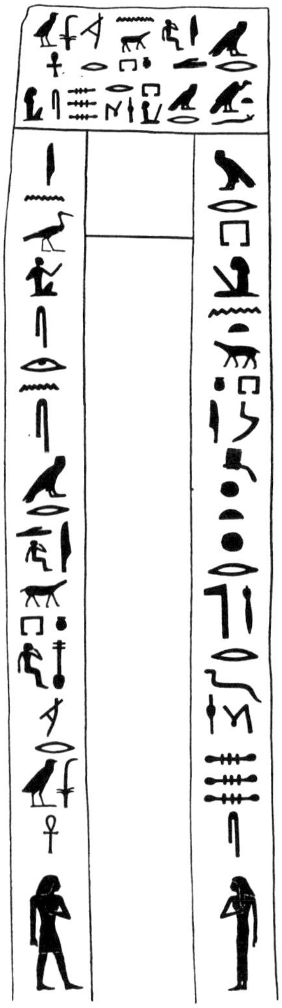

FIGURE 16
Example 19. From Hassan, *Gîza* I, fig. 184, p. 112

FIGURE 17
Example 20. From Junker, *Gîza* V, fig. 40, p. 145

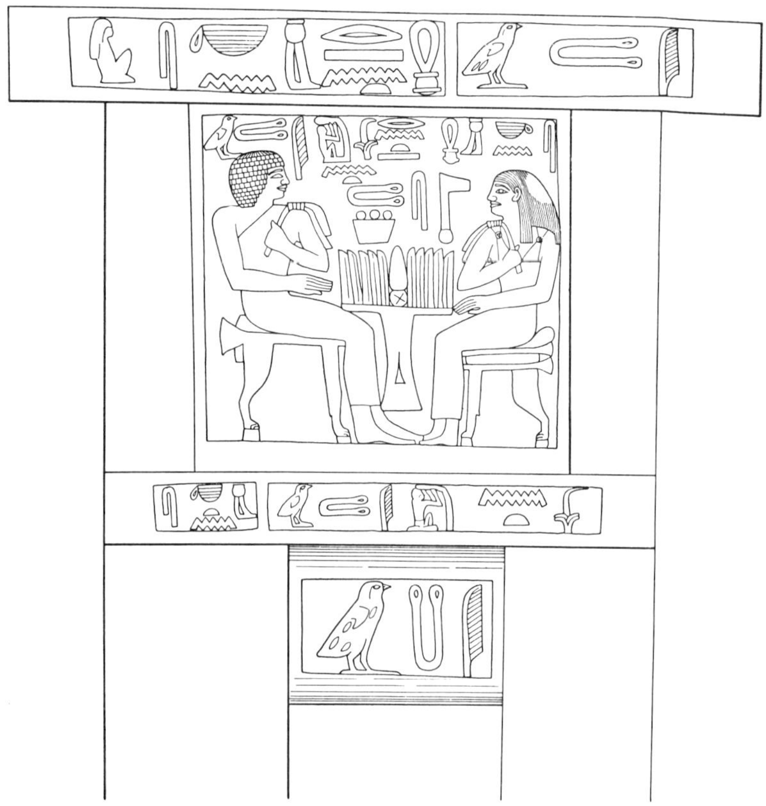

determinative applied to her name only: on the crossbar and on the lintel.

(19) The architrave of a simple false door from the tomb of *Mr-św-ʿnḫ*, from which example 4 derives, names the owner and his mother, who are represented at the bottom of the jambs, with the determinative ( ) applied to her name only, and not to his (Figure 16).

(20) Of still later date, probably within the Sixth Dynasty, is the false door of *ʾItw* (Figure 17), which shows the owner seated opposite his wife. The architrave above this scene gives her name the determinative ( ) and not his, and to this extent it bears out the testimony of the preceding examples.[28] Unlike example 18, however, the name-determinative is not actually redundant because it appears at the end of the architrave that is furthest from the wife, and her name is repeated, without a determinative, above her figure. It may be significant that no determinative is added to her name on the architrave above her own false door (Junker, *Gîza* V, fig. 36, p. 139).

28. Note also the false door CG 1462, which similarly shows no representations of the owner and his wife and supplies no determinative to the owner's name, while his wife is identified as . In this case, however, the sign probably belongs to the word *st* in *St-nt-Ḥtḥr*; compare the writing of *S-n-ꜣḫty*, Junker, *Gîza* VI, fig. 36, p. 117. Another example worth mentioning here is *LD* II, pls. 10–11; the wife's name shows the determinative on the architrave above her false door (pl. 10) while, in a similar context (pl. 11), the name of her husband lacks it.

3. OTHER LINTELS AND ARCHITRAVES

There are also a number of cases in which an isolated lintel or architrave shows the same distinction between men and women in the use of name-determinatives. Some of them may have accompanied an offering scene, as in the case of examples 18 and 20, but even so, the determinative could not, strictly speaking, be called "redundant" any more than it could in the example that has just been considered.

(21) Name-determinatives are completely omitted on one of a pair of lintels (Figure 18)[29] that bear the names of "the Craftsman *Nfr*, the *Mitrt My*, and the Butcher of the Slaughterhouse *ʿIy-wꜣt*," but the second lintel adds a determinative to the name of the woman alone: . The drum lintels that were presumably placed beneath each of these (Figure 19) include the names of *Nfr* and *My* only, and they show the determinatives and , respectively, in both cases.[30]

(22) An architrave from Reisner's excavations at Giza, above the entrance of tomb G 1208 (Figure 20), [31] is inscribed for: "The Custodian of the King's Property (?) , *Wʿb*-priest of the King, *Ḥm-nṯr* Priest of Cheops, Inspector of the Boat(s?), Overseer of the Army, Overseer of the Pyramid *ꜣḫt-Ḫwfw*, Leader of the Phyles, *ꜣḫty-ḥtp*, and his wife the Custodian of the King's Property (?), *Mrt-it.ś*." She alone has the name-determinative: . One might take the owner of this inscription to be "*ꜣḫty-ḥtp's* wife . . . *Mrt-it.ś*," but, in view of the number of titles that precede his name, it seems more likely that the architrave primarily belongs to him.

(23) The lintel over the entrance of another tomb at Giza (Figure 21)[32] was inscribed for the "Sealer of the King's Granary *Nfr-ḥr-n-Ptḥ* (together with) his wife

29. Brussels E. 5268, 5271. These facsimiles were previously published in Henry G. Fischer, "The Butcher *Pḥ-r-nfr*," *Orientalia* 29 (1960) p. 171.

30. Brussels E. 5270 (previously reproduced in Fischer, "The Butcher *Pḥ-r-nfr*," p. 171) and Field Museum Chicago 31297, reproduced here by permission of Dr. James W. Van Stone, and by the Oriental Institute, who provided the photograph on which this drawing is based. This second lintel completes the writing as a variant of , the sign being incompletely preserved on its counterpart in Brussels. This hieroglyph is apparently a phonetic complement; compare , *Wb.* II, pl. 105 (18) and *mr*/*mi* with determinative , *Wb.* II, pl. 105 (19).

31. Based on a drawing and photograph kindly supplied by Dr. William K. Simpson.

32. From W. M. F. Petrie, *Gizeh and Rifeh* (London, 1907) pl. 7A; now in the Manchester Museum, 1617.

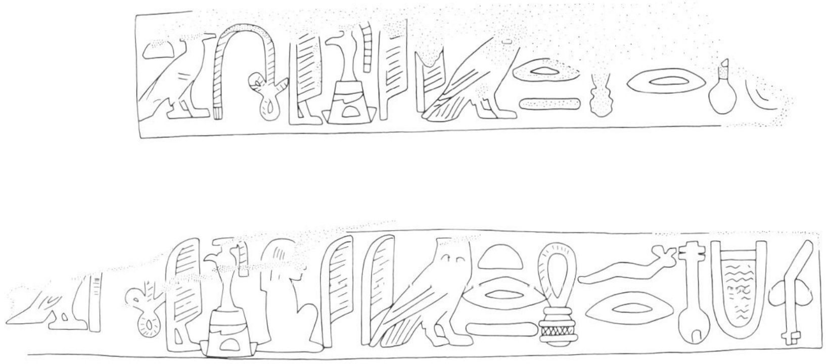

FIGURE 18
Example 21. Brussels, E. 5268 (above) and 5271

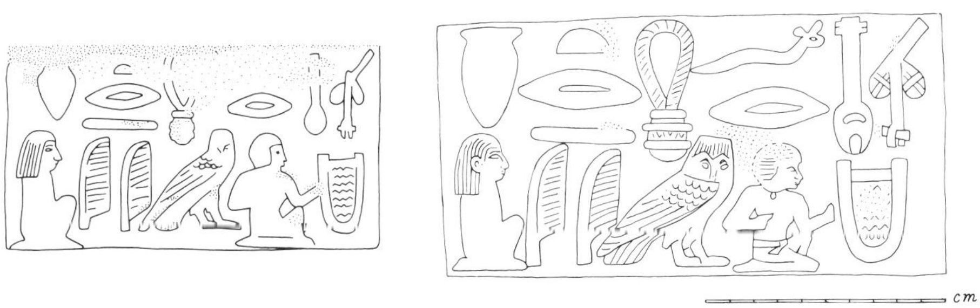

FIGURE 19
Brussels E. 5270 (left) and Field Museum, Chicago, 31297

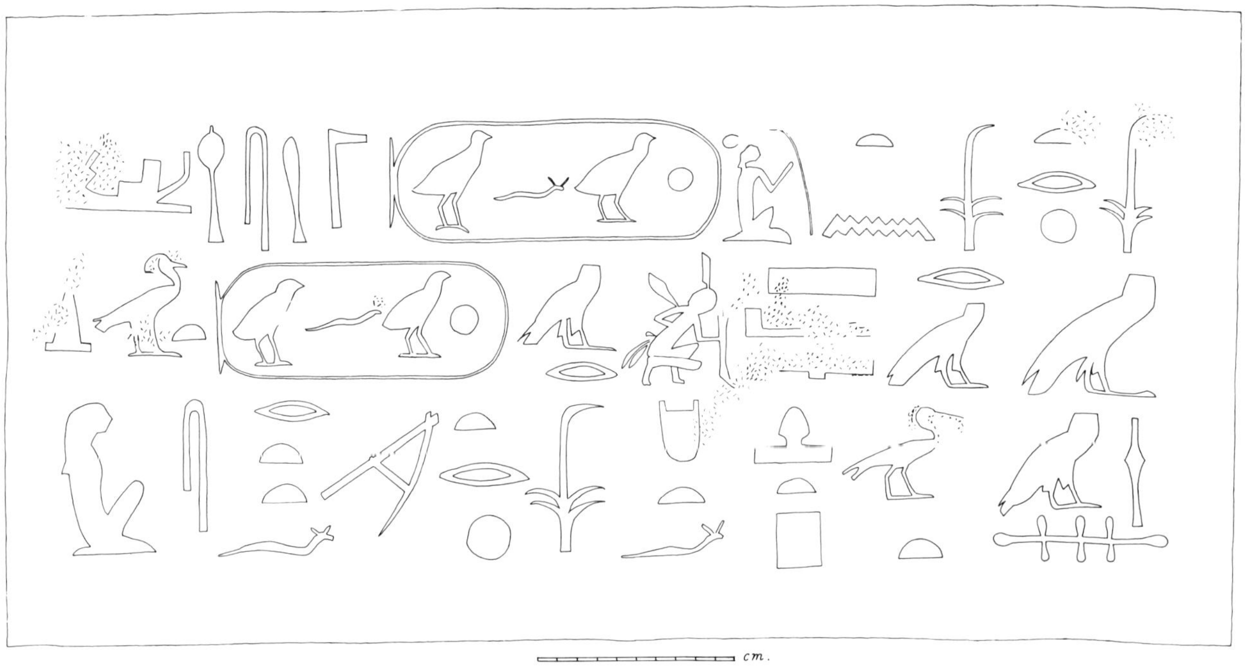

FIGURE 20
Example 22. From excavation records, Museum of Fine Arts, Boston

FIGURE 21
Example 23. From photograph, Petrie, *Gizeh and Rifeh*, pl. 7A

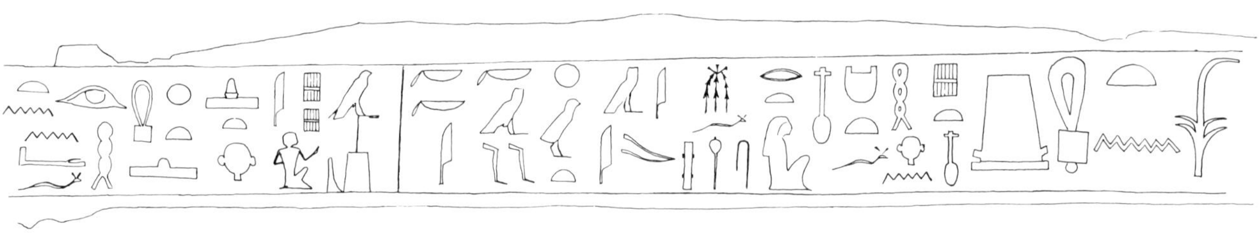

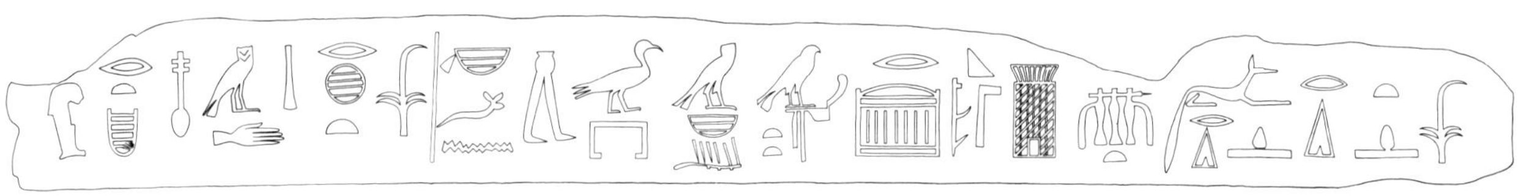

FIGURE 22
Example 24. From excavation records, Museum of Fine Arts, Boston

FIGURE 23
Example 25. From L*D* II, pl. 94a

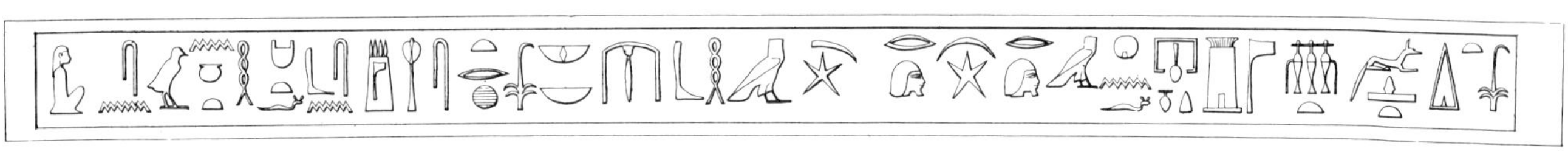

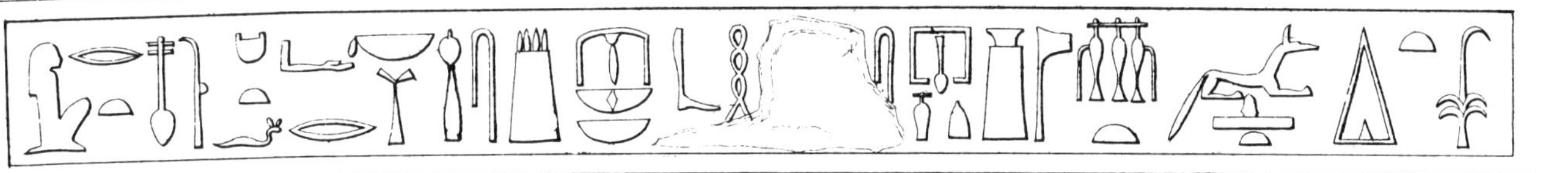

FIGURE 24
Example 26. From *LD* II, pl. 95c

Nfrt and his children, The Overseer of Crews *'Imi, Ḥwt, K³.i-m-rdwy, Kki.*" To the left is a statement: "the Stonemason *Ppi* is satisfied with the contract that I made with him." *Nfrt* has the determinative . The only other name that has one () is that of the stonemason, who is not a member of the family.

(24) Yet another lintel from Giza, found by Reisner in the vicinity of Giza tomb 1227 (Figure 22),[33] shows an offering formula and the name of the Estate Attendant (literally "Son of the House") *'In-k³.f*, who lacks a name-determinative, and a woman (presumably his wife), who has it. The offering formula is directed to the man "as possessor of reverence" (*m nb im³ḫ*) and the woman's title and name are separated from his by a vertical dividing line. In this case the addition of the determinative may have been reinforced by the form of the name, since *Mdw-nfrt* is probably the same as the masculine name *Mdw-nfr*, with the addition of the feminine ending *t*.[34] Perhaps the sign is to be read *ḥmt* "the woman," in which case the determinative is even more explainable in terms of the name itself. The addition of *ḥmt* may be compared to the words "she-ass" (Pyr. 323) and "wild cow" (Pyr. 389, 1370), to which Faulkner has recently called attention.[35]

(25) An architrave reused in one of the houses of Kafr el Batran, near the Giza cemetery (Figure 23) invokes offerings for "the inspector of the palace[36] *Śnb* and his wife *Ḥnwt.śn*," with a determinative () applied only to the name of the wife. It should be noted that he is explicitly designated as the primary recipient of offerings, since the formula concludes with the words *pri n.f ḫrw* "that the voice be emitted for him."

(26) A second architrave from the same place (Figure 24) shows the same use of the determinative after the wife's name alone (), but in this case the offering formula concludes with *pri* ⟨*n.*⟩*ś ḫrw* [*m*] *ḥb nb* "that the voice be emitted ⟨for⟩ her [on] every feast."[37] Thus the pair of names is to be interpreted as "the Inspector of the Palace *K³*(*.i*)-*'pr*'s wife *Rnpt-nfrt.*" In this particular instance the name-determinative might accordingly be regarded as the equivalent of a terminal representation; but a terminal representation is usually omitted on the smaller lintels and architraves of the type exemplified by nos. 18–22, 24–27, and a small-

33. Previously reproduced in Henry G. Fischer, "Old Kingdom Inscriptions in the Yale Gallery," *Mitteilungen des Instituts für Orientforschung* 7 (1960) fig. 1, p. 301.

34. Discussed in Fischer, "Old Kingdom Inscriptions," p. 301, note 5.

35. "*Ḥmt* 'woman' as a feminine suffix," *JEA* 58 (1972), p. 300. The sign also appears in a late Old Kingdom writing of the feminine title *mitrt* (: Junker, *Gîza* IX, p. 243) but here it seems to be the equivalent of ideographic as in the variant writing (CG 1707). Note also a further Middle Kingdom example, "the female children of the Count," in Newberry, *Beni Hasan* I, pl. 29.

36. The presence of the sign within cannot be verified; presumably the title in question is identical to the one in the following example, no. 26, and is to be compared with the more familiar titles and . Otherwise, as far as Old Kingdom sources are concerned, the monograph combining and usually occurs with the addition of (CG 1565 [wrongly transcribed in *Urk.* I, p. 83, line 11]; *Urk.* I, p. 52, line 8, p. 242, lines 1, 5; and especially , Firth and Gunn, *Teti Pyramid Cemeteries*, pp. 135, 148. Compare P. Kaplony, *Zeitschrift für Ägyptische Sprache und Altertumskunde* 88 (1962) p. 6, n. 3. It also replaces (*sḥ-nṯr*) in CG 1495 and evidently replaces (*ḥwt-nṯr*) in CG 1652 (Henry G. Fischer, "Monuments of the Old Kingdom in the Cairo Museum," *Chronique d'Egypte* 43 [1968] p. 311); possibly (*Urk.* I, p. 20, line 15) is the same as the second of these, but Elmar Edel, *Altägyptische Grammatik* I (Rome, 1955) §67, transliterates *nṯrj* "Kapelle."

37. For the emendation of ⟨*n.*⟩*ś* see the examples cited by Clère in "Le fonctionnement grammatical de l'expression *pri ḫrw* en ancien égyptien," *Mélanges Maspero* I (*Mémoires publiés par les membres de l'Institut Français d'Archéologie Orientale du Caire* LXVI) (Cairo, 1935–38) p. 761, note 1, and compare on the lintel of another woman from the same place: *LD* II, pl. 94 b.

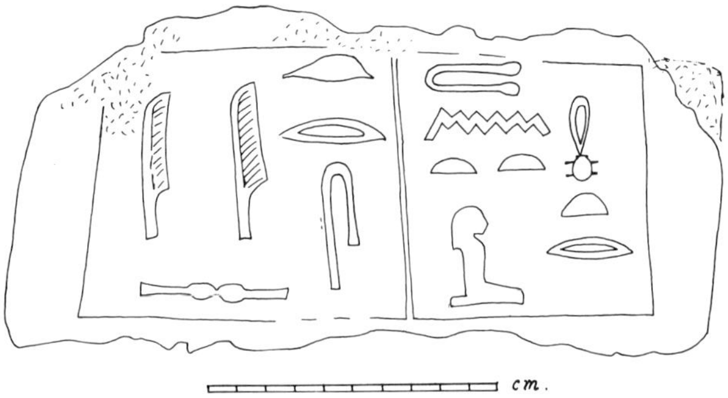

FIGURE 25
Example 28. University College, London, 8453

scale hieroglyphic determinative rarely serves this function.[38]

(27) A drum-lintel of unknown provenance in Cairo, CG 1751,[39] has an offering formula that shows masculine forms (*nb im*ꜣ*ḫ*. . . *i*ꜣ*w nfr wrt*) and is therefore primarily directed to the first of the two persons mentioned subsequently. His name, lacking a determinative, is *'Iy-nfrt*, and his title ( ) is obscure. The name that follows belongs to "the *mitrt Ṯntt*," followed by the determinative . She is presumably his wife, but their relationship is not specified.

(28) A small lintel of unknown provenance, University College, London 8453 (Figure 25),[40] bears the name of the *mitrt Ṯntt*, with the determinative , and, in a separate compartment, a name that is apparently masculine and lacks the determinative. The reading of the latter is problematic, but the final can hardly be anything but *s* "man" and I can suggest no explanation better than *'Iry-ś(w)-s* "The one who is made—he's a man!"[41]

It will be noted that all of the examples of known provenance (22–26) are from Giza. I feel doubtful that the date of no. 21 is as early as the Third Dynasty, as I have suggested previously, but I am uncertain how much later it may be. Klaus Baer has suggested that no. 22 is no earlier than the reign of Neferirkare in the Fifth Dynasty (*Rank and Title in the Old Kingdom* [Chicago, 1960] pp. 52 [10], 240). No. 23 is probably even later, as are all the rest.

4. CONCLUSIONS AND SEQUEL

The Old Kingdom evidence that has been presented is, in the first place, sufficient to establish the fact that women's names were frequently given a determinative in situations where a masculine name lacks it. The examples include some cases where the woman is evidently the owner of the monument (18, 19, 26). In no case, however, can it be proven that the monument did not come from the tomb of the man with whom she is associated, and that is certainly true in the case of no. 19 (the owner's mother). Furthermore the distinction is definitely known to occur on the husband's monument in several other instances (for example, 2, 8, 15, 16, 20, 23, 24, 25, 27).

It might be considered, then, whether the distinctive use of the feminine determinative derives from the idea that she is a secondary occupant of her husband's mastaba. But the same determinative is twice given to a daughter when a son lacks it (2, 4), and to a wife when it is omitted from the names of her sons (2, 8, 10, 11, 12, 13, 14, 15, 23). In the case of no. 23, however, a daughter lacks the determinative as well as a son. The last case is particularly interesting because another man, the builder of the tomb (and in all probability not a kinsman), does have a name-determinative.

Perhaps we should not place too much weight on the cases where the distinction in the use of the determinative is extended to other members of the family, but they suggest that two considerations were simultaneously operative: the first being a tendency to use a feminine determinative to distinguish the female entity from generic Man ( );[42] the second being a

38. One of the earliest examples, Junker, *Gîza* I, fig. 63, p. 252, follows a feminine name and may well be related to the examples under consideration. For masculine examples of later date from Giza see Junker, *Gîza* VIII, figs. 32, 60, pp. 75, 128; IX, fig. 72, p. 160; Hassan, *Gîza* II, fig. 34, p. 37; III, fig. 22, p. 23; VI, pt. 3, fig. 195, p. 199.

39. As described (without illustration) by Borchardt, *Denkmäler des Alten Reiches* II, p. 174.

40. The drawing is based on a photograph and tracing kindly supplied by Barbara Adams. I am obliged to Dr. D. M. Dixon for permission to publish it.

41. This would thus be a rare example of the passive participle used as predicate (Edel, *Altägyptische Grammatik* I, §644), with representing as in two other names, both of which also contain the word (Edel, *Altägyptische Grammatik* I, §167 dd).

42. Old Kingdom Egyptian does not always use the group as a determinative of *rmṯ* where the meaning is "men" in the generic sense; this may also be written (*Urk.* I, p. 71, line 3), (Hassan, *Gîza* IX, fig. 38, p. 88), or (*Urk.* I, p.

tendency to apply a determinative to the names of persons who are not so immediately present as the owner of the tomb.

The second consideration is reinforced by the fact that, in some cases, the statue of the owner was not felt to require any inscription whatever, taking its identity from the context of the tomb in which it was placed. And if, in such a case, the owner was a woman, her statue might omit her own name and show only that of her husband (Figure 12). Similarly the statue of a son, in his father's serdab, might allude to the father without mentioning his name since, here again (example 4), that identity is supplied by the context.[43] This study may, in fact, be regarded as a demonstration of the way in which every aspect of the context—archaeological, iconographic, and epigraphic—may affect a hieroglyphic inscription.

After the Old Kingdom, and particularly during the later part of the Eleventh Dynasty, redundant determinatives were more frequently applied to names on tomb stelae. The majority of the examples are from the Theban area—Dendera,[44] Thebes itself,[45] and Gebelein,[46] but a few cases are known from Naga ed-Deir,[47] and some of these are earlier than the others.[48] The later examples are sometimes to be explained by the semicursive character of the inscriptions, which tends to isolate them from the representations which they accompany.[49] In any case they are exceptional even in the Eleventh Dynasty; they rarely apply the determinative to the wife alone, and not to the owner;[50] and they do not seem to have had a lasting effect of any significance, once the country was reunited and older traditions were re-established.[51] A particularly conspicuous exception is to be found in Beni Hasan tomb 2, dating to the second reign of Dynasty XII, where the representations of the tomb owner's wife are identified as ,[52] while the determinative is consistently omitted from the name of the owner himself, even in those cases where he is not depicted.

I know of only four Middle Kingdom group-statues that omit the determinative after the owner's name and supply it to the name of his wife. The earliest and clearest example is an Eleventh Dynasty seated couple from Dendera who are named and

49, line 1, and *Kêmi* 15 (1959) pl. 1 [3], following p. 22), and, in addition there is the ideographic use of (*Urk.* I, p. 23, line 6, and often elsewhere), which may represent the same word or *s* (); compare Edel, *Altägyptische Grammatik* I, §53, and Raymond O. Faulkner, *The Plural and Dual in Old Egyptian* (Brussels, 1929) §30. The writing also occurs occasionally after the Old Kingdom: Jacques Vandier, *Mo'alla* (Cairo, 1950) p. 298; Norman de G. Davies, *The Tomb of Antefoker* (London, 1920) pl. 9.

43. Dr. Helmut Nickel informs me that a similar logic was more systematically applied to Viking tombstones; those marking an actual burial are uninscribed, while runic inscriptions identify the cenotaphs of those lost at sea. We must suppose, however, that the wife of *Mmi*/*Š3bw* was named elsewhere in her tomb chapel. The influence of the proprietary context is also to be recognized in the use of Old Kingdom epithets indicating seniority and juniority. In the event that father and son have the same name, a distinguishing epithet may be applied to the son's name ("junior") if—as is usually the case—he is shown in his father's tomb chapel. But in one case, where the father is shown in the son's tomb chapel, it is the older man who has the epithet; he is "senior." And if both are mentioned together in some other context, beyond their own funerary domain, each of them may receive an epithet; in one such example they are given the single name they have in common, which is followed by "senior and junior." The evidence is presented at the beginning of a forthcoming article, *Egyptian Studies* I: "Epithets of Seniority."

44. W. M. F. Petrie, *Dendereh* (London, 1900) pls. 11 (bottom left, bottom center, and right, second from bottom), 12 (right, second from bottom); J. d'E. 36423 (wife and daughter only), 44301, 44302 (= CG 20804).

45. J.-J. Clère and J. Vandier, *Textes de la Première Période Intermédiaire* (Brussels, 1948) §§ 2 (CG 20003, probably later than the end of Dyn. XI), 14 (Metropolitan Museum 14.2.7), 23 (British Museum 1203—wives only); Naville, *Deir el Bahari: XIth Dyn.* I, pl. 17 G, H; III, pls. 2–3, 9 D. Also CG 20007, which may well come from Thebes.

46. CG 1622, CG 1654 (wife only).

47. Dows Dunham, *Naga ed-Dêr Stelae of the First Intermediate Period* (London, 1937) nos. 45, 49, 70 (man, but not wife), 83 (same), 20 (wife only), 81 (wife only), CG 1648 (husband, not wife).

48. At least two examples (Dunham nos. 20 and 45) are evidently earlier than the end of Dyn. VIII.

49. For example, J. d'E. 44301 (from Dendera); Naville, *Deir el Bahari: XIth Dyn.* III, pls. 2–3, and the labels of some officials shown in an early Twelfth Dynasty tomb (Newberry, *Beni Hasan* I, pl. 13). An Old Kingdom example may also be cited, Toledo (Ohio) 49.4, where determinatives follow the names of a son and daughter who are represented in relief on the sides of a seated statue.

50. See above, notes 44–47; at Naga ed-Deir the determinative is sometimes applied to the husband alone.

51. Some later examples (besides CG 20003, mentioned above in note 45): CG 1597, 1753, 20518 (some of the captions); MMA 63.154 (captions of three daughters); Brooklyn Museum 37.1347E (captions of one of two men, and wives of both).

52. Newberry, *Beni Hasan* I, pls. 12, 18.

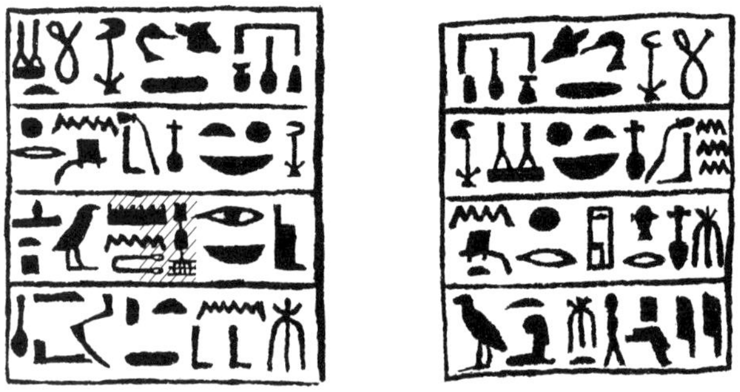

FIGURE 26
From Petrie, *Dendereh*, pl. 15

, *Mnṯw-ḥtp* born of *Bbt* and *Nfr-mśwt* born of *Ḥpy* (Figure 26).[53] It is difficult to form any definite conclusion about this period on the basis of such slender evidence, and the number of Middle Kingdom group-statues is so small, in comparison to earlier examples, and so much less adequately published, that no such conclusion may perhaps be possible for some time to come.

Statuary of the New Kingdom generally shows the determinative after the names of both husband and wife,[54] although one Eighteenth Dynasty example, probably dating to the reign of Tuthmosis IV, evidently perpetuates the old distinction (Figure 27).[55] The name of the husband (*'Imn-ḳd*) lacks a determinative while those of his wife (*Nbt-'Iwnt*) and daughter (*Mwt-nfrt*) in both cases end with 𓁐. The inscriptions on the backs and sides show no determinatives whatever.[56]

53. Ashmolean Museum E 1971: Petrie, *Dendereh*, pls. 15 (bottom right), 21. The other examples are Munich Glyptothek 99 (Hans Wolfgang Müller and Beatrix Löhr, *Staatliche Sammlung Ägyptischer Kunst* [Munich, 1972] p. 58, pl. 26); Louvre E. 19172 (Jacques Vandier, *Manuel d'archéologie égyptienne*, III. *La Statuaire* [Paris, 1958] pl. 85 [1]); Turayev, *Statui i Statuetki*, pp. 7–8.

54. As exemplified by CG 597, 613, 622, 628, 42126.

55. Metropolitan Museum 25.184.8, height 30 cm, described in W. C. Hayes, *Scepter of Egypt* II (New York, 1959) pp. 158–159.

56. The same distinction appears on at least two other New Kingdom statues, both in the Cairo Museum: CG 772 and 934, but in the first case both names show determinatives in the inscriptions on the back. All three examples are exceptional.

SOURCES ABBREVIATED

Abubakr, *Giza*—Abdel-Moneim Abubakr, *Excavations at Giza 1949–1950* (Cairo, 1953).

ASAE—*Annales du Service des Antiquités de l'Egypte.*

BMFA—*Bulletin of the Museum of Fine Arts (Boston).*

CG + number—Monuments in the Egyptian Museum, Cairo, numbers referring to *Catalogue général des antiquités égyptiennes du Musée du Caire:*

CG 1–1294: Ludwig Borchardt, *Statuen und Statuetten von Königen und Privatleuten* I-IV (Berlin, 1911–34);

CG 1295–1808: Ludwig Borchardt, *Denkmäler des Alten Reiches* I-II (Berlin, 1937–64);

CG 20001–20780: H. O. Lange and H. Schäfer, *Grab- und Denksteine des Mittleren Reichs* I-IV (Berlin, 1902–25);

CG 20804: unpublished continuation of CG 20001–20780 by J.-J. Clère.

CG 42126: Georges Legrain, *Statues et statuettes de rois et de particuliers* I (Cairo, 1906).

Curto, *Gli Scavi*—S. Curto, *Gli Scavi Italiani a El-Ghiza (1903)* (Rome, 1963).

Hassan, *Gîza*—S. Hassan, *Excavations at Gîza* I-X (Oxford, 1932; Cairo, 1936–60).

JEA—*Journal of Egyptian Archaeology.*

J. d'E. + number—Monuments in the Egyptian Museum, Cairo, unpublished unless otherwise noted.

Junker, *Gîza*—Hermann Junker, *Bericht über die von der Akademie der Wissenschaften in Wien . . . unternommenen Grabungen auf dem Friedhof des Alten Reiches bei den Pyramiden von Gîza* I-XII (Vienna, 1929–55).

LD—Lepsius, C. R., *Denkmaeler aus Aegypten und Aethiopien* (Berlin, 1849–59).

Naville, *Deir el Bahari: XIth Dyn.*—Edouard Naville, *The XIth Dynasty Temple at Deir el-Bahari* I-III (London, 1907–13).

Newberry, *Beni Hasan* I—Percy E. Newberry, *Beni Hasan* Part I (London, 1893).

Petrie, *Dendereh*—W. M. F. Petrie, *Dendereh* (London, 1900).

PN—Hermann Ranke, *Die Ägyptischen Personennamen* I-II (Glückstadt, 1935–[52]).

Pyr.—Kurt Sethe, *Die Altaegyptischen Pyramidentexte* (Leipzig, 1908, 1910).

Reisner, *Hist. Giza Necrop.*—George A. Reisner, *A History of the Giza Necropolis* I (Cambridge, Mass., 1942); Reisner and William Stevenson Smith, II (Cambridge, Mass., 1955).

Smith, *History of Sculpture and Painting*—William Stevenson Smith, *A History of Egyptian Sculpture and Painting in the Old Kingdom* (London, 1946).

Urk. I—Kurt Sethe, *Urkunden des Alten Reichs* (Leipzig, 1933).

Wb.—A. Erman and H. Grapow, *Wörterbuch der aegyptischen Sprache* I-V (Leipzig, 1926–31).

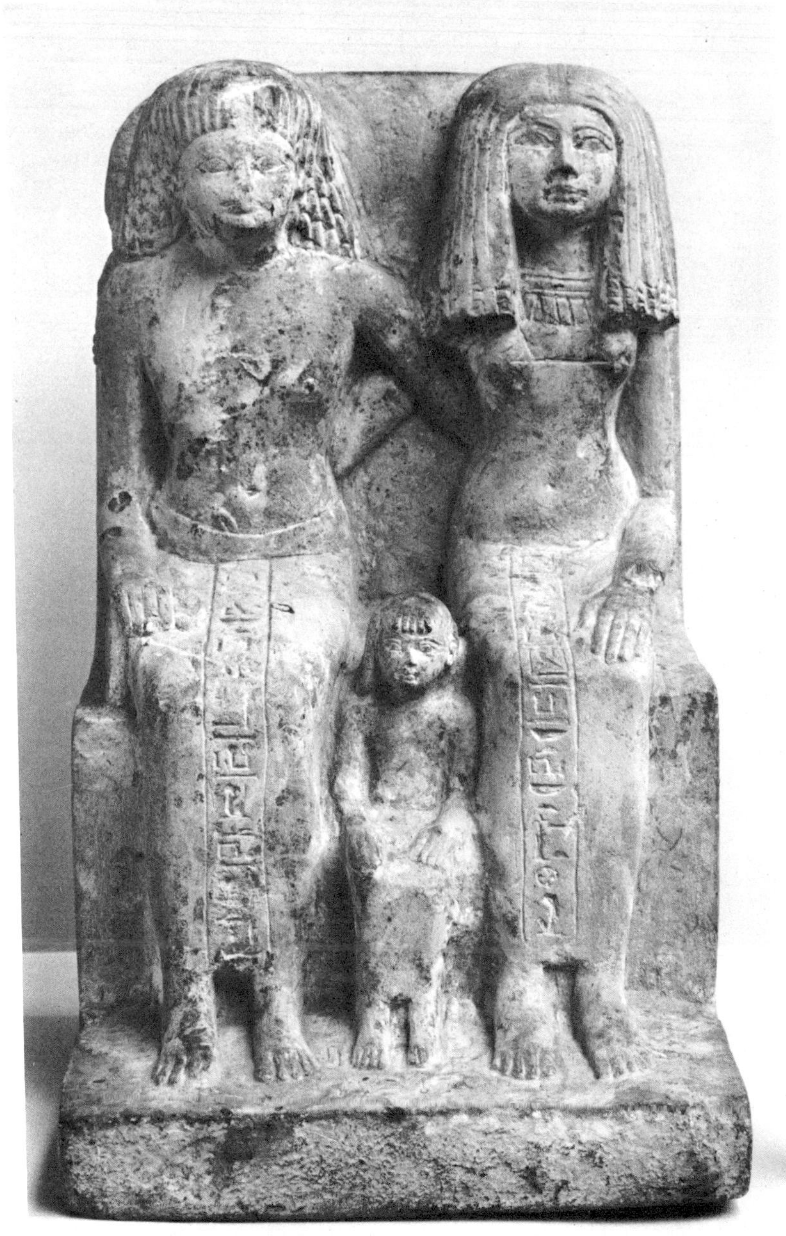

FIGURE 27
Eighteenth Dynasty couple with daughter. The Metropolitan Museum of Art. Gift of Mrs. S. W. Straus, 25.184.8

La Statue d'un Chef de Chanteurs d'Epoque Saïte

PROF. DR. HERMAN DE MEULENAERE

Seminarie voor Egyptologie, Hoger Institut, Rjksuniversiteit, Gent

La statue que nous publions ici est un chef d'oeuvre de l'art saïte, bien qu'à première vue, comme document, elle n'offre aucun intérêt particulier. C'est une statue acéphale, assez sérieusement endommagée aux épaules et aux bras, qui représente un homme agenouillé sur un socle et tenant devant ses genoux une tête hathorique. Achetée en 1924 par le Metropolitan Museum, elle y est inventoriée sous le n° 24.2.2.[1] Elle proviendrait du temple de Ptah à Memphis, dont les maigres vestiges sont recouverts par la palmeraie de Mitrahina, et aurait été retirée du trou qui a livré la célèbre statue de Horemheb, conservée au même musée.[2] Pratiquement inédite, elle a été brièvement décrite par H. G. Fischer[3] et citée à deux reprises par les auteurs du catalogue de l'exposition *Egyptian Sculpture of the Late Period.*[4]

Il ne nous semble pas nécessaire de nous arrêter ici à l'attitude du personnage puisque J.-J. Clère prépare un corpus des statues présentant un sistre hathorique.[5] Contentons-nous de remarquer que ce type de statue apparaît dans l'art égyptien du Nouvel Empire[6] et qu'il ne disparaît pas avant le 4e siècle av. J.-C.[7]

Pour déterminer l'âge de la pièce et avant de chercher d'éventuels critères de datation dans l'inscription, il convient de mettre en valeur deux détails importants. Observons d'abord le modelé du torse: le profond sillon vertical qui divise la poitrine en deux moitiés est caractéristique des oeuvres sculptées de la seconde moitié du 7e siècle av. J.-C.[8] Ce qui reste de la coiffure du personnage ne fait que confirmer cette datation provisoire. En effet, une trace minime au dessus du pilier dorsal indique que l'homme portait une perruque striée; or celle-ci, après avoir joui d'une grande faveur sous les Ethiopiens, cesse d'être utilisée

1. Faite en schiste vert-noir, la statue mesure 64 cm de haut, y compris le socle qui a 42 cm de long et 28 cm de large. Nous remercions vivement Virginia Burton, conservateur adjoint au Metropolitan Museum, qui nous a permis de la publier, et B. V. Bothmer, conservateur au Brooklyn Museum, qui nous a communiqué divers renseignements à son sujet.

2. Inv. 23.10.1, cf. Robert Hari, *Horemheb et la reine Moutnedjemet* (Genève, 1964) p. 42–45; pour la provenance présumée, voir en particulier Herbert E. Winlock, "Harmhab, Commander-in-chief of the Armies of Tutenkhamon," *Bulletin of the Metropolitan Museum of Art*, Part II (October, 1923) p. 4.

3. Henry George Fischer, "Anatomy in Egyptian Art," *Apollo* (September, 1965) p. 173–175, fig. 8.

4. *Egyptian Sculpture of the Late Period* (Brooklyn, 1960) p. 22, 35.

5. Jean-Jacques Clère, "Propos sur un corpus des statues sistrophores égyptiennes," *Zeitschrift für Aegyptische Sprache und Altertumskunde* 96 (1969) p. 1–4.

6. Jacques Vandier, *Manuel d'archéologie égyptienne* III (Paris, 1958) p. 464–465.

7. Les fragments Caire 1009 (Ludwig Borchardt, *Statuen und Statuetten von Königen und Privatleuten* IV [Berlin, 1934] p. 23), qui ne peuvent être antérieurs au 4e siècle av. J.-C., appartiennent à une des statues les plus récentes de ce type.

8. *Egyptian Sculpture of the Late Period*, p. 22, 35.

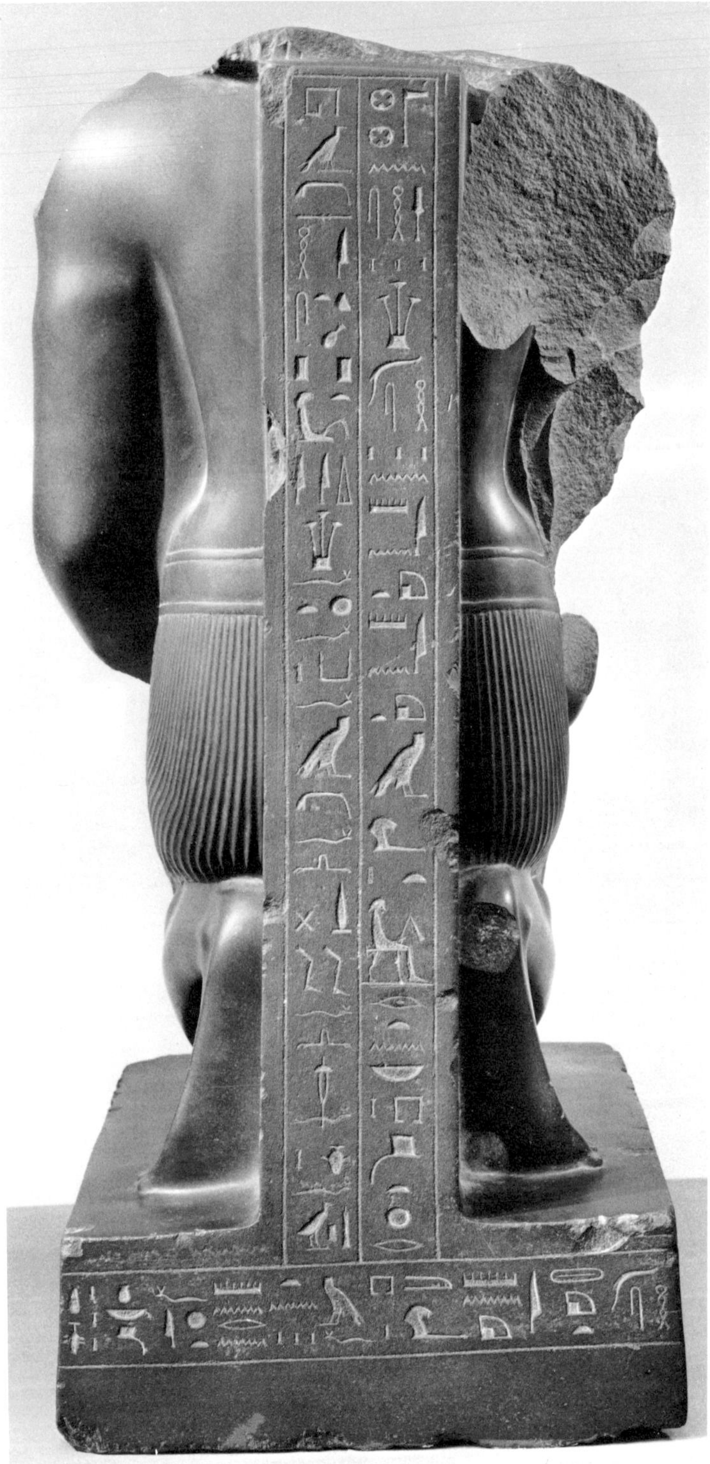

FIGURE I

Statue d'Amenemope-em-hat. The Metropolitan Museum of Art, Rogers Fund, 24.2.2. Inscription du pilier dorsal

à la fin du 7e siècle av. J.-C.[9] Bref, il semble bien que la statue appartient au règne de Psammétique I (664–610).

La perfection technique avec laquelle les textes ont été gravés et les formes soignées et nettes des hiéroglyphes suggèrent, elles aussi, que le propriétaire de la statue a vécu au commencement de l'époque saïte. Pour identifier celui-ci, il faut se reporter aux inscriptions du monument. Voyons ce que disent ces textes:

INSCRIPTION DU PILIER DORSAL (FIGURE I)

"1̣ Ô dieu local du directeur des chanteurs du Nord (*a*), chef des chanteurs d'Amen[em]ope (*b*), Amen-[em]ope-em-hat (*c*), né de la dame, vénérable auprès de 2̣ son époux (*d*), Ih-set-pep (*e*); (suit la formule saïte (*f*)"

(*a*) Le titre semble nouveau bien qu'on possède déjà quelques documents sur la hiérarchie des chanteurs (*ḥsw*) à l'époque saïte.[10] L'absence occasionnelle d'un déterminatif après *ḥsw* est signalée au *Wörterbuch der Aegyptischen Sprache* (Erman et Grapow), III, p. 165.

(*b*) Cette présence d'un culte d'Amon de Luxor à Memphis est étonnante. Il ne semble pas qu'on en ait signalé d'autres attestations. Mais est-il vraiment nécessaire de songer à Amon de Luxor? N'oublions pas qu'Ope (*'Ipt*) est le nom d'un sanctuaire osirien du nome héliopolite.[11] Il est possible qu'Amon y ait reçu un culte. C'est du moins ce que suggère un relief de Basse Epoque, découvert sur le site, où est mentionné un "prophète d'Amon-Rê qui réside à Héliopolis."[12] Parmi les membres du clergé d'Héliopolis, on rencontre, d'autre part, un certain nombre de personnages qui portent un nom formé sur celui d'Amon: Amenem-

9. Herman De Meulenaere, "Trois monuments de Basse Epoque," *Oudheidkundige Mededelingen uit het Rijksmuseum van Oudheden te Leiden* 44 (1963) p. 3.

10. Cf. Herman De Meulenaere, *Le surnom égyptien à la Basse Epoque* (Istanbul, 1966) p. 6.

11. Jean Yoyotte, "Prêtres et sanctuaires du nome héliopolite à la basse époque," *Bulletin de l'Institut Français d'Archéologie Orientale* 54 (1954) p. 91.

12. Francis Ll. Griffith, *The Antiquities of Tell el Yahûdîyeh* (London, 1890) pl. XXII, col. 24 (Caire JE 38824).

ope (Ipy),[13] Amenhotep,[14] et Ipy.[15] Comme les inscriptions de la statue contiennent, semble-t-il, d'autres réminiscences héliopolitaines (cf. infra), tout porte à croire que le culte évoqué dans la titulature d'Amenemope-em-hat n'a aucun rapport avec celui du temple de Luxor.

(*c*) C'est l'unique exemple de ce nom[16] que nous connaissons. Remarquons le déterminatif qui le suit: un personnage assis qui tient un sceptre sur les genoux. Si l'on établissait une statistique rigoureuse pour déterminer sa fréquence proportionnelle et, partant, sa valeur comme critère de datation à la Basse Epoque, elle révélerait sans aucun doute que son emploi est très répandu à l'époque où nous sommes tentés de situer la statue d'Amenemope-em-hat.

(*d*) Empruntée à l'Ancien Empire,[17] cette épithète a été remise en vogue par la renaissance saïte.[18]

(*e*) Il faut croire que la lecture du nom de la mère d'Amenemope-em-hat a singulièrement embarrassé Ranke puisque, contrairement à celui du propriétaire de la statue, il ne l'enregistre pas dans son dictionnaire. Il s'agit, en effet, d'un type de nom assez rarement attesté: *iḥ sṯy + nom divin* "agréablement parfumée est la divinité NN." Malgré la disposition quelque peu déconcertante des hiéroglyphes, on reconnaît facilement ces éléments sur la statue du Metropolitan Museum. L'adjectif *iḥ*[19] y est déterminé par le visage, vu de profil (Gardiner D 19). Le mot *sṯy*, "parfum," curieusement écrit pour former un cadrat parfait avec le signe qui précède, y est suivi, comme d'habitude, du déterminatif de la pustule (Gardiner Aa 2). Quant au nom divin, il se lit *Pp*. Sans entrer dans la discussion de cette appellation énigmatique qui a servi, à la Basse Epoque, à former des noms théophores de divers types,[20] nous ferons seulement remarquer qu'il est caractéristique de la Basse Egypte et qu'il fut particulièrement à la mode dans l'anthroponymie de la région d'Héliopolis.[21]

Les noms du type *iḥ sṯy + nom divin* sont uniquement féminins; voici les exemples que nous en avons relevé:

1. *'Iḥ-sṯy-'Imn* sur la stèle d'Ankhefenmout, conservée à Croydon;[22] il ne s'agit pas, comme l'a cru l'éditeur du monument, d'une dame Setamon, qui porterait le titre mystérieux *iḥḳ*.

2. *'Iḥ-sṯy-Pp*, le nom de la mère d'Amenemope-em-hat, ne nous est connu que par deux autres exemples, attestés respectivement sur une stèle, conservée à Francfort,[23] et sur un canope de l'ancienne collection N.-Cl. Peiresc dont nous ignorons le lieu de conservation actuel.[24]

3. *'Iḥ-sṯy-(Sḫmt, B3stt* ?) apparaît sur un bronze d'Harpocrate qui faisait autrefois partie de la collection Moïse Levy de Benzion au Caire; dans son catalogue manuscrit de la collection, conservé à la Fondation Egyptologique Reine Elisabeth de Bruxelles, J. Capart lui a assigné le nº 254. Le nom, dont la fin est

13. Gustave Lefebvre, "La statuette du Louvre E 10366," *Revue d'égyptologie* 1 (1933) p. 100–104.

14. Giovanni Kminek-Szedlo, *Catalogo di Antichità Egizie* (Torino, 1895) p. 158 (Bologna 1829, collationné sur photo).

15. George Steindorff, *Catalogue of the Egyptian Sculpture in the Walters Art Gallery* (Baltimore, 1946) pl. CXVI, 171C (Baltimore, Walters Art Gallery 171).

16. Hermann Ranke, *Die ägyptischen Personennamen* I (Glückstadt, 1935) p. 415, 7.

17. *Wörterbuch* II, *Belegstellen*, p. 724.

18. Ajouter à l'unique exemple, cité par le *Wörterbuch* II, *Belegstellen*, p. 724: Karl Piehl, "Doit-on accepter l'hypothèse d'un règne simultané d'Apriès et d'Amasis? *Zeitschrift für Aegyptische Sprache und Altertumskunde* 28 (1890) p. 10 (Stockholm 1); Henri Gauthier, *Cercueils anthropoïdes des prêtres de Montou* I (Le Caire, 1913) p. 495 (Caire 41068); Borchardt, *Statuen und Statuetten* IV, p. 137–138 (Caire 1269); British Museum 41516 (inédit); Anvers 284 (inédit).

19. *Wörterbuch* I, p. 120.

20. Ranke, *Personennamen*, signale les types suivants: *ir.f-n-ḥsj-n-pp* (p. 40, 12), *p3-dj-pp* (p. 123, 12; 126, 18, 19), *p3.f-ṯ3w-m-'wj-pp* (p. 127, 26), *ppjj-mr-itf.s* (p. 132, 4), *s3.t-pp* (p. 288, 17), *ṯs-pp-pr.ṯ* (p. 393, 27).

21. Voici les noms contenant l'élément *pp* que nous avons relevés sur des monuments héliopolitains: *ir.f-n-ḥsj-n-pp* (Alfred Wiedemann et Balthasar Pörtner, *Aegyptische Grabsteine und Denksteine aus verschiedenen Sammlungen* III [Strassburg, 1906] p. 32–35; la stèle provient vraisemblablement de la région de la première cataracte mais appartient à une famille héliopolitaine); *p3-dj-pp* (De Meulenaere, *Surnom*, p. 11, nº 30 et 31); *ṯs-pp-pr.t* Ahmed bey Kamal, "Rapport sur les fouilles faites dans la montagne de Sheikh Saïd," *Annales du Service des Antiquités de l'Egypte* 10 (1910) p. 154; Henri Gauthier, "A travers la Basse-Egypte," *Annales du Service des Antiquités de l'Egypte* 21 [1921] p. 33); *p3.s-ṯ3w-m-'wj-pp* (Steindorff, *Egyptian Sculpture*, pl. CXVI, 171B).

22. Eric Uphill, "The Stela of 'Ankhefenmut," *The Journal of Egyptian Archaeology* 43 (1957) p. 1–2, pl. I.

23. Wiedemann et Pörtner, *Aegyptische Grabsteine*, p. 32–35.

24. Jurgis Baltrušaitis, *La quête d'Isis* (Paris, 1967) p. 105, fig. 6.

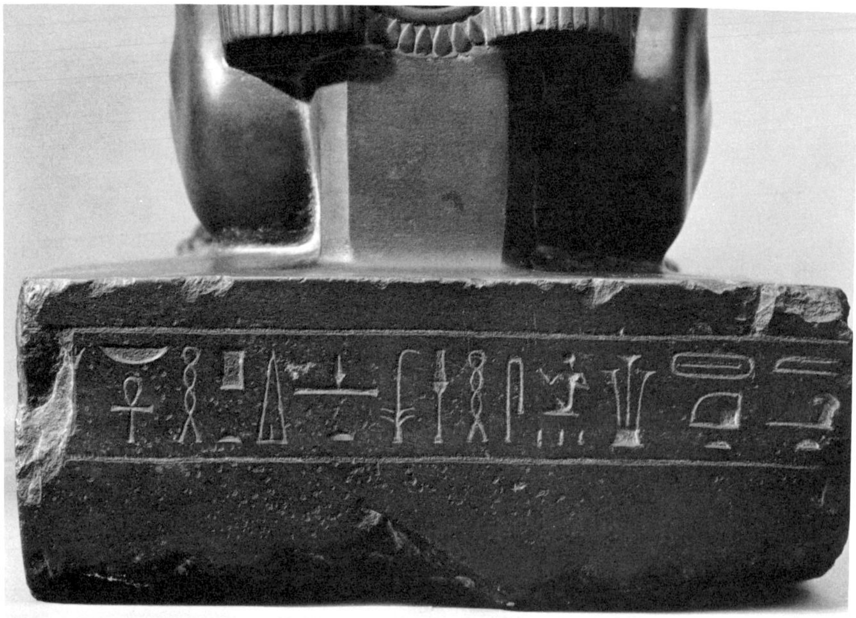

FIGURE 2 Inscription du socle, face

FIGURE 3 Inscription du socle, suite (à gauche du lecteur)

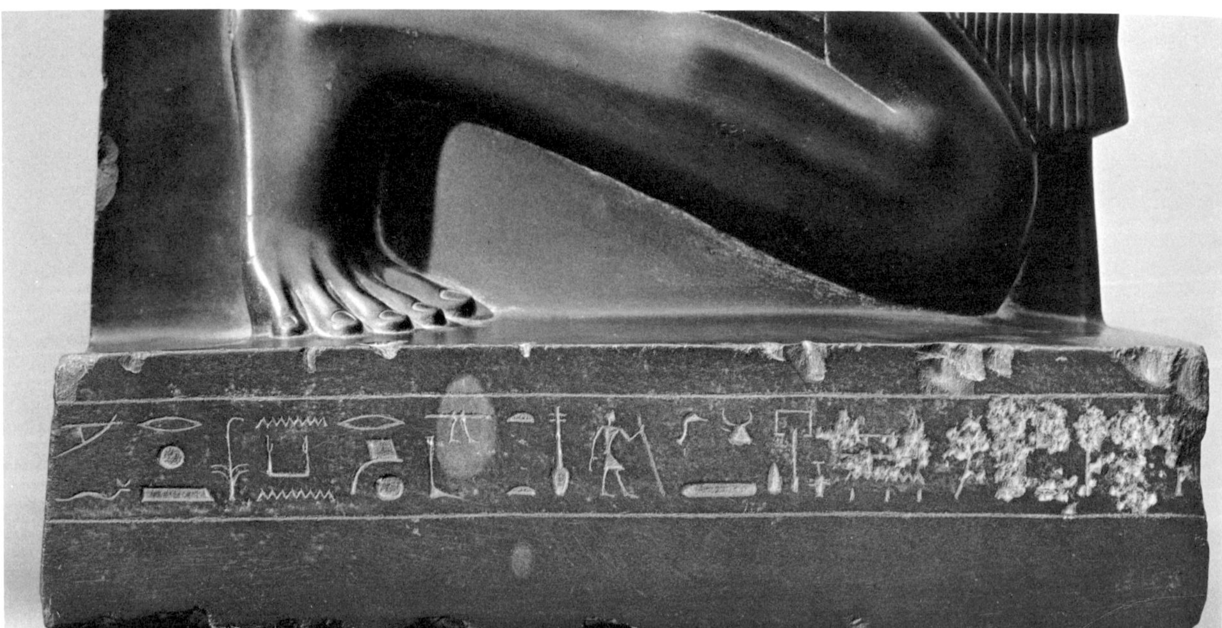

détruite, appartient à une femme, épouse d'un nommé Pétébast et mère d'un nommé Pétémihôs.[25]

Le contenu religieux des noms que nous venons d'analyser est intéressant. Que des anthroponymes formés sur le parfum que dégagent les divinités soient uniquement réservés à des femmes, ne doit pas nous étonner: dans l'épisode de la naissance divine d'Aménophis III, représentée dans le temple de Luxor, Amon ne s'est-il pas uni à la reine-mère après l'avoir éveillée par son divin parfum?[26]

(*f*) Celle-ci commence par une orthographe tout à fait exceptionnelle [hiéroglyphes] au lieu de l'habituel *di.tw*.

INSCRIPTION DU SOCLE (FIGURES 2–4)

(→)[27] "Proscynème à Ptah, seigneur d'Ankh[taoui] (*a*), et à Sekhmet, la grande, l'aimée de Ptah, pour qu'ils donnent (*b*), une offrande: pain, bière, bétail et volaille, une belle vieillesse, arriver à l'état d'*imakhou*, pour le *ka* connu véritable du roi, son aimé, le chef des chanteurs, Amenemope-em-hat."

(←) "Le directeur des chanteurs du Nord, Amenemope-em-hat, né de Ih-set-pep (*c*), il dit: ô Provisions alimentaires, ô Grands qui présidez aux Maisons Hautes et qui procurez du pain à Ptah, puissiez-vous [me] donner du pain et de la bière (*d*), [car] je suis son *imakhou*; alors vos noms demeureront dans son temple."

(*a*) Comme semble l'indiquer une trace du premier signe, la lacune à l'angle droit du socle était occupée par le groupe [hiéroglyphes] *t³wy*.[28]

(*b*) La partie que nous avons soulignée dans la traduction a été martelée. D'après les traces, on est tenté de restituer [hiéroglyphes]. On ne saurait préciser exactement la cause de ce martelage intentionnel du

25. En se fondant sur l'onomastique, on pourrait supposer que ce bronze provient de Léontopolis (cf. Jean Yoyotte, "La ville de Taremou (Tell el-Muqdâm)," *Bulletin de l'Institut Français d'Archéologie Orientale* 52 [1953] p. 190–192).

26. Sur le parfum des dieux, cf. en particulier Hellmut Brunner, *Die Geburt des Gottkönigs* (Wiesbaden, 1964) p. 50–51.

27. La flèche indique quel est, sur l'original, la direction de l'écriture.

28. Sur Ankhtaoui, voir Maj Sandman-Holmberg, *The God Ptah* (Lund, 1946) p. 214–215.

FIGURE 4 Inscription du socle, suite (à droite du lecteur)

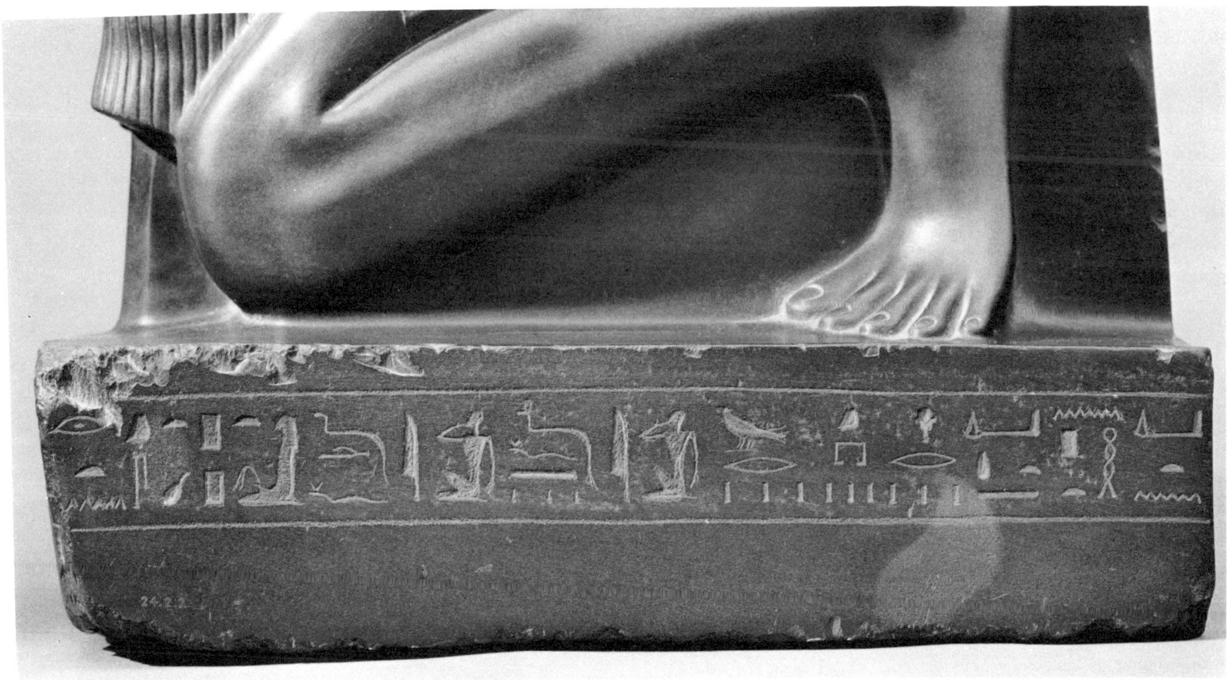

nom de la déesse Sekhmet; il ne semble pas que d'autres cas en aient été signalés.

(*c*) L'orthographe du nom confère au signe la valeur *iḥ*, apparemment nouvelle.

(*d*) Cette formule est empruntée au Livre des Morts, chapitre 106, dont les versions les plus anciennes, contrairement à celles du Nouvel Empire, ont Héliopolis comme lieu de l'action.[29] Les "Maisons Hautes" (*prw ḥryw*) sont connues comme se trouvant dans le voisinage de cette ville.[30]

La statue d'Amenemope-em-hat, malgré les mutilations qu'elle a subies, est un document d'un caractère assez inhabituel. Bien qu'elles consistent en formules traditionnelles, les inscriptions qui la couvrent ont fourni des données importantes pour l'anthroponymie égyptienne de Basse Epoque et ont permis, notamment, d'établir définitivement la lecture et le sens d'un nom propre curieux, mal défini jusqu'à présent. Le martelage du nom de la déesse Sekhmet et les allusions héliopolitaines, discrètement dissimulées dans l'onomastique, la titulature et la demande d'offrandes, posent d'autre part des problèmes d'ordre religieux qui méritent de retenir l'attention. Si les informations qu'on en tire demeurent provisoirement assez imprécises, on peut espérer qu'un examen approfondi de la question conduira à la découverte d'éléments qui seront susceptibles de l'éclaircir.

SUMMARY

The statue published here is a masterpiece of Saite art, although at first sight it does not offer any particular interest as a document. A headless figure, rather badly damaged at shoulders and arms, it represents a man kneeling on a base and holding a Hathor head before him. It was bought in 1924 by the Metropolitan Museum, and comes from the temple of Ptah at Memphis. Virtually unpublished, it was briefly discussed by H. G. Fischer and twice mentioned by the authors of *Egyptian Sculpture of the Late Period.*

Two iconographic criteria for the date are first considered. Both the deep vertical furrow that divides the chest and the traces of the striated wig are characteristic of works made in the second half of the seventh century B.C. These details would appear to date the statue in the reign of Psamtik I (664–610). The technical perfection with which the texts were carved, and the neat, careful forms of the hieroglyphs also suggest a date at the beginning of the Saite Period.

A translation of the inscription on the back pillar brings out these points: The title of the owner, Director of Singers of the North, is apparently hitherto unknown. The mention of a cult of Amen(em)ope probably refers, not to Luxor, but to Heliopolis; this suggestion is reinforced by the existence of other references to the worship of Amon at that site, and by the fact that the inscriptions of the statue seem to contain other Heliopolitan references. The name of the owner, Amen(em)ope-em-hat, is not known elsewhere. The determinative of his name, a seated person holding a scepter, is very frequent in the period to which the statue has been assigned. The name of the owner's mother, Ih-set-pep, is shown to be a rare type: *iḥ sṯy* + *divine name*, "pleasantly fragrant is the divinity NN." The divine name in this case is read *Pp*; it is characteristic of the Late Period, and was especially popular in theophoric names of the region of Heliopolis. Names referring to the perfume emitted by the gods are given only to women.

The inscriptions on the base are translated, including a section of the text referring to Sakhmet, which was deliberately hammered out. This is a unique case of mutilation of the goddess' name, and the reason for it is unknown. The writing of Ih-set-pep on the base gives the sign the value *iḥ*, which is apparently new. Part of the formula, with a mention of "High Mansions," is borrowed from chapter 106 of the Book of the Dead, the oldest versions of which refer to Heliopolis.

29. Charles Kuentz, "Le chapitre 106 du Livre des Morts," *Bulletin de l'Institut Français d'Archéologie Orientale* 30 (1931) p. 844–852.

30. Yoyotte, "Prêtres et sanctuaires," p. 96, note 1.

The Statue of Amenemope-em-hat[1]

EDNA R. RUSSMANN

Assistant, Department of Egyptian Art, The Metropolitan Museum of Art

THE STATUE whose inscriptions have been analyzed by Herman De Meulenaere in the preceding article is of such high quality that one cannot help particularly regretting the fact that it has lost its head. But this defect has the compensatory advantage of focusing attention on the modeling of the body. In its overall character, as well as in its details, the statue is a consummate example of the artistic trends, both of its period and of the part of Egypt where it was made (Figures 1–3).[2]

Carved in a dark green schist[3] that has a few lighter patches characteristic of this stone (for example, on the left breast and below the right eye of the Hathor head), and polished to a velvety surface typical of the early Late Period,[4] the statue is modeled with great attention to certain details of anatomy. The break at the neck has left enough traces at the back to show that the figure wore a striated wig that fell to the level of the shoulders.[5] The transition from neck to trunk is rather abrupt: the two meet in a clearly demarcated, rounded

1. Even more than their earlier counterparts, Egyptian statues of the Late Period suffer from inadequate publication or no publication at all. Since this study is primarily concerned with the minute details that make up a style and that can be judged only by a comparison of many contemporary objects, it could not have been undertaken had I not had the good fortune of being allowed access to the photographic files of the Corpus of Late Egyptian Sculpture at The Brooklyn Museum. I am grateful to Bernard V. Bothmer, Curator of Egyptian and Classical Art, for granting me permission to use them extensively in the preparation of this article; the extent of my debt will be apparent in the many references in the notes. Where possible I have added bibliographical references to CLES citations, especially when the statues are illustrated, though the picture may not show the detail under discussion. I am deeply indebted to Henry G. Fischer for numerous ideas and references; in many respects I am simply expanding his remarks on the statue under discussion in his article "Anatomy in Egyptian Art," cited in notes 7 and 8. I also wish to thank Dr. Fischer and Professor Bothmer for reading the article in manuscript and for their many helpful suggestions.

2. Metropolitan Museum of Art, accession 24.2.2. The height is 64 cm. The base measures 28 cm. wide, 42 cm. deep, 10.5 cm. high. The area of the break at the neck is 12.7 cm. deep at the middle of the back pillar and 19.8 cm. wide at its widest part. For bibliography on the statue see De Meulenaere's notes 3 and 4.

3. As it is called in standard Egyptological usage. Technically, it is a sedimentary rock, a greywacke; see A. Lucas, *Ancient Egyptian Materials and Industries* (London, 4th ed., rev. and enlarged, 1962) pp. 419–420.

4. In contrast to the highly polished harder stones preferred in later times: Bernard V. Bothmer et al., *Egyptian Sculpture of the Late Period* (Brooklyn, 1960), p. 5. Since the term "early Late Period" will be used repeatedly in this article, I should define my use of it at the outset. The Late Period proper is generally taken to extend from the XXVth Dynasty, ca. 740–656 B.C., to the end of Ptolemaic rule in 30 B.C. (Bothmer's periodization in *ESLP*, pp. xxx–xxxi, includes even the Roman Period, 30 B.C.–A.D. 324, when Egypt was no longer an independent political entity). Since the concern here is with art history rather than political periods, "early Late Period" refers to the XXVth Dynasty and the first reign of Dynasty XXVI, that of Psamtik I. The works of this brief span form, on the whole, a coherent body. Similarly, by "early XXVIth Dynasty" and "early Saite" I mean works dating to Psamtik I, but do not exclude pieces that may be slightly later, insofar as they reflect the earlier style rather than the new currents that first become visible during the reign of Psamtik II. This terminology is a matter of necessity as well as of convenience, for many works still cannot be more precisely dated.

5. The striated wig was once thought to have been confined to Dynasty XXV and the first two reigns of Dynasty XXVI (*ESLP*, p. 2), but at least two statues are now known that show its use in the time of Apries: Cairo J.E. 38021 (CLES; unpublished) and Lausanne Eg. 9 (CLES; for bibliographical references see note 60). In general, however, its appearance on a XXVIth Dynasty statue suggests a date early in the period.

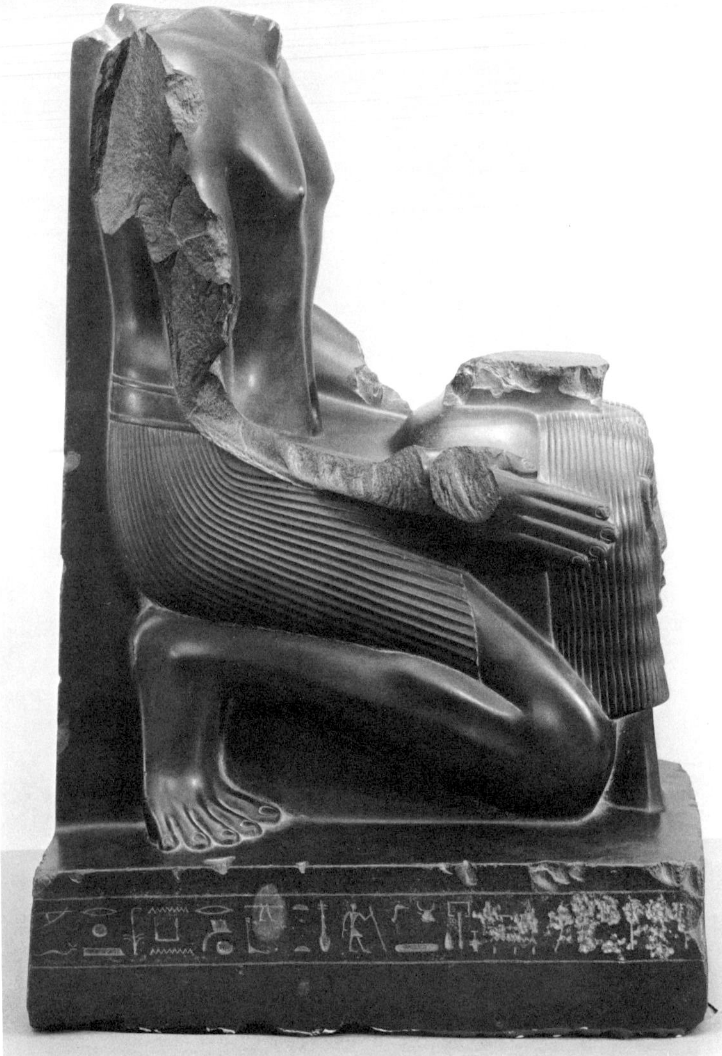

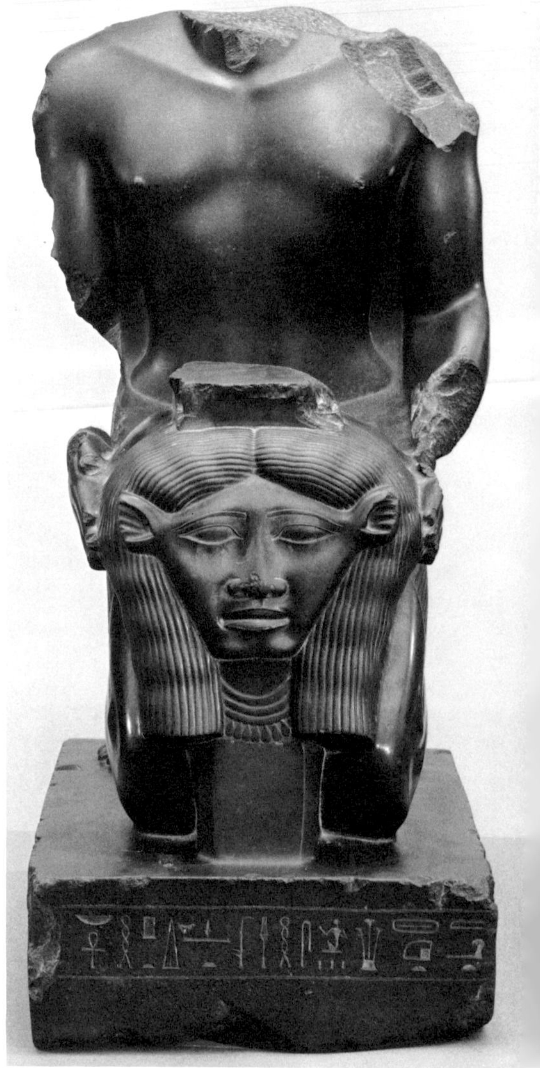

FIGURES 1–3
Kneeling statue of Amenemope-em-hat. Early XXVIth Dynasty. The Metropolitan Museum of Art, Rogers Fund, 24.2.2

line, characteristic of Egyptian sculpture. Set well under the neck, but no lower than they usually appear, are the collarbones, carved as obliquely curving ridges with the sternal notch well marked.[6] The rounded pectorals, with protuberant nipples, are quite prominent, their projection emphasized by the receding line of the lower torso. They are separated by a broad, shallow depression that runs the length of the trunk, becoming most noticeable in the area just above the round navel. The rib cage is indicated only very lightly, as a slight rounding in the receding line of the torso, and the abdomen, though differentiated from the hips, is very flat. The impression is one, not only of muscularity, but of considerable tension, as if the figure had taken a deep breath and was holding it, pulling in his stomach at the same time.[7]

The same muscularity is evident in the shoulders and arms, despite the damage they have suffered. The left shoulder has been broken at the front and the right shoulder at the back, but we can still see the way in which their broadness curves into the bulging muscles of the upper arm. This bulge is particularly apparent

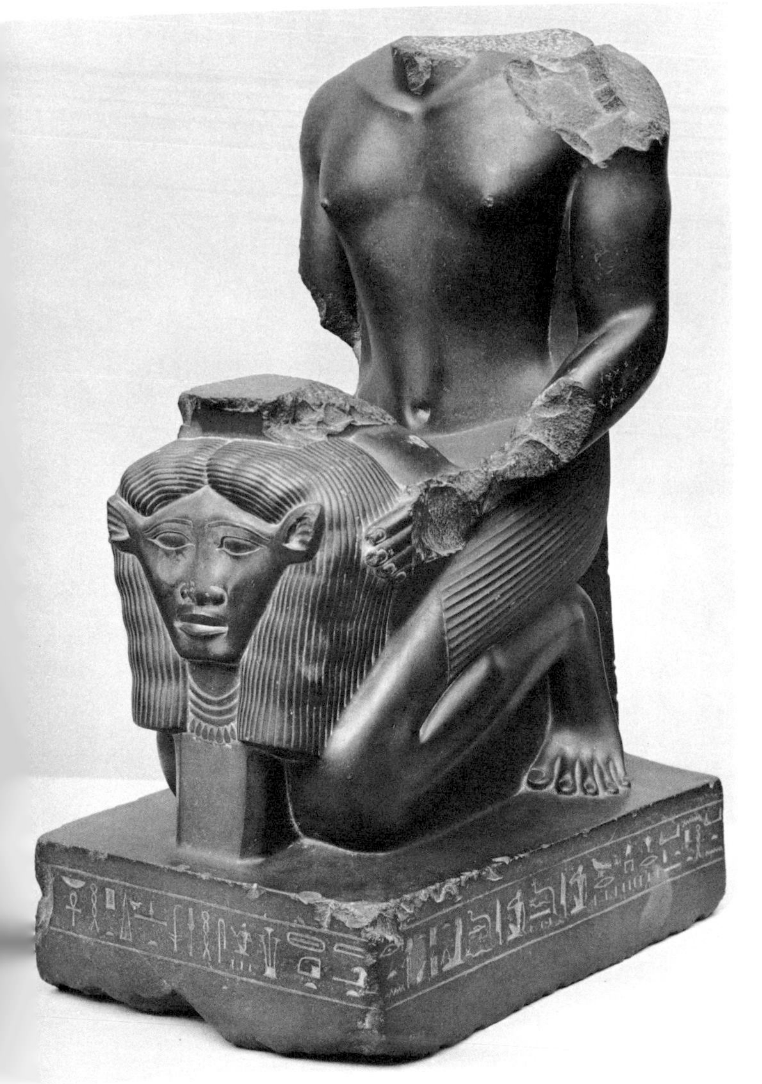

from the back (De Meulenaere's Figure 1) where, on the left side, one can also see a slight bunching of the flesh of the arm slightly below the armpit. The lower arms have suffered badly, the left one being lost for over half its length along with most of the hand, and the right one broken off altogether from slightly above the elbow. But enough remains of the left forearm to show how the muscle is tensed below the elbow, creating an oblique, almost angular surface. A curious contrast to the tension and muscularity of the body is formed by the hands, particularly the right one, which is almost fully preserved. They are modeled with equal care, the nails being clearly shown and the cuticles subtly indicated, but they are flat and lifeless, without any hint of bones, tendons, or joints. Such a "hieroglyphic" hand, little more than a symbolic notation for its real-life counterpart, is characteristic of even the most carefully modeled Egyptian sculptures, especially when the hand, as here, is flat, rather than flexed or fisted.

The figure wears a short pleated kilt, as we can clearly see at both sides, where the pleats are indicated by fluting. But at the front the lap is treated as a smooth flat shelf. Nor is there at the front any indication of the belt that can be seen behind the arms.

The legs show the same combination of broad generalizing treatment and attention to specific anatomical details: the kneecaps are large smooth convex surfaces without any indication of the bone structure, but the bulge of flesh at the inner fold of each knee, caused by its bending, is carefully modeled, to the point of slight

6. This unnaturally slanted collarbone is typically Lower Egyptian; it may be well observed on a statue of a Mendesian official contemporary with the piece under discussion, Palermo 145 (Henri Wild, "Statue d'un noble mendésien du règne de Psamétik Ier," *BIFAO* 60 [1960] pp. 43–67, pls. I–V, especially pl. II; *ESLP*, no. 20, pl. 18). In this case, however, the sternal notch is not indicated. On the other hand, the sternal notch is well marked, although the collarbones themselves are very faint, on Baltimore, Walters Art Gallery 22.79 (George Steindorff, *Catalogue of the Egyptian Sculpture in the Walters Art Gallery* [Baltimore, 1946] no. 154, pl. 24). The slant tends to be less pronounced in Upper Egyptian sculpture, where the collarbones are sometimes nearly horizontal (*ESLP*, pp. 29–30). Though often more prominent than in earlier periods, the collarbones are by no means always indicated, even on works of high quality; they do not seem to be present, for example, on Cairo C.G. 647 (Mentuemhat, Dyn. XXV/XXVI: Ludwig Borchardt, *Statuen und Statuetten von Königen und Privatleuten im Museum von Kairo* [*Catalogue général des antiquités égyptiennes du Musée du Caire*] II [Berlin, 1925] pl. 119), on Cairo C.G. 42243 (a son of Mentuemhat: Georges Legrain, *Statues et statuettes de rois et de particuliers* [*Catalogue général*] III [Cairo, 1914] pl. XLIX) or on British Museum 1132, datable to Psamtik I and probably from Karnak (CLES; *The Illustrated London News* 234, no. 6246 [Feb. 21, 1959] p. 313 [illustrated]; Herman De Meulenaere, *Orientalistische Literaturzeitung* 55 [1960] col. 129; De Meulenaere, "La famille des vizirs Nespamedou et Nespakachouty," *Chronique d'Egypte* 38 [1963] p. 73 f). Although collarbones are often represented on Theban sculptures, it is my impression that they are somewhat less frequent, and certainly less prominent, on the better works than they are in the north.

7. This tension has been noted by Henry G. Fischer in "Anatomy in Egyptian Art," *Apollo* 82 (Sept., 1965) p. 173.

exaggeration. Two muscles are clearly shown on the lower leg, the peroneus longus, forming a ridge down its length, and the gastrocnemius or calf muscle.[8] Representation of the latter, as we shall see, is quite rare in Egyptian sculpture. The peroneus longus terminates in the rounded projection of the anklebone. The feet are fairly high-arched, and the toes are quite naturalistically splayed. But, like the fingers, they appear boneless and jointless, although the nails are painstakingly marked. They are, in fact, typical Egyptian feet.[9]

The object held by Amenemope-em-hat is an architectonic element, consisting of a rectangular post with beveled corners, surmounted by a capital in the shape of the head of the goddess Hathor, on which rests an abacus. The whole forms a cult symbol of Hathor (Figure 4).[10] Although the presentation of an emblem of this deity by a kneeling statue enjoyed a certain popularity during the reign of Psamtik I,[11] most such statues hold a Hathor sistrum.[12]

The modeling of the emblem has received as much attention as that of the figure itself. The heavy striated wig of the goddess, with its soft undulations running at

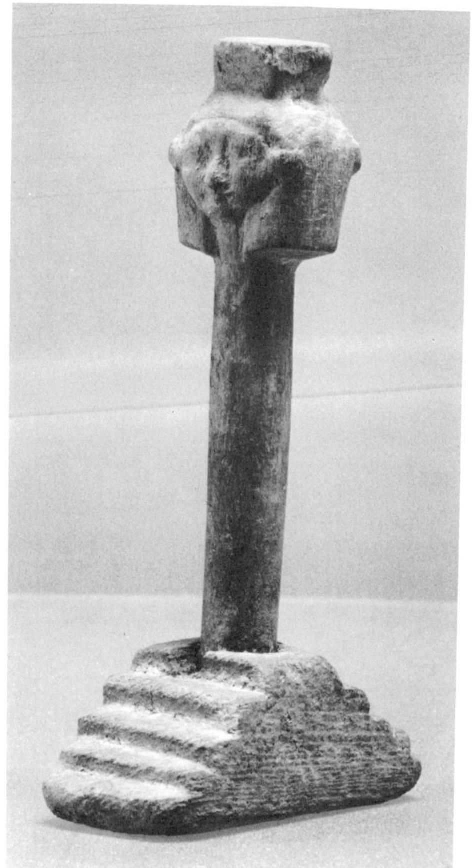

FIGURE 4

Hathor symbol found at Deir el Bahri (photo: Metropolitan Museum)

8. Both the calf muscle and the skin fold at the knee were observed by Fischer, "Anatomy," p. 173.

9. The feet occasionally receive a little more attention in this period than has been devoted to them in the present example. The cuticles of the toenails are indicated on Brussels E. 8039 (CLES; unpublished); Copenhagen Thorvaldsen's Museum 356, which must have been a very carefully modeled work, to judge from the lower body, which is all that survives (CLES; Henry Madsen, "Les inscriptions égyptiennes du Musée Thorvaldsen à Copenhague," *Sphinx* 13 [1910] p. 56, no. 356); and Durham 509, also a very fine work (CLES; S. Birch, *Catalogue of the Collection of Egyptian Antiquities at Alnwick Castle* [London, 1880] pp. 69–71, pl. A, right [opposite p. 72; drawing]. The toes are widely separated and unusually splayed on East Berlin 10289, where the knees are also farther apart than usual (CLES; Königliche Museen zu Berlin, *Ausführliches Verzeichnis der Aegyptischen Altertümer* [Berlin, 1899] p. 258 [not illustrated]). Occasionally the toes are not splayed; on Cairo J.E. 37425 this causes an awkward inward bend to the little toe (CLES; unpublished). On a few statues the tops of the toes are rounded and well differentiated from the flat, depressed surfaces of the nails: Cairo J.E. 36908 (asymmetrically squatting: CLES; Hermann Kees, "Der Vezir Hori, Sohn des Jutjek," *ZÄS* 83 [1958] pl. XIIb; Kenneth A. Kitchen, *The Third Intermediate Period in Egypt [1100–650 B.C.]* [Warminster, 1973] §194, p. 228. Both mistakenly give the number as 86908.); J.E. 37425 (CLES); Durham 509 (CLES). But even these do not approach the degree of naturalism that occurs sporadically in other periods, such as the quite realistically rendered toes of the early XXVIIth Dynasty statue of Hekatefnakht, Louvre E. 25499 (CLES; Jacques Vandier, "La statue de Hekatefnakht," *La Revue du Louvre* 14 [1964] pp. 57–66).

10. This example was found at Deir el Bahri (Herbert E. Winlock, "The Museum's Excavations at Thebes," *Bulletin of the Metropolitan Museum of Art*, Part II, *The Egyptian Expedition 1922–1923* [Dec., 1923], fig. 34, p. 39; dated by the excavator to the XVIIIth Dynasty). Though far more crudely worked, it is strikingly similar to the object held by the statue under discussion, differing chiefly in the facts that, like a true Hathor column, it appears to have two heads of the goddess, and that it is mounted on a stepped base.

11. *ESLP*, p. 16. Perhaps there is some connection between the appearance of such statues and the fact, noted by Labib Habachi, that Hathor capitals are popular in temple architecture during the XXVIth Dynasty, whereas they are less often used from Dynasty XIX through Dynasty XXV (*Tell Basta* [*Supplément aux ASAE*, Cahier no. 22] [Cairo, 1957] p. 66).

12. J. J. Clère, who is making a study of sistrophorous statues, seems to feel that such variations are of no great significance, since the face of the goddess is the most important element ("Propos sur un corpus des statues sistrophores égyptiennes," *ZÄS* 96 [1969] p. 2). And indeed, the distinction between Hathor sistrum and Hathor capital is often very indistinct, for the sistrum clearly incorporates a Hathor capital, and the capital is typically surmounted by a superstructure which has elements of the sistrum.

right angles to the striations, shows the closest sort of simulation of wavy tresses known to ancient Egyptian conventions. The necklace, carved on the post under her chin, is cut with precision. But the cow-eared face, though modeled with great finesse and refinement, has a curious, flattened look, particularly evident in the nose, which is very flat and therefore also seems extremely broad at the nostrils. All the features, when studied individually, share in the general disproportion: the plane of the eyes and their plastic brows is too flat; the area between eye and nose is too depressed; the cheeks seem to push in on the nose and on the mouth, which is too wide for the sharply narrowed jaw; the square chin is excessively short. In fact, the head, although modeled in the round, is conceived two-dimensionally and handled with the same conventions usually applied to Egyptian representations of the full face in relief.[13] This is quite deliberate, for it is not really the head of the goddess that is depicted, but her symbol on a capital. The fact that relief, rather than sculptural, conventions are normally applied to such capitals may indicate that a mask of the goddess is represented, or perhaps, with typical Egyptian logic, that a face was applied to the stone block which formed the actual supporting element.[14] In any case, the avoidance of naturalistic, three-dimensional modeling emphasizes the abstract, symbolic quality of the emblem.

The pose of a figure kneeling and holding before it the emblem or image of a deity is not an innovation of the Late Period, but it is by no means one of the most ancient types of Egyptian statuary. Although kneeling figures exist from the earliest period on,[15] the theo-

13. The technical difficulties arising from the attempt to reproduce essentially three-dimensional forms in relief, and the conventions established in the attempt to cope with them, may clearly be seen in the frontal figure represented on a relief from Giza now in the Boston Museum of Fine Arts: William Stevenson Smith, *A History of Egyptian Sculpture and Painting in the Old Kingdom* (London, 2nd ed., 1949) pl. 57c, dated by Smith to the VIth Dynasty (p. 190). Once established, the conventions remained applicable to all faces represented frontally in relief; thus they are also used in the XXVIth Dynasty for the faces of large anthropoid stone sarcophagi (Marie-Louise Buhl, *The Late Egyptian Anthropoid Stone Sarcophagi* [Copenhagen, 1959] no. A, 5, fig. 3 [Leiden 149]; no. A, 7, fig. 5 [MMA 07.229.1, here shown in profile view]; no. B, a1, fig. 4 [Boston 30.834]). The same treatment is accorded the full-face hieroglyph *ḥr* throughout its history. See, for example, the representations collected by Karol Myśliwiec in "A propos des signes hiéroglyphiques '*ḥr*' et '*tp*'," *ZÄS* 98 (1972) figs. 2, 3, 5, 7, 9, 12, 13, 14. His conclusion (pp. 86, 96) that the hieroglyph represents a foreigner seems to me most unlikely, for the peculiarities of the face are precisely those we have already noted on a Hathor capital and on representations of Egyptians at various periods.

14. Certainly the Hathor capital was not conceived as a full head. As Eugen von Mercklin notes in "Das aegyptische Figuralkapitell," *Studies Presented to David Moore Robinson* (Saint Louis, 1951) pp. 198–199, the majority of such capitals have either two or four faces of the goddess; he quotes (p. 198) von Bissing's interesting comment that the Hathor capital is a "Pfeiler, gegen den das Kultbild gelehnt ist." Von Mercklin's illustrations in *Antike Figuralkapitelle* (Berlin, 1962) figs. 1–39, give a good idea of the Hathor mask as it appears on capitals of various periods. For similar Hathor heads on sistra held by statues of this period, see, for example, Cairo C.G. 646 (CLES; Borchardt, *Statuen* II, pl. 119), British Museum 1132+1225 (CLES; for other references, see note 6), Louvre E. 25388 (CLES; François Lenormant, *Collection de feu M. Raifé* [Hôtel Drouot, March 18–23, 1867] p. 2, no. 5 [not illustrated]).

15. The history of the kneeling statue in Egyptian art prior to the XVIIIth Dynasty is a curious one. Throughout this long period there is not, to my knowledge, a single example clearly made to represent the owner in his own right, in tomb or temple. The IInd or IIIrd Dynasty kneeling man Cairo C.G. 1 (Edward L. B. Terrace and Henry G. Fischer, *Treasures of the Cairo Museum* [London, 1970] no. 2, pp. 25–28) was most likely, as Fischer has observed (p. 25), a funerary priest of royal cults; it is noteworthy that the statue was found at Memphis; it was probably put in a temple of the owner's service, rather than in his tomb. Even greater subservience is indicated in the placement of the kneeling funerary priest Cairo C.G. 119 (Borchardt, *Statuen* I, pl. 26): it was deposited in his master's tomb and was, for all practical purposes, a servant figure. A still greater degree of humility marks the little figures kneeling to present vessels; these begin in the Archaic Period (Zaki Y. Saad, *Royal Excavations at Helwan [1945–1947]* [*Supplément aux ASAE*, Cahier 14] [Cairo, 1951] pl. xxiv; ivory; the figure represented is a hunchback) and continue into the Middle Kingdom (MMA 22.1.124: Bodil Hornemann, *Types of Ancient Egyptian Statuary* III [Copenhagen, 1957] no. 640; faience, representing a dwarf); one might also mention the numerous servant statues kneeling to grind grain (James H. Breasted Jr., *Egyptian Servant Statues* [*Bollingen Series* XIII] [Washington, D.C., 1948] pls. 15–21), and kneeling bound captives, such as MMA 47.2 (William C. Hayes, *The Scepter of Egypt* I [New York, 1953] fig. 67, p. 114). There seems little doubt that a connotation of servitude was attached to the pose, rendering it unsuitable for representation of the deceased. Nevertheless, it could be applied to the king as servant of the gods: the Brooklyn statuette 39.121 depicts Pepy I kneeling and holding out two *nw* pots. This pose is very rare before Dynasty XVIII, but it is repeated twice without variation in the Middle Kingdom (Jacques Vandier, *Manuel d'archéologie égyptienne* III *La statuaire* [Paris, 1958] pp. 221, 683, referring to Cairo C.G. 42013 [Sesostris III] and Karnak-Nord E. 133 [Amenemhat III]), suggesting that a specific ritual was involved. The kneeling statue of Queen Sobkneferu, from the end of the XIIth Dynasty, is apparently too damaged for one to be sure of the position of the hands. Vandier believes they rested flat on the thighs (*Manuel* III, p. 215, note 2), but Labib Habachi thinks it possible that they held vessels (Habachi, "Khatâ'na-Qantîr: Importance," *ASAE* 52 [1952–54] p. 459; the statue is illustrated in his pl. viiB).

phoric kneeling statue has its origins in the early Eighteenth Dynasty, when both Hatshepsut and her great official Senenmut had themselves portrayed in this fashion.[16] From such exalted beginnings the pose no doubt acquired a high status for, following a period of lesser popularity in the later Eighteenth Dynasty,[17] it was frequent in the later New Kingdom and Third Intermediate Period for statues of large size and careful work.[18] The Late Period inherited it without interruption; in fact, many of the earliest examples, especially at Thebes, reproduce not only the pose but also the elaborate pleated, long-skirted costume of the earlier examples.[19] But such fussy dress did not accord with the severer principles of a period that, in general, looked further back in time for its models, and almost from the beginning of the Late Period we find the New Kingdom pose rendered in the costume of a much earlier and simpler time: a short kilt, often the pleated *šndyt*, with chest and arms bare of any ornaments.[20] In keeping with its period, our statue wears the *šndyt*, for the short kilt quickly prevailed, apparently during the reign of Psamtik I. Not until the Persians conquered Egypt, establishing a dynasty now called the Twenty-seventh, was a kneeling figure again shown wearing a long skirt. But then it was the peculiar garment, wrapped high on the chest, that the Persians may have introduced.[21]

These remarks on the costume of kneeling figures have brought us to a tendency well known for the early Late Period, the borrowing from styles of the past, which is known as archaism.[22] This archaizing fashion affected almost all aspects of the art of the Twenty-fifth and early Twenty-sixth Dynasties.

16. Hatshepsut: MMA 23.3.1, 23.3.2. Senenmut: Cairo C.G. 579 (Borchardt, *Statuen* II, pl. 99), Cairo J.E. 34582 [Bernard V. Bothmer, "More Statues of Senenmut," *Brooklyn Museum Annual* XI [1969–70] figs. 15–18, pp. 140–142); Brooklyn 67.68 (Bothmer, "More Statues," fig. 1, pp. 125–143; the article also discusses two examples in private collections); Louvre E. 11037. The importance of such statues may be realized in the fact that Senenmut himself apparently commissioned a copy of one of them (the copy is MMA 48.149.7; see William C. Hayes, "Varia from the Time of Hatshepsut," *Mitteilungen des Deutschen Archäologischen Instituts, Abteilung Kairo* 15 [1957] pp. 84–88). For a discussion of the significance of statues representing private people holding images see Hans Bonnet, "Herkunft und Bedeutung der naophoren Statue," *Mitteilungen des Deutschen Archäologischen Instituts, Abteilung Kairo* 17 (1961) pp. 91–98. Bonnet makes some telling points in looking to cult practices, and in particular festival processions, as origins for the type. One wonders, however, whether "genugsam Gelegenheiten . . . bei denen man in die Knie sank" (p. 96) are sufficient to account for the adoption of the kneeling pose at this time, especially since, as he himself points out, this kind of explanation is not very satisfactory for the naophorous block statue.

17. Examples can be cited, however, for the reigns of Amenhotep II (Cairo C.G. 935: Borchardt, *Statuen* III, pl. 158), Tuthmosis IV (Brooklyn L93.88.2) and Amenhotep III (Cairo C.G. 901: Borchardt, *Statuen* III, pl. 156).

18. Dynasties XIX and XX: Brooklyn 36.615; numerous examples in Cairo: Legrain, *Statues* II (Cairo, 1909), passim; MMA 33.2.1 (Hayes, *Scepter* II [New York, 1959] fig. 219, p. 351). Dynasty XXII: Cairo C.G. 42208 (Legrain, *Statues* III, pl. XV), C.G. 42229 (Legrain, *Statues* III, pls. XXXVI, XXXVII).

19. East Berlin 8806 (CLES; Labib Habachi, "A Statue of Bakennifi, Nomarch of Athribis," *Mitteilungen des Deutschen Archäologischen Instituts, Abteilung Kairo* 15 [1957] p. 73); Cairo C.G. 1056 (CLES; Borchardt, *Statuen* IV, p. 41: illustrated with a sketch); Cairo C.G. 42245 (CLES; Legrain, *Statues* III, pl. LI); Louvre E. 25388 (CLES; Lenormant, *Coll. A. Raifé*, p. 2, no. 5); Saint Louis 221:24 (CLES; *ESLP* no. 3, pl. 3). Most of these examples belong to the brief span conventionally labeled Dynasty XXV/XXVI. Cairo C.G. 42245, for example, was made for one Horsiese, a brother of the great Mentuemhat who flourished both under the Kushites and Psamtik I: the statue could have been made in either dynasty. That the continuation of this costume spanned both dynasties is proved by the Saint Louis statue, where XXVth Dynasty Divine Consorts are named, which make it datable to the time of Taharqa, and by the Louvre piece, which not only represents a well-known official of Psamtik I, but also has the cartouche of that king.

20. The same Horsiese of note 19 also had himself represented in this fashion: Cairo C.G. 42244 (Legrain, *Statues* III, pl. L) and so did his brother, Mentuemhat, Cairo C.G. 42237, holding a stela (Legrain, *Statues* III, pl. XLVII); he wears a necklace, consisting of a pendant hung from several strands of beads.

21. For the form and dates of this skirt see *ESLP*, pp. 75, 76; Bernard Bothmer has recently called attention to the continued representation of the garment in the fourth century ("The Head That Grew a Face," *Miscellanea Wilbouriana 1* [Brooklyn, 1972] p. 30). Its representation on kneeling figures of the XXVIIth Dynasty include Cairo C.G. 726 (*ESLP*, no. 65, pls. 61–62) and Louvre E. 25499 (Vandier, "La statue," figs. 1–3).

22. See *ESLP*, p. xxxvii and passim, especially p. 30. Much work needs to be done on Egyptian archaism and imitation of the past in all periods. Besides the well-known proclivity of the initiators of a new era in Egyptian history for systematically looking to the great monuments of the past, especially in royal art, there are sporadic and seemingly isolated instances throughout. We do not know, for example, why Amenhotep, son of Hapu, had himself portrayed, under Amenhotep III, in Middle Kingdom guise, complete to pose, costume, and a very creditable imitation of a late XIIth Dynasty face (Cairo C.G. 42127: Legrain, *Statues* I [Cairo, 1906], pl. LXXVI. Another of his statues also shows him with a Middle Kingdom wig: Cairo C.G. 551: Borchardt, *Statuen* II, pl. 92. Its pose may also invoke the Middle Kingdom; compare the statues of Sesostris III found at Deir el Bahri: one is illustrated in E. A. Wallis Budge, *Egyptian Sculptures in the British Museum*

Having so long a past on which to draw, the Egyptians of this period were fairly eclectic in their borrowing. They rejected much of the late New Kingdom tradition, which had been handed down through the Third Intermediate Period,[23] and turned instead to the two great preceding periods. From the Middle Kingdom they took a few statue types, such as the seated cloaked figure[24] and the seated crosslegged scribe with legs covered by a long skirt.[25] The distinctive Middle Kingdom wig with pointed lappets appears,[26] and the heavy-lidded face so well known from the later Twelfth Dynasty enjoys a brief vogue.[27]

Even more striking, however, is the attempt to simulate the art of the Old Kingdom. It shows itself in the revival of the crosslegged scribal pose for important officials,[28] in the preference we have noted for the most characteristic Old Kingdom costume, the short kilt, and in the representation of certain types of long unused wigs.[29] But the sculptors of the early Late Period were not concerned simply to reproduce obsolete details of fashion. They sought to recreate the spirit of the earlier works, their purity and above all their strength.[30] What they saw in the early art, and the ways in which they utilized it, make a fascinating chapter in the history of art.

We have observed that the torso of the Metropolitan statue is bisected by a broad shallow groove running its length. This somewhat unnaturalistic manner of organizing the trunk, known on other sculptures of the early Twenty-sixth Dynasty,[31] is characteristic of the

[London, 1914] pl. xi). The XIXth and XXth Dynasties are full of such throwbacks: Sety I recalls the style of Tuthmosis III (MMA 22.2.21; Hayes, *Scepter* II, fig. 210, p. 335); Bakenkhonsu, under Ramesses II, borrows a specific peculiarity of representing the eye from the time of Amenhotep III (Munich Gl. W. A. F. 38: Hans Wolfgang Müller, *Die ägyptische Sammlung des bayerischen Staates* [Munich, 1966] fig. 38); Ramesses III imitates (almost to the point of caricature) the features of Tutankhamun (Boston 75.10: Vandier, *Manuel* III, p. 402, note 4, pl. cxxx, 2), to name only a few of the most obvious examples. Many, no doubt, have not even been recognized.

23. That it is a deliberate rejection is emphasized by the brief survival of such details as the elaborate double wig with its striated and echeloned patterns. Carried over into the early XXVth Dynasty (British Museum 1514: CLES; Jean Leclant, *Enquêtes sur les sacerdoces et les sanctuaires égyptiens à l'époque dite "éthiopienne,"* [Cairo, 1954] V B, pp. 78–83, pls. xviii–xxii), it occurs occasionally until the time of Psamtik I (British Museum 1132: CLES; for bibliography see note 6), then disappears from the scene. See also *ESLP*, p. 12.

24. Examples are given in *ESLP*, p. 2; since the works listed here that have a provenance are both Theban, one should perhaps also mention the Memphite example discussed elsewhere in *ESLP* (no. 10, pp. 11–12). A seated cloaked statue is the subject of Irmgard Woldering's "Zur Plastik der Äthiopenzeit," *ZÄS* 80 (1955) pp. 70–73.

25. British Museum 1514 (CLES; for bibliography see note 23), early XXVth Dynasty. Note that the Middle Kingdom pose is here combined with a New Kingdom double wig.

26. Leningrad, Hermitage 18112, dated to the reign of Psamtik I (CLES; I. A. Lapis and M. E. Mat'e, *Drevneegipetskaia Skul'ptura v Sobranii Gosudarstvennogo Ermitazha* [Moscow, 1969] pl. 70, no. 108, pp. 106–107 [with further bibliography]).

27. Cairo J.E. 37866 (Leclant, *Enquêtes*, pls. i–iv; the head is quite well illustrated in Woldering, "Zur Plastik," pl. viii, fig. 3); Richmond 51-19-3 (*ESLP*, no. 8, p. 9, pl. 8; also see the discussion of this phenomenon, with further examples, on pp. 2, 8).

28. *ESLP*, pp. xxxvii, 23; I cannot help wondering if the high status of this pose, which is used for large and important sculpture (such as Cairo J.E. 37341: CLES; Rudolf Anthes, "Der Berliner Hocker des Petamenophis," *ZÄS* 73 [1937] p. 30, no. 4; Palermo 145: Wild, "Statue d'un noble mendésien," pp. 43–67, pls. i–v; Richmond 51-19-4: "Herald of the King," *Bulletin of the Virginia Museum of Fine Arts* 25, no. 8 [April, 1965] pp. 1–2), is not conferred to some extent by its use in the New Kingdom to represent the highest officials in the land. Such statues as the two belonging to Amenhotep, son of Hapu (Cairo J.E. 44861: Terrace and Fischer, *Treasures*, no. 25, pp. 117–120, and J.E. 44862), that of Horemheb (MMA 23.10.1: Hayes, *Scepter* II, fig. 190, p. 305), and the pair made for the vizier Paramessu (Cairo J.E. 44863, 44864) must have been visible and well known; indeed, the Amenhotep and Paramessu statues were still in situ when excavated at Karnak (Georges Legrain, *Au pylône d'Harmhabi à Karnak*, *ASAE* 14 [1914] pp. 15–16, pls. i–iii).

29. Such as the striated wig half covering the ears, on a head found at the temple of Mut at Karnak (Sale Catalogue, *An Important Group of Ancient Egyptian Sculpture*, Christie, Manson and Woods, Dec. 5, 1972, no. 4); or the short echeloned wig: East Berlin 8803 (CLES; *Ausführliches Verzeichnis*, p. 83 [not illustrated]); Louvre A 89 (CLES; Bernard V. Bothmer, "Apotheosis in Late Egyptian Sculpture," *Kêmi* 20 [1970], no. x, pl. xi, fig. 18); both of the latter are standing statues.

30. The thoroughness of this attempt to reproduce both the spirit and details of Old Kingdom works is best seen in the standing statues. One of the most interesting is Louvre A 89 (CLES; Bothmer, "Apotheosis," no. x, pl. xi, fig. 18), datable to Dynasty XXV and possibly from Heliopolis. It was probably an Old Kingdom model that led the owner to have himself shown with a woman standing beside him, for women are not often represented in this period (*ESLP*, p. xxxvii). The bipartite modeling of the torso, the muscular arms, everything is in the best Old Kingdom tradition (see notes 32, 35). Even such a tiny detail as the indication of ridges across the sternum has been taken over from the prototype. (For an Old Kingdom example of this feature, MMA, 48.111, see Fischer, "Anatomy," p. 172 and fig. 6, p. 173.)

31. Other examples of the median line rendered as a broad depression may be found in *ESLP*, nos. 18 and 19, pl. 16.

period; it clearly derives from the narrower line that divides the torso of all fine Old Kingdom statues.[32] There can be no doubt that the torso of our figure is meant to recall those of the Old Kingdom; the firmness and reticence of the modeling and the lack of emphasis on the rib cage strongly recall Old Kingdom models.[33] But there is considerable difference between the torso of Amenemope-em-hat and his Old Kingdom predecessors. The pectorals are more prominent than is usually the case earlier, and the sharply receding line beneath them is a late development. The flattened stomach is very far removed from the Old Kingdom models.[34] The result is that, whereas an Old Kingdom torso gives an impression of equilibrium, even of a healthy relaxation, the later work is taut and strained. There is a sense, also reflected in the limbs, of almost painful tension.

The tensed forearm of the Metropolitan statue provides another example of borrowing from the Old Kingdom. From the Fourth Dynasty on the muscles of the lower arm are often quite prominently marked, not only when the fist is clenched,[35] but even when, on seated statues, one hand rests palm down on the thigh, and one might expect to find the corresponding forearm relaxed.[36] The emphasis, therefore, is on the muscularity of the arm, but a certain effect of tautness is produced. This effect is much reduced in the Middle Kingdom; although the muscle continues to be indicated, both when the hand is fisted and when it is open,[37] the modeling tends to be considerably more subdued. The generally slacker body modeling of the New Kingdom dispenses with the forearm muscle. When the kneeling figure holding a large object appears in this period the arms, like the hands, are represented as perfectly relaxed.[38]

The early Late Period revival of the tensed forearm is most successful on examples that are closest to Old Kingdom types, especially on the standing figure. When the fists are clenched, the effect, though often somewhat exaggerated, is not dissimilar to the prototypes.[39] But its application to the theophoric kneeling pose[40] creates an effect of strain unlike anything found

32. Such as the Vth Dynasty Ranofer (Cairo C.G. 19), well illustrated in *Encyclopédie photographique de l'art, Le Musée du Caire* (Éditions 'TEL,' 1949) pl. 23. This narrow median line appears on early Late Period standing figures: Boston 07.494 (*ESLP*, no. 9, pl. 9); Cairo J.E. 38045 (CLES; Bothmer, "Apotheosis," no. XII, pl. XI, fig. 20); Cairo J.E. 39403, 39404 (representing Taharqa: Jean Leclant, *Recherches sur les monuments thébains de la XXVe dynastie dite éthiopienne* [Cairo, 1965] pls. LXIV, LXV); Louvre A 89 (CLES; Bothmer, "Apotheosis," no. X, pl. XI, fig. 18).

33. Thus I must take issue with the view expressed in *ESLP*, p. XXXV, that bipartite torso modeling in the early Late Period derives from Middle Kingdom sculpture. On the statue of Sesostris I (MMA 25.6; Hayes, *Scepter* I, fig. 110, p. 180; Fischer, "Anatomy," fig. 1, p. 169), cited in *ESLP*, p. 11, as a prototype, the median line is quite subdued and the rounding of the rib cage even hints at a tripartite organization of the torso; the whole is much more subtle and rounded than Old Kingdom sculpture. Professor Bothmer himself, in class and in conversation, has often spoken of the Old Kingdom elements in such statues as the one under discussion.

34. Nor have I been able to find very close parallels for this particular feature on statues contemporary with the Metropolitan piece. It is, however, a detail very difficult to observe in photographs.

35. A few obvious examples are the right arm of the seated Chephren (Cairo C.G. 14: Borchardt, *Statuen* I, pl. 4), the arms of the king in the Mycerinus dyad (Boston 11.1738: Cyril Aldred, *Old Kingdom Art in Ancient Egypt* [London, 1949] fig. 26) and of Ranofer on the statue cited in note 32.

36. The arms are equally tense, for example, on the seated Vth Dynasty Nykare, although one hand is fisted and the other flat (MMA 52.19: Hayes, *Scepter* I, frontispiece). Some Old Kingdom seated figures, especially those from royal workshops, show a clear differentiation between the arms of the fisted and the relaxed hands: thus the Mycerinus colossus (Boston 09.204: Smith, *History of Egyptian Sculpture*, pl. 13b), but also the nonroyal statue Cairo C.G. 85 (Borchardt, *Statuen* I, pl. 19). The higher profile of the right arm in such cases apparently reflects the fact that the fist is upright with the little finger at the bottom, so that the arm is turned, radius and ulna being lined up vertically. This differentiation on seated statues may also be observed in the Middle Kingdom when the fist is held vertically (MMA 33.1.1: Vandier, *Manuel* III, pl. LXXVII, 2), but the arms are equally flat when the fisted hand rests palm down.

37. As, for example, on the beautifully modeled seated Sesostris I, MMA 25.6. For views of the two arms, compare the illustrations in Hayes, *Scepter* I, fig. 110, p. 180, and Fischer, "Anatomy," fig. 1, p. 169.

38. This appears to be true of all the examples cited in notes 16–18, except for Cairo C.G. 571, where the surface of the arm is too broken to be observed.

39. The muscles are especially noticeable on the standing statues Cairo C.G. 42243 (CLES; Legrain, *Statues* III, pl. XLIX; generally over-muscled), Louvre A 89 (CLES; Bothmer, "Apotheosis," no. X, pl. XI, fig. 18) and Boston 07.494 (CLES; *ESLP*, no. 9, pl. 9). A peculiarity of the arms of the last-named statue is the marking of the elbows at the back as two circles. The same detail may be observed on another statue of the same man, Cairo J.E. 36991 (CLES; unpublished; mentioned in *ESLP*, p. 11) and on Louvre A 111, which is datable to Psamtik I (CLES; Charles Boreux, *Guide-catalogue sommaire. Musée National du Louvre. Département des Antiquités Égyptiennes* II [Paris, 1932] p. 463 [not illustrated]).

40. On kneeling statues the tensed forearm is customarily indi-

in the Old Kingdom. It is as if the hands were being pressed tightly against the object they hold; it is not a pose one would want to keep for all eternity. The detail represents another departure from the spirit of the model, even though the outward form is revived.

The striving for tension in Amenemope-em-hat's figure is probably the result of an effort to impart a sense of vitality and life. It impelled the sculptor, not only to exaggerate his borrowings, but even to add new details not to be found in the prototypes. The clearest example of this elaboration on the model is to be seen in the muscles of the leg.

A strong, muscular lower leg was part of the ideal of the perfect Old Kingdom body. Strength was conveyed by the rather curious convention of marking the long muscles as a series of vertical grooves and ridges, sometimes quite sharply faceted.[41] Behind them the bulging calf was often indicated in a fairly naturalistic manner.[42] The importance of the lower limbs may be seen in the fact that the legs are sometimes treated with some detail on statues where the modeling of the rest of the body is rather summary.[43] The emphasis on the legs and their stylization as well were revived in standing figures of the early Late Period.[44] A similar treatment was accorded kneeling statues, once they were freed from the long, concealing skirts. But the several ridges and grooves of the standing statues' legs are reduced to a single ridge, usually quite pronounced, connecting with and ending in the ankle bone.[45] The area above this ridge often bulges slightly, marking the calf.[46] The sculptor of the Metropolitan statue, however, has gone one step further. He has indicated the calf muscle as a separate entity, with the lower end clearly defined. The recognition of this particular muscle is without precedent in Egyptian art of any earlier period.

The representation of the calf muscle was not invented for this statue, however. The earliest surviving

cated by a ridge that creates an angular surface, as on the statue under discussion. The feature is not always as pronounced, however, as on the Metropolitan piece. Examples are British Museum 41561 (CLES; unpublished; mentioned in *ESLP*, p. 20), Louvre E. 9417 (CLES; unpublished; mentioned in *ESLP*, pp. 38, 44); Turin 3043 (CLES; unpublished). Exactly the same stylization is used when the hands rest flat on the thighs: Athens N.M. 8 (CLES; Karl Piehl, "Textes égyptiens inédits," *Proceedings of the Society of Biblical Archaeology* 10 [1888] p. 532, no. 4; D. Mallet, "Quelques monuments égyptiens du Musée d'Athènes," *Recueil de Travaux* 18 [1896] p. 10, no. 1267; inscriptions only); East Berlin 10289 (CLES; Staatliche Museen zu Berlin, *Führer durch das Berliner Ägyptische Museum* [Berlin, 1961] p. 77 [not illustrated]); Copenhagen, Ny Carlsberg Glyptothek 591 (Otto Koefoed-Petersen, *Catalogue des statues et statuettes égyptiennes* [Copenhagen, 1950] pl. 117); Leiden 1942/11.5 (W. D. van Wijngaarden, "Een Granieten Beeld uit de Saïtische Tijd," *Oudheidkundige Mededelingen uit het Rijksmuseum van Oudheden te Leiden* n.s. 29 [1948] pl. 1, pp. 1–2). Occasionally the muscle is more specifically marked: on Moscow 4997 (CLES; V. V. Pavlov, *Egipetskaia Skul'ptura* [Moscow, 1949] pl. 47), its ridge is set off from the rest of the arm by a shallow groove, and on Louvre E. 5778 the ridge is curved and very prominent (CLES; unpublished).

41. As on the preserved leg of a standing statue of Chephren, Cairo C.G. 16 (Borchardt, *Statuen* I, pl. 4), or the standing Mycerinus from his triads (as Cairo J.E. 40679: Terrace and Fischer, *Treasures*, no. 7, p. 46).

42. As, for example, on the Vth Dynasty statue of Ranofer, cited in note 32; the legs are best seen in Terrace and Fischer, *Treasures*, no. 10, p. 59.

43. Examples from Borchardt, *Statuen* I, include Cairo C.G. 76 (pl. 17), C.G. 137 (pl. 31), C.G. 146 (pl. 33), C.G. 172 (pl. 38).

44. For example, on the statue of Horemakhet, Dynasty XXV/XXVI, Cairo C.G. 42204 (Terrace and Fischer, *Treasures*, no. 36, p. 159). The calf is especially pronounced, and even seems to be set off by grooves on a contemporary statue representing a son of Mentuemhat, Cairo C.G. 42243 (CLES; Legrain, *Statues* III, pl. XLIX). The bulge of the calf may be very pronounced on other poses, for example, on the asymmetrically squatting statue Cairo J.E. 36908 (CLES; see note 9 for bibliographical references), and often on cross-legged scribe statues, most notably on the powerful, unstylized legs of Cairo J.E. 37341 (CLES; Anthes, "Der Berliner Hocker," p. 30, no. 4).

45. The ridge is unusually broad and rounded on Durham 509 (CLES; for bibliography see note 9). Sometimes it is formed by parallel grooves, as on Cairo C.G. 42237 (CLES; Legrain, *Statues* III, pl. XLVII) and Zagazig 171 (CLES; unpublished). So nearly omnipresent is it on kneeling statues that it may be well to mention the few cases where it could not be observed: Cairo J.E. 36987 (CLES; unpublished), J.E. 37855 (CLES; unpublished), Lyon, Collection Varille I (CLES; Paul Tresson, "Sur deux monuments égyptiens inédits," *Kêmi* 4 [1931] pp. 126–144, pls. VIIb, VIII, IX), Louvre N. 5406 (CLES; Boreux, *Catalogue-Guide* II, p. 453 [not illustrated]; Paul Pierret, *Recueil d'inscriptions inédites du Musée Égyptien du Louvre* II [Paris, 1878] p. 13). The convention did not originate with the Late Period; it is one of the few carry-overs from the New Kingdom, for it occurs on kneeling figures from Senenmut on: it may be seen on the statue of Senenmut, Brooklyn 67.68, despite the fact that he wears a long skirt (Bothmer, "More Statues," fig. 1; the detail is not visible on the photograph). Usually the skirt hides all leg modeling, but the continuation of the detail may be seen on Brooklyn 36.615 (Dynasty XIX: a son of Ramesses II).

46. As on Cairo C.G. 656 (CLES; Borchardt, *Statuen* III, pl. 121), Cairo J.E. 36674 (CLES; unpublished), J.E. 42880 (CLES), Copenhagen, Ny Carlsberg Glyptothek 591 (CLES; Koefoed-Petersen, *Catalogue des statues*, pl. 117), Rome, Vatican 167 (CLES; *ESLP*, no. 56, pl. 51, fig. 123).

FIGURE 5
Kneeling statue of Pedimahes. End of XXVth Dynasty. Moscow, Pushkin Museum, 4993. (Photo: courtesy CLES)

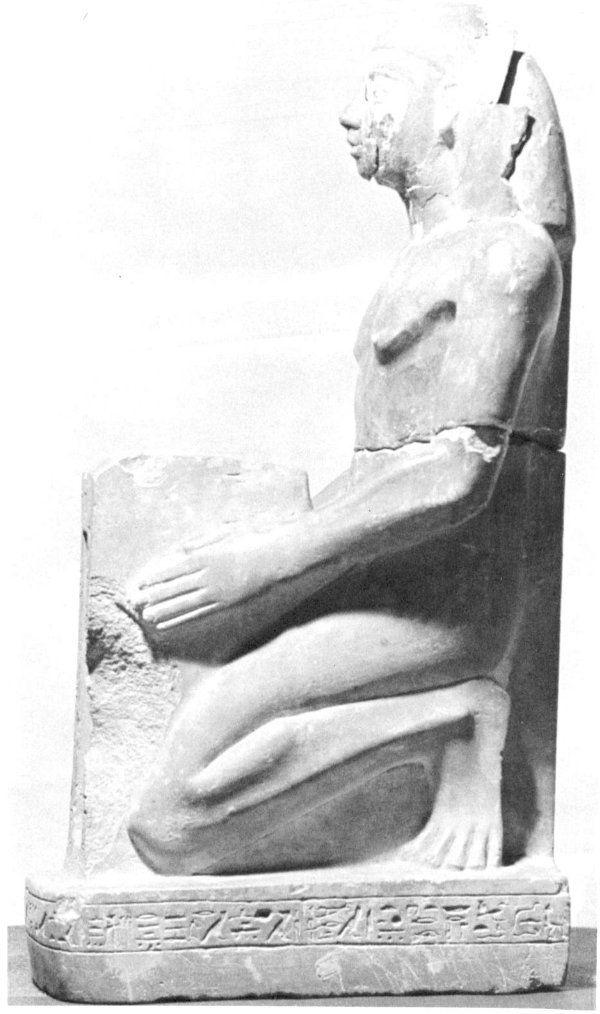

example I have been able to find is on a statue believed to date to the end of the Twenty-fifth Dynasty (Figure 5).[47] It was made for a man named Pedimahes,[48] and is a product of Lower Egypt, coming from Tell el Muqdam, the ancient Leontopolis.[49] As the illustration shows, it is not an especially attractive statue, nor is the workmanship of the best quality. Though the muscle is shown, it is clearly as a convention rather than the result of direct observation; there is, for example, no attempt to show the bulge of flesh at the inside of the knee.

Thus it seems probable that Pedimahes' statue was made to follow the example of better works, very likely products of the royal workshops, which were usually the sources of innovation in Egyptian style, especially when close observation and attention to detail were involved. That the muscle was indicated on royal statues in the early Twenty-sixth Dynasty is shown by a badly damaged kneeling figure of Psamtik I in Copenhagen (Figure 6),[50] where the detailing of the calf muscle is in keeping with the care exhibited in the decoration of the wide belt. Indeed, most of the statues that display the gastrocnemius muscle are made with some care, and many, like Amenemope-em-hat's, are of the highest quality. One finds, for example, that, in most cases where the torso is preserved, the collarbones are marked—by no means an invariable feature of Late Period Egyptian sculpture.[51]

Originating in the north and, we may suppose, in a royal workshop, the convention was quickly picked up in Thebes. It appears on a statue from the Karnak Cachette, of the end of the Twenty-fifth or beginning of the Twenty-sixth Dynasty.[52] But it did not win acceptance in the south: to the best of my knowledge this is the only example with a Theban provenance.

Two early Twenty-sixth Dynasty statues whose provenance is not known, one in Paris and one in Moscow, show again the connection between representation of the calf muscle and detailed modeling of the body generally.[53] On both the collarbones are strongly marked, and on the Paris statue even a fold of flesh at the armpit

47. Moscow 4993. A front view of this statue is illustrated in Bothmer, "Apotheosis," pl. VIII, fig. 6. For its probable date, see the Bothmer article, p. 42.

48. Another statue of this man, Brooklyn 64.146, is discussed in Bothmer, "Apotheosis," and illustrated in his pls. VI and VII.

49. Jean Yoyotte, "La ville de 'Taremou' (Tell el-Muqdâm)," *BIFAO* 52 (1953) no. 5, pp. 180–181, 185.

50. Nationalmuseet AAb 211: CLES; Marie-Louise Buhl, "Antiksamlingens Betydeligste Orientalia Erkvervet efter 1851," *Fra Nationalmuseets Arbejdsmark* (1952) p. 80, fig. 2 (front view); Hans Wolfgang Müller, "Ein Königsbildnis der 26. Dynastie mit der 'Blauen Krone' im Museo Civico zu Bologna," *ZÄS* 80 (1955) p. 54, fig. 1b (back view).

51. See note 6.

52. Cairo J.E. 38061, Dynasty XXV/XXVI, from the Karnak Cachette (CLES; Hornemann, *Types* III, no. 563; Herman De Meulenaere, "Les monuments du culte des rois Nectanébo," *Chronique d'Égypte* 35 [1960] p. 102, n. 6 [inscription]).

53. Paris, Petit Palais 308 (CLES; unpublished; mentioned in *ESLP*, see note 54) and Moscow 4997 (CLES; Pavlov, *Egipetskaia Skul'ptura*, pl. 47).

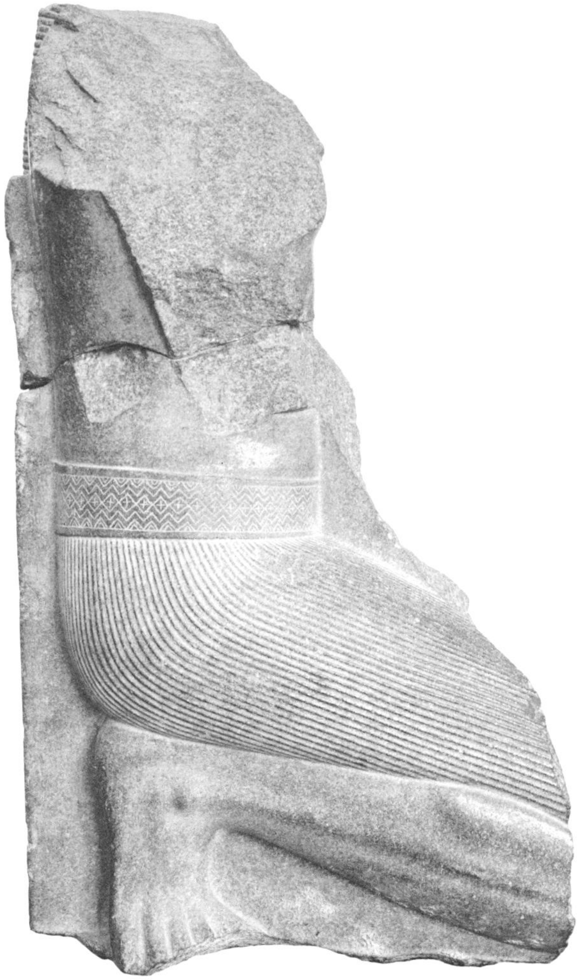

FIGURE 6

Kneeling statue of Psamtik I. Copenhagen, Nationalmuseet Antiksamlingen, AAb 211. (Photo: courtesy Nationalmuseet Antiksamlingen)

is indicated.[54] Both also show, to some degree, the bunching of skin at the bend of the knee, which the Karnak example apparently lacks. This skin fold, as well as the calf muscle, is also to be observed on two contemporary statues of which only the lower bodies are preserved.[55]

These examples show that by the end of the reign of Psamtik I the representation of the calf muscle was an accepted, if rather rare, feature for kneeling statues of some quality. It appears at least once during the short reign of Necho II.[56] Continued representations later in the dynasty show that the detail remained characteristic of northern rather than of southern sculpture. It appears on the statue of General Hor, an official of Psamtik II, which was found at Tell el Yahudieh in the Delta.[57] Also datable to the reign of Psamtik II are the two statues of Nekhthorheb on which the calf muscle is shown (Figure 7).[58] It is not known where these pieces were found, but a Lower Egyptian origin seems virtually assured for both.[59] Still later in the dynasty, datable to the reign of Apries, and also from

54. There are a number of unusual details on this interesting statue. Besides the face, discussed by Bothmer in *ESLP*, p. 20, one might mention the bulge of the collarbones at the front, the deep slit of the sternal notch, and the large, teardrop-shaped navel.

55. Hannover 1935.200.512, preserved from the hips down (CLES; unpublished) and Turin Cat. 3021, preserved from the waist down (CLES; Eberhard Otto, *Die biographischen Inschriften der ägyptischen Spätzeit* [Leiden, 1954] no. 42, p. 128). The Turin statue may come from Mostaï in the Delta, according to Jean Yoyotte in *Annuaire de l'École Pratique des Hautes Études* V^{e} section *Sciences religieuses* (1967–1968) p. 104.

56. East Berlin 11332 (CLES; *Ausführliches Verzeichnis*, pp. 256–257 [not illustrated]; Herman De Meulenaere, *Le surnom égyptien à la Basse Époque* [Istanbul, 1966] no. 45, p. 15). The northern connections of the owner of this statue are shown by a figure of Isis inscribed for him, from Sais, Cairo C.G. 39303 (Georges Daressy, *Statues de divinités* [*Catalogue général*] [Cairo, 1906] p. 326).

57. Manchester 3570, preserved from the waist down (CLES; W. M. F. Petrie, *Hyksos and Israelite Cities* [London, 1906] pls. 15, 20, pp. 18–19; De Meulenaere, *Le surnom*, no. 57, p. 18).

58. The statue illustrated is Louvre A 94. Its importance for Egyptian art history is considerable, for it represents one of the earliest examples in the dynasty of tripartite torso modeling (*ESLP*, p. 54). The bibliography for this piece is extensive; for references see De Meulenaere, *Le surnom*, no. 44, p. 14. The second statue of Nekhthorheb is British Museum 1646 (CLES; *The Cambridge Ancient History*, Volume of Plates II [Cambridge, 1928] pp. 118–119, fig. b). The date of these monuments has been established by G. Posener in "La date de la Statue A 94 du Louvre," *Revue d'Égyptologie* 6 (1951) pp. 234–235.

59. The inscription of Louvre A 94 invokes Thoth of both *Ḫmnw*, well known as Hermopolis Magna in Upper Egypt, present-day Ashmunein (Alan H. Gardiner, *Ancient Egyptian Onomastica* II [Oxford, 1947] pp. 79*–80*) and *Bʿḥ*, identified as the Delta Hermopolis, capital of the XVth nome of Lower Egypt, the modern Tell el Baqlieh (Henri Gauthier, *Dictionnaire des noms géographiques* II [n.p., 1925] p. 16; see also Labib Habachi, "Notes on the Delta Hermopolis," *ASAE* 53 [1955] pp. 441–480, and Yoyotte in *Annuaire* V^{e} section [1969–1970] p. 180). It is the Delta Hermopolis, however, that is named on the dominant right side of the statue. And the name *Ḫmnw* possibly in this case also refers to the Delta town, rather than its better-known Upper Egyptian counter-

FIGURE 7

Kneeling statue of Nekhthorheb. Dynasty XXVI, reign of Psamtik II. Paris, Musée du Louvre, A 94. (Photo: courtesy the Louvre)

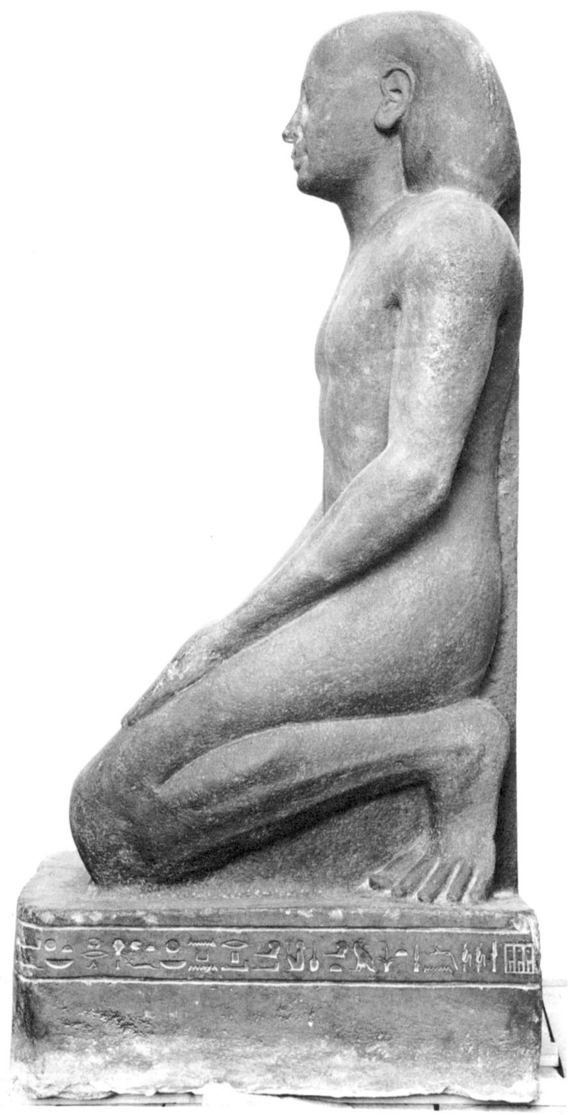

the north, are two more statues with calf muscles marked. One is in Lausanne and one in London.[60] Both of these are rather perfunctory and schematic in their modeling; on the Lausanne statue the collar-bones, though indicated, are rudimentary. This work is also one of the last datable examples of the striated wig,[61] so perhaps it was even intended to be a little old-fashioned.

It is interesting that, of the fifteen statues where the calf muscle could be observed,[62] only one is known to come from Thebes. The precise differences between northern and southern art in this period are difficult to describe, but they undoubtedly exist.[63] In light of what we know, it is not surprising that this detail was apparently a northern development. In the north there seems to have been a closer observation of the body and a more studied attempt to reproduce the sense of skin and flesh. The impulse is apparent in such very different examples as our statue with its extreme tautness and the relaxed, fleshy softness of the asymmetrically squatting Bes.[64] The south was more traditional in its approach to the body, more bound by the conventions. Theban statues tend to be much more "stony" than their northern counterparts, even when attempts are made to render fleshiness.[65]

I cannot pretend to have observed all the examples

part, for a mention of "Thoth, lord of *Ḫmnw*" has been found at Tell el Baqlieh with apparent local reference (Edouard Naville, *Ahnas el Medineh* [London, 1894] p. 24). Yoyotte, however, would apparently discount any special geographic significance in Delta references to Thoth of *Ḫmnw*; see his comments on a similar writing found at Tarrana in *Annuaire* Ve section (1969–1970), p. 184. That the provenance of the statue is indeed Tell el Baqlieh is confirmed in an unpublished study by Yoyotte, in the possession of Bernard V. Bothmer, where he lists it under this site. Nekhthorheb also had ties to Sais. The funerary formula of British Museum 1646 invokes Neith and Osiris at Sais, and another of his monuments was found there (Cairo C.G. 39275: Poseneṛ, "La date," p. 234).

60. Lausanne Eg. 9, head and arms broken off. From the region of Tell el Balamun (communication of Herman De Meulenaere to B. V. Bothmer) (CLES; Henri Wild, *Antiquités égyptiennes de la collection du Dr. Widmer* [Lausanne, 1956] pl. v, pp. 15–16; Emma Brunner-Traut, "Die Tübinger Statuette aus der Zeit des Apries," *ZÄS* 82 [1957–1958] no. 8, p. 95; De Meulenaere, *Le surnom*, no. 55, p. 17). British Museum 83, head and shoulders gone; possibly from Heliopolis (CLES; Brunner-Traut, "Die Tübinger Statuette," no. 6, pl. IV, p. 94 [with further bibliography].)

61. See note 5.

62. A final example, which cannot be more closely dated than the XXVIth Dynasty, and the provenance of which is not known, is Vienna 5772. It is headless and unfinished (CLES; unpublished).

63. This virtually unexplored topic is touched on in *ESLP*, especially pp. 29–31. That different tendencies should have existed is not surprising, given the political realities of the period: see Kenneth A. Kitchen, *Third Intermediate Period*, §356, pp. 395–396; §365, pp. 404–405.

64. Lisbon, Gulbenkian 158 (*ESLP*, no. 29, pl. 27, pp. 34–35). Note also the idiosyncratic treatment of the corolla of the nipples.

65. I am thinking particularly of the standing figure of Irigadiganen (Cairo J.E. 38018: *Encyclopédie photographique de l'art. Le*

of defined calf muscles on statues of the Twenty-fifth and Twenty-sixth Dynasties. Even had photographs of all extant works been available, it is the sort of detail that becomes invisible under inopportune angles of lighting.[66] But the examples I have found show that it seems to have developed shortly before the time when our statue was made; it continued throughout most of the Twenty-sixth Dynasty, but was never common, and it apparently disappeared before the end of the dynasty. I know no examples datable to Amasis, and in the Twenty-seventh Dynasty, though kneeling figures wearing short skirts are sometimes represented,[67] there seems to be no attempt to show the muscle.

But this feature had still not quite disappeared from Egyptian art, for it surfaces at least once more, in the fourth century B.C., on a kneeling statuette (Figure 8).[68] In this case, however, it is most perfunctory, merely an incised line that sets the calf off from the rest of the leg and curves to mark the lower end of the muscle. We are now very far from the Saite version—and yet, perhaps, not so far, for this little figure is one of the clearest examples of the archaistic trend of the Thirtieth and Thirty-first Dynasties. Looking to their past, as we have seen the Egyptians were so wont to do, these sculptors went no further back than the Twenty-sixth Dynasty for their models.[69] With its striated wig, its pleated kilt, and its sketchy calf muscle, the Chicago statuette must have derived from a sculpture very like the one discussed here.

Like its inscriptions, the style of the Metropolitan statue places it firmly into the early part of the Twenty-sixth Dynasty. Further comparisons, especially if parallels for the flattened stomach can be found, may help to refine this dating, but in the present state of our knowledge we cannot be more precise. In the modeling of the calf muscle the figure suggests its northern origin. With its careful workmanship and—apart from the head—its relatively good state of preservation, the statue is one of the finest examples of the art of this period.

FIGURE 8
Kneeling statuette of Wesirnakht, fourth century B.C. The Art Institute of Chicago, 10.243. (Photo: courtesy The Art Institute of Chicago)

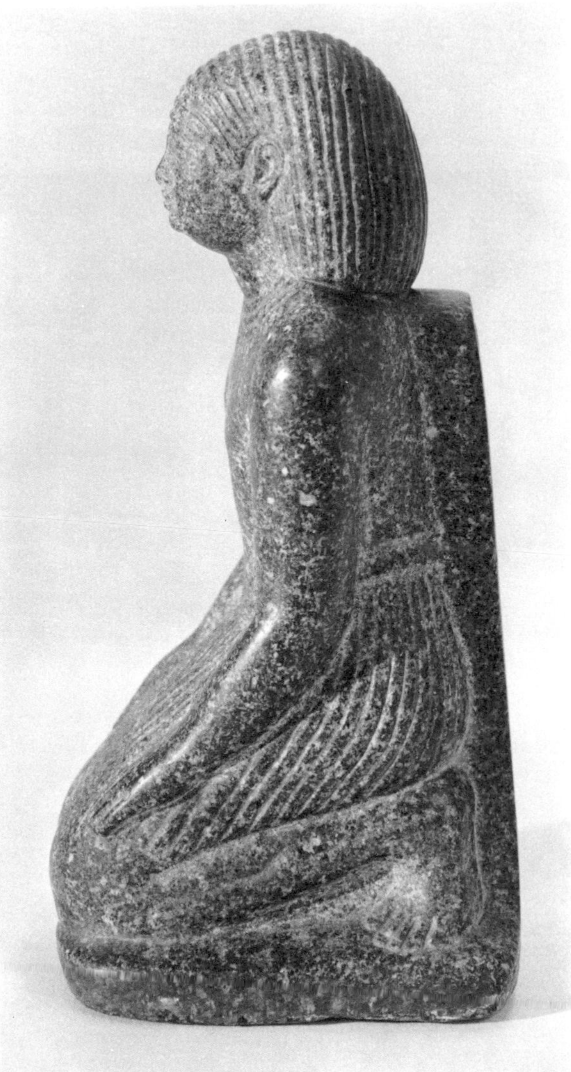

Musée du Caire [Éditions 'TEL,' 1949] pl. 173) and the asymmetrically squatting Harwa (Cairo J.E. 37386: Battiscombe Gunn and R. Engelbach, "The Statues of Harwa," *BIFAO* 30 [1931] pls. I–II; similar statues of the same man on pl. III).

66. For example, the calf muscle on Manchester 3570 (note 57), clearly visible in Petrie's publication, can scarcely be seen in that museum's photograph on file in CLES.

67. Cleveland 3955.20 (*ESLP*, no. 61, pl. 58, figs. 143–145); Louvre E. 25390+E. 25475 (*ESLP*, no. 57, pls. 54–55, figs. 132–134); Toronto 969.137.1 (W. B. Emery, "Preliminary Report on the Excavations at North Saqqâra 1966–7," *Journal of Egyptian Archaeology* 53 [1967] pl. XXIII, 1–2, p. 143); Turin Cat. 3034 (CLES; G. Maspero, "Rapport . . . sur une mission en Italie," *Recueil de Travaux* 4 [1883] p. 149, no. XXXVIII [inscription only]).

68. Chicago Art Institute 10.243 (*ESLP*, no. 91, pl. 85, figs. 226–227).

69. Thus their products are called archaistic, for they are patterned on works that are themselves archaizing; they are twice removed from the original. See *ESLP*, p. xxxvii and the remarks on the Chicago statuette, *ESLP*, pp. 114–116.

ADDENDUM: The frequent occurrence of archaism in Egyptian art, particularly art of the Late Period, and the problems involved in recognizing and evaluating it, have been much discussed in the above pages. A statue that came to my attention only after the manuscript had been completed serves to illustrate these points only too well. It is a Fifth Dynasty statue in wood representing one Akhtyhotep, found in his tomb at Saqqara. (Abd el-Hamid Zayed, "Le tombeau d'Akhtihotep à Saqqara," *ASAE* 55 [1958] pp. 127–137. The statue under discussion is briefly referred to, along with other statuary from the tomb, on p. 136; it is illustrated on pls. IX, XII, XIII, and XV. The size is not given). Although the piece is, in most respects, typical for the period, the workmanship is excellent. Its great interest for our purposes lies in the fact that the gastrocnemius muscle is clearly indicated on the back of the right leg. The advanced left leg has a bulging calf, but there is apparently no trace of the muscle (the different conformations of the two legs may be seen on Zayed's pls. XIII and XV). It would seem that we have here another example of the often subtle naturalism of the finest Old Kingdom sculpture: presumably the right leg is being tensed in the moment just before the heel is lifted off the ground to take another step.

This observation of an early representation of the calf muscle makes it seem quite probable that its depiction in the Late Period was not, as I had thought, an innovation. On the contrary, for this detail, as for so many others, the sculptors had revived an Old Kingdom usage; and, just as in the case of the tensed forearm muscle, they applied it to a different, and altogether less appropriate, pose. The detail can never have been common; it would seem, therefore, that sculptors of the early Late Period sought out the finest of Old Kingdom works as models. But the naturalism and close observation embodied in such pieces were of less interest to them than the depictions of individual muscles which they used quite arbitrarily to heighten the effect of tension in their sculpture. It may also be significant that Akhtyhotep's statue comes from the Memphite necropolis: exemplars from the same cemetery may account for the fact that representation of the calf muscle seems to be concentrated at Memphis and the Delta sites.

SOURCES ABBREVIATED

ASAE—Annales du Service des Antiquités de l'Égypte
BIFAO—Bulletin de l'Institut Français d'Archéologie Orientale
CLES—Corpus of Late Egyptian Sculpture, Department of Egyptian and Classical Art, The Brooklyn Museum
ESLP—Bernard V. Bothmer et al., *Egyptian Sculpture of the Late Period* (Brooklyn, 1960)
ZÄS—*Zeitschrift für Ägyptische Sprache und Altertumskunde*

The Mark of a Second Hand on Ancient Egyptian Antiquities

HENRY G. FISCHER

Lila Acheson Wallace Curator in Egyptology, The Metropolitan Museum of Art

A SURVEY OF THE QUESTION

WHILE THE SURVIVAL and present condition of ancient Egyptian monuments is largely a matter of chance and has little to do with their form or the content of their inscriptions, they often prove to have been altered for very specific reasons. In order of chronological sequence there are, first of all, the strictly contemporaneous changes made by the artist himself or by his supervisors and fellow craftsmen, to revise a scene or composition.[1] In some cases—and most conspicuously in the case of inscriptions—these alterations are clearly corrections,[2] eliminating errors by the deletion, insertion, or transposition of signs. All three possibilities are well illustrated by titularies. A Twelfth Dynasty stela shows a deletion in "hereditary prince, count, treasurer of the King of Lower Egypt, sole companion," restoring the expected sequence of this honorific series by the elimination of a title that was introduced at the wrong point.[3] Another inscription of somewhat earlier date, having omitted the second half of the last title of this series, has repaired the omission by superimposing the missing signs on the first half: .[4] In a still earlier example, from the

1. See, for example, Wm. S. Smith, *A History of Egyptian Sculpture and Painting in the Old Kingdom*, p. 252; Dows Dunham, "A 'Palimpsest' on an Egyptian Mastaba Wall," *AJA* 39 (1935) pp. 300–309; Wm. C. Hayes, *Scepter of Egypt* I, fig. 59, p. 103 (cf. Wm. C. Hayes, "Egyptian Tomb Reliefs of the Old Kingdom," *BMMA* 4 [1946] p. 174; the traces of the original scene are not visible in J. E. Quibell, *Excavations at Saqqara* [*1907–08*] pl. 64); H. G. Fischer, *Dendera in the Third Millennium B.C.*, p. 113, pl. 13. Some examples reflect a transition from earlier to later style: E. Brunner-Traut, "Zur Tübinger Mastaba Seschemnofers III," *MDIK* 15 (1957) pp. 18–30; H. G. Fischer, "Relief Fragments from Deir el Bahri," *Yale University Art Gallery Bulletin* 24, no. 2 (Oct., 1958) pp. 32–35.

2. An interesting survey of textual corrections in the funerary spells of a Twelfth Dynasty burial chamber is presented by Wm. C. Hayes, *Texts in the Mastabeh of Se'n-Wosret-'ankh at Lisht*, pp. 25–27. An equally systematic survey of corrections in a later New Kingdom temple has been made by John A. Wilson, "Ancient text corrections in Medinet Habu," *ÄZ* 68 (1932) pp. 48–56.

3. Berlin 1204: *LD* II, 135 (h); *Aegyptische Inschriften* I, 171, where it is denied that any signs were ever inscribed in the lacuna; H. Schäfer, *Die Mysterien des Osiris in Abydos* (Sethe, *Untersuchungen* IV) p. 10, where it is stated that signs have been erased, although no traces remain. For other changes in titles see Jéquier, *Monument funéraire de Pepi II*, II, pl. 109 (, with last two signs deleted); H. Fischer, "Three Old Kingdom Palimpsests in the Louvre," *ÄZ* 86 (1961) pp. 22–28 (replaced by).

4. Petrie, *Athribis*, pl. 13. For the addition of omitted signs in titles see also H. Fischer, *Inscriptions from the Coptite Nome*, pp. 19–20, fig. 2. Similar additions occur in the funerary formulae of a Sixth Dynasty coffin as described and illustrated in Firth and Gunn, *Teti Pyramid Cemeteries*, p. 99, pl. 58 (1).

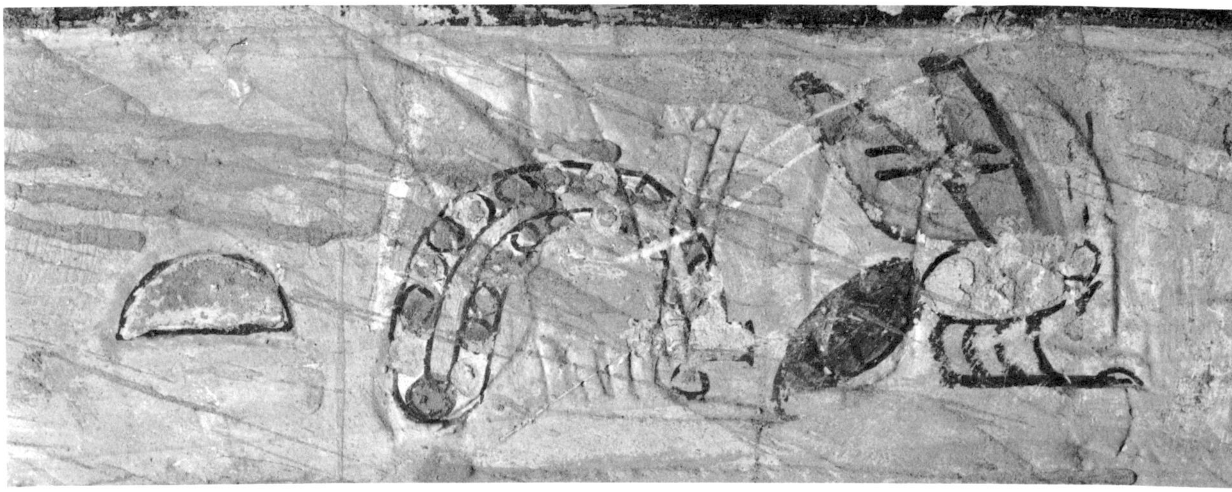

FIGURE 1
Detail from tomb chapel of Meḥu at Saqqara

Sixth Dynasty tomb chapel of Meḥu at Saqqara (Figure 1),[5] the sculptor has transposed and in the penultimate title of the same series, or rather has failed to apply "honorific transposition" to the sequence, so that the "King of Lower Egypt" fails to take precedence; this oversight has been rectified by the painter, who imposed the correct sequence on the wrong one, completely disregarding the original outline. Sometimes a bizarre composite results from erasures that were effected by filling an incised sign with plaster and recarving the new surface. In such cases the plaster has frequently been lost, leaving a result such as the two-headed goose in the Ramesside inscription shown in Figure 2,[6] which represents a reorientation of the group , "Son of Re."

Secondly, there are the alterations—often not much later in date—that were made to eliminate the memory of an individual, and his survival beyond death, by erasing his image,[7] his name,[8] and perhaps

5. For this tomb see Zaki Saad, "A Preliminary Report on the Excavations at Saqqara 1939–1940," *ASAE* 40 (1941) pp. 687–690. I am indebted to the late Zakaria Ghoneim for the photograph used here.

6. University Museum, Philadelphia, E 635; the figure is taken from Philippus Miller, "A Statue of Ramesses II," *JEA* 25 (1939) pl. 3 (2) following p. 4.

7. E.g., Étienne Drioton, "Une Mutilation d'image avec motif," *Archiv Orientalni* 20 (1952) pp. 351–355. The image is less commonly erased than the name (see next note), but in the case of one late Old Kingdom tomb (Jéquier, *Tombeaux des particuliers*, fig. 117, p. 103, pl. 12) the name is erased in the burial chamber, whereas the false door aboveground shows the heads of the figures destroyed while the name is left intact (*ibid.*, fig. 114, p. 99). The same is true of the figures in an adjacent chapel (fig. 116, p. 101), but the burial chamber has been spared completely. In other cases the mutilation is still more selective; A. Klasens describes the figure of a man which shows deep incisions across the neck ("A Stela of the Second Dynasty," *Oudheidkundige Mededelingen* 46 [1965] p. 3, pl. 1). The mutilation of images in the New Kingdom is discussed by Alan Schulman in "Some Remarks on the Alleged 'Fall' of Senmut," *JARCE* 8 (1969–70) pp. 29–48, especially p. 36. Further examples of this period are described by Norman Davies in several of his publications of Theban tombs: *Tombs of Two Officials*, p. 2 (tomb 75); *Ḳen-Amūn*, p. 4; *Rekh-mi-rēʿ*, p. 7; *Ḥuy*, p. 7; *Puyemrê*, pp. 22–26 (the last two subsequently restored, as mentioned in note 42 below). Queen Hatshepsut's statues offer the most striking example of methodical destruction (as described by H. E. Winlock, *Excavations at Deir el Baḥri*, pp. 77, 141–142), although it is no longer believed that they were destroyed immediately after her death; cf. the article of Schulman pp. 33–35, and note 8 below.

8. E.g., Junker, *Gîza* IV, pp. 6–7; the name of a wife is eliminated, as also in Cairo CG 1482. Sometimes the name of an attendant is systematically deleted: A. Blackman, *Meir* V, p. 25, note 1. Other examples: Firth and Gunn, *Teti Pyramid Cemeteries*, p. 150 and pls. 14 (3), 65 (10), p. 270 and pl. 14 (c) (headrests); Jéquier, *Pyramides des reines*, fig. 35, p. 58 (offering slab); CG 447 (statue). Royal examples are of particular interest to the historian; besides the well-known erasures of the name of Hatshepsut, most recently discussed by Nims, "The date of the dishonoring of Hatshepsut," *ÄZ* 93 (1966) pp. 97–100, see, for example, Yoyotte, "Le martelage des noms royaux éthiopiens par Psammétique II," *RdE* 8 (1951) pp. 215–239, and Sauneron, "Les querelles impériales vues à travers les scènes du temple d'Esné," *BIFAO* 51 (1952) pp. 111–121. Other ramifications of this subject are discussed by G. Posener, "Les criminels débaptisés et les morts sans noms," *RdE* 5 (1946) pp. 51–56.

some of his titles[9] as well. But this motive is not necessarily involved if, in such cases, the deleted names and titles have been replaced by those of another individual, indicating a change of ownership by fair means or foul. The reuse of a tomb or monument could, on occasion, require a change in the representations as well as the inscriptions; a man's form might replace that of a woman (Figure 3),[10] or vice versa,[11] a young man might replace an old one[12] or, more rarely, a royal monument might be remodeled for the use of a commoner.[13]

In some cases names were added to figures that were not originally accompanied by any identification. Funerary priests of the Old Kingdom took this means to associate themselves permanently with the tomb chapel in which they served, and if no other alternative were available they might even apply their names to representations of ordinary laborers.[14] A more exceptional example is to be seen in the temple of Ramesses III at Medinet Habu, where a number of nameless princes (borrowed from the reliefs of the more prolific Ramesses II) subsequently acquired the identity of his Twentieth Dynasty successors.[15]

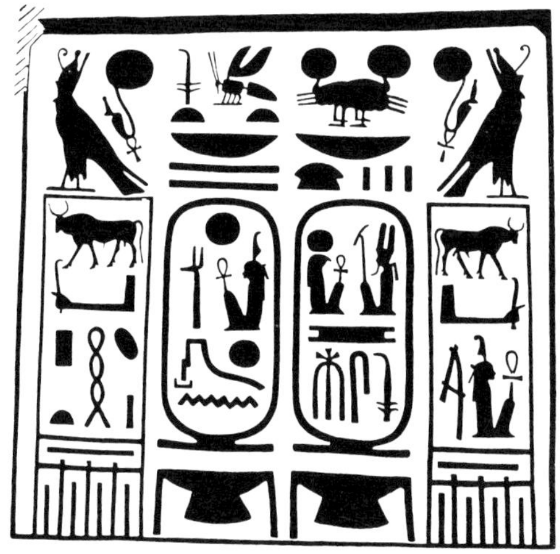

FIGURE 2
Inscription of Ramesses II on statue, University Museum E 635

Here, parenthetically, one may note the deliberate breakage of objects when they were placed in the tomb, a practice that was limited to pots, stone vessels, bows, and staves.[16] Of greater interest is the

9. Jéquier, *Tombeax des particuliers*, figs. 41, 43, 44, pp. 37–40, pl. 3; the honorific titles are selectively erased along with the name *Šnỉ*.

10. Reisner's Giza tomb 2001; cf. H. Fischer, "Three Palimpsests," *ÄZ* 86 (1961) p. 28, note 5. The drawing has been made from a 35 mm. transparency.

11. Louvre E 17233: article cited in preceding note, fig. 2, pp. 23, 28–29. Also Macramallah, *Mastaba d'Idout*, pp. 1–2, pl. 6.

12. MMA 08.201.1: H. Fischer, "A Scribe of the Army in a Saqqara Mastaba of the Early Fifth Dynasty," *JNES* 18 (1959) pp. 245–246, fig. 10 (f).

13. Reworked statuette of king, MMA 22.1.1638: H. Fischer, "Two Royal Monuments of the Middle Kingdom Restored," *BMMA* 22 (1964) pp. 235–239. A similar reuse seems probable in the case of a Middle Kingdom queen, the uraeus of which has been carefully chiseled away, Walters Art Gallery 22.376: George Steindorff, *Catalogue of Egyptian Sculpture in the Walters Art Gallery*, no. 65, pl. 10. The reverse of this situation appears in royal reliefs of the Fifth Dynasty, where the figure of an official in the retinue of King Sahure has been altered to represent Sahure's successor Neferirkare: L. Borchardt, *Grabdenkmal des Königs Saꜣḥureʿ* II, p. 32, pls. 17, 33–34, 48.

14. E.g., Firth and Gunn, *Teti Pyramid Cemeteries*, p. 114; Mariette, *Mastabas*, p. 315.

15. K. Seele, "Ramesses VI and the Medinet Habu Procession of the Princes," *JNES* 19 (1960), pp. 184–204; also, more recently, Wm. J. Murnane Jr., "The 'King Ramesses' of the Medinet Habu Procession of Princes," *JARCE* 9 (1971–72), pp. 121–131. Cf. the introduction of the name of Neferirkare in the pyramid temple of Sahure (end of note 13 above).

16. L. V. Grinsell, "The Breaking of Objects as a Funerary Rite," *Folklore* 72 (1961) pp. 480–482; 84 (1973) pp. 111–114; for the breaking of staves and bows see also A. C. Mace and H. E. Winlock, *The Tomb of Senebtisi*, pp. 77, 80, 92–93.

FIGURE 3
Revised figure in Giza tomb 2001

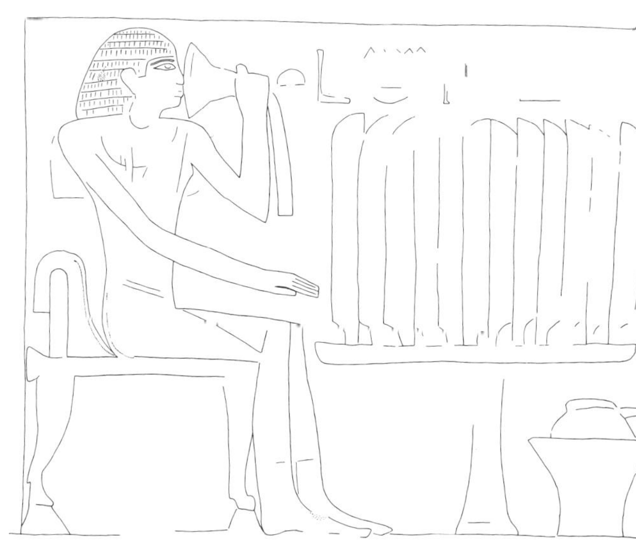

FIGURE 4
Name of Alexander in tomb of Sen-nufer, with drawing of pectoral amulet

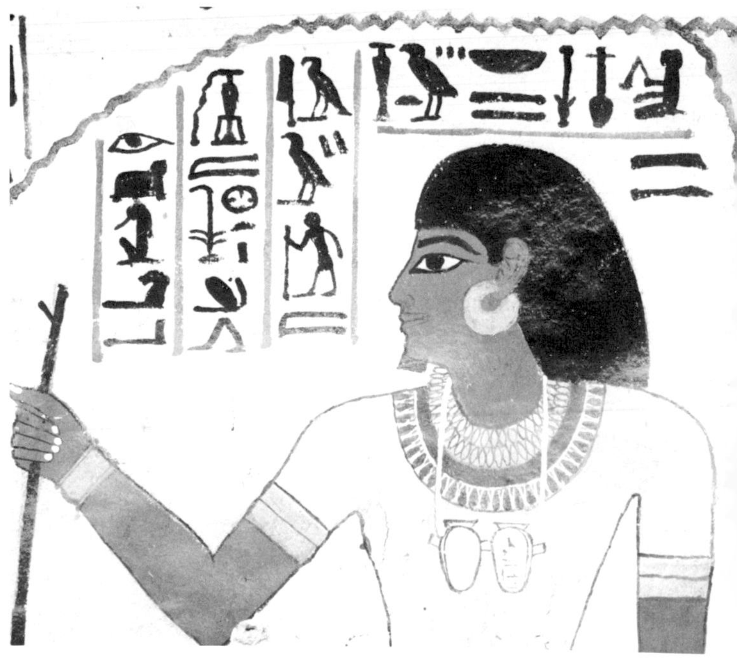

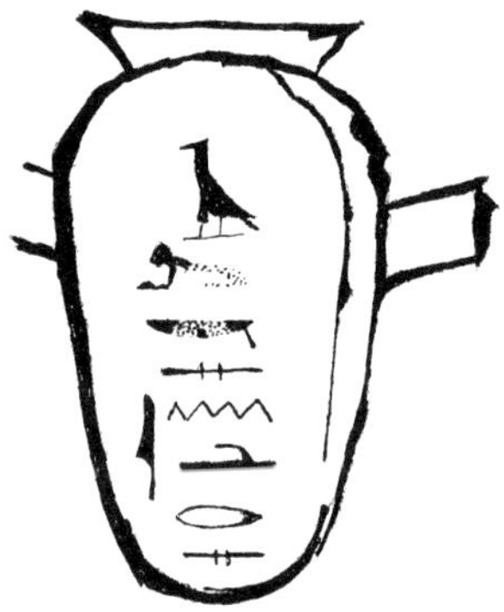

FIGURE 5
Inscription of Lepsius on the Great Pyramid, A.D. 1842

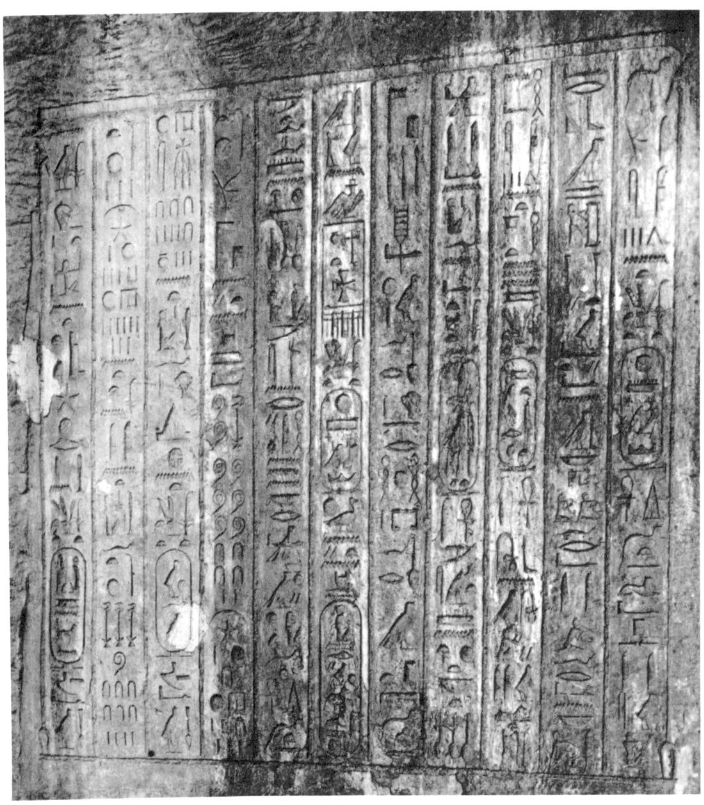

gradual erasure that ocurred as texts on temple statuary were repeatedly read by ancient visitors and, at the same time, fingered.[17]

Thirdly, there are the reuses of monuments that have taken place after a considerable span of time, when the personality of the original owners had become too remote to excite either resentment or respect, although their works might still be esteemed as works of art or as antiquities. The first extensive reuse of this kind is Ramesses II's usurpation of monuments belonging to his royal predecessors, and it is significant that he and his son Khaemwase also showed an interest in restoring earlier tombs and temples.[18] In

17. Cairo CG 42126; J 44861: E. L. B. Terrace and H. Fischer, *Treasures of the Cairo Museum*, pp. 113, 117.

18. For the restorations of Ramesses II see E. Naville, *Temple of Deir el Bahari* VI, p. 11; *The XIth Dynasty Temple at Deir el Bahari* I, pp. 17, 24; II, p. 2, pl. 5 (D); Hassan, *Gîza* VIII, pp. 7–9, where he also remarks on his depredations at Giza. Khaemwase left inscriptions commemorating his restorations at the pyramids of Djoser (Lauer, *La Pyramide à Degrés: Compléments* III, p. 52), Shepseskaf (Jéquier, *Mastabat Faraoun*, fig. 7, p. 12), and Unis (Drioton and Lauer, "Une inscription de Khamouas sur la face sud de la pyramide d'Ounas à Saqqarah," *ASAE* 37 [1937] pp. 201–211; also Lauer, *ASAE* 54 (1956–57) pp. 114–116). This subject is comprehensively discussed in Chap. XII of Farouk Gomaà, *Chaemwese, Sohn Ramses' II.*, Wiesbaden, 1973, which appeared after this article went to press.

the succeeding Libyan Period the usurpation of earlier statues was taken up by nonroyal persons as well, as exemplified by the first of the following studies.[19]

The graffiti of ancient Egyptian tourists, who left their names on older tombs and temples along with a few words of admiration, seem to be limited to the New Kingdom,[20] and the oldest monument that bears such inscriptions is the pyramid complex of Djoser.[21] The Greeks and Romans visited the monuments as tourists in the more literal sense of the word, again leaving graffiti behind them. One of the most curious indications of their visits is to be seen in the Theban tomb of Sen-nufer, whose pectoral amulet—a double heart—is neatly inscribed with a hieroglyphic writing of the name Alexander (Figure 4).[22] A second curiosity, of much more recent date (Figure 5), is the hieroglyphic inscription which Richard Lepsius carved upon the Cheops pyramid to commemorate his archaeological and epigraphic expedition of 1842–45.[23]

A certain number of inscriptions and reliefs of all periods also show "marginalia" of later date—most frequently a detail or hieroglyph that someone felt impelled to copy to try his skill or merely to pass the time.[24] Figure 6 shows two examples of this kind from the left-hand wall of the entrance passage in Perinebi's tomb chapel; they appear at the back of the passage, where both could have been copied from the scenes and inscriptions within. In some cases such sketches may have been the work of professional artists who were copying the scenes, and further evidence of such copying is attested by painted grids which were superimposed on paintings and reliefs at a much later date.[25] Again the oldest reliefs that show such grids are those of Djoser,[26] and it is generally assumed that in this case the grids were added during the Saite Period, some 2000 years later.[27]

It is more difficult to situate the effects of religion, magic, and superstition in this chronological summary. The most immediate example is the modification of hieroglyphs in burial chambers of the Sixth Dynasty, where all sorts of representations of living creatures were suppressed, in whole or in part, to protect the deceased from their presence.[28] In most cases these modifications were planned in advance, but they were

19. See below, p. 17 and note 65.

20. W. Helck, "Die Bedeutung der ägyptischen Besucherinschriften," *ZDMG* 102 (1952) pp. 39–46; D. Wildung, "Besucherinschriften," in Helck-Otto, *Lexikon* I/5, pp. 766–767.

21. Firth and Quibell, *Step Pyramid*, pl. 83, pp. 77–85.

22. Theban tomb 96: P. Virey, "La tombe des vignes à Thèbes," *Rec. trav.* 22 (1900) pp. 84–85. The detail shown here is taken from a negative of the Metropolitan Museum's epigraphic expedition.

23. From a photograph taken by Albert Lythgoe prior to 1906. For details see Georges Goyon, *Inscriptions et Graffiti des voyageurs sur la Grande Pyramide*, pp. lxxvi-lxxvii, 82, pl. 117. The inscription is visible at the upper right of J. Capart and M. Werbrouck, *Memphis*, fig. 50, p. 53.

24. E.g., Newberry, *Beni Hasan* I, pl. 10; Fischer, *Inscriptions from the Coptite Nome*, pp. 19–20, fig. 2; Fischer, *Dendera*, p. 193, fig. 37, pl. 23c; also an incised sketch on University Museum, Philadelphia, E 13575, the right side of the gateway of Merneptah. For a Coptic sketch in a New Kingdom tomb see N. de G. Davies, *BMMA* 17 (Dec. 1922, Pt. II), p. 56, fig. 9. A sketch of the Queen of Punt (N. de G. Davies, *BMMA* 25 [Dec. 1930, Pt. II], pp. 30–31) should be included in this category, although it appears on a detached flake of limestone rather than on the margin of the original scene at Deir el Bahri.

25. These are to be distinguished from the so-called "proportion squares." See the remarks of E. Mackay concerning Theban tomb 93 in *JEA* 4 (1917), pp. 74, 75, 84; also C. Ransom Williams, *Decoration of the Tomb of Per-nēb*, p. 10, note 31.

26. Firth and Quibell, *Step Pyramid*, pls. 15–16, p. 5.

27. Cf. I. E. S. Edwards, *The Pyramids of Egypt*, revised ed. 1961, p. 79.

28. P. Lacau, "Suppressions et modifications de signes dans les textes funéraires," *ÄZ* 51 (1913) pp. 1–64; "Suppression des noms divins dans les textes de la chambre funéraire," *ASAE* 26 (1926) pp. 69–81; B. Gunn in Firth and Gunn, *Teti Pyramid Cemeteries*, pp. 171–177.

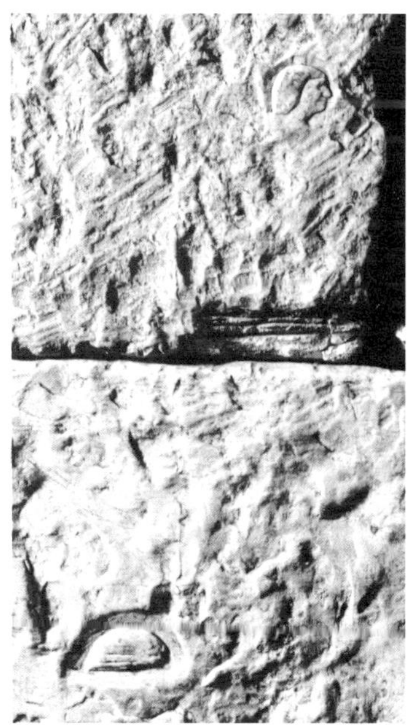

FIGURE 6
Isolated hieroglyphs in tomb chapel, MMA 13.183.3

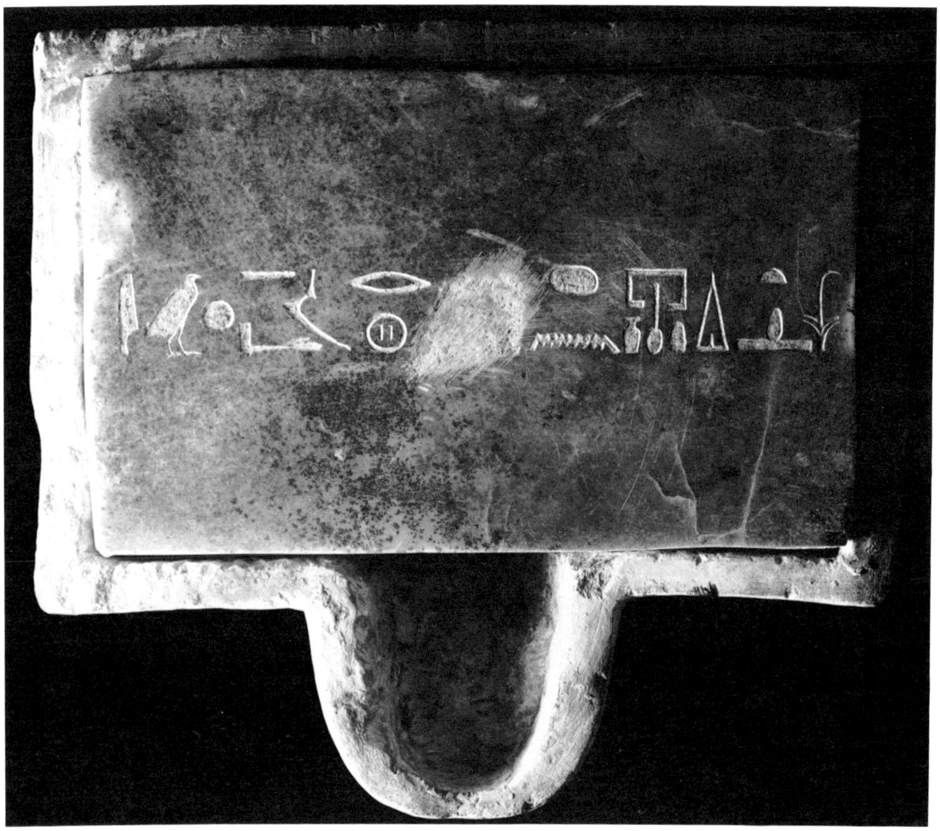

FIGURE 7
Erasure of 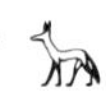 on a covered offering basin from Saqqara

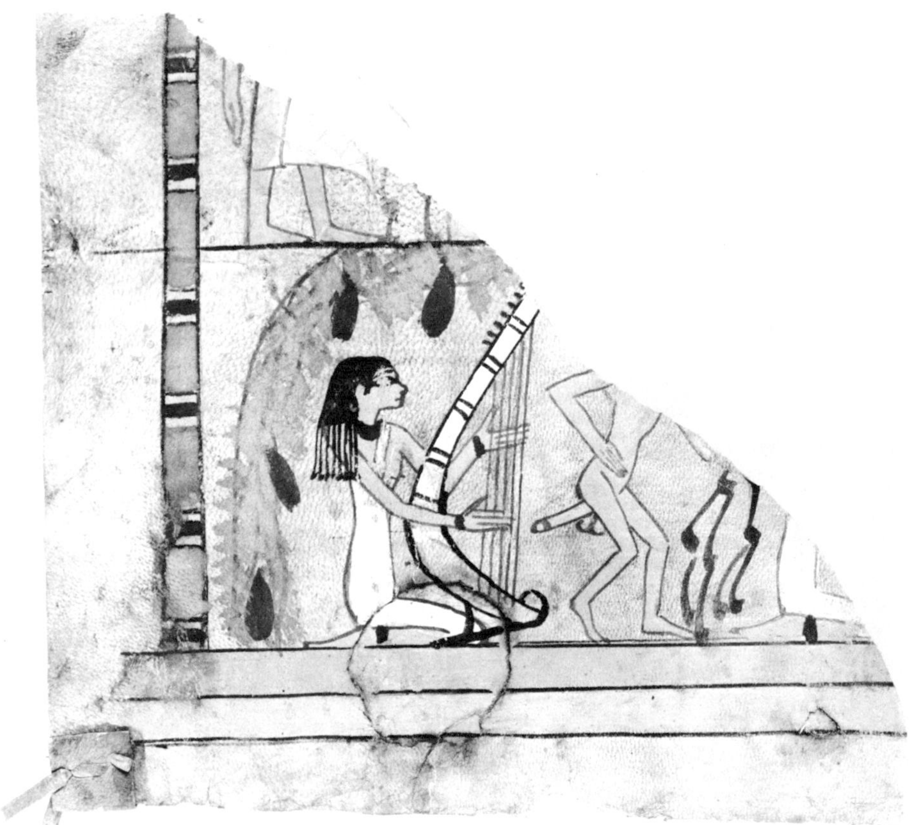

FIGURE 8
Painted leather fragment from Deir el Bahri, MMA 31.3.98

occasionally introduced as an afterthought.[29] That is probably the explanation of the erasure shown in Figure 7,[30] where the first sign of the title has evidently been eliminated.[31] A longer interval is involved in the erasure of the name of the god Amun by the Eighteenth Dynasty Atenists,[32] as in the case of the much later persecution of the god Seth.[33] But these very selective modifications can hardly be compared with the more recent ravages of Christian and Islamic iconoclasm[34] or Christian morality, as attested not only in the Coptic Period[35] but also in the reign of Queen Victoria. Ancient Egypt has left extraordinarily little to offend moral susceptibilities, and there is virtually nothing that could be called obscene prior to the famous Turin Papyrus dating to the end of the New Kingdom.[36] The earlier tombs and temples treat the theme of procreation forthrightly, although human intercourse is scarcely represented except in schematic and hieroglyphic fashion. The one exception, a more literal hieroglyphic representation in an early Middle Kingdom tomb chapel at Beni Hasan, was censored by a Victorian visitor,[37] and the same censorship is still frequently imposed on the emblematic virility of ithyphallic gods such as Min of Coptos.[38] It is exemplified in the Metropolitan Museum by a painted fragment of the Eighteenth Dynasty that is described as an "erotic dance". On the basis of that judgment, the genitals of a naked dancer were painted out, and the original state of the painting can only be seen from a photograph that was made prior to censorship (Figure 8).[39]

29. In the last two discussions cited in the preceding note Lacau, p. 72, so interprets the erasure (with plaster) of in the offering formula of a Sixth Dynasty coffin; and Gunn, p. 174, similarly interprets the replacement of by on the contemporary coffin of Mereruka. The same explanation has been applied to a group of Eleventh Dynasty scarabs that were mutilated before being placed in the tomb of their owner: H. G. Fischer, *Ancient Egyptian Representations of Turtles*, p. 18.

30. From the photographic archives of the Egyptian Department of Antiquities at Saqqara, through the kindness of the late Zakaria Ghoneim. The size and material are unknown to me, but it appears to be made of calcite, and it probably is related to the category of calcite offering slabs that were frequently placed in Sixth Dynasty burial chambers (H. Fischer, *Dendera*, pp. 107–108).

31. It should be noted that this sign is not ordinarily eliminated; see Gunn, discussion cited in note 28, p. 173, note a; but it is once replaced by phonetic signs in Pyr. 319 (T), as noted by Lacau, "Suppressions et modifications," p. 38.

32. In some cases the deletions involved much more than the name of Amun, and only the hieroglyphic sign of the sun (☉) was spared (N. de Garis Davies, *BMMA* 18 (Dec. 1923, Pt. II) fig. 9, p. 45). One may compare the occurrences of the sign "god," which was likewise spared in an erased inscription of the Old Kingdom: Hassan, *Gîza* VI, Pt. 3, p. 166. The Atenists, on the other hand, sometimes erased the plural of the word for "god" because of its association with Amun, who was "king of the gods": Davies, *Tomb of Ramose*, p. 4.

33. Breasted, "The Philosophy of a Memphite Priest," *ÄZ* 39 (1901) p. 40, note 6, points out that this degree of hostility must have begun after the Eighth Century B.C. since the name of Seth is chiseled out on the Twenty-fifth Dynasty Shabako Stone. The image of Seth was also eliminated, in some cases, by transforming it into another divinity: G. Legrain, "Une Statue du dieu Set," *Rec. trav.* 16 (1894) pp. 167–169 (and O. Koefoed-Petersen, *Catalogue des Statues et Statuettes*, no. 83, pls. 95–97). One may also compare the case of a protodynastic turtle the eyes and paws of which were mutilated at a much later date—most probably at the end of the Dynastic Period (H. G. Fischer, *Ancient Egyptian Representations of Turtles*, pp. 13, 18–20).

34. Sauneron, *Le Temple d'Esna* (*Esna* III), pp. xxiv-xxvii, describes how "à une époque difficile à dater exactement, mais postérieure au 'paganisme', les hommes ont réagi devant des images ou des signes hiéroglyphiques dont le sens leur échappait, mais qui leur semblaient chargés de pouvoir." Doctrinal iconoclasm was probably equally selective; L. Habachi, "The Destruction of Temples in Egypt," in *Medieval and Middle Eastern Studies in Honor of Aziz Suryol Atiya*, pp. 192–198, points out that the process was gradual, and is not specifically attributable to Christianity. Cf. also Alan Schulman, *JARCE* 8 (1969–70) p. 37.

35. All the female figures of Theban tomb 56 were expunged by an anchorite who used it as a dwelling: N. de G. Davies, *BMMA* 17 (Dec. 1922, Pt. II), p. 56.

36. This has very recently been published in entirety for the first time: Jos. A. Omlin, *Der Papyrus 55001 und seine Satirisch-erotischen Zeichnungen und Inschriften*, Turin, 1973. There are, in addition, a certain number of contemporaneous ostraca in the same spirit (L. Keimer, *Études d'Égyptologie* III, pp. 4–9), and an apparently licentious figurine of much earlier date (Dyn. XIII?) from Lisht is discussed by Elizabeth Riefstahl, "An Enigmatic Faience Figure," *Miscellanea Wilbouriana* 1 (1972), 137–143. It might be thought that the "Fall von Prüderie aus der Ramessidenzeit" debated by S. Schott, *ÄZ* 75 (1939) pp. 100–106, reflects a complementary aspect of prurient interest, but that conclusion seems doubtful. As N. de Garis Davies makes clear in his publication of the tomb in question, *Seven Private Tombs*, pp. 5–8, the reuse of the Eighteenth Dynasty paintings not only added clothing of naked ladies, but also entailed the remodeling of furniture—all in an attempt to adjust outmoded features to current fashion. That view does not seem seriously incompatible with Schott's final conclusions.

37. A unique hieroglyph, showing a couple on a bed, recorded by Lepsius in 1842 (*LD* II, 143 [b]), no longer showed the couple when Newberry copied it, about fifty years later (*Beni Hasan* II, pl. 14).

38. See, for example, Petrie, *Koptos* (1896) pls. 6 (6), 9, 22.

39. MMA 31.3.98. The description is used by Wm. C. Hayes, *Scepter* II, p. 167, and his fig. 92. shows the painting in its retouched condition.

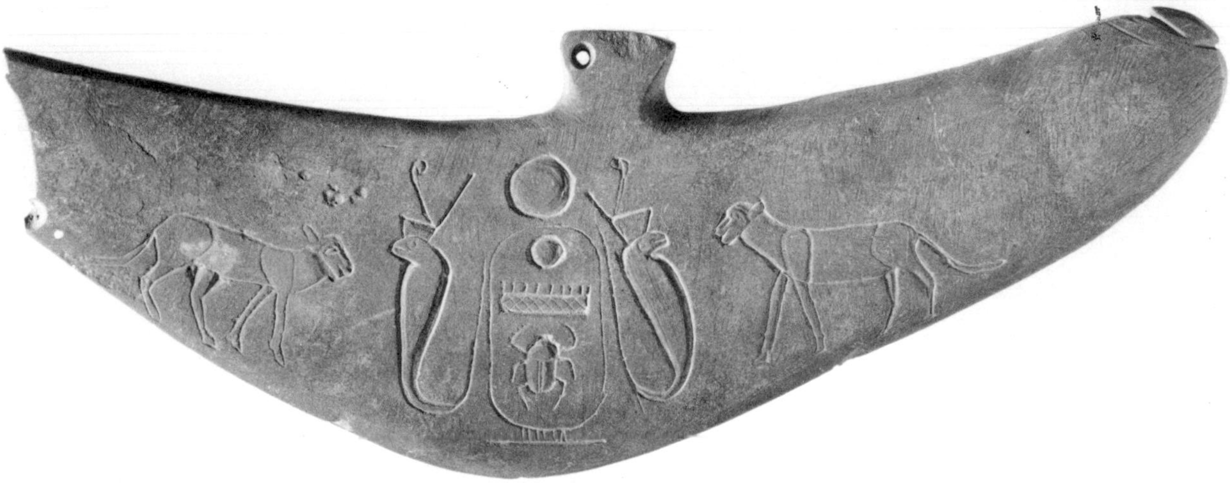

FIGURE 9
Predynastic palette with modern decoration, Leiden

The repair and restoration of monuments was likewise practiced at all periods of antiquity, as in the present day. Sometimes the repairs may have been required even before the work was complete, as in the case of stone statuary which was apt, as the work proceeded, to reveal a flaw or weakness that required an insertion.[40] And wood paneling might show knot-holes or splits that had to be patched with "dutchmen".[41] Obviously such repairs, like the corrections and revisions mentioned earlier, must be considered an integral part of the original workmanship. After a lapse of time, however, a repair or restoration may depart from the style of the original,[42] even to the point of becoming anachronistic, as in the case of the plaited beard of a divinity that was supplied to the great sphinx of Giza in the Nineteenth Dynasty;[43] the original beard was certainly the unplaited variety that was worn by kings, but in the Nineteenth Dynasty this monument was considered a god, its association with Chephren having been forgotten. Similarly, the fragments of a wooden coffin that bears the name of Chephren's successor, Mycerinus, and was accordingly attributed to the Fourth Dynasty, was eventually dated to the Twenty-sixth Dynasty on the basis of the style, orthography, and phrasing of the texts.[44] The "restoration" of this royal coffin was a totally new production, and the same was often true of temples that were "renewed" by total replacement. Even when the restoration called for nothing more than fresh paint,[45] one cannot be sure that the earlier colors and details were matched conscientiously.

Coming down to more recent times, there are countless examples of Egyptian antiquities that have been restored in a manner that not only departs from

40. MMA 25.6, a basalt statue of Sesostris I, lacks the head, which was carved separately and fastened by means of a tenon (Wm. C. Hayes, *Scepter* I, pp. 180–181); MMA 22.5.2, a diorite statue of Amenophis III (*Scepter* II, p. 235) has lost an inset at the back of the throne.

41. The veneer of MMA 68.58, an early Eighteenth Dynasty chair (*BMMA* 27 [1968] p. 90) shows several almost invisible patches of this kind.

42. Davies, *Tomb of Puyemrê* I, pp. 23–26. Compare also Davies and Gardiner, *Tomb of Ḥuy*, p. 7, and the usurped and repainted scenes of Theban tomb 45, as described in note 36 above.

43. Howard Vyse, *Operations Carried on at the Pyramids of Gizeh in 1837* III, pl. following p. 108.

44. *Ibid.* II, p. 93; cf. I. E. S. Edwards, *A Handbook to the Egyptian Mummies and Coffins exhibited in the British Museum* (1938) pp. 21–23, pl. 8. S. Birch (*ÄZ* 7 [1869] pp. 49–51) seems to be the first to have suggested the correct dating; see also Sethe, *ÄZ* 30 (1892) pp. 94–98.

45. As stated in a Thirteenth Dynasty biography which records the repainting of reliefs dating to the beginning of the previous dynasty, two centuries earlier: Louvre C 12 (Sethe, *Ägyptische Lesestücke*, p. 76).

the spirit of the original but—to a greater or lesser degree—has destroyed it as well.[46] In some cases such restoration can only be detected by very close scrutiny and research, as exemplified by the last of the following studies. In other cases the result is glaringly apparent, and there is probably no example that is more shocking than the one presented in the second of the studies. This case may well be unique, however, in that the "restoration" was applied to a portion of a statue, completely disregarding the existence of the other parts, which had doubtless been lost from sight. With this example we come to the category of fraudulent alterations or additions designed to lend interest to antiquities of negligible value. There are limestone reliefs that are only very marginally ancient[47] and predynastic pots and palettes the decoration of which is wholly modern (Figure 9).[48] The most mischievous alterations, however, are those which seek to augment the market value of an antiquity by adding a well-known name where none originally existed. One of the most outrageous examples of this kind is a Seventeenth Dynasty statuette of a woman that was excavated at Thebes in the winter of 1898–99 (Figure 10).[49] Its worth was subsequently impaired by the loss of the feet and base, which were already detached when it was found, and the upper left portion of the head, which had already been weakened by a deep chip in the forehead. This was evidently its condition when it came into the possession of an unscrupulous semischolarly collector who erased the

46. A missing head may be replaced by one from another statue (J. Cooney, "A Reexamination of Some Egyptian Antiquities," *Brooklyn Museum Bulletin* 11, no. 3 [Spring 1950], figs. 1–2, p. 13 ff.) or by a newly made head (*ibid.*, fig. 3, p. 16 ff.) or new features may be carved on a battered face (J. J. Clère, "The Statue of an Egyptian Priest," *Museum Notes, Museum of Art, Rhode Island School of Design* 9, no. 4 (May 1952) p. 1; B. V. Bothmer, "The Head That Grew a Face," *Miscellanea Wilbouriana* 1 [1972] pp. 25–31). Another example of this kind is probably to be seen in Louvre E 11057 (P. Barguet, *Chronique d'Égypte* 28 [1953] pp. 23–27), a statue of Senmut holding a coil of rope; all the inscriptions were erased, presumably so that the statue could be usurped by someone else, but a new inscription was never added. The ram's head on top of the coil of rope, emblematic of Khnum, was also attacked—probably, as Barguet says, in the reign of Akhenaton—because of its resemblance to the ram of Amun. But its transformation into a human face may well be a modern restoration.

47. J. D. Cooney, "Assorted Errors in Art Collecting," *Expedition* 6/1 (Fall 1963), displays (p. 25, fig. 6) a fragment of Amarna relief to which the head of a queen has been added in recent years; another New Kingdom relief, showing ancient inscription and a modern head, is illustrated by L. Borchardt, "Ägyptische 'Altertümer', die ich für neuzeitlich halte," supplement to *ÄZ* 66/1 (1931) pl. 2 (12). Spurious repainting has also been applied to ancient monuments in modern times; see, for example, Cooney, *Amarna Reliefs from Hermopolis in American Collections*, pp. 1–2.

48. Rijksmuseum van Oudheden, Leiden F 1938/10.23, schist, length 23.8 cm.; reproduced by the kind permission of the director, Dr. A. Klasens. For further details see H. G. Fischer, *Ancient Egyptian Representations of Turtles*, p. 20, note 54. Further discussions of this class of forgeries are presented by G. Brunton, "Modern Painting on Predynastic Pots," *ASAE* 34 (1934), pp. 149–156, and A. J. Arkell, "Modern designs on predynastic slate palettes," *JEA* 41 (1955) p. 126.

49. Northampton, Spiegelberg, and Newberry, *Theban Necropolis*, p. 17, pls. 15 (2, 5), 16 (1, 2).

FIGURE 10
Seventeenth Dynasty statuette from Thebes

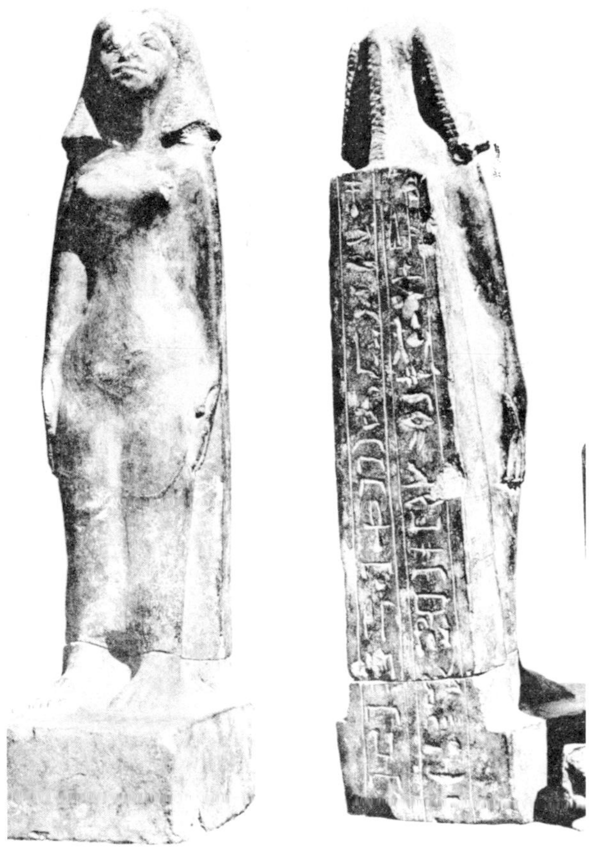

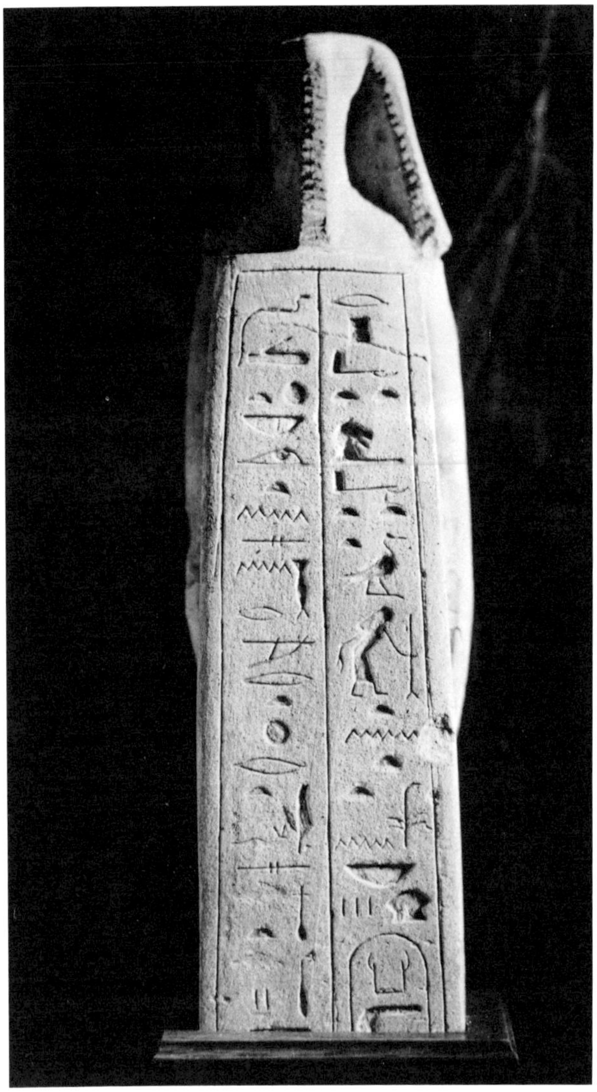

FIGURE 11

Altered inscription on statuette in Figure 10

inscription on the backpillar—a conventional offering formula—and substituted a new one (Figure 11).[50] Evidently taking a cue from a suggestion made by Gauthier in his *Livre des Rois*,[51] the new inscription purports to belong to "The Hereditary Princess and Countess, the eldest daughter of the King of Upper Egypt, Lord of Diadems Ka[mose] . . . She Who Says a Thing and It is Done for Her, Sweet of Love in the Sight of Her Father, Nefertiry . . . ."[52]

Finally, there are those monuments which have not been affected by spurious restoration but have served as a model for modern copies that may be difficult to detect as forgeries—particularly if the original is not available for comparison.[53] If such a comparison is possible, however, the difference usually becomes apparent at a glance. Figure 12 shows an early Twelfth Dynasty stela in Florence[54] beside a facsimile of its counterpart in Athens (Figure 13),[55] the latter a slavish but inept imitation of the first, again revealing the mark of a later hand.

A REUSED STATUETTE OF THE TWELFTH DYNASTY FROM BYBLOS

The statuette shown in Figures 14–16 (MMA 68.101) is of greenish schist (greywacke) and stands 15.65 cm. high. The base, feet, and lower part of the legs are now missing; the original height must have been about 20 cm. It represents a standing man, the left leg advanced as usual; his right hand is held palm downward upon the flat and slightly flaring front of a

50. Now in another private collection, published by permission of the owner. I am indebted to Wm. K. Simpson for bringing this piece to my attention. The identification of the statue is confirmed beyond question by comparing the accidental chips and irregularities such as the vein in the stone which appears on the thighs, or a pit behind the lock of hair that falls on the right shoulder; a larger pit at the right edge of the backpillar was reduced in depth and area by the erasure of the old inscription.

51. Vol. II, p. 167 (XV).

52. These phrases have probably been pieced together from various sources, such as the titulary of Queen Ahmose, Gauthier, *Livre des Rois* II, 224. The Middle Kingdom writing of *ỉryt-pʿt* seems questionable, as does the inclusion (and writing) of *ḥ3tyt-ʿ*. The sign 𓏏 has been substituted for 𓇋 in the name *Nfrt-ỉry*. Otherwise the new inscription is fairly plausible—so much so that its antiquity might well be debated if the statuette had not been published in its original state.

53. An example of this kind is discussed by W. Spiegelberg, "Eine merkwürdige Fälschung," *ÄZ* 58 (1923) pp. 158–160.

54. Florence 6364: Sergio Bosticco, *Le Stele egiziane dall'Antico al Nuovo Regno*, no. 17. I am indebted to Dr. Bosticco for the photograph and for his permission to use it here.

55. B. Pörtner, *Aegyptische Grabsteine und Denksteine aus Athen und Konstantinopel*, no. 17, pl. 5. The material is described as black granite! Antiquites of smaller size are frequently duplicated by casting them in metal or clay; an early example of this kind is presented in H. G. Fischer, "A Frequently Copied Scarab," *JARCE* 2 (1963) pp. 39–41. I have also seen, in the hands of a private collector, a duplicate of the small silver sphinx of Seqenenre in the Mariemont Museum (B. van de Walle, "Antiquités Égyptiennes" in *Les Antiquités . . . du Musée de Mariemont* [Brussels, 1952] p. 34, no. E 55 [136], pl. 9); this reproduces every detail of the other, including damaged areas.

long kilt, and the other arm is folded, again palm downward, upon his chest. He wears a striated, shoulder-length wig that is drawn back behind his ears. The brows are indicated in relief, and a "cosmetic line" in relief projects from the outer corners of the eyes, both of which show traces of an incised pupil. His lips are evidently thick and everted, but these are badly worn away, and the nose has fared even worse.

The simple attire admits a date fairly early in the Twelfth Dynasty, and so too the gesture of reverence, which is known from at least one Old Kingdom example,[56] although it is much more frequently attested in Twelfth Dynasty statuary.[57] The same conclu-

56. Cairo J 52081: Engelbach, *ASAE* 38 (1938) p. 285, pl. 37 (2) on p. 291 (a hunchbacked retainer from the serdab of *Mitry*); compare Abd el Hamid Zayed, *Trois Études* (Cairo, 1956) p. 15. For the gesture see Hellmuth Müller, *MDIK* 7 (1937) p. 102. This gesture also occurs in Cairo J 66620 (Hassan, *Gîza* I, pl. 72), where it is one of a pair, the second statue mirroring the attitude of the first. Apart from some scribal statues with hands crossed upon the chest, most of the other Old Kingdom examples represent women, and in most cases it is the right hand that is raised.

57. The most comparable examples are Louvre E 17365 (Vandier *Manuel d'archéologie* III, pl. 78 [2]); Walters Art Gallery 71.509, Steindorff, *Catalogue of Egyptian Sculpture*, pl. 11 (46); CG 434 (Vandier, *op. cit.*, pl. 76 [3]). The left hand is similarly raised in many other cases, the figures standing, seated, or cross-legged. And in some cases both arms are crossed upon the chest, as in the Old Kingdom.

FIGURE 12
Middle Kingdom stela in Florence, Museo Archeologico 6364

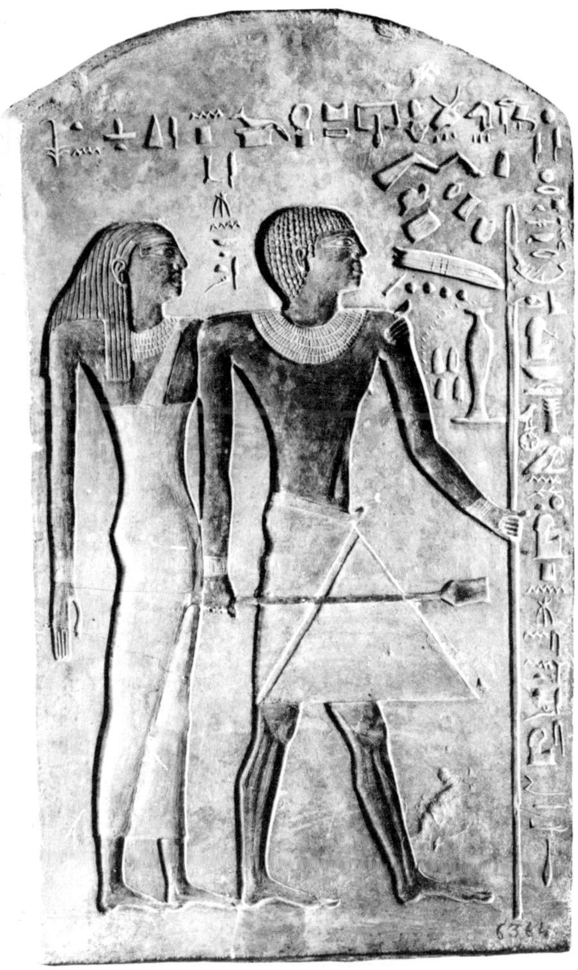

FIGURE 13
Modern copy in Athens

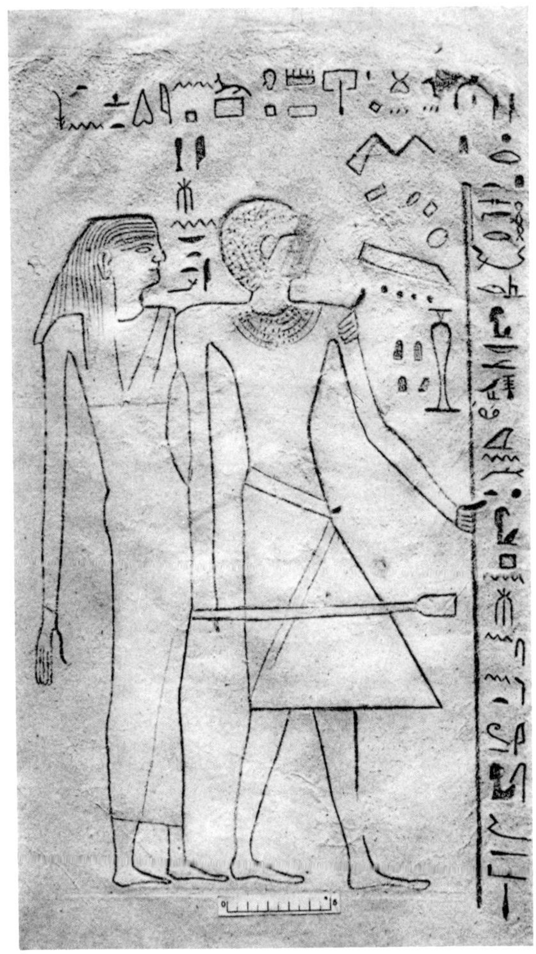

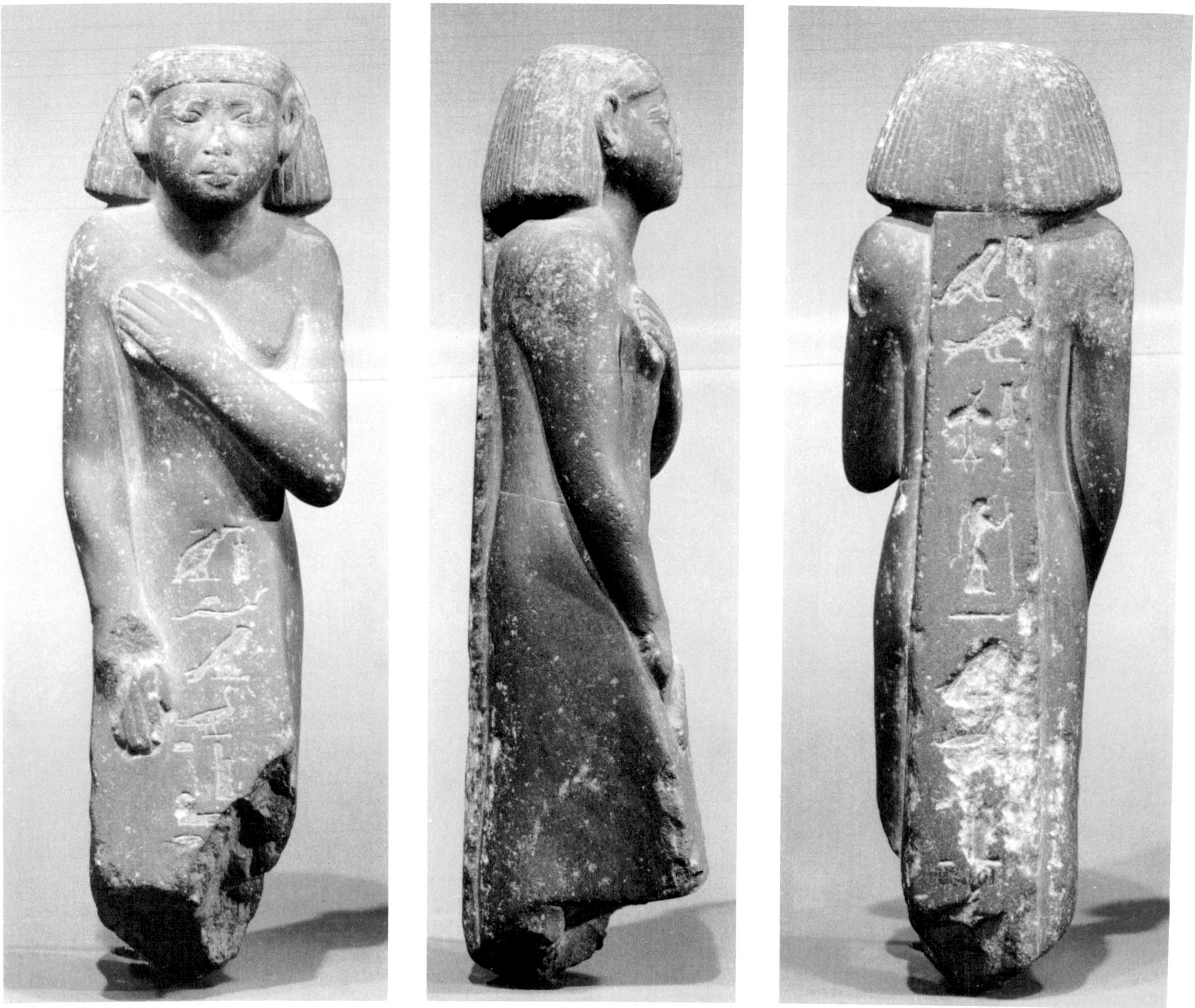

FIGURES 14, 15, 16 Reused Middle Kingdom statuette, MMA 68.101

sion is likewise suggested by the features; although the large ears indicate that the date is no earlier than the reign of Sesostris I,[58] a date much later than that reign seems unlikely in view of the shape of the brows, the thick lips, and the presence of the cosmetic line. H. W. Müller has pointed out that the last detail does not appear in private statuary until the Eleventh Dynasty and the beginning of the Twelfth.[59] It occurs on the face of a limestone statue from the tomb of Ibu at Qau,[60] generally dated to the reign of Amenemhet III and it occasionally appears on reliefs of the later Twelfth Dynasty,[61] but is not common on either royal or private statuary of that time.[62]

The original inscriptions, on the kilt and backpillar, have been completely removed, and this erasure has all but eliminated the upper edge of the kilt along with

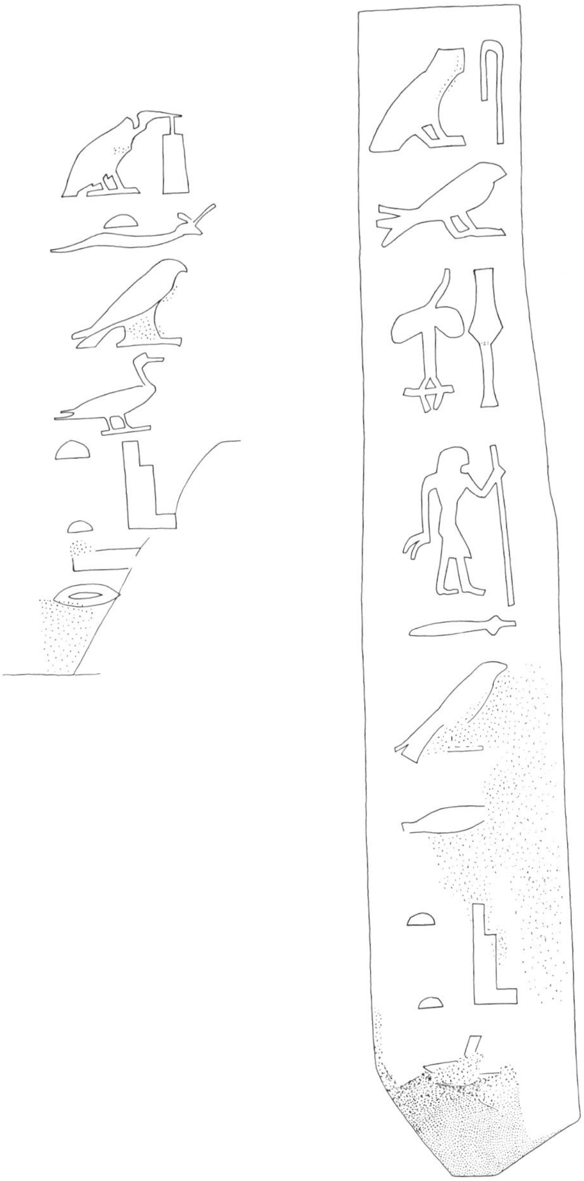

FIGURE 17
Inscriptions of MMA 68.101

the band above it. The newly polished surfaces display the inscriptions (Figure 17) of a much later individual: (front) "The *'Iwn-mwt.f*-priest Horsiese, justified"; (back) "The *Sm*-Priest, Greatest of Those Who Direct the Craftsmen, the Great Chief Horsiese, just[ified]." The second group of titles combines the function of the High Priest of Ptah at Memphis with the lineage of the Great Chiefs of the Meshwesh, and this narrows the identification down to two Memphite high priests named Horsiese who officiated in the Twenty-first and Twenty-second Dynasties, respectively.[63] Of these two, the later one seems the more probable choice in view of the abbreviated form of the title "Great Chief"; for the reference to "the Meshwesh" probably did not begin to be dropped until the later years of the Libyan Period.[64]

The usurpation of a Twelfth Dynasty statuette by an official of the Libyan Period recalls the identical case of a Twenty-second Dynasty commissioner from Palestine who reused a statuette of only slightly later date than the one in the Metropolitan Museum, originally belonging to a vizier.[65] The kilt is shorter than the one customarily worn by a vizier, but it does not seem likely that the pair of straps is to be interpreted in any other way. For the original date, I would suggest the reign of Amenemhet III. While the

58. See Aldred, *MMJ* 3 (1970) p. 37, discussing examples of royal portraiture.

59. In *Festgabe für Dr. Walter Will*, 124, 136. The Munich head (ÄS 5570, pl. 1) does not appear to represent an earlier example; it is very like the sphinx head of Sesostris I from Karnak (Evers, *Staat aus dem Stein*, pl. 33; Aldred, *MMJ* 3 [1970] fig. 17, p. 38).

60. Steckeweh, *Die Fürstengräber von Qau*, pl. 15a; illustrated more clearly in Scamuzzi, *Egyptian Art*, pl. 18.

61. For example, Newberry, *El Bersheh* I, pl. 10 (temp. Sesostris III; cf. Smith, *AJA* 55 [1951] pls. 18, 20); Petrie, *Antaeopolis*, pl. 27 (*W3ḥ-k3* II, presumably temp. Amenemhet III).

62. This feature apparently reappears in the Seventeenth Dynasty statue of Prince Ahmose in the Louvre (E 15682; *JEA* 10 [1924] pl. 18), but it was evidently little used in Eighteenth Dynasty private statuary until the reign of Hatshepsut (e.g., CG 42116: Terrace and Fischer, *Treasures of the Cairo Museum*, pp. 97, 100).

63. The first (Dyn. 21, temp. Psusennes) is known from Berlin 23673, 1, 13 (Borchardt, "Die Mittel zur zeitlichen Festlegung," *Quellen und Forschung zur Zeitbestimmung der ägyptischen Geschichte*, Bd. 2 [1935] p. 99, pls. 2–2a) and Louvre 96 (Malinine et al., *Catalogue des Stèles du Sérapéum* I, no. 52). The second (Dyn. 22, temp. Pimay) is known from two other stelae in the Louvre (*ibid.*, nos. 22, 23). Cf. K. Kitchen, *Third Intermediate Period*, §151–152 (Horsiese J) and §155–156 (Horsiese H).

64. Yoyotte, "Les Principautés du Delta au temps de l'anarchie libyenne," *Mélanges Maspero* I, 4e fasc., 123 (§3). The complete title is given to Padiese, the father of Horsiese H on Serapeum stela 23 (Malinine et al., *Catalogue des Stèles du Sérapéum* I, p. 23). Neither version of the title is present in the titulary of a later Memphite High Priest named Horsiese (Dyn. 26: CG 1212).

65. Walters Art Gallery 22.203; Steindorff, *JEA* 25 (1939) pp. 30–33 and *Catalogue of the Egyptian Sculpture in the Walters Art Gallery*, no. 145, p. 49, pl. 95. For the interpretation of the title see A. Alt, *BiOr* 9 (1952) pp. 163–164. Several Eighteenth Dynasty statues were also reinscribed in this dynasty: CG 42194, 42206, 42207.

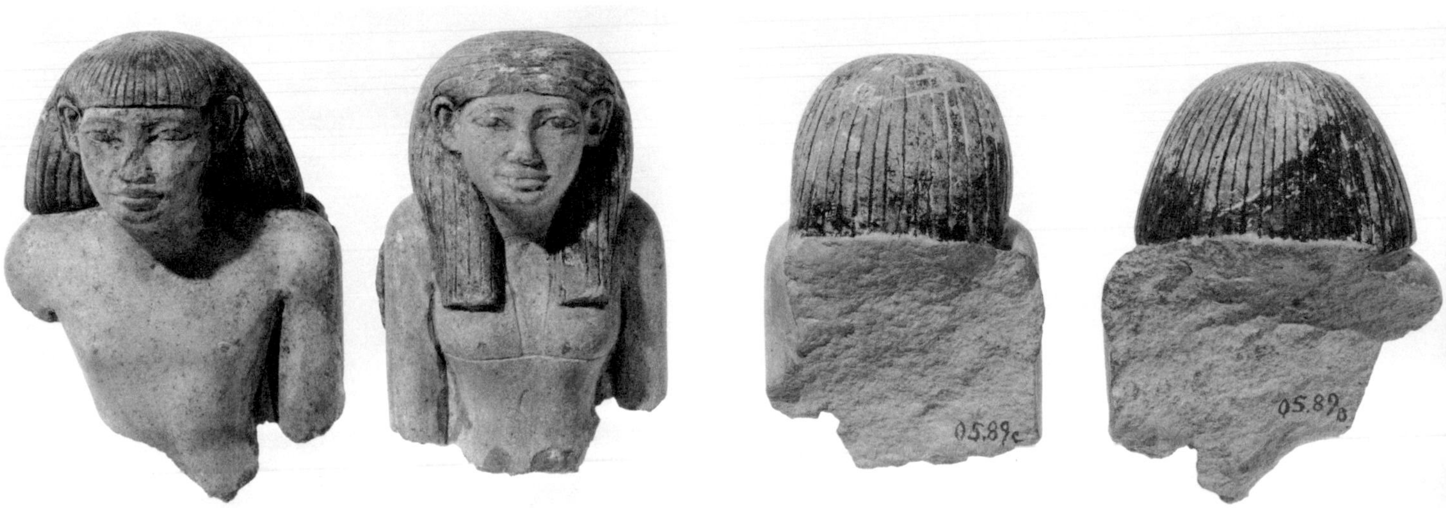

FIGURES 18, 19 Upper parts of Twelfth Dynasty dyad in Boston, MFA 05.89b–c

statuette of the Palestinian commissioner was found in the Egyptian Delta, that of his Memphite contemporary is reported, conversely, to come from the shores of northern Syria, specifically Byblos. It was purchased in Beirut by a European dealer who sold it to the Metropolitan Museum a short time thereafter. One need not, of course, be surprised to find a Middle Kingdom statuette in Byblos, for this site, and the surrounding region, have yielded many other examples of that period.[66] But it is difficult to say whether this one was reinscribed in Lebanon, or whether it went there after the later name was added.

FIGURE 20 Fragments as assembled in Boston, MFA 05.89a–c

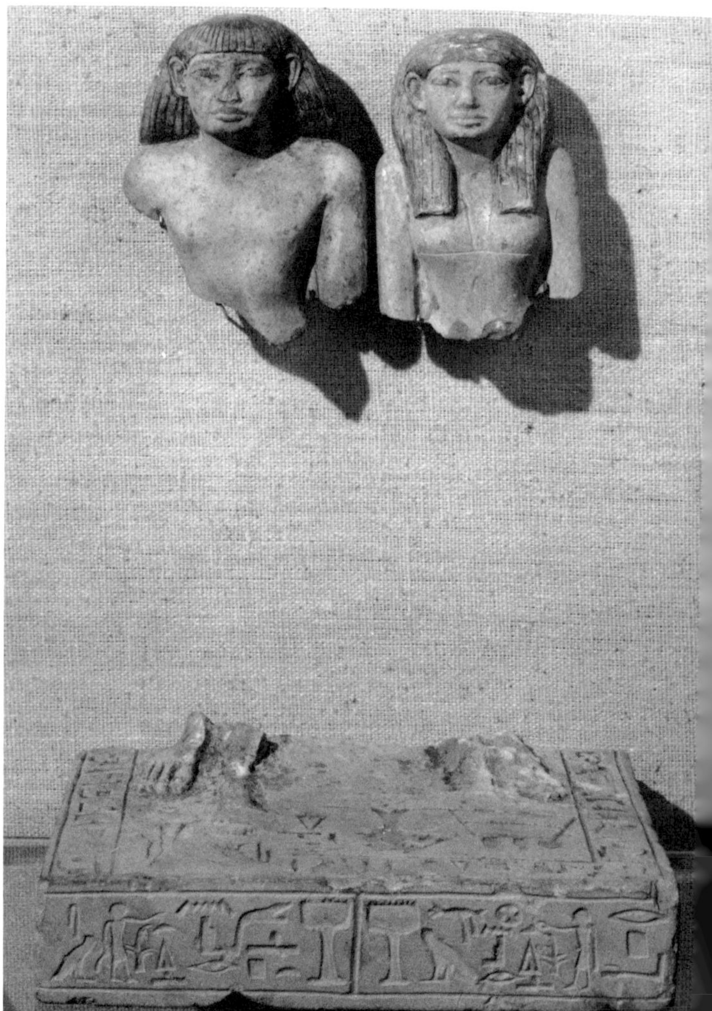

A DISMEMBERED DYAD OF THE TWELFTH DYNASTY

The fragments

In the fall of 1905 Theodore Davis gave the Boston Museum of Fine Arts three fragments of a Middle Kingdom limestone statuette representing a certain

66. Most of this evidence is reviewed by John Wilson in *AJSL* 58 (1941) pp. 225–236. In addition a fragmentary Middle Kingdom statuette was found at Byblos (Montet, *Byblos et l'Égypte*, p. 252, fig. 112), and two more fragmentary statuettes of the same period, purchased from a dealer in Beirut and said to come from Qatna, are in the Metropolitan Museum: 67.226, 68.101.

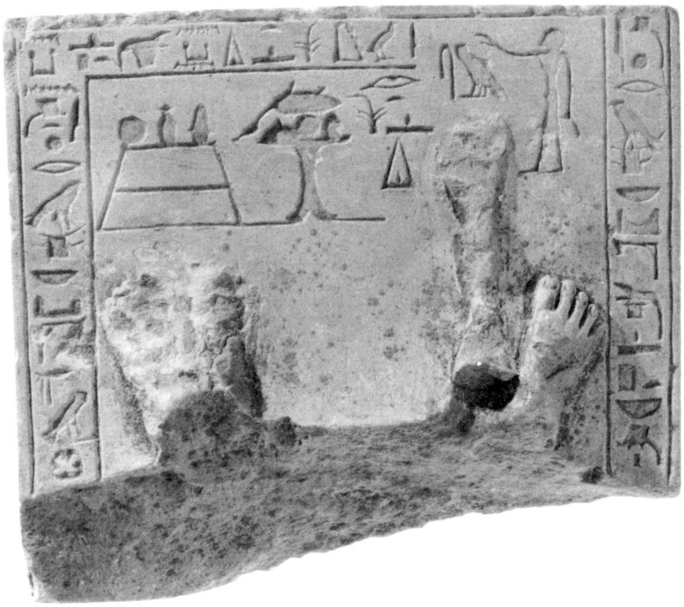

FIGURE 21
Upper surface of base, MFA 05.89a

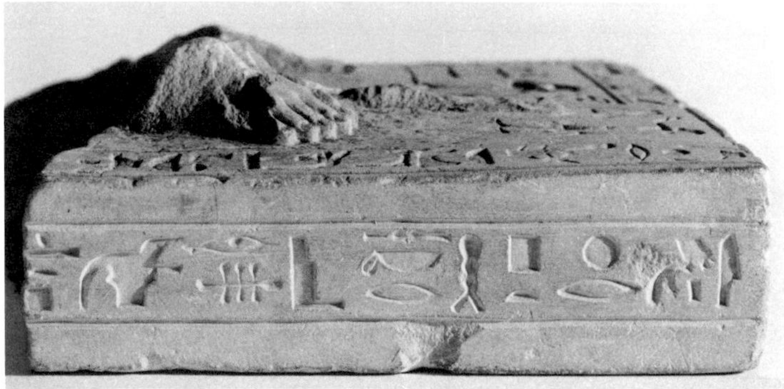

FIGURE 22
Proper right edge of base

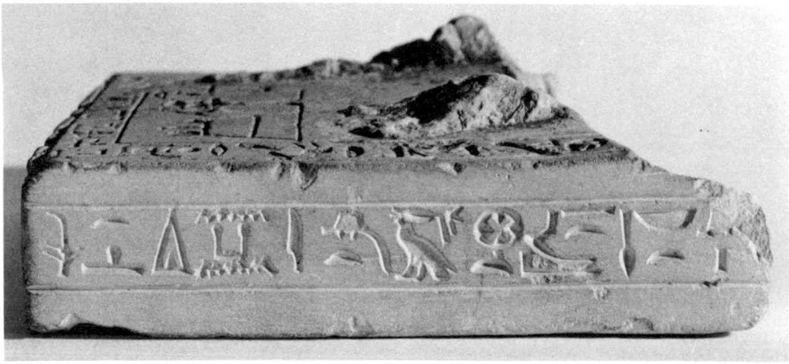

FIGURE 23
Proper left side of base

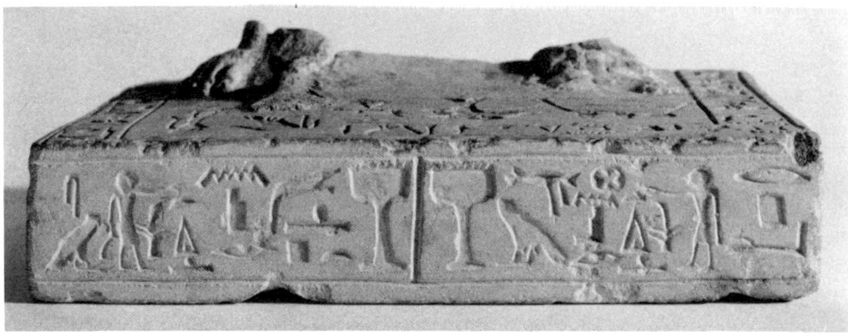

FIGURE 24
Front edge of base

Sobk-ḥotpe and his wife Shedi-em-niwe (05.89a-c; Figures 18–24).[67] The man wears only a kilt, of which nothing is preserved, and a striated shoulder-length wig, she a long close-fitting dress with shoulder straps and a long tripartite wig. To judge from the physiognomies and the style of her wig, the date lies within the first half of the Twelfth Dynasty, but is not so early as the first reign, or even, perhaps, so early as the first two reigns; thus the range is most probably the fifty years of Amenemhet II–Sesostris II, centering on 1900 B.C.

The backpillar, which terminated just below the level of the shoulders, is completely missing, as is the back edge of the base, which shows the battered remnants of both pairs of feet. Otherwise the surface of the base is in good condition, and the inscriptions, on the top, front, and sides, are almost completely preserved.

A second limestone statuette belonging to a Sobk-ḥotpe and Shedi-em-niwe is described by Weigall in *Rec. trav.* 29 (1907), p. 217. It was acquired by Sir Flinders Petrie and is now in the Egyptology Department of University College, London (U.C. 14346). Since the name of the woman is not attested elsewhere, and since the name of the man is preceded, in both

67. Fragment a (the man) is 9.5 cm. high; fragment b (the woman) is 9 cm.; the base (c) is 3.2 cm. high at the edge.

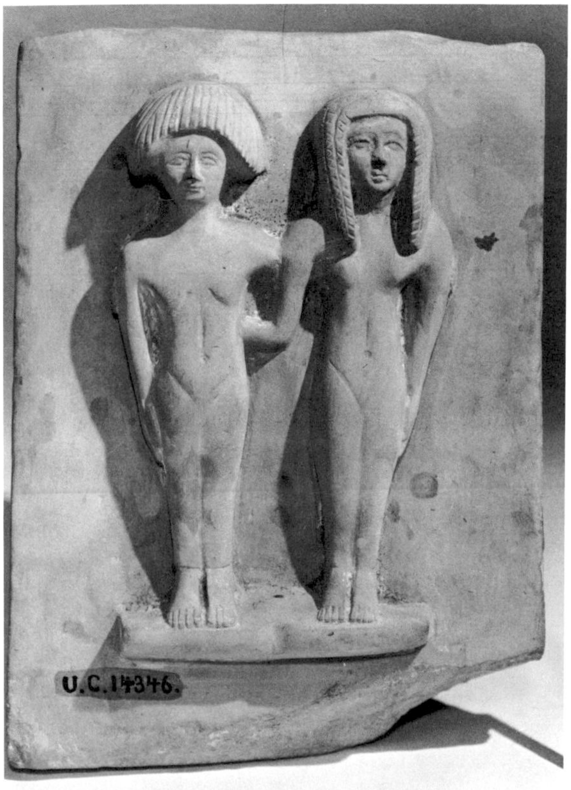

FIGURE 25
Reworked central portion of dyad, University College 14346

FIGURE 26
Proper right side of reworked fragment

FIGURE 27
Proper left side of reworked fragment

cases, by an identical title, and one that is scarcely less exceptional, it is immediately evident that both monuments belong to the same individuals. When all the evidence was assembled, moreover, including photographs (Figures 25–27) and facsimiles of the inscriptions (Figure 28),[68] the second statuette proved to be both more and less closely related to the other than was anticipated. The inscriptions on each side of the backpillar complete those on the base so precisely that there can be no doubt that they belong to the same monument, which stood about 29 cm. high when complete. The figures, on the other hand, have nothing to do with the other fragments; they are not only a forgery, but a forgery that imitates the style of a later period.[69] They have been carved from those parts of original sculpture that remained on the backpillar when the other pieces, now in Boston, were detached. In this way two statuettes were produced from one, and the spurious sculpture that was carved from the least interesting of the four fragments was authenticated by its ancient inscriptions.

68. I am indebted to Suzanne Chapman for providing information, rubbings of the inscriptions, and photographs of the Boston fragments, and to Mrs. Barbara Adams for a rubbing and photographs of the fragment in London. All this material has been used in preparing the drawings for Figures 27, 28. The photographs are published with the kind permission of Dows Dunham, of the Boston Museum of Fine Arts, and H. S. Smith, formerly Curator of Egyptian Antiquities at University College.

69. The interlaced arms are not known before the New Kingdom, as first observed by Spiegelberg, "Note on the Feminine Character of the New Empire," *JEA* 15 (1929) p. 199. For other examples see Vandier, *Manuel d'archéologie* III, pp. 310, 440, 441, 447.

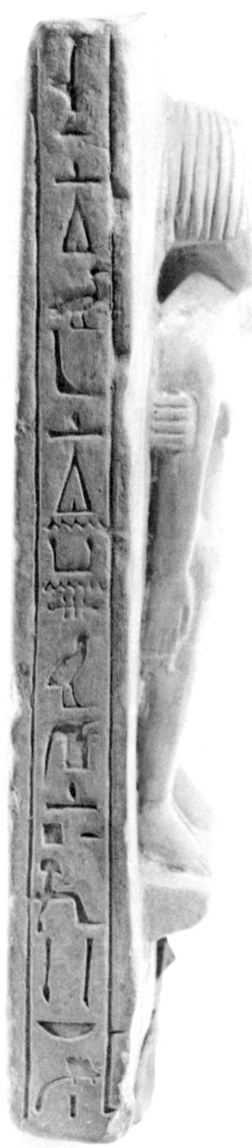

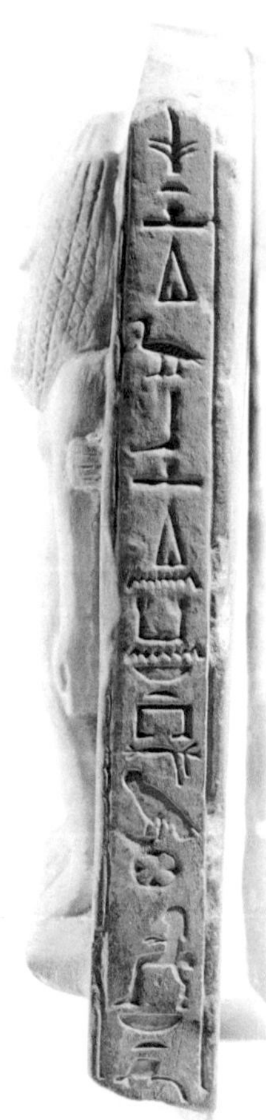

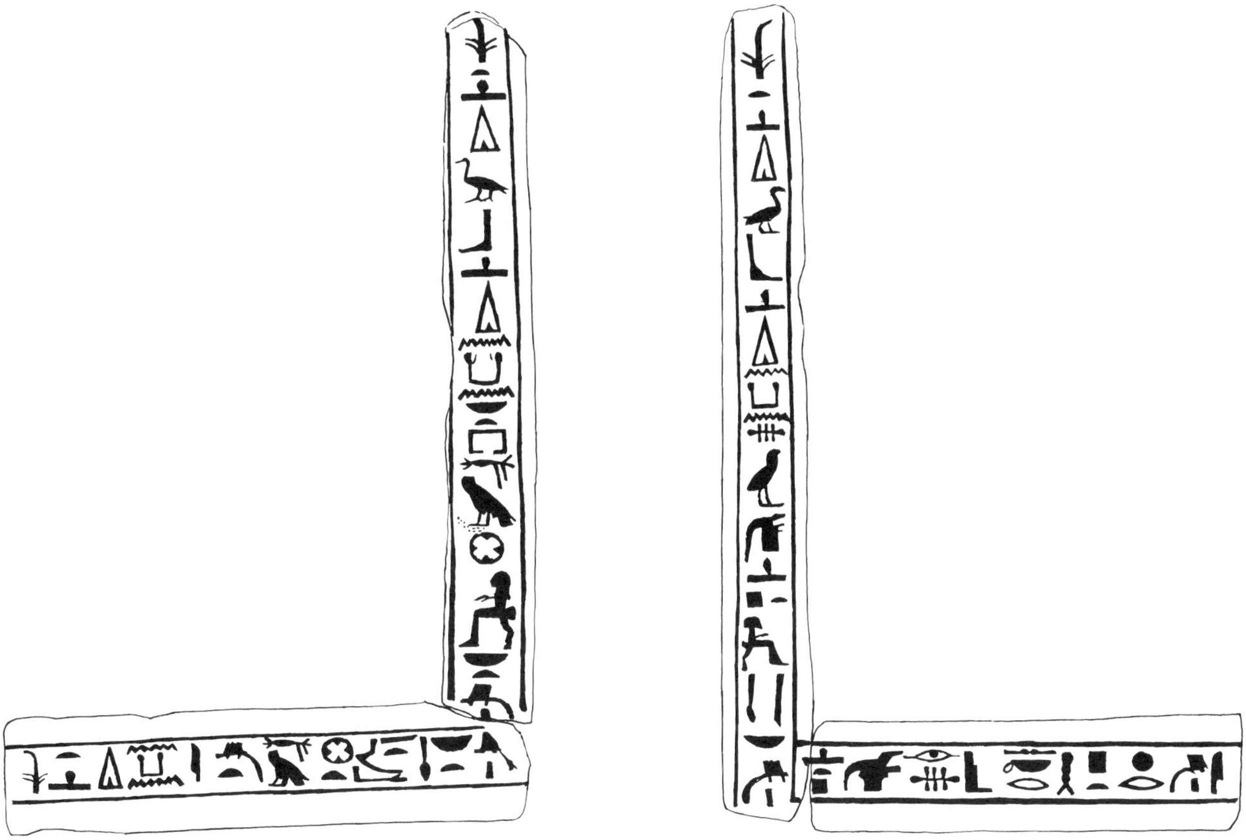

FIGURE 28
Facsimile of inscriptions of Boston and London fragments of dyad, reassembled

FIGURE 29
Facsimile of front and upper surface of base (latter inverted)

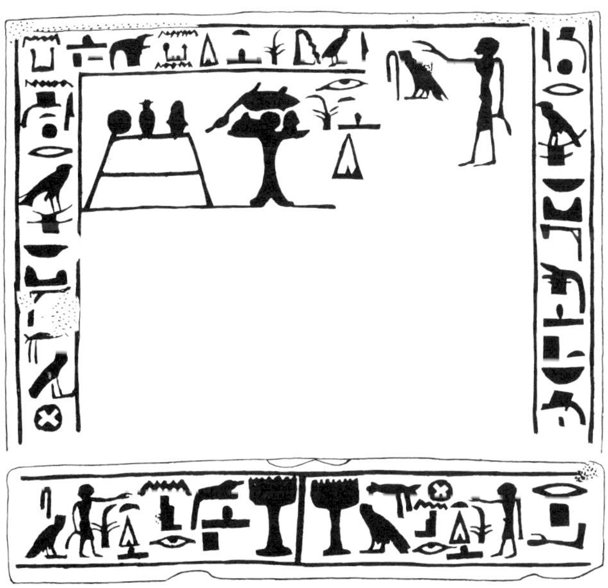

The inscriptions

All the representations and inscriptions on the base and backpillar lack inner detail and are filled with blue paint. Those on the top of the base (Figures 21, 29) are oriented so that they address the statuettes to which they refer, and are upside-down when viewed from the front.[70] A relatively large figure at the upper

70. This orientation is most unusual. Offering tables commonly show the [hieroglyph] -sign so that it faces the recipient (false door or statue), but the inscription is almost always oriented so that it can be read by those making the offering; the offering slab of Queen *Wḏbtn*, dating to the late Sixth Dynasty, exceptionally orients the [hieroglyph] -sign and inscription so that both face the pyramid (Jéquier, *Pyramide d'Oudjebten*, fig. 7, p. 15, pl. 13 [2]), and a few other offering slabs similarly show the inscription and [hieroglyph] -sign oriented in the same direction; although these were not found *in situ*, it is probable that the inscriptions also faced the offering niche in these cases: Jéquier, *Monument funéraire de Pepi II*, III, figs. 78, 80, p. 75; Cairo CG 23007 (with name of King *Nb-ḥpt-Rʿ* Mentuhotep; cf. Habachi, *MDIK* 19 [1963] p. 32, fig. 12). But in those cases where statues are associated with offering tables, the

right stands with one hand raised in a gesture of invocation, the other hand holding what is evidently the tail of the leopard skin customarily worn by the *sm*(*t*)-priest.[71] He is in fact labeled *sm*(*t*), and his action is described as "making an 'offering that the king gives'"; the whole of this might also be read: "Making an offering . . . (by) the *smt*-priest." Two tables placed before him are laden with the offerings he invokes: a circular tray on a tall stand bears three loaves of varied shape as well as a goose; a rectangular stand supports two more loaves, flanking a jar. These representations are arranged at different levels so as to fill the space left by the feet of the standing couple.

At the top edge, and continuing down the left side, is the invocation which the *sm*(*t*)-priest pronounces: "It is pure[72]—an offering that the king gives to the spirit of *Sbk-ḥtp* and to the spirit of her who is revered with Nemty,[73] Lord of the Twelfth U.E. Nome,[74] *Šdi-m-niwt*."[75] The corresponding column on the opposite side reads: "He who is revered with Nemty, Lord of the Twelfth U.E. Nome, *Sbk-ḥtp*, possessor of reverence."

The proper right and left sides of the base and backpillar (Figure 28) contain the following phrases: (right) "One revered with Ptah-Sokar, the Osiris,[76] the Magician(?)[77] *Sbk-ḥtp*"; "An offering that the king gives, and an offering that Geb gives to the Magician(?) *Sbk-ḥtp* justified, possessor of reverence"; (left) "An offering that the king gives to the spirit of *Šdi-m-niwt*, justified, possessor of reverence"; "An offering that the king gives, and an offering that Geb gives to the spirit of the Mistress of the House *Šdi-m-niwt*, possessor of reverence."

The front edge of the base (Figures 24, 29) is divided in two halves, the hieroglyphs being oriented toward the center. On both sides, near the outer corners, the standing figure of a priest makes a gesture of invocation toward one of a pair of offering tables at the center. The sequence of the inscriptions is retrograde, reading inward, and the one on the left reads: "The *sm*(*t*)-priest (he says), 'An offering that the king gives, to the Osiris *Sbk-ḥtp*.'" The corresponding inscription on the right is: "The *iry-pʿt*-priest (he says), 'An offering that the king gives, to the Osiris *Šdi-m-niwt*.'"

It will be noted that the *iry-pʿt*-priest, in contrast to his counterpart, does not hold his garment and therefore does not appear to wear a leopard skin. In royal offering scenes of the New Kingdom (Figures 30, 31)[78] this officiant similarly lacks the leopard skin and follows the *sm*(*t*)-priest just as, in the present case, he occupies the subordinate right-hand side of the base and gives the invocation for the wife, while the *sm*(*t*)-priest is on the left side, associated with the man. Probably the *iry-pʿt* also figured in the funerary cult of Twelfth Dynasty kings, but their pyramids have unfortunately left only a few fragments of relief, so that the evidence is sadly incomplete. At any rate the two functions of *sm*(*t*) and *iry-pʿt* seem to be united in the late Twelfth Dynasty tomb chapel of *Wḫ-ḥtp* at Meir, where numerous other usurpations of royal prerogatives may be observed. The officiant in question is clad in a leopard skin (Figure 32)[79] and is accompanied by the caption 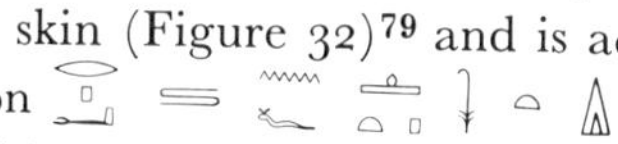 "the *iry-pʿt* who offers him an 'offering that the king gives.'"

orientation is always normal: Louvre E 11573 (Vandier, *Manuel* III, pl. 85 [4]); Turin 3082 (*ibid.*, pl. 83 [3]); Petrie and Brunton, *Sedment* II, pl. 51; MMA 22.1.107a–b (A. C. Mace, *BMMA* 16 [Nov. 1921, Pt. II] p. 13, fig. 14); Brooklyn 57.140 (Bothmer, *Brooklyn Museum Bulletin* 20/4 [Fall 1959] fig. 2, p. 13).

71. For similar examples of the costume cf. Blackman, *Meir* VI, pl. 17; de Morgan, *Fouilles à Dahchour 1894*, pl. 11; *1894–95*, pl. 14; Griffith, *Siût and Dêr Rîfeh*, pl. 2. For the reading of *sm*(*t*) see Gardiner, *Ancient Egyptian Onomastica* I, 39* ff.

72. Cf. *irt ḥtp-di-nswt in ḥry ḥbt: iw wʿb n kȝ.s* (Newberry, *Beni Hasan* I, pl. 18); also Tylor and Griffith, *Paheri*, pl. 6: the son, clad in the leopard skin, offers *prt ḫrw m ḫt nbt iw wʿb* "funerary offerings consisting of everything—it is pure."

73. For the reading of the name of this divinity as *Nmty* rather than *ʿnty*, see O. D. Berlev, *Vestnik Drevnej Istorii* 1 (1969) pp. 3–30.

74. For the writing of the nome emblem see below, p. 26.

75. This name is highly unusual. A masculine example is known from Dyn. XX (Ranke, *PN* II, p. 319 [16]) and names of the pattern NN-*m-niwt* are common from the late New Kingdom onward (*ibid.*, p. 50, notes 1, 2; p. 51, note 1) when *niwt* presumably refers to Thebes; but it can hardly have that meaning in this case in view of the date.

76. Note that this epithet also occurs before the names of both the man and his wife on the front of the base, in the more usual context of funerary offerings; cf. *ÄZ* 90 (1963) pp. 37–38.

77. *Sȝ*(*w*); discussed below, pp. 26–27.

78. Figure 30 is from Naville, *The Temple of Deir el Bahari* IV, pl. 110 (cf. pl. 112). Figure 31 is from Winlock, *Bas-Reliefs from the Temple of Rameses I at Abydos*, pl. 9.

79. Blackman, *Meir* VI, pl 15.

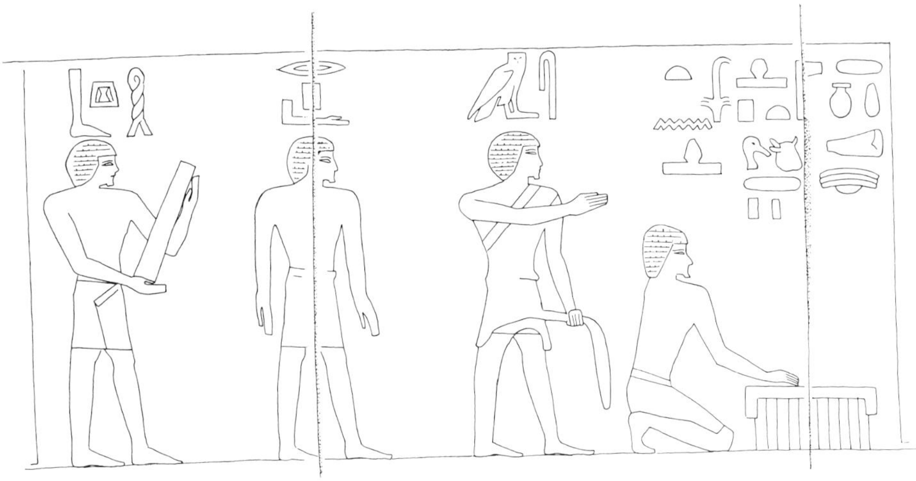

FIGURE 30
Detail of offering scene in temple of Hatshepsut at Deir el Bahri. After Naville

FIGURE 31
Detail of offering scene in reliefs of Ramesses I from Abydos. After Winlock

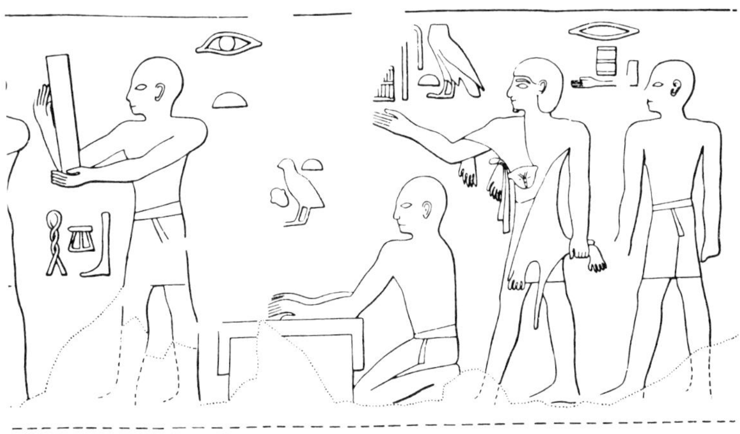

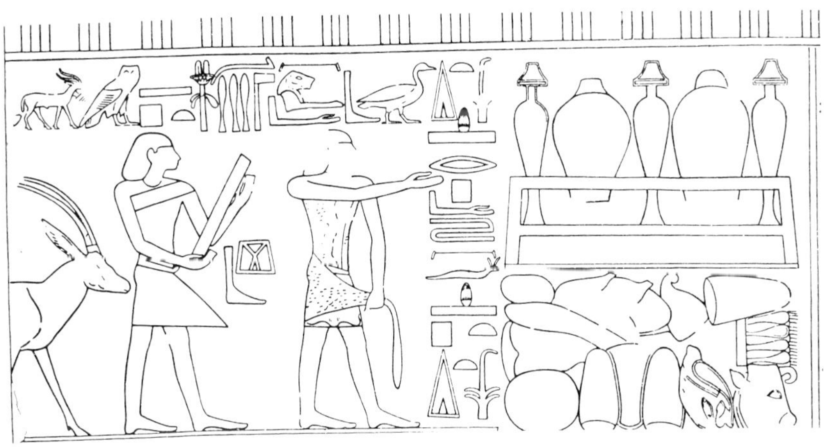

FIGURE 32
Twelfth Dynasty offering scene from Meir. After Blackman

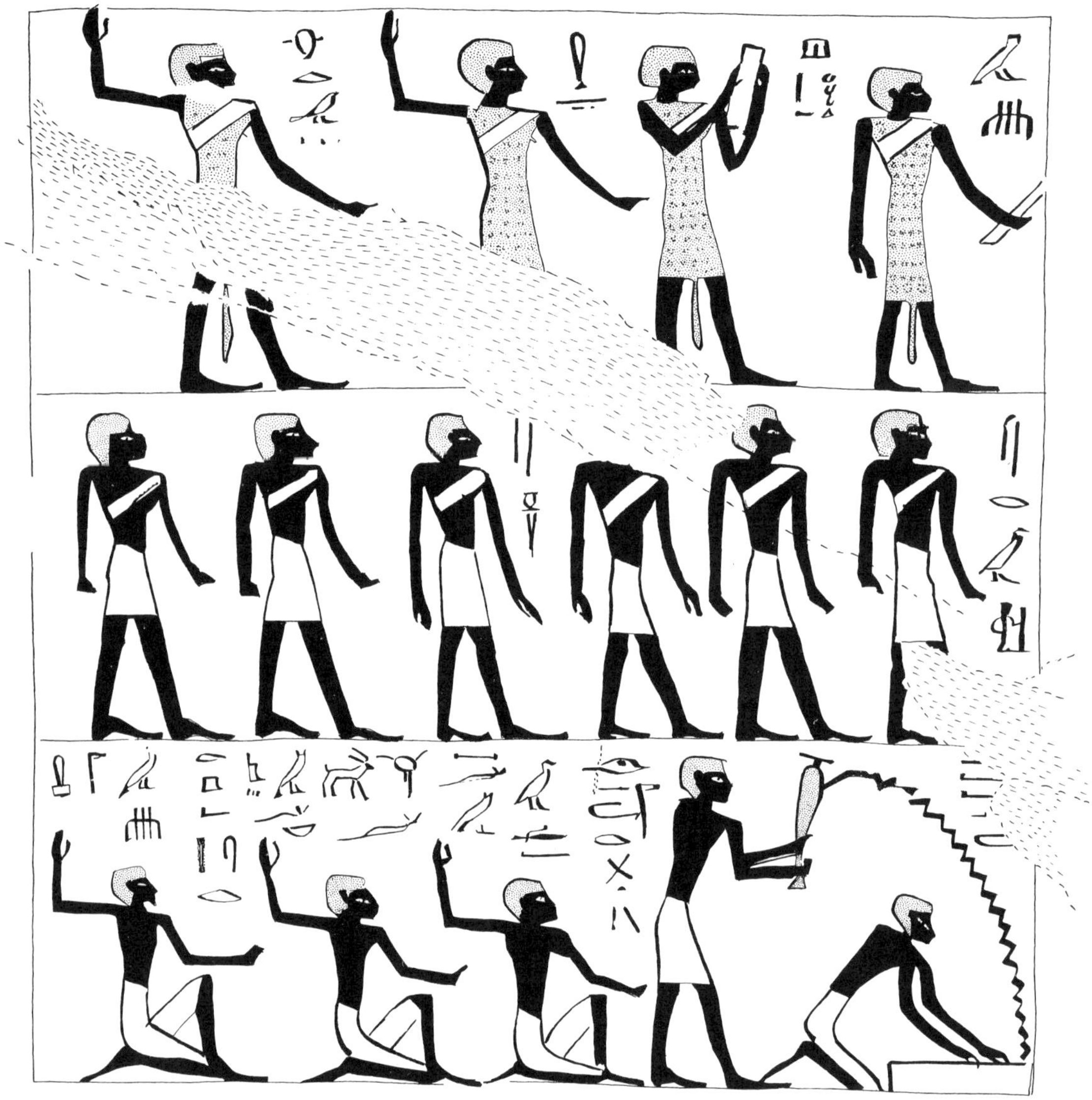

FIGURE 33
Twelfth Dynasty offering scene on a coffin from Asyut

Even earlier evidence for the appearance of the *iry-p‘t* in a funerary context is provided by a coffin from Asyut, the date of which cannot be much later than the beginning of the Twelfth Dynasty.[80] On the inside of the back, directly opposite the representation of the false door, is a most unusual scene (Figure 33)[81] representing three registers of funerary officiants. The uppermost series, wearing the leopard skin as well as the lector priest's bandoleer, are labeled *imy-ḫnt*, *ḥry ḥbt*, *ḥm-t3*, and *ḥry-wrw* "the chamberlain, the lector priest, the 'servant of the earth,' and 'one who is over the great.'"[82] The second series of officiants, wearing the bandoleer, are labeled *śrw* and *śmr(w)* "officials

80. On the dating of the Asyut coffins see Schenkel, *Frühmittelägyptische Studien*, §44a.

81. Drawn from the photograph in Chassinat and Palanque, *Une campagne de fouilles dans la nécropole d'Assiout*, p. 68, fig. 4, pl. 19. According to de Buck, *CT* II, p. xiii, note 9, the coffin is in the Louvre, but the back, containing the scene described here, is not to be found.

82. The last two designations are exceedingly rare but occur again in the Eighteenth Dynasty: Davies, *Five Theban Tombs*, pls. 7, 9, 10. The *ḥry-wr* also appears in Davies, *Rekh-mi-rē‘*, pls. 80–82; on pl. 80 he is accompanied by the *íry-p‘t*.

and companions." The officiants in the lowermost register lack the leopard skin and bandoleer. Two of them "pour water," while the last three kneel, making a gesture of incantation; the caption above these three figures reads: "making incense (on) the fire, offering to him in his rank and dignity, and in all his places,[83] (by) the *iry-p*ʿ*t*, the chamberlain, the seal-bearer of the god."[84]

The use of the prestigious title *iry-p*ʿ*t* by a funerary officiant is readily explained by its hereditary aspect; it conveys the idea of the heir and survivor that is the fundamental idea of priesthood in ancient Egypt, whether it relates to the gods or the dead. Evidently the *iry-p*ʿ*t*-priest plays the role of Horus, the heir of his father Osiris, and of his grandfather Geb.[85]

The retrograde arrangement of the texts on the front of the base will be discussed in a forthcoming monograph on the orientation of hieroglyphic inscriptions. For the present it is sufficient to say that it primarily relates to other retrograde inscriptions that involve a speech, and more particularly a speech that concludes with the name of the person who is addressed. The use of retrograde sequence on this part of the monument is also appropriate because it enables the orientation of the hieroglyphs to correspond to that of the inscriptions on the sides of the base, yet directs the offering formulae to the center. In this respect it is closely related to Middle Kingdom offering slabs that frequently apply the same procedure to the texts at the bottom edge.[86]

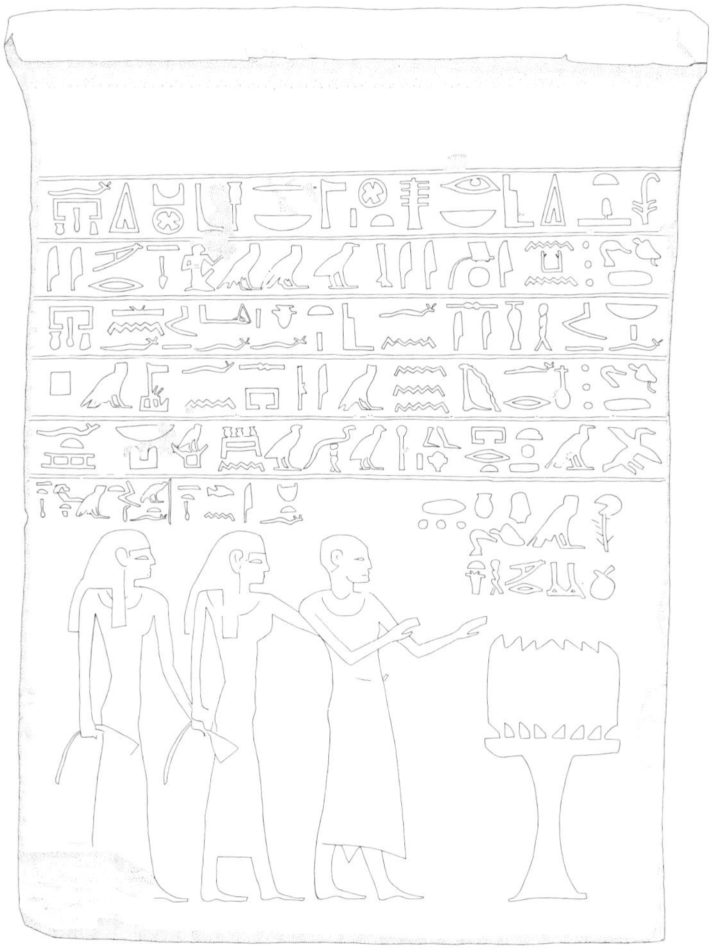

FIGURE 34
Brussels E 2161

The provenance

Both the owner and his wife are "revered with [hieroglyphs]," which certainly refers to the Twelfth Nome of Upper Egypt or to its capital. A Middle Kingdom stela in Brussels (Figure 34)[87] invokes offerings which

83. Cf. CG 1486 (Dyn. XII, Dahshur): "an offering that the king gives in all thy dignities (*m s*ʿ*ḥw.k nbw*) and in all thy places which thou lovest." Also Boston MFA 13.4333, Dyn. VI (H. Fischer, *Dendera*, Pl. 30 [b]): "in his name, in his dignity, in his rank."

84. The last of the designations is an administrative title that acquired a secondary meaning in the context of the funerary ritual: cf. Sauneron, *BIFAO* 51 (1952) pp. 137–171, who does not, however, include this example.

85. The funerary use of the title is not mentioned by Gardiner *Onomastica* I, p. 14* ff., who somewhat misleadingly states that "crown-prince" was "the only meaning still alive in Ramesside times." For the hereditary aspect see, in addition to Gardiner's remarks, those of Helck, "*Rp*ʿ*t* auf dem Thron des *Gb*," *Orientalia* 19 (1950) pp. 416–434. Again the priestly function is not discussed (even the case of *ʾIi-ḥr-nfrt*, p. 427, who presided over the Osirian mysteries as *s*ꜣ*-mr.f* "the loving son"), but Helck aptly quotes Pyr. 1458e (*CT* I, 179e/i): "Thou (Osiris) art the Great One, Lord of Abydos . . . Thoth has given him the throne of Geb, but Horus is the *iry-p*ʿ*t*." Elsewhere in the Pyramid Texts Geb is called the "*iry-p*ʿ*t* of the gods," and his son Osiris is called the "*iry-p*ʿ*t* of Geb."

86. I have summarized these uses of retrograde sequence in "L'Orientation des textes," *Textes et langages de l'Égypte pharaonique* I (Cairo, 1973) pp. 21–23.

87. Brussels E 2161. Drawn from the photograph reproduced in the sales catalogue *Antiquités . . . appartenant à P. Philip* (Paris, 1905) no. 38. A hand copy of the text is given by Speleers, *Recueil des inscriptions*, p. 17 (75); this is to be added to the evidence presented by Gardiner, *Ancient Egyptian Onomastica* II, 69*–70*. The stela is said to come from Gebelein, but that provenance hardly seems possible in view of the internal evidence provided by the inscriptions.

"come forth upon the altar of "; the owner's mother is *M3tit-m-ḥ3t*, a theophoric name referring to the lioness goddess, who was worshiped along with the falcon god and is the sole divinity attributed to in the nome list of the Karnak shrine of Sesostris I.[88] Both divinities are known from the Old Kingdom tombs of Deir el Gebrawi,[89] but the capital was evidently located about fifteen kilometers to the southeast, at Atwala; this site has yielded a Thirteenth Dynasty fragment of relief from the temple of and a late offering slab (CG 20037) that invokes offerings in the name of .[90] The cemeteries near Atwala were persistently looted at the end of the last century, and these operations may well have produced both the statuette, which was presented in 1905, and the stela, which was auctioned in the same year.[91]

The writing of the nome emblem as is not known elsewhere, but the omission of is probably not accidental, since it occurs in the epithet of both husband and wife. If it is not an accident, this omission would mean that the terminal is a phonetic complement, and would thus provide further support for the reading *3tft*, which Kees has proposed in *MDIK* 20 (1965), pp. 107–108. It has already been noted that the reading of , formerly read *ʿnty*, is evidently to be read *Nmty*, as proposed by Berlev.

The title S3w

The sole title of Sobk-ḥotpe, written and , occurs only very rarely in precisely this form. The *Wörterbuch* (III, 414 [4]) cites the Twelfth Dynasty stela CG 20597 for as a title, and probably rightly so: Lange and Schäfer (*Grab- und Denksteine* III, p. 156) take this as part of a name, reading the whole as , but their transcription in II, p. 237, shows , i.e., the title *s3(w)* plus the common name *Nb(.i)-pw* (Ranke, *PN* I, 184 [14]). The title also precedes the name of a certain *Ssn* in Sinai inscription 105 (temp. Amenemhet III). In neither case does the context suggest the meaning, but occurs again in an Eighteenth Dynasty scene representing funerary ceremonies; here an attendant labeled follows another who is (Davies, *Five Theban Tombs*, pl. 2); this last is one of the several designations of magicians (Gardiner, *PSBA* 39 [1917], p. 44) and is known from the Old and Middle Kingdoms in the form (Hassan, *Gîza* II, figs. 17, 22, 25, 27) and (Sinai inscr. 90). The Sinai inscriptions also provide evidence for persons called who are at the same time doctors and are therefore equally clearly *s3w* in the sense of "protector" or "magician" (inscr. 117a, 121, where also occurs as an independent title), and the same association is attested in the Ebers Papyrus (99, 2–3; cf. Gardiner, *o.c.*, 33).

The question is whether the substitution of for would be expected in a title as early as the Twelfth Dynasty. Names like *Sbk-m-s3.f* show such a substitution in Middle Kingdom inscriptions (Ranke, *PN* I, p. 304 [7–9] and cf. p. 69 [23–26] and p. 384 [19–22]), and conversely, the title is written on at least one stela that appears to date to the Twelfth Dynasty—CG 20162—while "overseer of gangs (of workers)," which generally takes this form in Sinai inscriptions (nos. 92, 136, 137, 143, 412, 502), is repeatedly written in no. 85, dating to Amenemhet III.

It seems doubtful, however, that the Sinai example of means "magician" in view of a rock inscription at Aswan (Petrie's no. 286) which seems to refer to the same individual,[92] mentioning his father in this case rather than his mother:

Sinai 105 [?] [ ]

Aswan 286

The meaning of is obscure, but may represent a nisbe-form *ḫnwty*, as it evidently does in the Old Kingdom title "one who is within the workhouse of Ptah."[93] If so, *ḫnwty-s3* would be syn-

88. Lacau and Chevrier, *Une Chapelle de Sésostris Ier*, pl. 3. Here and in *MDIK* 20 (1965) pl. 35, the sign above resembles a knife and is so interpreted by Kees on p. 103, but it is simply the left side of , the missing portion of which has been filled with plaster. Here it may also be noted that the example of , which is quoted by Spiegelberg, *Rec. trav.* 25 (1903) p. 185, and is there identified as U.E. Nome 12, is actually (a crocodile), as T. G. H. James has kindly informed me.

89. Davies, *Deir el Gebrâwi* I, pls. 8, 23; II, pl. 26 (*M3tit*); II, pls. 21, 24 (both divinities).

90. Ahmed Kamal, *ASAE* 3 (1902) pp. 80–81.

91. See note 87 above.

92. Petrie, *Season in Egypt*, pl. 11. In Petrie's copy the signs have mistakenly been fused together.

93. Cairo CG 191. I doubt that *ḫnwt* "Werkstatt" (*Wb.* III, 368[13]) is involved in either case, and it should be noted that the *Wb.* errs in citing *Urk.* I 148 (read p. 149); this is "Residence." The other evidence is no earlier than the New Kingdom.

onymous with the aforementioned title *imy-s3* "one who is within a corps (of workers),"[94] and this in turn would support the interpretation of *s3w*, in the other case, as "ganger," which is the meaning tentatively suggested in Peet-Gardiner-Černý, *Sinai*, p. 109.

I find it difficult, however, to believe that the translation "ganger" is applicable in the present case. A person of so humble a rank would hardly have been able to purchase a statuette of the quality that Sobkḥotpe was able to afford. For this reason alone one may conclude that he was more probably a "magician."

AN EIGHTEENTH DYNASTY DYAD WITH AN ALTERED INSCRIPTION

The sculpture

Representations of corpulent men are well known in relief and statuary from the Fourth Dynasty onward, and a relief of only slightly later date contrasts the obesity of a middle-aged husband with the youthful slimness of his wife.[95] Such a contrast is rarely presented in either relief or statuary, however, and the example shown here (Figures 35–38) may be the earliest of its kind in three dimensions. The closest comparison is provided by the statue of Bak and his wife, dating to the Amarna Period (Figure 39),[96] although a second New Kingdom example (Figure 40) is closer in date and more comparable in respect to attire.[97]

The difference between the proportions of the man and woman is accentuated if they are viewed from the side, as is the difference in attitude. The feet of the woman remain together, as dictated by earlier tradition, and unlike later statuary of the New Kingdom in which women more usually extend the left foot at least slightly, echoing the more decisively advanced foot that is characteristic of men.[98] These differences are mitigated by the massive backing from which the two figures emerge, and by the equally massive base on which they stand. A harmonious effect is also struck by the mass and contour of the woman's wig, which—since her husband is wigless[99]—nicely balances the lower and larger mass of his flaring kilt.

Despite the fact that it stands only 29.7 cm. high, the balanced simplicity of the statuette creates an impression of monumentality that is in keeping with the hard dark stone from which it is made.[100] In this respect it seems to continue the style and taste of the later Middle Kingdom. The faces, however, have acquired the slightly squinting blandness of the early New Kingdom, and seem rather masklike compared to the more expressive physiognomies of the Twelfth Dynasty. The interlaced arms of the couple represent an entirely new feature, as far as representations of husband and wife are concerned, and this may be one of the earliest examples.[101]

The form of the wife's wig is similar to those of the early New Kingdom, consisting of long braided strands

94. Compare 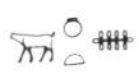 and  (var. 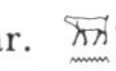), which, according to *Wb.* III, 373 (3), is known from the Ptolemaic Period in reference to priests or sages and is presumably to be interpreted as "one who is within the (priestly) phyle(s)."

95. Fischer, "A Scribe of the Army in a Saqqara Mastaba of the Early Fifth Dynasty," *JNES* 18 (1959) pp. 243–248, fig. 8.

96. Berlin (Charlottenburg) 1/63: W. Kaiser, *Jahrbuch der Stiftung Preußischer Kulterbesitz* 2 (1963) p. 133 ff; *Ägyptisches Museum Berlin* (Berlin, 1967) no. 766.

97. Pushkin Museum, Moscow, 2099. In his *Manuel d'archéologie* III, pp. 495, 504, Vandier dates this statuette, along with another, representing the same man's wife, to the reign of Tuthmosis I. Lacking the publication in which the texts are presented (Turaiev, *Statues et statuettes de la Collection Golénischef*, nos. 46–47), I have obtained further information from Professor Vandier, including a reference to Porter-Moss, *Topographical Bibliography* I (2nd ed.), Pt. 1, p. 414, where the statuettes are identified as coming from Theban tomb 345. A slightly later date is possible, however; Kees *ÄZ* 85 [1960] (p. 47) believes the tomb to be "etwa Hatschepsut," but this would not necessarily mean a difference of more than eight years, while a date within the reign of Tuthmosis I would still be about fifty years later than the beginning of the Eighteenth Dynasty. Further illustrations of the statuettes (in addition to those mentioned by Porter-Moss) are to be found in S. Khodzhash, *Egipetskoe Iskusstvo v Gosudarstvennom Musee Izobrazitelnikh Iskusstvo Imeni A. S. Pushkina* (Moscow, 1971) pls. 34–37; Irmgard Woldering, *Gods Men and Pharaohs* (Fribourg, Switzerland, n.d.) p. 134.

98. Cf., for example, MMA 24.7.1424 (Hayes, *Scepter* II, fig. 31, p. 62), with one foot very slightly advanced, and the earlier statuette MMA 16.10.369 (*Scepter* II, fig. 5, p. 15), with the feet together; also Figure 40.

99. A usual feature in representations of portly aging men; see *JNES* 18 (1959), p. 245 (article cited in note 95 above).

100. The stone has been identified by Pieter Meyers as gabbro, but it might also be called diorite (or dioritic-gabbro).

101. See note 69 above. Groups belonging to the preceding Second Intermediate Period generally show clasped hands, as exemplified by MMA 16.10.369 (Hayes, *Scepter* II, fig. 5, p. 15) and Northampton, Spiegelberg, Newberry, *Theban Necropolis*, pl. 15 (1, 3).

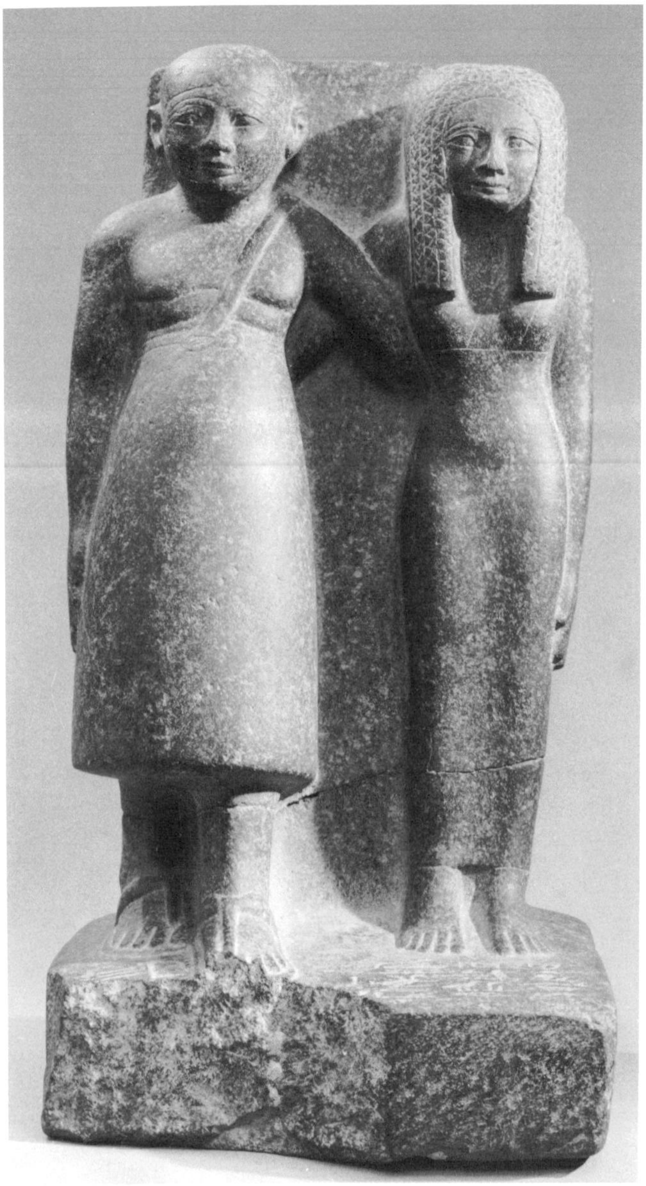

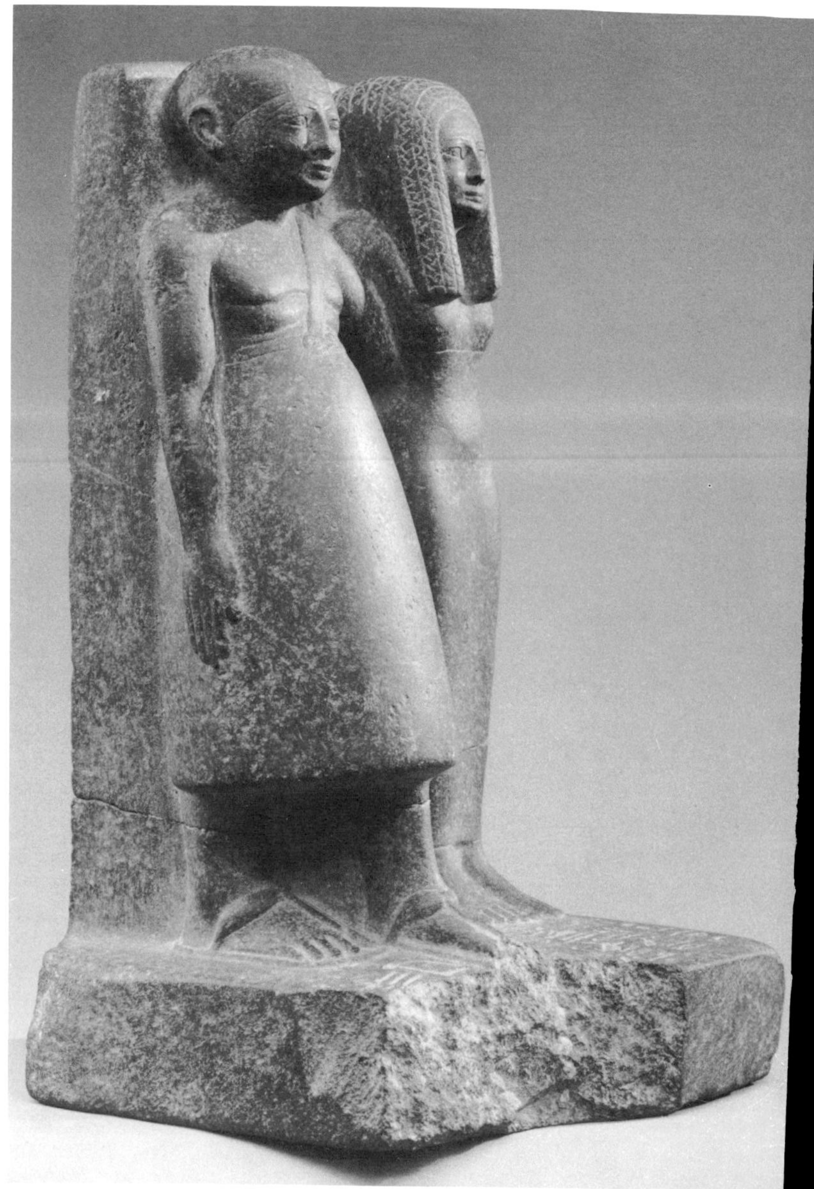

FIGURES 35, 36, 37, 38 Eighteenth Dynasty dyad, MMA 62.186

but the crown of her head shows a lozenge-shaped blank area (Figure 41) for which I can find no parallel; presumably it is related to the median band, or pair of bands, that appears on most women's wigs of the early Eighteenth Dynasty (e.g., Figure 40).[102]

The clothing shows none of the changes that begin to appear in the mid-Eighteenth Dynasty, since the statue is presumably of earlier manufacture. The single strap of the wife's dress is extremely uncommon in statuary, but is occasionally found in two-dimensional representations from the Old Kingdom onward,[103] and is more frequently seen on those of the early New

102. See Vandier, *Manuel* III, p. 254. Possibly this detail represents a "skull plate" (Arabic ḳurṣ) like that of the headdress shown in Winlock, *Treasure of Three Egyptian Princesses*, p. 14, pl. 4.

103. For the Old Kingdom see Staehelin, *Untersuchungen zur ägyptischen Tracht*, p. 168, who cites Oriental Institute, *Mereruka*, pl. 94; Junker, *Gîza* X, figs. 44–45, pl. 18a; CG 250. For the Middle Kingdom see Blackman, *Meir* II, pl. 3, and CG 20456, 20754.

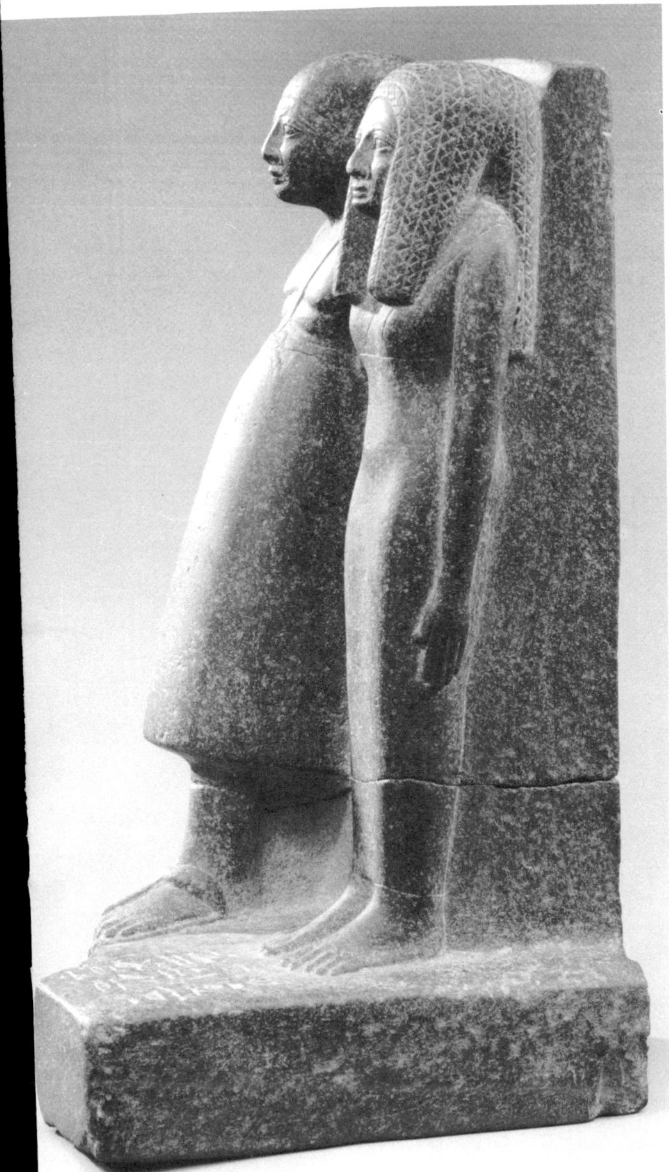

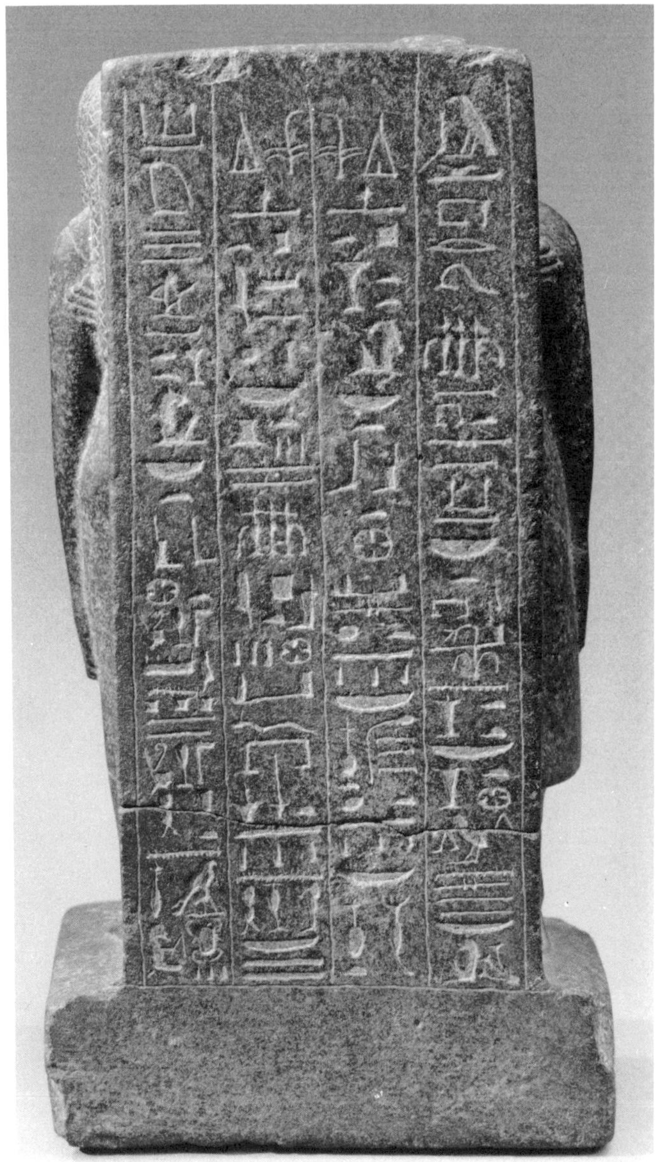

Kingdom.[104] It is considerably more surprising to find a single, narrower strap repeated in the husband's attire; while single straps are not unknown in earlier representations of men, they generally belong to the costume of workers or soldiers and are bandoleers, not intended to support the kilt.[105] Normally the long kilt lacks any support of this kind whatever except in the case of the vizier's harness, as attested from the late Middle Kingdom onward—a cord passed behind the neck and fastened at two points on the front edge.[106] In the present case the fastening of the kilt, which

104. E.g., MMA 19.3.33 (Hayes, *Scepter* II, fig. 7, p. 19); 12.182.3 (*ibid.*, fig. 93, p. 169); Davies, *Rekh-mi-rēʿ*, pls. 9, 63, 64, 66, 67, 73.

105. For soldiers and workmen see Fischer, *Kush* 9 (1961) p. 66, note 48. The Middle Kingdom examples in Lange and Schäfer, *Grab- und Denksteine*, all represent the costume of the lector priest: CG 20246, 20404, 20515, and all the cases shown in Pt. IV, pls. 62–63 except 427 (a soldier).

106. Vandier, *Manuel* III, p. 250; for examples of the vizier's straps on stelae see CG 20102, 20690.

seems to derive from the Old Kingdom dress bow, is also unexpected, although there are some other New Kingdom examples where this knot is revived in connection with the archaic half-goffered kilt.[107] And the very loose form of the knot is probably unique. There is, however, one other early New Kingdom example of a long kilt with single strap and knot—the wooden statuette in the Pushkin Museum, Moscow (Figure 40).

Inscriptions

The inscriptions on the base (Figure 42) identify the couple, but his name is lost, leaving only a title that preceded it: "*wꜥb*-priest." She is "His wife, the Mistress of the House, Yotes-resu,[a] who is called Tjare."[b]

107. See Engelbach, *ASAE* 29 (1929) p. 45, referring to CG 42125 and cf. also CG 42132.

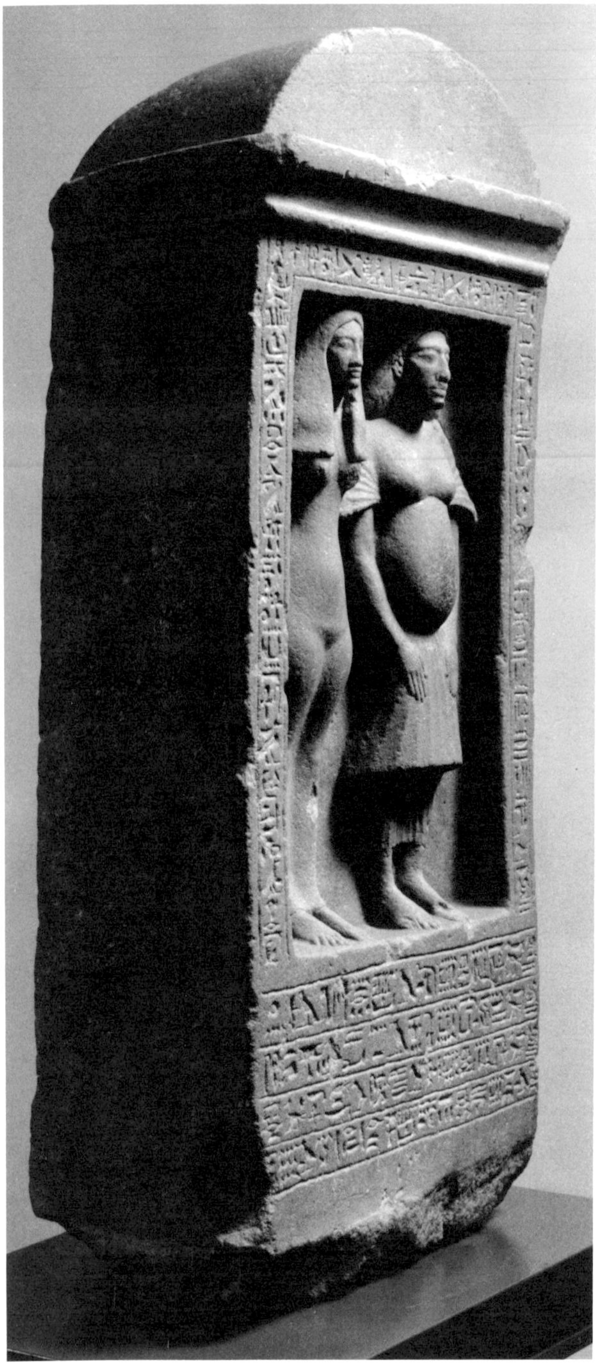

FIGURE 39
Eighteenth Dynasty dyad, Amarna Period, Berlin (West) 1/63

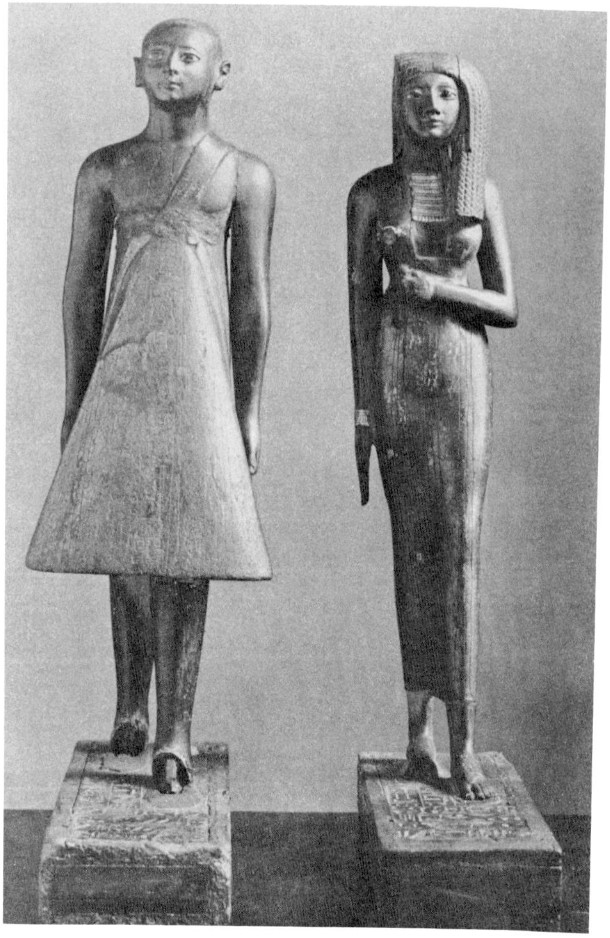

FIGURE 40
Eighteenth Dynasty dyad, Pushkin Museum, Moscow 2099

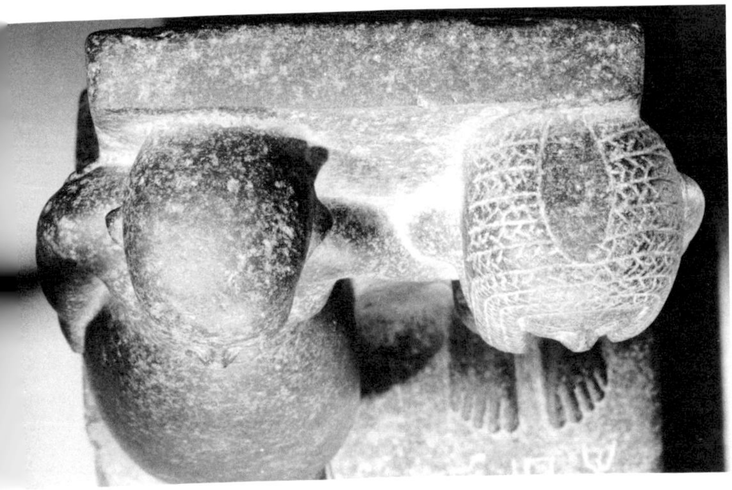

FIGURE 41
Detail of woman's headdress, MMA 62.186

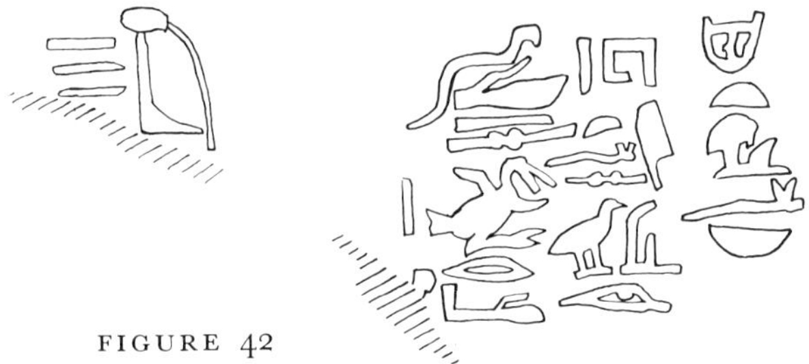

FIGURE 42
Inscription on base of MMA 62.186

FIGURE 43
Inscription on backpillar of MMA 62.186

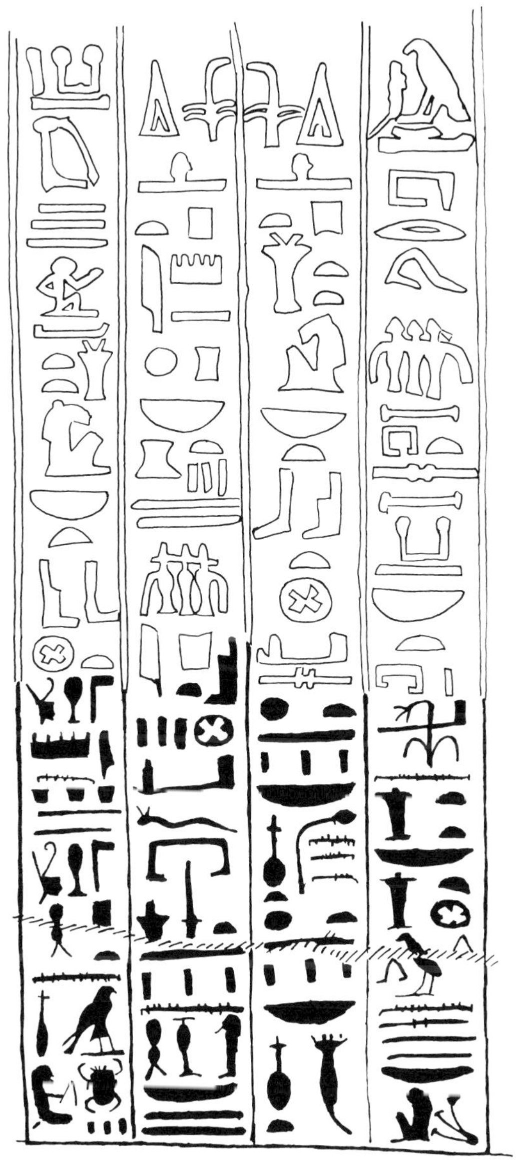

The inscription on the back (Figure 43) comprises four vertical columns, the left pair referring to the husband, the right pair referring to his wife. The lower part of the surface, including the entire width of the backpillar and more than three-fifths of its height, has been ground down to eliminate the original signs and a new inscription has replaced this portion of the old one. The substituted signs have a fresher look than those on the base, but this contrast is less apparent on the upper portion of the backpillar since the signs there have been scraped out to reduce the contrast. Otherwise the signs at the top of the backpillar correspond to the style of those on the front. There are, however, some slight alterations in the group 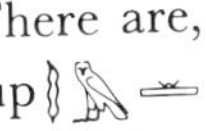 at the upper right.

Although the secondary inscription is more or less suited to the lines above it, it has produced a lack of continuity between the first and second column of each pair. This problem is indicated, in the following translation, by a series of dots and by a partial restoration of the original context, while the whole of the secondary inscription is distinguished by italics:

(Left, 1) An offering that the king gives (to) Amun[c] Lord of Thrones-of-the-Two-Lands, Presiding over Karnak, *that he may give funerary offerings to One who is Praised of the Lord of the Two Lands*[d] . . . (2) . . . [to] the spirit of the *w*ʿ*b*-priest of Bastet, Mistress of Bubastis, *the Priest of Amun (Lord) of Thrones-of-the-Two-Lands, the priest of Ptah, Na-nefer-kheperu.*[e]

(Right, 1) An offering that the king gives (to) Bastet, Mistress of Bubastis, that she may give *everything goodly and pure, everything goodly and sweet*[f] . . . (2) . . . and the pleasant [breath] that goes forth from her,[g] to the Mistress of the House, *the Chantress of Bastet, Mistress of Bubastis, Iw-nes-neb-tawy*,[h] *justified*.

Comments on the inscriptions

(a) Ranke, *PN* I, p. 51 (14); attested in the Middle Kingdom and Dyn. XVIII.

(b) Not attested in *PN*.

(c) Although the surface is slightly pitted in this area, there does not seem to have been any attempt to erase the name of Amun. The reversal of the divine name may be intended to make it face the titles and name of the deceased recipient of offerings; at all events the reversal is evidently intentional, for it departs from the usual rightward orientation. This reversal would in turn imply that the goddess Bastet faces him too.[108]

(d) The epithet *ḥsy* is common (*Wb.* III, 156 [7]), although I do not have a parallel for *nb tȝwy* in this phrase, nor can I cite another example of the determinative . This must be the equivalent of , which, again according to *Wb.*, occurs after the New Kingdom; it derives from *ḥsy* as a designation of temple statues (*Wb.* III, 157).

(e) Not attested in *PN*. It is theoretically possible, but not very probable, that the name is to be read *Ny-Ḥr-nfr-ḫprw*, in which case it would refer to the Horus Nefer-kheperu, Nubkheperre Intef VII of the Seventeenth Dynasty. And if the first element is *nȝ*, it is equally difficult to recognize a reference to either of the two Eighteenth Dynasty kings who called themselves *Nfr-ḫprw-Rʿ*, as Tuthmosis III sometimes did, following his nomen, or Amenophis IV, as his prenomen, although one Amarna name, 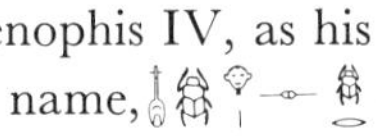 [109] apparently refers to the name of Amenophis IV as *Nfr-ḫpr(w)* (Ranke, *PN* I, 199 [12]), and one might perhaps compare 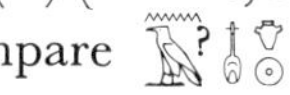 which Ranke interprets as *Nȝ-nfr-[nfr-?]ib-rʿ* (*PN* I, 169 [25]). But, as Ranke notes in *PN* II, 82, names of this pattern (*nȝ*+adjectival verb) did not come into use until the Twenty-second Dynasty.

(f) Barta, *Aufbau*, pp. 90, 175, 213 (Bitte 15a) quotes three examples dating to the early Eighteenth Dynasty, the Second Intermediate Period, and the Graeco-Roman Period, for *iḫt nbt nfrt wʿbt iḫt nbt nḏmt bnrt*. Several other similar examples may be cited from New Kingdom stelae in the Cairo Museum: CG 34101, 34102, 34117, 34168, all of which combine *nfrt wʿbt* on the one hand and *nḏmt bnrt* on the other. Some Eighteenth Dynasty examples also combine *iḫt nbt nfrt wʿbt* and *iḫt nbt nfrt bnrt*, as in the present case (Davies, *Griffith Studies*, pls. 39, 40; and *Menkheperrasonb*, pl. 29), and another has *ḫt nbt nfrt nḏmt* . . . *ḫt nbt nfrt wʿbt* (CG 42138), but none shows the sequence *ḫt nfrt bnrt nḏmt* and only one example has come to light (Barta, *Aufbau*, p. 197) that shows the sequence *bnrt nḏmt* instead of *nḏmt bnrt*.

(g) Since *nḏmt bnrt* is the normal sequence when these two words occur together (see preceding comment), it does not seem likely that *bnrt nḏmt* is to be read here, and it is even more improbable that this combination would follow *nfrt*. Furthermore both *nḏm* and the following participle *pri* lack a feminine ending. Although *pri* might nonetheless refer to *ḫt nfrt* (as in CG 605 and J. E. Quibell, *Excavations at Saqqara* [1908–10], pl. 86 [1]), *prrt* is the expected form. It is therefore virtually certain that *nḏm pri* belongs to the common formula *ṯȝw nḏm pri ḫnt.s* (or *ḫnt.f*, if the divinity is masculine); cf. Barta, *Aufbau*, pp. 116 (Bitte 78a), 146 (78b, 79b), 165 (78a), where *pri m* (or *pri m ḫnt*) sometimes replaces *pri ḫnt*.[110] Note also the reversal of the feet in 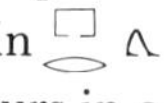, which is probably not accidental since it occurs in a number of other cases,[111] one of which involves the same phrase:

108. Some analogous examples will be found in my forthcoming *The Orientation of Egyptian Hieroglyphs* §35.

109. Ranke, referring to Bouriant et al., *Culte d'Atonou*, p. 79, also gives the writing 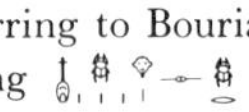, but I can find no evidence of this.

110. Presumably the meaning is the same in both cases (compare *Wb.* III, 303); I doubt that Barta can be right in translating *pri ḫnt.s* as "die vor ihr hervorkommt." For further examples see BM 1513 (*Hieroglyphic Texts* V, pl. 29); Quibell, *Ramesseum*, pl. 27 (1), which has *m ḫnt.f*; CG 42121; Tylor and Griffith, *Paheri*, pl. 1 (left). All of them invoke "*his* (the god's) pleasant breath which comes forth from him" (*ṯȝw.f nḏm pri ḫnt*[*.f*]).

111. The evidence will be presented in *The Orientation of Egyptian Hieroglyphs*, §42.

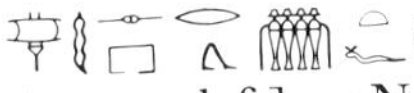 (Petrie, *Gizeh and Rifeh*, pls. 27B [bottom left], 27N [1]).

(h) Not attested in Ranke, *PN*; evidently 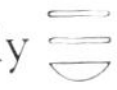 is a mistake for 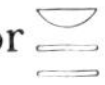.

Conclusions

In view of the lack of continuity between the first and second column in each half of this inscription, it is unlikely that the reinscribed portion is the work of an ancient Egyptian, and this conclusion is reinforced by several other considerations. In the first place the alterations do not seem to have served any practical purpose; they can hardly be regarded as a correction or restoration,[112] and it is equally difficult to believe that they represent a later usurpation, for in that case one would expect the names on the base of the statue to have been changed; it is those inscriptions, after all, that most directly "determine" the statue's identity. Even if one makes the unlikely assumption that a later individual merely wished to share the statue with the original owner by usurping the funerary formulae on the back, he would have applied the changes to the titles and names alone and not to an entire segment of the inscription that, on the one hand, leaves some of the original titles unaltered and, on the other hand, includes portions of the funerary formulae that are not only irrelevant to the presumed change of ownership but actually, as a result of the changes, have become less intelligible.

The only other purpose that these changes could have served is a prosthetic one. Presumably the lower part of the inscription was more scarred and pitted than the upper portion, and this may have been the point of impact when the statue was broken into two pieces, although a corner has also been detached from the left front corner of the base. Once the surface had been smoothed down, the "restorer" had to complete the inscription by adding new signs. He did not—as in another case which I have discussed elsewhere[113]—attempt to fill in the space with hieroglyphs imitated from the original; instead he copied another ancient text that was somewhat different in style[114] but must otherwise have seemed to have filled the need felicitously. The most conspicuous stylistic difference is the form of the sign , which is written 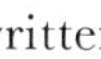 or in the upper part of the four columns and on the base, and is in all four columns within the reworked area. Other differences appear in the phrases identifying Amun and Bastet:

(top) 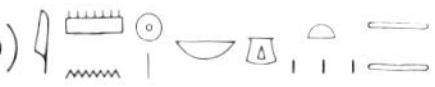 (top) 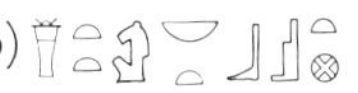

(bottom) 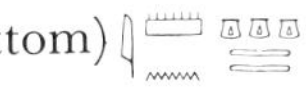 (bottom) 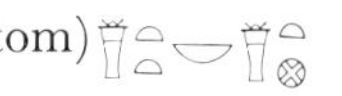

In both cases the lower part of the inscription shows greater brevity. These points of consistency suggest that the substituted text was copied from a single inscription rather than from several sources. The copyist evidently followed the original very closely, but he did not understand the logic of the reversal in the first of the left-hand pair of columns, and reversed the remaining signs so that their orientation was the same. Obviously the copy cannot be trusted in every detail, and one would like to verify some of the orthographic peculiarities, such as 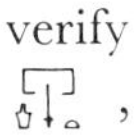, 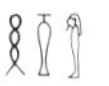, and 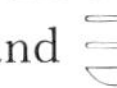 (the last presumably representing *nb t3wy*).

If the presumably modern restorer worked from a single inscription and if—as the woman's title indicates—the second inscription came from Bubastis, it is interesting that the man is a priest of Amun and Ptah, for these gods, however important in their own right, are not known to have had a cult in that city.[115] A relatively late date is suggested by 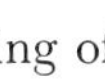 as a writing of *m3ʿt-ḫrw* after the woman's name. According to W. Erichsen's study of the epithet in question, the use of  is first attested in the Amarna Period, but does not

112. The restoration of extensive portions of the texts on a statue is attested by CG 42114. A stela of the same person—Senmut—was similarly effaced and extensively restored: Helck, *ÄZ* 85 (1960), pp. 23–34, believes that the erasures were made by the Atenists and the restorations by Horemheb or Seti I. That explanation is excluded in the present case because the name of Amun was left intact.

113. "The inscription of *'In-it.f*, born of *Tfi*," *JNES* 19 (1960), pp. 258–260.

114. Cf. A. Wiedemann, *PSBA* 33 (1911) pp. 167–168, concerning a statue in Athens the inscription of which is a forgery "copied from a genuine inscription which is unknown to us."

115. For their mention there see Labib Habachi, *Tell Basta*, pp. 111–117; it is assumed that, in most cases, the evidence involves monuments brought from other places.

become common until the Nineteenth Dynasty and later.[116] The man's name, if correctly read as Nanefer-kheperu, is even more distinctly later, since names of this pattern did not become current until the Twenty-second Dynasty. The writing of *ḥsy* as also suggests this late a date.[117]

116. *Acta Orientalia* 6 (1928) p. 272; Spiegelberg, *Rec. trav.* 26 (1904) p. 49, had already come to very nearly the same conclusion.

117. Another relatively late feature is the writing of in the name *Iw-n.s-nb-tȝwy*, which does not seem to become common before Dyn. XIX (e.g., CG 561, 606). The form of — is occasionally attested after the New Kingdom: relatively late examples are to be found in Petrie, *Abydos* III, pl. 25 (left), and Randall-Maciver and Mace, *El Amrah and Abydos*, pl. 31/D7, the latter dating to the Libyan Period. But it is also known earlier, in the Middle Kingdom (Petrie, *Diospolis Parva*, pl. 27, bottom right; Steckeweh, *Die Fürstengräber von Qâw*, pl. 14 [a]; Carnarvon and Carter, *Five Years' Explorations at Thebes*, pl. 49 [MMA 26.7.1438]), and Second Intermediate Period (Petrie, *Koptos*, pl. 8 [Dyn. 17]; BM 40958 [*Hieroglyphic Texts* V, pl. 19]); also in the Old Kingdom, e.g., CG 1495 and Junker, *Gîza* IV, pls. 4–8.

SOURCES ABBREVIATED

AJA—*American Journal of Archaeology*

AJSL—*American Journal of Semitic Languages*

ASAE—*Annales du Service des Antiquités de l'Égypte*

ÄZ—*Zeitschrift für Ägyptische Sprache und Altertumskunde*

BIFAO—*Bulletin de l'Institut Français d'Archéologie Orientale*

BiOr—*Bibliotheca Orientalis*

BM—*British Museum*

BMMA—*Bulletin of the Metropolitan Museum of Art*

CG+number—Monuments in the Egyptian Museum, Cairo, numbers referring to *Catalogue général des antiquités égyptiennes du Musée du Caire*:

- CG 1–1294: Ludwig Borchardt, *Statuen und Statuetten von Königen und Privatleuten* I-IV (Berlin, 1911–34);
- CG 1295–1808: Ludwig Borchardt, *Denkmäler des Alten Reiches* I-II (Berlin, 1937–64);
- CG 20001–20780: H. O. Lange and H. Schäfer, *Grab- und Denksteine der Mittleren Reichs* I-IV (Berlin, 1902–25);
- CG 23001–23256: Ahmed Kamal, *Tables d'offrandes* I-II (Cairo, 1906–09);
- CG 42001–42191: Georges Legrain, *Statues et statuettes de rois et de particuliers* I-II (Cairo, 1906–09)

CT—A. de Buck, *The Egyptian Coffin Texts*, 7 vols. (*Oriental Institute Publications*, Chicago, 1935–61)

JARCE—*Journal of the American Research Center in Egypt*

JEA—*Journal of Egyptian Archaeology*

JNES—*Journal of Near Eastern Studies*

LD—C. R. Lepsius, *Denkmaeler aus Aegypten und Aethiopien* (Berlin, n.d.)

MDIK—*Mitteilungen des Deutschen Archäologischen Instituts Abteilung Kairo*

MMA—*Metropolitan Museum of Art*

MMJ—*Metropolitan Museum Journal*

PSBA—*Proceedings of the Society of Biblical Archaeology*

Ranke, *PN*— H. Ranke, *Die ägyptischen Personennamen* (Glückstadt, 1935, [1952])

RdE—*Revue d'Égyptologie*

Rec. trav.—*Recueil de travaux relatifs à la philologie et à l'archéologie égyptiennes et assyriennes*

ZDMG—*Zeitschrift der Deutschen Morgenländischen Gesellschaft*

An Elusive Shape within the Fisted Hands of Egyptian Statues

HENRY G. FISCHER

Lila Acheson Wallace Curator in Egyptology, The Metropolitan Museum of Art

THE PROBLEM

No feature of Egyptian sculpture has so often perplexed its present-day admirers as the peglike objects that are held in the fisted hands of male statues. This curious detail first appears in the right hand of the limestone statue of *Ḥm-iwnw* in Hildesheim, dating to the reign of Cheops (Figure 1),[1] but it is absent in that of the slightly earlier statue of *Rꜥ-ḥtp* in Cairo (CG 3). Beginning, then, in the second reign of the Fourth Dynasty, its use extends throughout the Old Kingdom and down through the entire course of ancient Egyptian history, until, at length, it is carried over into the series of archaic Greek kouroi.[2]

There is fairly general agreement on one point: these objects are particularly characteristic of statuary in stone, a material that does not lend itself to attenuated projections such as the staff and baton that are often held by men as represented in relief and—as separate attachments—in standing statues made of more resilient material, notably wood. Such elements could, of course, have been represented in stone by showing them

FIGURE 1
Right hand of the statue of *Ḥm-iwnw* (photo: courtesy Roemer-Pelizaeus Museum, Hildesheim)

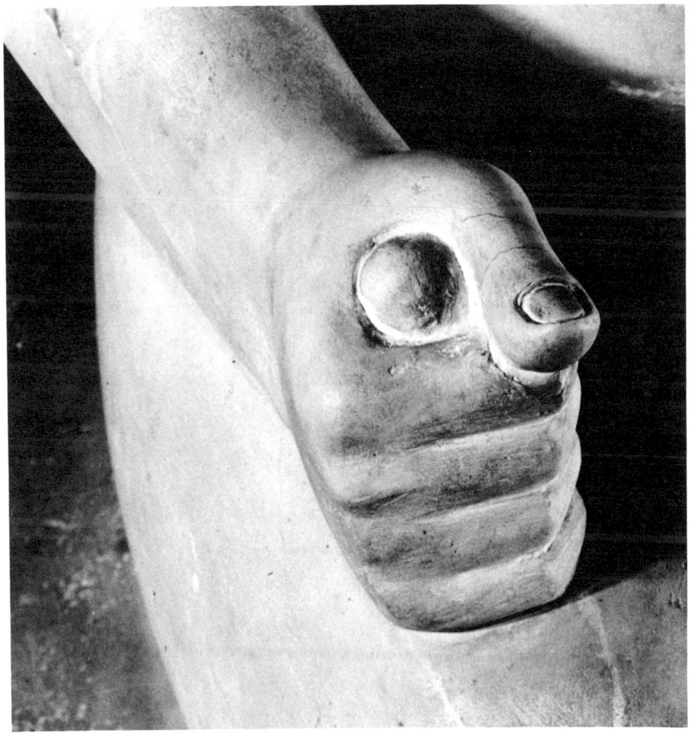

1. Roemer-Pelizaeus Museum 1962. For this detail I am indebted to Dr. Arne Eggebrecht. See also Junker, *Gîza*, I, pp. 153–157, pls. 18–22.
2. See Gisela M. A. Richter, *Kouroi* (New York, 1942) p. 5, and the reference to Anthes at end of note 4, below.

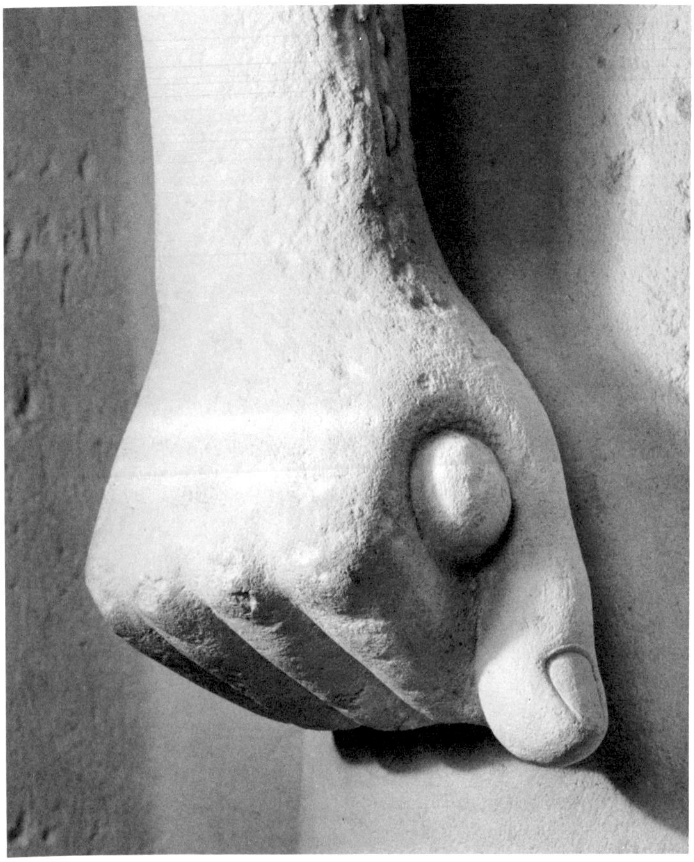

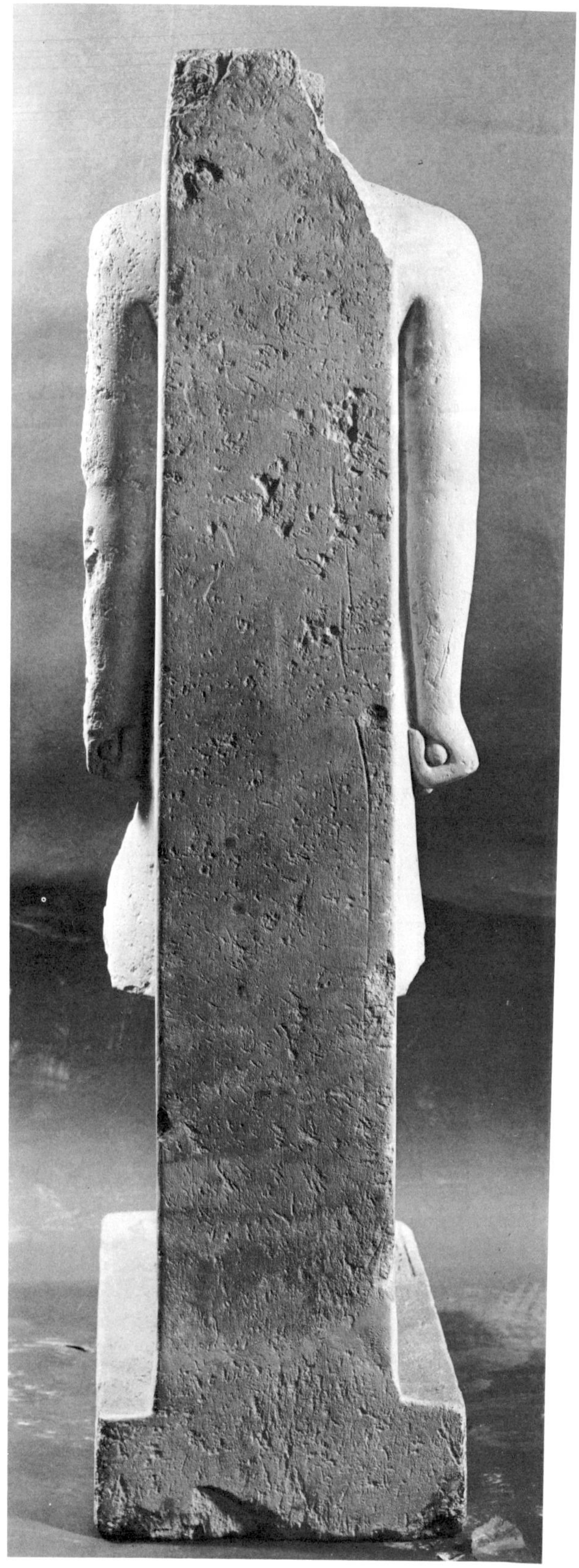

FIGURE 2
Right hand of the statue of *Bꜣ-bꜣ.f.* The Metropolitan Museum of Art, Fletcher Fund, 64.66.2

FIGURE 3
Bꜣ-bꜣ.f from rear

close to the body, as was done in the case of the Third Dynasty statues of *Zpꜣ* in the Louvre.[3] But this solution imposed a stiffness of attitude that was subsequently avoided by sculptors of any competence. The Egyptian statues of the Old Kingdom and later are usually relaxed, assuming an attitude that might, with greatest ease and comfort, be maintained for eternity. The resultant disengagement of the limbs meant, in turn, that the connective areas currently described as "negative space" (or more appropriately by the German "Zwischenraum") were used to a greater extent and

3. André Vigneau, *Encyclopédie photographique de l'art,* I: *Musée du Louvre,* (Éditions "Tel," Paris [1935]), pl. 6.

with increased resourcefulness. It was in the Fourth Dynasty that the characteristic reinforcement now termed a "back-pillar" was supplied, in contrast to the aforementioned statues of *Zpꜣ*, which lack it.

Consequently the peglike objects have frequently been regarded simply as another manifestation of "negative space."[4] As a rule, however, they form rounded projections at both ends (Figures 2, 3),[5] whereas the areas of negative space are characteristically cut back to a lower level than the elements they reinforce. The back-pillar cannot be cited as a comparable exception because, although it is sometimes painted black (i.e., the color applied to negative space) along with the upper surface of the base in standing statues,[6] it may also, in the case of seated limestone statues, be painted red in imitation of wood or granite, along with the rectangular block on which the figure is seated.[7] More significantly, in the case of a number of standing statues the back-pillar is painted red[8] or yellow[9] (the latter more clearly in imitation of wood) in contrast to the black surface of the base. This adjunct was accordingly regarded as a concrete, supportive element, fully justifying its modern designation.[10]

Of the alternative explanations for the elusive shape, the most persuasive is one that Spiegelberg proposed in 1906,[11] and which has been reiterated in recent years. Comparing standing statues of stone and wood, Spiegelberg concludes that the peglike objects in the hands of the former are a truncated version of the staff and baton that are held by the latter. In recent publications they are sometimes described as "emblematic staves," a term initiated by Bernard V. Bothmer.[12]

If the functional reason for the usage is beyond question, and if it also seems highly likely that a specific object is represented, it is nonetheless impossible to agree with Spiegelberg's explanation, for it incurs an objection that has not—to my knowledge—been raised against it previously,[13] but is nonetheless conclusive.

4. Borchardt, *Statuen und Statuetten* p. 6 (no. 5): "Hohlräume der Fäuste"; p. 8 (no. 7): "Hohlungen in den Händen." F. W. von Bissing, *Denkmäler ägyptischer Sculptur*, text (Munich, 1914) no. 4: "Hohlraum der Faust." H. Schäfer in Schäfer and Andrae, *Die Kunst des alten Orients* (Berlin, 1925) p. 44. George Steindorff, *Catalogue of the Egyptian Sculpture in the Walters Art Gallery* (Baltimore, 1946) p. 6. Elisabeth Staehelin. *Untersuchungen zur ägyptischen Tracht im Alten Reich* (*MÄS* 8, 1966) p. 161. See also Rudolph Anthes, "Affinity and Difference between Egyptian and Greek Sculpture and Thought," *Proceedings of the American Philosophical Society* 107 (1963) p. 64: "Since this bit of stone was meaningless otherwise, we must assume that it was left for either technical or aesthetic reason, or both."

5. A typical Fifth Dynasty example from Giza. Other examples are occasionally rounded in front only (CG 18, 24, 47, 52) or show no projection (CG 70, 126, 132, 178, 180, 192, 211, 235). Such cases are very much in the minority, however.

6. About 18 examples noted by Borchardt: CG 5, 6, 47, 54, 55 (seated), 77, 81, 88, 90 (?), 97, 98, 100 (seated), 111, 129, 132, 133, 158, 212.

7. About five examples noted by Borchardt: CG 22, 44, 91, 94 (?), 101.

8. Five examples noted by Borchardt: CG 20, 125, 278, 284, 372. In two other cases this element is blue gray, imitating darker stone (CG 143, 205).

9. Six examples noted by Borchardt: CG 23, 50, 51, 96, 99, 151.

10. In some cases it is replaced by a wall-like backing (CG 18, 19, 20, 29, 47, 52, 89, 90). This, like the narrower back-pillar, does not always extend above shoulder level, and for that reason Bernard V. Bothmer is inclined to doubt that back-pillars were simply intended as structural support (Brooklyn Institute of Arts and Sciences, *Egyptian Sculpture of the Late Period* [New York, 1960] p. xxxiv). In at least one New Kingdom statuette, representing Amenophis III, the back-pillar is carved to represent the hieroglyph meaning "stability" and "permanence" (𓊽): MMA 30.8.74; W. C. Hayes, *The Scepter of Egypt*, II (Cambridge, Mass., 1959) p. 237, fig. 142.

11. W. Spiegelberg, "Der 'Steinkern' in der Hand von Statuen," *Recueil de travaux relatifs à la philologie et à l'archéologie égyptiennes et assyriennes* 28 (1906) pp. 174–176. His view is accepted by Anwar Shoukry, *Die Privatgrabstatue im Alten Reich* (*ASAE* Suppl. No. 15 [Cairo, 1951]) p. 129.

12. "A Wooden Statue of Dynasty VI," *BMFA* 46 (1948) p. 34; more extensively discussed in "Notes on the Mycerinus Triad," *BMFA* 48 (1950) p. 15; there is no mention of Spiegelberg in either case, and the idea is put forward as a new one. So also Brooklyn Institute of Arts and Sciences, *Egyptian Sculpture of the Late Period*, p. 10. J. Vandier, *Manuel d'archéologie égyptienne*, III (Paris, 1958) p. 19, refers to Bothmer's view and partially agrees: the object in question is described as "un bâton, très court, mais probablement moins court que sur les statues égyptiennes." The same view is followed more explicitly by E. L. B. Terrace in Terrace and Fischer, *Treasures of Egyptian Art from the Cairo Museum* (London, 1970) p. 48.

13. The only detailed argument that has been presented against it is that of Staehelin, *Untersuchungen zur ägyptischen Tracht*, p. 161; she adduces the allegedly dark color of the objects and the fact that women sometimes hold them. Although, in my opinion, the example shown in her fig. 3 is not of ancient manufacture, valid examples are to be found in a Hildesheim statue (G. Roeder, *Die Denkmäler des Pelizaeus-Museums zu Hildesheim* [Berlin, 1921] fig. 10) and CG 135 (cf. B. Hornemann, *Types of Ancient Egyptian Statuary*, IV [Munksgaard, 1966] no. 1056), as well as in one of the Mycerinus triads (Cairo J. 46499: G. A. Reisner, *Mycerinus* [Cambridge, Mass., 1931] pl. 45). In some other cases it appears in the hands of prisoners (esp. Cairo J. 51729, although this feature is not apparent in G. Jéquier's *Le Monument funéraire de Pepi II*, III [Cairo, 1940] pl. 47 [right]), or a child (Leiden D. 125: P. Boeser, A. and J. Holwerda, *Beschreibung der aegyptischen Sammlung* I: *Denkmäler des Alten Reiches, Atlas* [The Hague, 1908] pl. 24). And the object is also

In all of the extraordinarily abundant evidence for ancient Egyptian iconography there is not a single comparable example of symbolic abstraction. One of the most salient aspects of pharaonic art, in fact, is its adherence to concrete and naturalistic detail. This point is most strikingly attested by the fact that hieroglyphic pictographs continued to be employed for monumental inscriptions, despite the virtually simultaneous development of hieratic, which tended to become more abbreviated and cursive. As the individual hieroglyphs demonstrate, the Egyptian artist was willing to isolate parts, to combine them as seen from different points of view, and to alter their scale and proportions. But the result is consistently clear and recognizable, and the departures from retinal reality were generally designed for precisely that reason—to produce greater clarity and comprehension.

The hieroglyphic representation of one of the alleged "emblematic staves" is a case in point. The sign alters the proportions of width and length in order to differentiate the two ends as distinctly as possible—one knobbed (i.e., larger and bulbous, with a beveled edge), the other flat and narrower. It is hardly possible that this truncated form would not appear in the hands of statues if it had actually been intended, particularly if one takes account of the very close interrelationship of Egyptian art and hieroglyphic writing. The so-called emblematic staves not only fail to make the distinction between the two ends of the alleged staff, but also fail to distinguish the staff from its supposed counterpart, the scepter, the end of which is shaped quite differently; in hieroglyphs these are given equal length, but are contrasted as follows: (Figure 4).[14] Furthermore the peglike objects sometimes appear in the hands of kings, and in this case one would have to suppose the elimination of a further distinction between a staff and mace ( ) or between the crook and flail ( ).

Although Spiegelberg does not overlook the important consideration of color, his observations on this score are meager and rather suspect. That shortcoming is understandable, for descriptions of polychromy on statues are sadly deficient even in recent publications, such as Junker's *Gîza*, and it is by no means easy to identify traces of pigment under ordinary lighting conditions in museum installations. For this reason, my own observations are also limited, but, taken together with the observations made by Ludwig Borchardt in his *Statuen und Statuetten*, the evidence seems sufficient to indicate a range of possibilities that evidently excludes the staff and baton from further consideration.

Borchardt's observations are clearly affected by the fact that he considered the peglike object to represent the "hollow of the fist" and therefore merely "negative space." Unless he observed definite traces of color on the rounded ends, this detail evidently received no attention, and, conversely, it is impossible to say to what extent he observed traces of pigment on these areas when he states that in general the negative space of a certain statue is black. In some instances—such as CG 20—the surface of the limestone seems to have been left unpainted in contrast to the surrounding dark reddish paint on the hand itself, but Borchardt's sole description of a similar distinction is that of CG 145, which specifies "freie Räume, mit Ausnahme der Höhlungen der Fäuste." In addition to these two cases, Borchardt records that thirteen statues have peglike

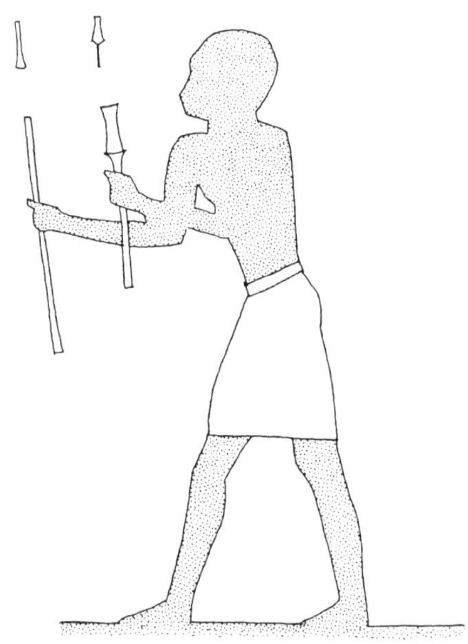

FIGURE 4
Offering bearer holding staff and scepter. After Newberry

occasionally found in the hands of naked boys and youths: MFA 06.1881 (*HESPOK*, pl. 24 [d]); CG 143, Cairo J. 57019; Junker, *Gîza*, VII, pl. 10.

14. From an early Middle Kingdom procession of offering bearers: P. E. Newberry, *Beni Hasan*, II (London, 1893) pl. 7.

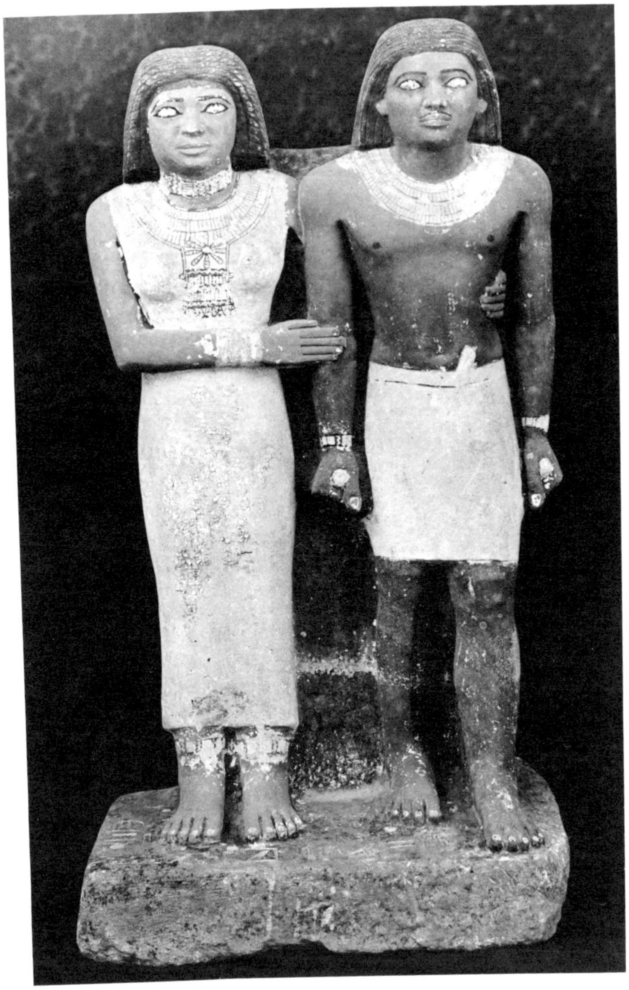

FIGURE 5

Statue of *Mśi* and *Śnnw*. Cairo J. 38670. Excavation-record photograph, Museum of Fine Arts, Boston (photo: courtesy Museum of Fine Arts)

objects that are white, while the negative space is black (CG 80, 88, 98, 101, 129, 133, 151, 185, 191, 192), unspecified (CG 60, 370), or white (CG 219).

From my own observation I have noted that the peglike objects are similarly white (or, in the case of limestone statues, unpainted) in many instances: Brooklyn 53.222; MFA 06.1876, 06.1885,[15] 12.1484 (probably),[16] 21.2598,[17] 31.777,[18] 47.1455;[19] Univ. Mus. E 13515,[20] 14301;[21] Cairo J. 38670 (Figure 5),[22] 66618,[23] 66619,[24] 87804.[25] A few more examples may be found in publications: Univ. Calif. 6-19775,[26] statues in the tombs of *'Irw-kȝ-Ptḥ*[27] and *Mrr-w(.i)-kȝ(.i)*[28] at Saqqara (with white negative space in both cases),[29] Hildesheim 418,[30] and the statue illustrated in J. E. Quibell and A. G. K. Hayter, *Teti Pyramid, North Side* (Cairo, 1927) pl. 29, where the objects in question are much lighter in contrast to the red hands and the yellow goffering of the kilt.[31]

In a few other cases the peglike objects are the same hue as the dark red or reddish brown hand that holds them, but, in contrast to the foregoing cases, these are more probably to be explained as negligence on the part of the painter: MFA 21.2596, 21.25999; Univ. Mus. E 2551 (?); Cairo J. 66620, CG 27, 28. In the last case the color is described as yellow brown, again matching the skin, but I have not personally observed any that are black.[32] I know of no certain cases where the objects are yellow.

15. For MFA 06.1876 and 06.1885, *HESPOK*, p. 69; the latter illustrated in pl. 24 (c).

16. For MFA 12.1484, *HESPOK*, pl. 21 (d).

17. For MFA 21.2598, *HESPOK*, p. 74.

18. For MFA 31.777, *HESPOK*, p. 76.

19. Not pale yellow as described by Bothmer, *BMFA* 46 (1948) p. 34.

20. See Alan Rowe in Clarence Fisher, *The Minor Cemetery at Giza* (Philadelphia, 1924) pp. 135–136, pl. 42.

21. Unpublished: standing limestone statue of a man named Khenu, purchased in 1925 and said to come from Saqqara.

22. See *HESPOK*, p. 69 pl. 24 (b). The photograph is published with the permission of Dr. Wm. K. Simpson.

23. Hassan, *Gîza*, I, pl. 70.

24. Hassan, *Gîza*, I, pl. 73.

25. Hassan, *Gîza*, V, pl. 53 (A).

26. H. F. Lutz, *Egyptian Statues and Statuettes in the Museum of Anthropology of the University of California* (Leipzig, 1930) p. 23 (referring to pl. 34 a).

27. B. de Rachewiltz, *The Rock Tomb of Irw-Kȝ-Ptḥ* (Leiden, 1960) frontispiece and p. 9. More clearly seen in Cyril Aldred, *Egypt to the End of the Old Kingdom* (London, 1965) fig. 100.

28. *Mereruka*, II, pl. 148.

29. The use of white "negative space" evidently tends to occur in the case of statues that, like these two examples, are located within niches; so too BM 1165, which also has white objects in the hands: E. A. W. Budge, *British Museum: A Guide to the Egyptian Galleries (Sculpture)* (London, 1909) p. 21, and T. G. H. James, *Hieroglyphic Texts from Egyptian Stelae* I, 2nd ed. (London, 1961) pl. 4. In this case, however, the base of the niche is painted red.

30. Hans Kayser, *Die ägyptischen Altertümer* (Hildesheim, 1973) color plate 2, p. 47.

31. Other examples of this kind might also be cited; Abdel-Moneim Abu-Bakr, *Excavations at Giza 1949–1950* (Cairo, 1953) pl. 50; Junker, *Gîza*, VI, pl. 17; in neither case is the color described in detail.

32. W. Wolf so describes CG 19 (*Die Kunst Aegyptens* [Stuttgart, 1957] p. 158) but this does not coincide with my own observations or those of Borchardt, who says the color is red, matching the surrounding color of the skin.

If the objects in question represented staves, one would certainly expect their color to be yellow in most cases, although red might also be considered a secondary possibility. And the large proportion of white examples (those listed above add up to at least thirty-two) would be totally unexplained. This proportion evidently greatly exceeds the relatively rare incidence of white as the color of negative space; Borchardt notes five or six cases of white negative space,[33] as compared with ninety-nine that show the normal use of black.

It may be added that Heinrich Schäfer seems to be the only scholar who has previously characterized the color of the "elusive shape" as white,[34] but Perrot and Chipiez and their German translator, Richard Pietschmann, were evidently of the same opinion, for they identified the object in question as a roll of papyrus[35] and as a loop of cloth.[36] These explanations, although they have long since been discarded,[37] deserve closer consideration.

THE PROPOSED SOLUTION

The form of the "elusive shape" is displayed most clearly in a few seated statues that turn the fisted hand so that both rounded ends are outlined upon the lap. Examples like Figure 6 confirm the concrete reality of

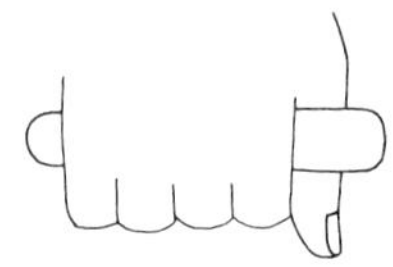

FIGURE 6
Right hand of statue of *Ptḥ-šps̀s̀*. CG 164. After Borchardt

this object;[38] if it seems improbable that the rounded protuberances would represent negative space in freestanding sculpture, it is altogether inconceivable that negative space would assume such a form in relief, against a flat surface. The predominantly rounded ends also exclude the possibility that the object ordinarily represents a roll of papyrus, although that possibility is suggested by some two-dimensional representations of standing statues,[39] as well as by a seated statue that exceptionally shows this object as a white cylindrical shape with flat ends.[40] It must, of course, be admitted that the convention, once it had become established, could occasionally have been reinterpreted in more than one sense.

But the only object in the repertory of Old Kingdom iconography that corresponds to the more usual form of the "elusive shape," both in contour and color, is a bolt of cloth, as represented by the hieroglyph 𓈀. This sign is explained as a "garment" in Gardiner's Sign List,[41] but is actually a folded length of linen, and it is accordingly rounded at both ends as compared with the hieroglyph 𓋴, which shows a cloth that is only partly folded.[42] Both modes of representing cloth appear in Old Kingdom scenes that depict linen being delivered by the weavers and their supervisors (Figure 7).[43]

A handkerchief in the form of 𓋴 is often seen in the hands of two-dimensional representations of the tomb owner, and it is apt to replace 𓈀 in the right hand of seated statues, where the free ends of the cloth can be readily displayed in relief upon the surface of the kilt, as noted earlier.[44] In the case of standing statues, the

33. CG 18, 27, 31 (?), 37, 49, as well as 219, mentioned earlier. Even more rarely the color is red or red brown (CG 8, 44) or gray blue (CG 649).

34. H. Schäfer, *Von ägyptischer Kunst*, 4th ed. (Wiesbaden, 1963) p. 52.

35. G. Perrot and C. Chipiez, *Histoire de l'art dans l'antiquité*, I (Paris, 1882) p. 655.

36. Perrot and Chipiez, trans. Pietschmann, *Geschichte der Kunst im Alterthum: Aegypten* (Leipzig, 1884) p. 855 (Anhang zu S. 595). This view is cited and rejected by Bissing, *Denkmäler ägyptischer Sculptur*, text, no. 4.

37. The interpretation as a roll of papyrus has again been suggested fairly recently, however, by Henri Wild in "Statue de Hor-néfer au Musée des Beaux-Arts de Lausanne," *Bulletin de l'Institut français d'Archéologie orientale* 54 (1954) p. 174.

38. Borchardt says CG 164 and 177 are the same. The same is also true of CG 649 and Hassan, *Gîza*, I, pl. 70 (Cairo J. 66618); II, pls. 19, 21 (2, 3).

39. Most clearly in Junker, *Gîza*, XI, fig. 99, p. 248. Cf. *Mereruka*, I, pls. 29, 30, 39 (the latter perhaps an incomplete representation of ⇸— as in the figure shown above it), and *LD* II, pl. 64 bis (b), where the object appears to be rounded at either end.

40. MFA 06.1885, cited among the white examples presented earlier (note 15, above).

41. Adapted from N 18; this follows S 26 in the Sign List (A. H. Gardiner, *Egyptian Grammar*, 3rd ed. [London, 1957] p. 507).

42. Sign List S 29.

43. From *LD* II, pl. 103 (a); also reproduced by Junker, *Gîza*, V, fig. 10, p. 49. Another example is in A. M. Blackman and M. R. Apted, *The Rock Tombs of Meir*, V (London, 1953) pl. 15.

44. CG 9, 10, 14, 15, 17 (all Chephren), 26, 30, 41, 46, 49, 55, 63, 67, 69, 84, 123; Hassan, *Gîza*, II, pls. 1, 2 (3, 4); Junker, *Gîza*, VI, pl. 7; Cairo J. 48076; Louvre A 43.

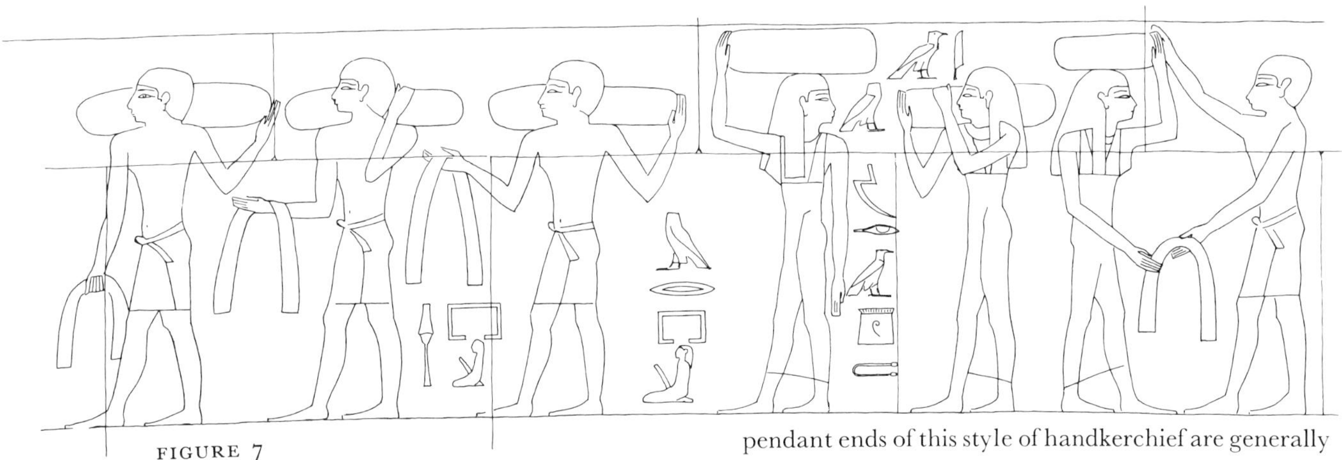

FIGURE 7
Relief from tomb of *Ptḥ-ḥtp*, Saqqara. After Lepsius

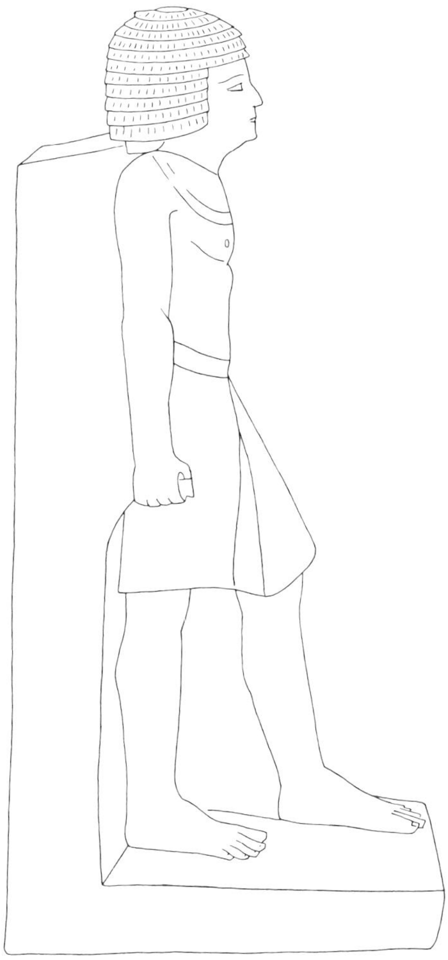

FIGURE 8
Statue of *Rˁ-wr*. Cairo J. 66622. After Hornemann

pendant ends of this style of handkerchief are generally avoided unless the statue is made of a material such as wood, which permits projections to be introduced with less danger of breakage. But in at least two standing statues of stone the same form is suggested by making a curved connection with the back-pillar (Figure 8).[45] Another stone statue, in the Metropolitan Museum, more surprisingly makes the same connection by extending the object in the hand straight backward, and this evidently represents rather than (Figure 9).[46]

Both representations of cloth, as seen in the hands of statues, are "hieroglyphic" in that they reduce a flat object to a thin strip—Figure 10, a, b instead of c, d. The thin strip then assumes a tubular form when transferred to three dimensions. In view of their hieroglyphic aspect, they may well display that disregard of scale that is particularly characteristic of hieroglyphs, although it also pertains to Egyptian art in general, which is itself an extension of the hieroglyphic system. While relatively small handkerchiefs were doubtless used on some occasions, representations such as Figure 11[47] show that a much larger cloth was carried,

45. B. Hornemann, *Types of Ancient Egyptian Statuary*, I (Munksgaard, n.d.) no. 125. Also Cairo J. 66616, Hornemann, V (Munksgaard, 1966) no. 1361. Front views of both appear in Hassan, *Gîza*, I, pls. 21 (Cairo J. 66622) and 22 (Cairo J. 66616).

46. Another view is shown by H. Fischer, "Redundant Determinatives in the Old Kingdom," *MMJ* 8 (1973) p. 14, and by Nora Scott in "Memy-Sabu and His Wife," *BMMA* (1948–49) p. 96.

47. From Selim Hassan, "Excavations at Saqqara 1937–1938," *ASAE* 38 (1938) p. 520, pl. 96. See also Vigneau, *Encyclopédie photographique de l'art*, I, pl. 27. The tomb owner is also shown with such a cloth over the shoulder: *LD* II, pls. 9, 12 (same in Hassan, *Gîza*, IV, fig. 77, p. 135), 19, 106; Junker, *Gîza*, II, fig. 22, p. 156; also Staehelin, *Untersuchungen zur ägyptischen Tracht*, p. 194 and notes

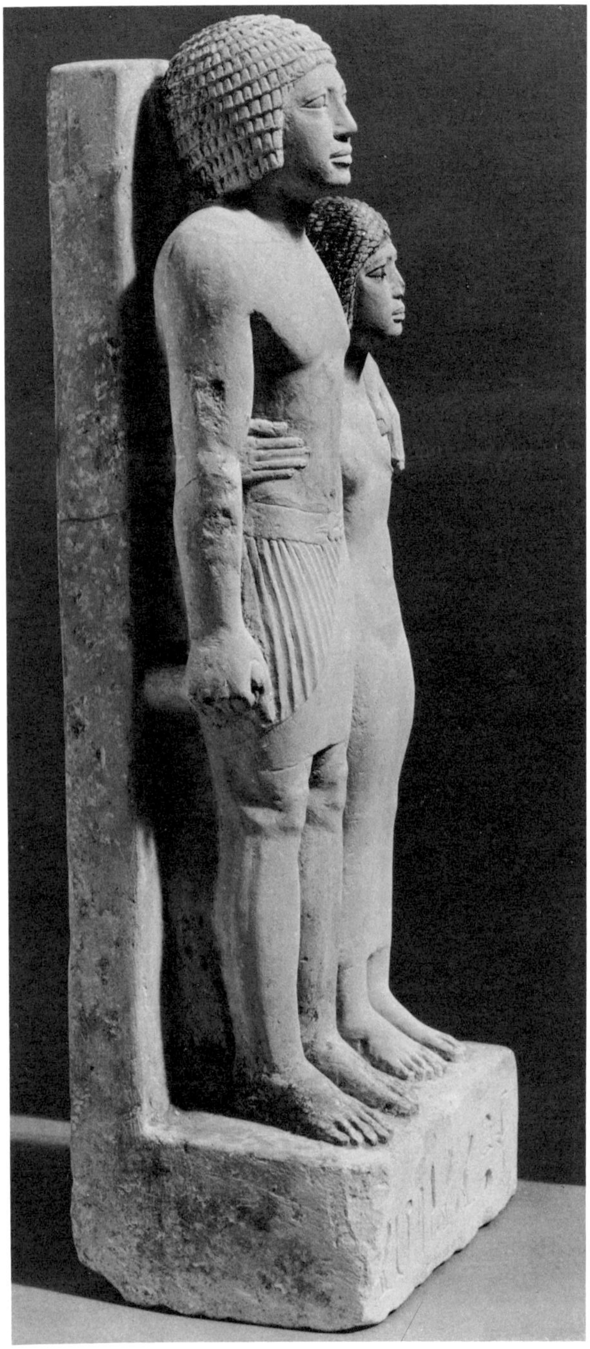

FIGURE 9

Statue of *Mmỉ/Śꜣbw* and his wife. The Metropolitan Museum of Art, Rogers Fund, 48.111

slung over the shoulder. A relief from one of Mariette's mastabas at Saqqara, illustrated here for the first time (Figures 12–14),[48] shows a cloth of this size that has been folded up and placed under one arm. The lower edge of the folded cloth is broken at the rear, and partly restored with plaster; but a portion of the original surface of the stone is visible only a short distance below the break, and from this it is evident that the cloth did not originally show a pair of pendant ends, curving downward. It is apparently the exact counterpart, on a larger scale, of the object that is under discussion.[49]

The date of this relief is probably no earlier than the mid-Fifth Dynasty, but there is every reason to believe that the hieroglyph ⊂⊃, representing a bolt of cloth, was familiar to sculptors in the early Fourth Dynasty, when it made its first appearance in the hands of statues. The earliest evidence derives from offering lists, where it figures among the various determinatives

6, 7. This use of the cloth reappears in Ramesside tombs (N. de G. Davies, *Two Ramesside Tombs at Thebes* [New York, 1927] pl. 37; N. de G. Davies, *Tomb of Nefer-ḥotep at Thebes*, I [New York, 1933] pl. 27), which also show a folded cloth used as a head covering (*Nefer-ḥotep*, I, pls. 16, 47; N. de G. Davies, *Seven Private Tombs at Ḳurnah* [London, 1948] pl. 30).

48. Published with the kind permission of the owner, Dr. Endre Ungar of Mexico City. From Mariette's B4: see A. Mariette, *Les Mastabas de l'Ancien Empire* (Paris, 1889) pp. 95–96, where the titles may be seen more completely. The left jamb measures 40 × 124.2 cms., the right 37.5 × 126.5. The location of tomb B4 is discussed by W. S. Smith in G. A. Reisner, *Development of the Egyptian Tomb* (Cambridge, Mass., 1936) p. 398. For the unusual pair of tabs that project below the kilt of the right-hand figure, see Staehelin, *Untersuchungen zur ägyptischen Tracht*, p. 15 and note 3. For the belt on the leopard skin of the left-hand figure, see the same work, p. 45, note 7; also James, *Hieroglyphic Texts*, I, 2nd ed., pls. 3 (3), 12 (2).

49. One might be tempted to regard this as the scribal kit called a *ḥryt-ꜥ*, literally "that which is under the arm (or hand)"; but such kits are generally less elongated, and made of wood (W. F. M. Petrie, *Medum* [London, 1892] pl. 13; M. A. Murray, *Saqqara Mastabas*, I [London, 1905] pl. 2); furthermore, they were evidently too large to be placed under the arm, as shown by representations of a man carrying one on his shoulder, S. Curto, *Gli Scavi Italiani a El-Ghiza* (Rome, 1963) fig. 7, pl. 7; *LD* II, pl. 105 (2); *ASAE* 16 (1916) p. 259.

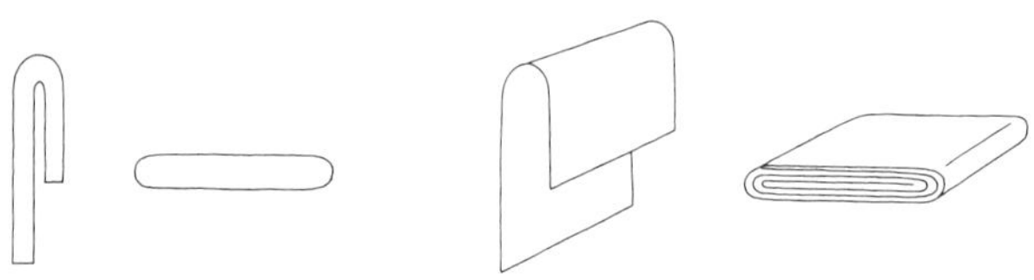

a b c d

FIGURE 10

Hieroglyphs representing folded cloth, with perspective interpretation

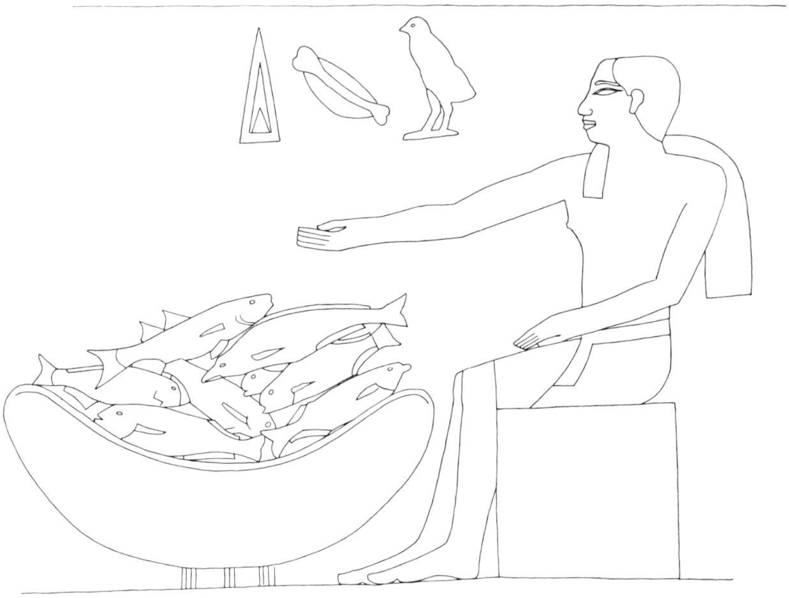

FIGURE 11

Relief from Unis pyramid causeway. After Hassan

of (Figure 15).[50] Some of the variants show an elongated rectangular form, probably representing a chest or pile of cloths, as is seen more clearly from later Old Kingdom representations of bolts of linen (Figure 16).[51] A few early examples show a tie at the center, and in some cases the determinative is reduced to the tie alone: . Some sort of binding, at the ends or at the center, is also applied to the form , as again illustrated by detailed representations.[52] This form is applied not only to *szf* but also to several other terms for cloth in the Abu Sir papyri, dating to the end of the Fifth Dynasty.[53] It is particularly well known in , *dꜣiw*, a word that is first attested in the Sixth Dynasty and is generally taken to mean "kilt" but primarily means "bolt of cloth."[54] From the Eleventh Dynasty onward *dꜣiw* is written ideographically as . The hieroglyph in question also appears

50. Fig. 15 a: Zaky Y. Saad, *Ceiling Stelae in Second Dynasty Tombs* (*ASAE* Suppl. No. 21 [Cairo, 1957]) no. 19, pl. 23. Fig. 15 b: *Ceiling Stelae*, no. 25, pl. 30. This earliest attested example of occurs relatively late in the series of Helwan stelae, and most probably belongs to Dyn. III; see Drioton's comments in the same work, pp. xv, xvi, and P. Kaplony, *Die Inschriften der ägyptischen Frühzeit* (*Ägyptologische Abhandlungen*, 8 [Wiesbaden, 1963]) pp. 331, 343–351. Figs. 15 c, d: CG 1385, 1386 (both dating to end of Dyn. III). Fig. 15 e: G. A. Reisner, *A History of the Giza Necropolis*, I (Cambridge, Mass., 1942) pl. 39 (a) (Dyn. IV, temp. Cheops). Fig. 15 f: same work, pl. 31 (c) (Dyn. IV, temp. Chephren). Fig. 15 g: Berlin 1107G, *Aegyptische Inschriften aus den Königlichen Museen zu Berlin*, I (Leipzig, 1913) p. 99 (early Dyn. V; see Junker, *Giza*, II, pp. 121–131). Fig. 15 h: A.-M. Abu-Bakr, *Excavations at Giza, 1949–1950*, fig. 10, facing p. 14 and pl. 10 (B) (Dyn. V ?). Fig. 15 i: P. Posener-Kriéger and J. de Cenival, *Hieratic Papyri in the British Museum*, V: *The Abu Sir Papyri* (London, 1968) pl. 47, and similarly pls. 41, 49, 50, 51, 92, 93 (end of Dyn. V). Fig. 15 j: A. M. Blackman, *Rock Tombs of Meir*, IV (London, 1924) pl. 20, p. 48 (Dyn. VI). Another hieratic writing of *szf* with the determinative is to be found in A. M. Moussa and H. Altenmüller, *The Tomb of Nefer and Ka-hay* (Mainz am Rhein, 1971) fig. 11, p. 44 (late Dyn. V). The same determinative occurs in the related word , Pyr. 265c, at the end of Dyn. V: K. Sethe, *Die Altaegyptischen Pyramidentexte*, I (Leipzig, 1908) p. 144. Sethe (*Dramatische Texte zu altaegyptischen Mysterienspielen* [Leipzig, 1928] p. 216), discussing this word, rightly concludes that the determinative is a "Zeugballen," a bolt of cloth. W. S. Smith ("The Old Kingdom Linen List," *ÄZ* 71 [1935] p. 149) may also be right in concluding that *szf* represents a narrow width of cloth, but, less happily, he believes that this narrowness is represented by the determinative.

51. Fig. 16a is from Blackman, *The Rock Tombs of Meir*, IV, pl. 19. Other examples: G. Jéquier, *Tombeaux de particuliers contemporains de Pépi II* (Cairo, 1929) fig. 17, p. 19; fig. 18, p. 20; fig. 50, p. 46, etc.

52. Fig. 16b is from C. Firth and B. Gunn, *Teti Pyramid Cemeteries*, II (Cairo, 1926) pl. 6 (B, D). Fig. 16c is from T. G. H. James and M. R. Apted, *The Mastaba of Khentika Called Ikhekhi* (London, 1953) pl. 38.

53. Posener-Kriéger and Cenival, *Hieratic Papyri in the British Museum*, V: *nfr(w)*, pls. 14, 47, 50, 51, 92, 93; *ḥnk*, pls. 41, 47, 49; *pꜣk*, pl. 47; *nwt* and *mnw*, pl. 51; *sṯꜣ*, pl. 49; *šzpt*, pl. 15.

54. Elisabeth Staehelin has independently come to the same conclusion in "Bindung und Entbindung," *ÄZ* 96 (1970) pp. 125–133, and her careful survey of the evidence leaves little more to be said; a few more references will be presented elsewhere, in an article of mine in the *Journal of the American Research Center in Egypt* 13.

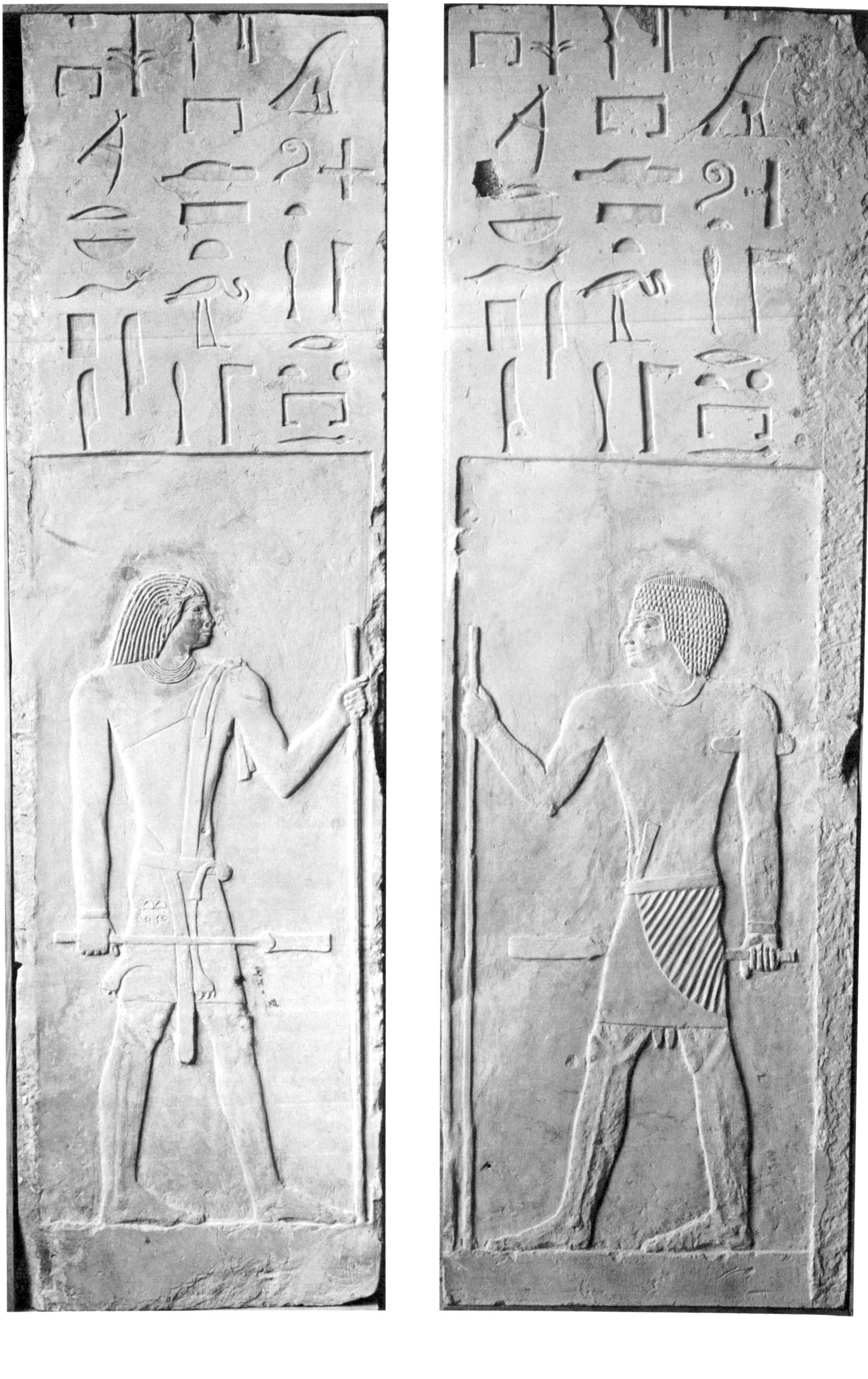

FIGURES 12, 13 (LEFT)
Reliefs from tomb of *'Ipi*, Saqqara (photo: courtesy Dr. Endre Ungar)

FIGURE 14
Detail of relief, Figure 13

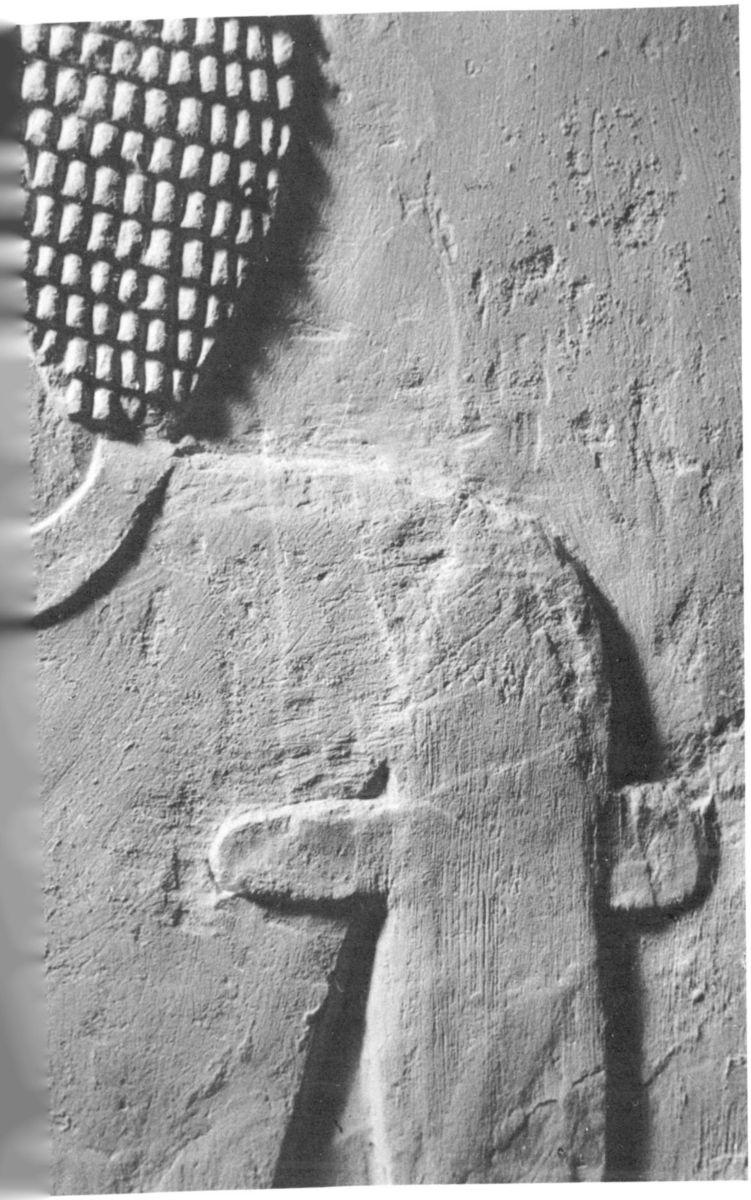

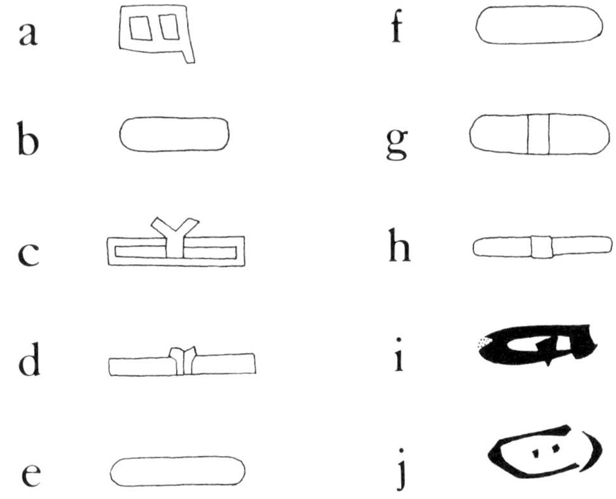

FIGURE 15
Variants of the hieroglyph representing a bolt of cloth

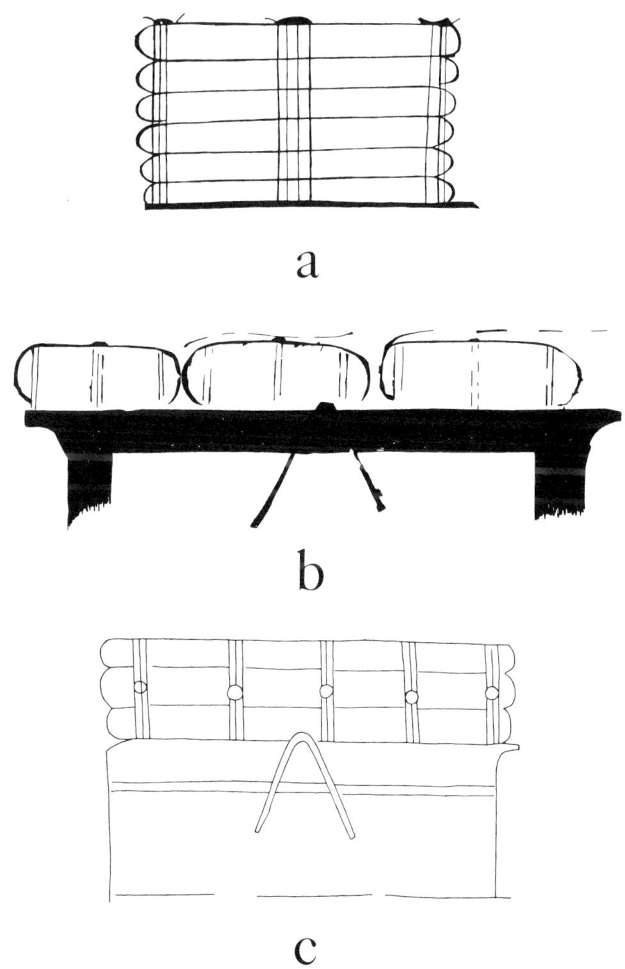

FIGURE 16 (RIGHT)
Bolts of cloth as represented among offerings in Old Kingdom burial chambers

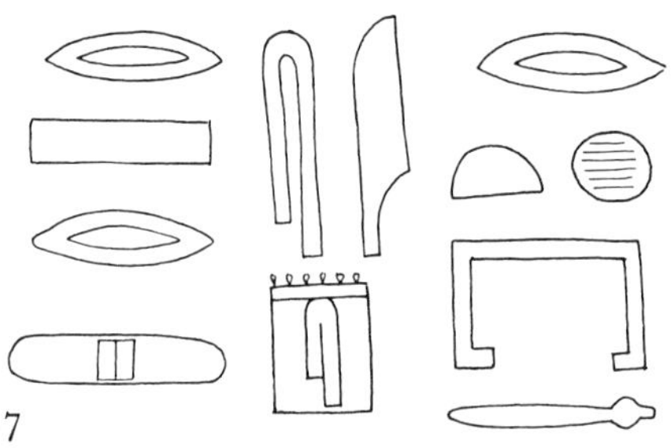

FIGURE 17

Titles from the tomb of *Nfr-kꜣ.i*, Giza, based on photograph (photo: courtesy Museo Egiziano, Turin)

in some later Old Kingdom variant writings of the title "overseer of the wardrobe."[55] And finally, a particularly interesting occurrence of is to be found in a title that is probably not much later than the beginning of the Fifth Dynasty (Figure 17).[56] The orthography offers some difficulties, but I suggest that it is to be read , *iry šśr,* "keeper of linen."[57] The last sign is certainly not a loaf of bread, as has previously been suggested.[58] The last two signs may both be regarded as generic determinatives.[59] Possibly, however, the sign may have a more specific meaning, in which case the title would mean "keeper of bolts of linen."

If cloth has, by its very nature, an elusive shape, assuming, among other shapes, the one that is found in the hands of Egyptian statues, it also lends itself to a variety of uses. Thus it is not surprising to find a piece of cloth occasionally in the hands of women, children, or prisoners (see Note 13), who would not ordinarily be expected to hold a staff or baton.

Finally it should be noted that the "elusive shape" is to be distinguished from the wide-ended object () that was sometimes carried by the king. This is colored yellow[60] and represents a container for documents.[61] Something very similar exceptionally appears in the

55. Several examples in Sixth Dynasty tomb chapels near the Unis pyramid causeway: A. Barsanti, "Le mastaba de Samnofir," *ASAE* 1 (1900) p. 152 (also in Z. Y. Saad, *Royal Excavations at Saqqara and Helwan [1941–1945]* [Cairo, 1947] p. 56, pl. 18); other examples unpublished: , , etc.

56. Curto, *Gli Scavi Italiani a El-Ghiza,* fig. 22 and pl. 2. I am indebted to Professor Curto for the photograph from which my drawing was made. Another detail from the same tomb is discussed in "Redundant Determinatives in the Old Kingdom," *MMJ* 8 (1973) pp. 16–18.

57. *'Iry šśr(w)* is otherwise known from BM 130 (James, *Hieroglyphic Texts,* pl. 14); CG 1564, Cairo J. 37731 (the latter on a basin from Reisner's tomb G 1351). In the first two cases the title is accompanied by *iry ḫt pr ꜥꜣ* "keeper of property of the Great House," just as in the present example. The use of instead of is unexpected in an Old Kingdom inscription, although another case occurs in the tomb of *Mrr-w(.i)-kꜣ(.i)* (: *Mereruka,* I, pl. 8); it is more frequent in the Twelfth Dynasty (e.g., , BM 839, *Hieroglyphic Texts . . . in the British Museum,* II, pl. 7). Curto, *Gli Scavi Italiani a El-Ghiza,* p. 14, takes as a writing of , citing *Wb.* I, 127; the interchange of and would be quite unexpected, however, in the midst of reliefs and inscriptions that are carefully designed and executed. Nor is there any parallel for his interpretation of the entire title: *(jrj-jḫt pr-ꜥꜣ) jš ḥbšjrj šjrj t* "addetto alle cose del Palazzo (e) el guardaroba, addetto ai giardini, addetto al pane."

58. See preceding note. The sign representing a loaf of bread is similar to this in hieratic (Posener-Kriéger and Cenival, *Hieratic Papyri in the British Museum,* V, pls. 34, 36, 39, 40, 41, etc.), but the detailed hieroglyphic equivalent is more like (Junker, *Gîza,* II, fig. 15, p. 146), which more usually lengthens to at the end of the Old Kingdom (H. Fischer, *Dendera in the Third Millennium B.C.* [Locust Valley, N. Y., 1968]) p. 81 [13]; also G. Jéquier, *Les Pyramides des reines Neit et Apouit* [Cairo, 1933] figs. 4, 12, pp. 11, 30). But elongated examples of (without internal detail) occur as the determinative of *psn*-bread as early as Dyn. IV (*Journal of Egyptian Archaeology* 19 [1933] pl. 23); also Dyn. V (Mariette, *Mastabas,* p. 300); Dyn. VI (James and Apted, *Mastaba of Khentika,* pl. 9 [33], with two vertical strokes at the bottom edge, not as high as shown in the publication); perhaps this form typifies the particular loaf in question. A form like does occur as a generic determinative for food in at least one small-scale hieroglyphic inscription of the late Old Kingdom (C. Fisher, *The Minor Cemetery at Giza,* pl. 50[2]; not, however, Mariette, *Mastabas,* p. 348, which is Cairo CG 1304); the variant is clearly influenced by semicursive writing and such an influence is unlikely in the present case.

59. One may perhaps compare cases where the related title *imy-r šśr* is written with both and , the first of which represents a sack for clothing, the second a generic determinative for cloth: Mariette, *Mastabas,* p. 307 (and CG 1484), 252 (and Hilda F. Petrie and M. A. Murray, *Seven Memphite Tomb Chapels* [London, 1952] pl. 14). The group occurs once in the Abu Sir papyri, but the preceding signs are lost: Posener-Kriéger and Cenival, *Hieratic Papyri in the British Museum,* V, pl. 15. Both these hieroglyphs are combined, apparently as determinatives, in a Middle Kingdom coffin which lists, among various kinds of cloth: (sic) , , *pꜣḳt, irtyw, mrw* (W. F. M. Petrie and G. Brunton, *Sedment,* I [London, 1924] pl. 18).

60. As in L. Borchardt, *Das Grabdenkmal des Königs Śaꜣḥu-reꜥ,* II (Leipzig, 1913) pl. 42; see also Jéquier, as cited in following note.

61. W. Spiegelberg, "Varia," *ÄZ* 53 (1917) pp. 101–104; G. Jéquier, *Les Frises d'objets des sarcophages du Moyen Empire* (*MIFAO* 47 [Cairo, 1921]) pp. 281–282; B. V. Bothmer, "Notes on the Mycerinus Triad," *BMFA* 48 (1950) pp. 15–16 and fig. 5, p. 12.

hand of a nonroyal individual in an Old Kingdom relief[62] and a Twelfth Dynasty statue;[63] in the latter case it is white, and is held in the left hand, while the right hand holds a white folded cloth. The same combination of objects is, more appropriately, held by royal statues of the Twelfth Dynasty.[64] Royal statues of the Eighteenth Dynasty show a more cylindrical container, the ends slightly concave, held in both hands,[65] while those of the Nineteenth Dynasty revert to something closer to the original form.[66] Cylindrical objects with flat ends occasionally appear in the hands of nonroyal statues of the later dynasties,[67] and these may perhaps represent rolls of papyrus rather than the cases in which such documents were placed.

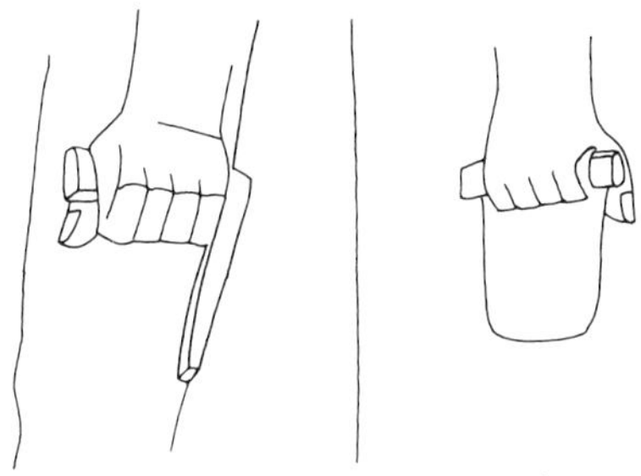

FIGURE 18
Details of statues, Ramesses II (a), Seti II (b)

62. H. Wild, *Le Tombeau de Ti*, Pt. III (Cairo, 1966) pl. 171; see also Staehelin, *Untersuchungen zur ägyptischen Tracht*, p. 162, but note that her second example, a relief on the base of CG 376, shows a son holding a papyrus roll.

63. W. M. F. Petrie, *Gizeh and Rifeh* (London, 1907) pl. 10 E, and M. A. Murray, *The Tomb of Two Brothers* (Manchester, 1910) p. 16, pl. 21 (7).

64. Cairo J. 38286, J. 38287, Sesostris I (the former in C. Aldred, *Middle Kingdom Art in Ancient Egypt* [London, 1950] fig. 27); CG 42011, Sesostris III. In the last case, the container is more or less cylindrical; so too CG 42026 (despite Lacau's description), representing Sesostris IV, and CG 386, representing Sobekemsef I, both of Dyn. XIII.

65. CG 42053, 42054, both Tuthmosis III, and 42077, representing Amenophis II; the last is best illustrated in Terrace and Fischer, *Treasures of Egyptian Art from the Cairo Museum*, pp. 110–111

66. The object is held horizontally on the lap of the seated statue of Ramesses II in Turin (R. Anthes, *Aegyptische Plastik in Meisterwerken* [Stuttgart, 1954] pls. 4–5). The colossal statue of Ramesses II in Cairo Station Square (L. Habachi, *Features of the Deification of Ramesses II* [Glückstadt, 1969] pl. 14) holds this object in the right hand, while the object in the left hand may represent a piece of cloth, as shown in the accompanying sketch (Figure 18a). Possibly, however, the pendant end represents a flap to close the case, and the same detail is perhaps to be recognized in the right hand of Louvre A 24, a statue of Seti II (Figure 18b), although Spiegelberg (*ÄZ* 53 [1917] p. 104) interprets this as the document that the case ordinarily concealed. This statue is illustrated in Charles Boreux, *Musée National du Louvre, Département des Antiquités Égyptiennes, Guide-Catalogue Sommaire* (Paris, 1932), pl. 2.

67. Cairo J. 37150 (H. Kees, *ÄZ* 84 [1959] pp. 54–67, pl. 2, dating to Dyn. XXV; better illustrated in J. Yoyotte, *Treasures of the Pharaohs* [Geneva, 1968] p. 190); CG 42243, dating to Dyn. XXVI.

SOURCES ABBREVIATED

ASAE—*Annales du Service des Antiquités de l'Égypte*
ÄZ—*Zeitschrift für ägyptische Sprache und Altertumskunde*
BM—British Museum
BMFA—*Bulletin of the Museum of Fine Arts* (Boston)
BMMA—*Bulletin of The Metropolitan Museum of Art*
Borchardt, *Statuen und Statuetten.* See CG + number
Cairo J. + number—Monuments in the Egyptian Museum, Cairo, unpublished unless otherwise noted
CG + number—Monuments in the Egyptian Museum, Cairo, numbers referring to *Catalogue général des antiquités égyptiennes du Musée du Caire:*
- CG 1–1294: Ludwig Borchardt, *Statuen und Statuetten von Königen und Privatleuten im Museum von Kairo* I–IV (Berlin, 1911–34);
- CG 1295–1808: Ludwig Borchardt, *Denkmäler des Alten Reiches*, I–II (Berlin, 1937–64);
- CG 42001–42250: Georges Legrain. *Statues et statuettes de rois et de particuliers*, I–III (Cairo, 1906–14)

Hassan, *Gîza*—Selim Hassan, *Excavations at Gîza*, I–X (Oxford–Cairo, 1932–60)
HESPOK—W. S. Smith, *A History of Egyptian Sculpture and Painting in the Old Kingdom* (London, 1946)
Junker, *Gîza*—H. Junker, *Gîza* (*Akademie der Wissenschaften in Wien, Philosophisch-historische Klasse. Denkschriften*), I–XII (Vienna, 1929–55)
LD—C. R. Lepsius, ed., *Denkmäler aus Ägypten und Äthiopien*, I–XII (Berlin, 1849–59)
MÄS—*Münchner Ägyptologische Studien, Münchner Universitäts-Schriften, Philosophische Fakultät* (Berlin)
Mereruka—University of Chicago, *Oriental Institute Publications* 31, 39, *The Mastaba of Mereruka*, I–II (Chicago, 1938)
MFA—Museum of Fine Arts, Boston
MIFAO—*Mémoires publiés par les membres de l'Institut français d'Archéologie orientale* (Cairo)
MMA—The Metropolitan Museum of Art
Univ. Mus.—University Museum, University of Pennsylvania, Philadelphia
Wb.—A. Erman and H. Grapow, eds., *Wörterbuch der Ägyptischen Sprache*, I–V (Leipzig, 1926–31)

Some Early Monuments from Busiris, in the Egyptian Delta

HENRY G. FISCHER

Lila Acheson Wallace Curator in Egyptology, The Metropolitan Museum of Art

CONSIDERING HOW VERY frequently Osiris "Lord of Busiris" is invoked on funerary monuments from the Fifth Dynasty onward, it is remarkable how little evidence is known to have come from the native city of that all-important divinity. The fourth volume of the Porter-Moss *Topographical Bibliography* (Oxford, 1934), p. 44, mentions only three fragmentary monuments of the Twenty-second Dynasty and later, all published in E. H. Naville's *Mound of the Jew* (London, 1890), pl. 7 (A–C), and the list has been only very slightly augmented in the meantime.[1] For more than half a century, however, the Fitzwilliam Museum in Cambridge has housed a limestone false door (E 6.1909)[2] that clearly comes from Busiris and provides the earliest specific mention of the local temple, as well as a hitherto unknown local cult of Hathor (Figures 8, 9). The date of the monument, which will be examined more closely in the following pages, lies somewhere between the end of the Sixth Dynasty and the beginning of the Twelfth, and I am inclined to attribute it to the end of the Heracleopolitan Period. In addition, Labib Habachi has called my attention to a group of inscribed monuments from the same site that have been known for an almost equal number of years, albeit to a very few persons. The oldest of them is evidently of somewhat greater antiquity than the false door in Cambridge; three others are Eleventh Dynasty and a fourth is only slightly later than these. They were excavated by Ali El Manzalawy on his property at Kom el Akhdar, two kilometers west of Abusir village, in 1928. Sami Gabra inspected them for the Department of Antiquities in the following year and Dr. Habachi re-examined them in 1943, when he was able to take photographs. These have most generously been put at my disposal and three of them—a limestone slab, a limestone false door, and a fragmentary limestone offering slab—are illustrated and described here.[3]

1. Bernard Bothmer describes the cemetery in *ARCE Newsletter* 18 (June 15, 1955), pp. 5–6; for further references to the cult, see Gardiner, *Ancient Egyptian Onomastica* II (Oxford, 1947) pp. 176*–180*. It may noted that J. Gwyn Griffiths is inclined to doubt that the cult of Osiris emanated from Busiris rather than Abydos: *The Origins of Osiris* (*MÄS* 9 [1966]) pp. 86, 119. On p. 90, however, he concedes that, although Andjety preceded Osiris as the god of the Busirite Nome, "Osiris may have begun as a subordinate deity in Busiris." In favor of his Lower Egyptian origin, it should be emphasized that the Upper Egyptian crown was acquired by Osiris from Khentiamentiu at a relatively late date—not before the Eleventh Dynasty (*JAOS* 76 [1956] p. 101, note 11). On the other hand, it is uncertain whether Khentiamentiu acquired the crook and flail from Andjety or whether both gods possessed this pair of attributes independently; they appear in a Sixth Dynasty determinative of Khentiamentiu which also shows the Upper Egyptian crown: 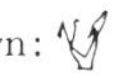 (Cairo CG 1574 and similarly Louvre C 160), and may derive from the iconography of the king, just as the crown does. See also Joachim Spiegel, *Die Götter von Abydos* (Wiesbaden, 1973) p. 7, who points out that even in the Middle Kingdom the Busirite origin of Osiris is strongly emphasized.

2. Given by F. W. Green in 1909. I am indebted to Dr. Caroline Peck for the photograph and to Miss Janine Bourriau for permission to publish it here.

3. The choice is limited to those from which it was possible to prepare a reasonably reliable line drawing.

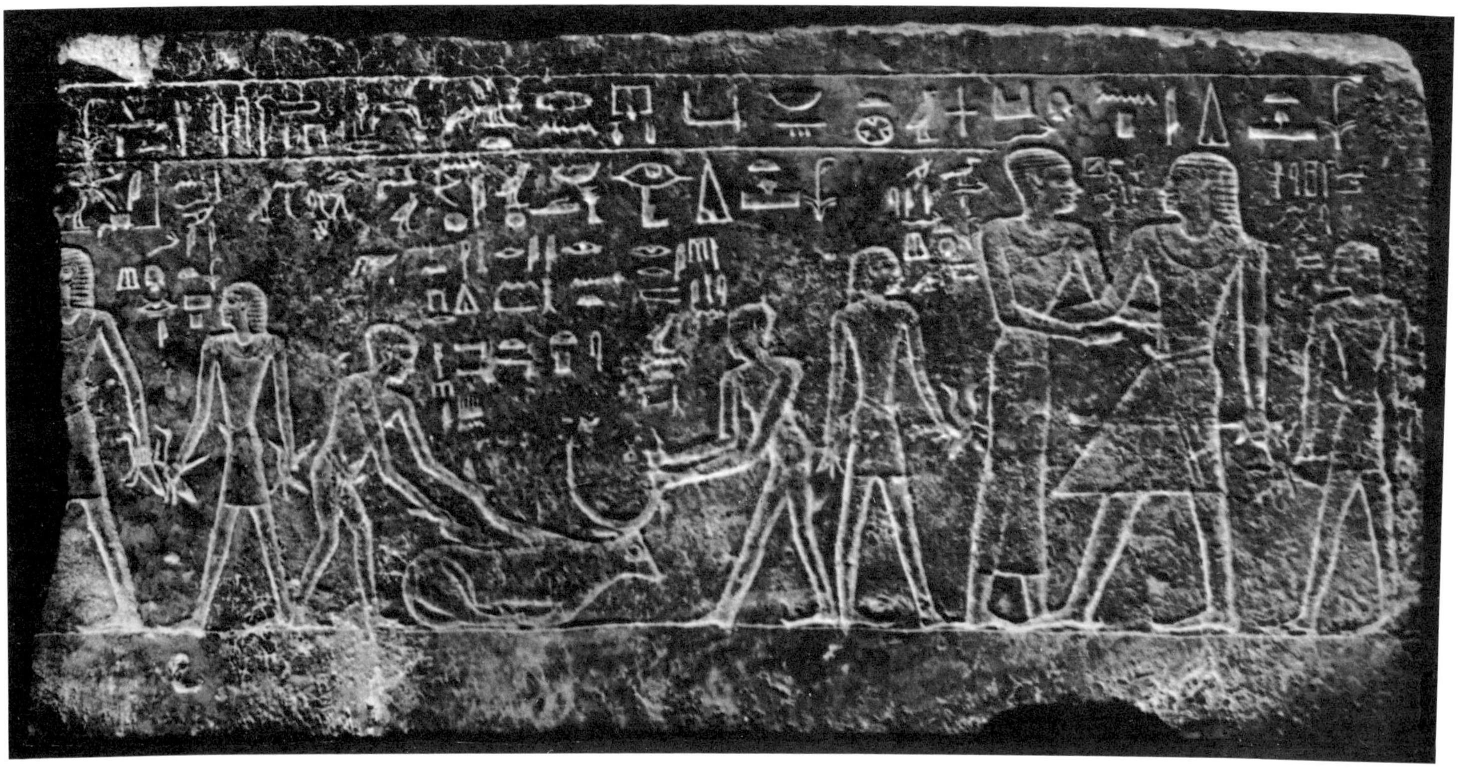

FIGURE 1
Old Kingdom architrave from Kom el Akhdar. (photo: courtesy Labib Habachi)

They require less commentary than does the Fitzwilliam Museum false door, and so are presented more concisely.

MONUMENTS FROM KOM EL AKHDAR

The oldest of the monuments (Figures 1, 2) is a limestone slab, measuring 102 cm. in length, 51 cm. in height and 11 cm. in thickness. The pair of offering bearers at the left (a, b) evidently advance toward a representation of the owner, now missing, which may have been accompanied by that of his wife. He is again shown with his wife at the right end (f, g), accompanied by two sons. These two groups are separated by a butchering scene (c, d). Although the figures are rather crude in style and workmanship, they are altogether in the tradition of the Old Kingdom. As in many Sixth Dynasty reliefs from Saqqara and Upper Egypt, the owner wears a shoulder-length wig, consisting of horizontal tiers of locks, while his wife's wig is short, following the contour of her head.[4] The titles are well known from monuments of the late Old Kingdom,[5] and the orthography generally conforms to what one would expect of that period, as exemplified by the writing of *imywt* with

4. Other examples: Firth and Gunn, *Teti Pyramid Cemeteries*, pl. 77; G. Jéquier, *Tombeaux de particuliers contemporains de Pepi II* (Cairo, 1929), fig. 129, p. 114; A. M. Blackman, *Rock Tombs of Meir* IV (London, 1924) pls. 4, 5, 9; W. M. F. Petrie, *Dendereh* (London, 1900) pls. 11, 11A ("Beba"); Fischer, *Coptite Nome*, pls. 5, 7, 8, 9, 11, 12; CG 1586 (from Akhmin: Fischer *Dendera*, pl. 30[a]); Cairo J 49803 (from Abydos: Frankfort, *JEA* 14 [1928] pl. 20[3]). More rarely women retain the older fashion of the long tripartite wig, and this again becomes more common on later monuments.

5. *Ḥḳ3-ḥwt* and *imy-r gś-pr* are particularly frequent on monuments of this period at Saqqara: see Jèquier, *Tombeaux de particuliers*, fig. 68, p. 60; figs. 80–83, pp. 71–74; *Monument funéraire de Pepi II* III (Cairo, 1940) figs. 73, 78, pp. 74–75; Lauer, *ASAE* 53 (1955) p. 155 and pl. 3. In such cases *ḥḳ3-ḥwt* precedes the honorific *śḏ3wty-bîty*, and Klaus Baer similarly lists *ḥḳ3-ḥwt* before *śḏ3wty bîty* in his latest series (VI G: *Rank and Title in the Old Kingdom* [Chicago, 1960] p. 239, based on a single source—N. de G. Davies, *Rock Tombs of Deir el Gebrâwi* I [London, 1902], pls. 3–19, 23). The Dendera inscriptions provide several cases of the sequence *śḏ3wty-bîty, ḥḳ3-ḥwt, śmr wꜥty:* Petrie, *Dendereh*, pls. 5, 5A ('*Idw* I), 6 ('*Idw* II), 11, 11A

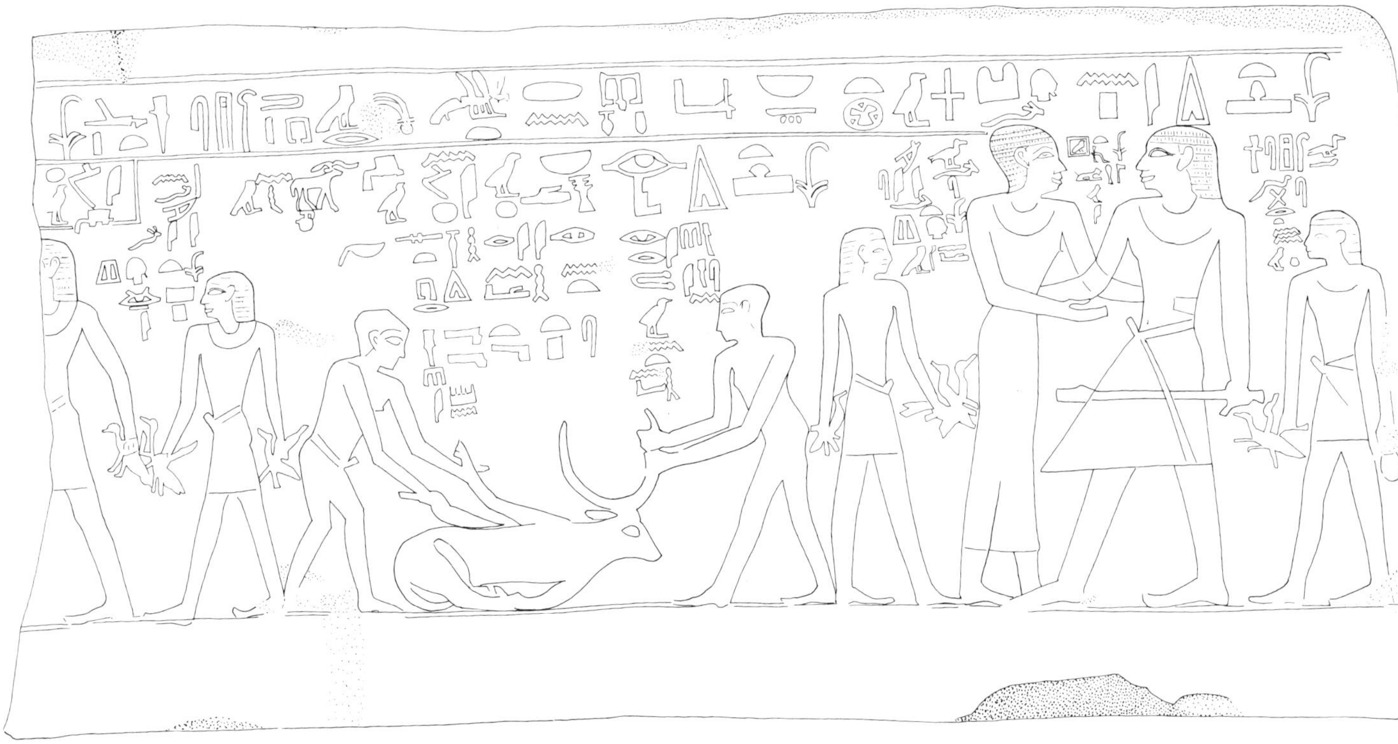

a b c d e f g h

FIGURE 2 Old Kingdom architrave from Kom el Akhdar

the determinative ⊗, rather than the later ◊,[6] and *imꜣḫw* rather than Eleventh Dynasty *imꜣḫy*.[7] The phonetic writing of *'Inpw*, however, suggests a relatively late date. This derives from the circumlocutions that were designed to eliminate the figures of men and animals in inscriptions adjacent to the burial.[8] It is found in coffins and burial chambers of the Sixth Dynasty, but probably did not begin to appear in the offering chamber or in other parts of the superstructure of the tomb, before the very end of the Old Kingdom, in Dynasty VIII.[9] If, in the present case, the phonetic writing had been intended to eliminate the figure of a jackal from an inscription near the body, it seems unlikely that a multitude of human figures would have been admitted in the same context.[10] It also seems unlikely that the slab lined one of the lateral walls of a burial chamber,

(*Bbi*), the last dating to the very end of Dyn. VI; similarly pls. 1–3 (*Mni*) and 7 (*Ṯꜣwti*), both of which are later than the Old Kingdom. Similarly Naga ed-Deir tomb N48 (*Ḥꜣgi*, Dyn. VIII) shows the same sequence, as seen from field records in the Museum of Fine Arts, Boston (for this nomarch see also *JAOS* 74 [1954] p. 33, and Caroline Peck, *Some Decorated Tombs at Naga ed-Dêr* [Ann Arbor, 1958] p. 127). So too the limestone sarcophagus of *Tti-išt.f* from Mendes (Chabân, *ASAE* 10 (1910] p. 28).

6. See note 78.

7. See p. 20, Comment h.

8. Firth and Gunn, *Teti Pyramid Cemeteries*, pp. 172–174.

9. The same purely phonetic writing, omitting *w*, occurs on two stelae of *Šnni*: Petrie, *Dendereh*, pls. 7, 7A; for the date, see Fischer, *Dendera*, pp. 113–115. The phonetic writing also occurs on the fragmentary false-door niche of *St-nt-Ppy* at Mendes: Christine Soghor, *JARCE* 6 (1967) fig. 9 following p. 28. See too Caroline Peck, *Some Decorated Tombs at Naga ed-Dêr*, pls. 11, 14, 15 (the last two cases written ..., all N3737, probably as late as Dyn. IX (Peck, p. 127); but ... occurs after *imꜣḫ ḫr* in N41, which is presumably earlier (Sayce, *Recueil de travaux relatifs à la philologie et à l'archéologie égyptiennes et assyriennes* 13 [1890] p. 64). The writing ... also appears on two false doors at Giza that may or may not antedate the end of the Sixth Dynasty: Junker, *Gîza* VII, fig. 104, p. 247; XI, fig. 40, p. 71.

10. See Junker, *Gîza* IV, p. 45, who points out that at Giza, unlike Saqqara and elsewhere, decorated burial chambers show figures and do not avoid human or animal hieroglyphs in the inscriptions. Even at Giza, however, hieroglyphs of this kind are avoided on Sixth Dynasty coffins: Junker, *Gîza* VII, p. 224; VIII, pp. 99–103.

although it may originally have been long enough to serve that purpose; an example at nearby Mendes indicates that the burial chambers in this area of the Delta resemble those of Saqqara, with the representations confined to offerings.[11] Almost certainly, then, it is an architrave from a tomb chapel, and the phonetic writing of Anubis is to be regarded as a late feature. The same conclusion is suggested by the degenerate form of (with three crossroads)[12] and (with three horizontal elements at the top,[13] the peculiar form of (the upper part formed separately)[14] and (with backward-slanting "horns").[15] Moreover, the hieroglyphs all face rightward, in accordance with the dominant orientation of texts, even where the figures to which they belong are turned toward the left. This too might be considered a late and degenerate feature, although it occurs on a provincial monument of the Sixth Dynasty that is as early as the reign of Merenre—namely the offering niche of *Ḳȝr* from Edfu.[16]

None of the iconographic elements is new, but the face-to-face embrace is known from only a few Old Kingdom monuments,[17] and here it is rendered rather less satisfactorily; the woman leans forward and it is not entirely clear which of the crisscrossed arms passes in front of the other.

Assuming that the monument is an architrave of rather unusual composition, I am inclined to date it no earlier than the very end of the Sixth Dynasty, admitting the possibility that it is as late as Dynasty VIII.

The inscriptions may be translated as follows:

Two horizontal lines at top: (1) An offering that the king gives and Anubis, Who Is Upon His Mountain, Who Is in the Place of Embalming, Lord of the Sacred Land, that invocation offerings go forth to the Chancellor of the King of Lower Egypt, the Overseer of the Work Center, the Estate Chief, Sole Companion and [Liegeman (?)] of the King [. . .?] the Revered [*Ḫnmw-nḏm(w)*][18] (2) An offering that the king gives, and Osiris, Lord of Busiris, to the Revered *Ḫnmw-nḏm(w)*.[19]

Figures at left: (a) [lost] (b) His brother, his beloved, the Liegeman *Špi*.[20]

Butchering scene: (d) The Director of the Dining Tent *Śȝbni*:[21] "Exert thyself, my companion!" (c) "I do as thou praisest, my companion; I cause the choice cuts to come forth"—the Director of the Dining Tent *Mni*.[22]

Group at right: (g, the owner, requires no caption) (f, his wife)[23] The Noblewoman of the King, Priestess of Hathor *Rwi*.[24] (e) His/her son, his/her beloved,[25] the Liegeman of the King *ꜥȝm*.[26] (h) His son, the Estate Chief and Companion *Śḏ-rtnnw* (?).[27]

11. The aforementioned tomb of *St-nt-Ppy:* Donald Hansen, *JARCE* 4 (1965) p. 36 and pl. 20; Christine Soghor, *JARCE* 6 (1967) p. 26 and pl. 17 (30). Two limestone burial chambers at Barnugi, near Damanhur, do show painted scenes including offering bearers and butchering, as well as representations of the owner, but these are evidently Twelfth Dynasty (C. C. Edgar in G. Maspero, *Le Musée égyptien* II [Cairo, 1907] pp. 112–113).

12. Occasionally exemplified by some very late Old Kingdom stelae from Abydos: Cairo CG 1615 (*JARCE* 1 [1962] fig. 3 on p. 21 and pl. 2); BM 128 (T. G. H. James, *Hieroglyphic Texts from Egyptian Stelae, etc.* I, 2nd ed. [London, 1961] pl. 34 [2]); Cairo CG 1592 (Brovarski, *JNES* 32 [1973] fig. 4, p. 460); CG 1645. Also Junker, *Gîza* VII, fig. 47, p. 127 and pl. 27(a).

13. A decidedly late feature at Dendera; Fischer, *Dendera*, p. 120. An example is possibly to be found in Hassan, *Gîza* VI, pt. 3, fig. 207, p. 209.

14. Not attested elsewhere, to my knowledge; some examples in Figure 9 may seem to show a slight resemblance, but this is illusory.

15. Otherwise most clearly exemplified by the Eighth Dynasty inscriptions of *Śnni:* Petrie, *Dendereh*, pls. 7, 7A; compare L. Keimer, *Études d'Égyptologie*, fasc. VII (Cairo, 1945), p. 5 and note 2.

16. Cairo J 43370 (Daressy, *ASAE* 17 [1917] pp. 130–140); this is only true of the false door proper, and not the architrave above it. Somewhat later examples of the same kind are to be found on stelae from Abydos: Cairo CG 1615, see note 12; Louvre C 198; Berlin 7512 (the latter two illustrated by Brovarski, *JNES* 32 [1973] figs. 5–6, pp. 462–463).

17. Fischer, *JNES* 18 (1959) p. 243, and *Egyptian Studies* I: *Varia* (New York, 1976) pp. 5, 9.

18. This is below the first line, but the frame indicates that it is a continuation.

19. Not listed in *PN*. Note that this theophoric name refers to the Upper Egyptian Khnum rather than to the ram of nearby Mendes, for the ram is clearly accompanied by rather than .

20. Compare *PN* I, p 325 (15).

21. Compare *PN* I, p. 299 (12).

22. Compare *PN* I, p. 151 (2).

23. As shown by the caption of the son behind her; see note 25.

24. Compare *PN* I, p. 220 (15).

25. This more explicit substitution for the third person plural suffix does not seem to be attested elsewhere.

26. Compare *PN* I, p. 59 (2), otherwise first attested in the Middle Kingdom, although a feminine example (*ꜥȝmt*) is known from the Thinite Nome on a stela that is evidently earlier than the Eleventh Dynasty—D. Dunham, *Naga-ed-Dêr Stelae* (Oxford, 1937) no. 87; this belongs to the group discussed by Vandier, *Revue d'Égyptologie* 2 (1936) pp. 49–51 (Schenkel's "Gruppe B": *Studien* §38b), which may be of Dyn. VIII or only slightly later. It is difficult to say whether the Busirite example indicates Asiatic blood or whether it simply reflects some aspect of the son's appearance. In the latter case, the peculiarly explicit reference to his parentage ("his/her son") may be designed to eliminate any misapprehension about his antecedents which the name would otherwise suggest. At all events

The limestone false door (Figures 3, 4) is one of three very similar monuments. This one measures 112 cm. in height, 62 cm. in width, and 47 cm. in thickness. The others measure 64 × 38 × 10 cm.[28] and 85 × 47 × 15 cm.[29] All three display a pair of *wḏꜣt*-eyes on the inner jambs, flanking the central niche, and the spaces on either side of the offering scene have been reduced to very small proportions.[30] The epithet "revered" is written and ,[31] the epithets *ikr* and *mꜣꜥ ḫrw*[32] follow the owner's name, and the initial words of "the Great God Lord of Abydos" are consistently written .[33] The abstract sign retains the old form . The location of the *wḏꜣt*-eyes is not otherwise known to occur before the reunification of Egypt,[34] but the spelling of "revered" suggests that the present example cannot be much earlier, and so too does the use of the epithet *mꜣꜥ ḫrw*. An even later date is indicated by the group and this conclusion is reinforced by the use of ideographic as a writing of "Hathor" on one of the other false doors.[29] Since late criteria must always, in such cases, outweigh the earlier ones, it seems likely that these false doors are not earlier than the last years of the Eleventh Dynasty, and that the *wḏꜣt*-eyes retained their older location longer at Busiris than they did elsewhere. The phrase "every good feast of the spirit" is peculiar to this particular monument.

The translations proceed from upper to lower elements and from left to right:

Outer frame: (1) An offering that the king gives, and Osiris, Lord of Busiris, Khentiamentiu the Great God, Lord of Abydos in all his places (2) that invocation offerings go forth to the Scribe of the God's Treasure in the House of Osiris,[35] the Overseer of the Army in (the Nome of) *ꜥnḏty*[36] (more specifically) Busiris,[37] the Re-

this name is probably related to the fact that Asiatics had established themselves in the adjacent eastern half of the Delta, as subsequently described in the Instructions of King Merykare. Compare the comments on the name of the second son, discussed in the following note.

27. Nothing analogous is known from *PN*, but one might perhaps compare *Ḥw-nḥsy* (*PN* I, p. 234 [21] and Cairo CG 1695), which Junker, *Gîza* I, p. 254, translates "Vernichter der Nubier." If *šd* "break" is used in the same sense as *ḥw*, then may be an ethnicon; this is reminiscent of the later , but it hardly seems possible that the group is to be read , as far as I can see from comparing the two photographs on which I have had to rely.

28. Belonging to a man named ; compare *PN* I, p. 259 (5) and note the replacement of by . He has the epithets *ikr* and *mꜣꜥ-ḫrw*, as well as some titles or epithets that are difficult to read and interpret.

29. Belonging to a priestess of Hathor () whose name is lost. For the title *hmt* compare Berlin 7716 (*Aegyptische Inschriften aus den Königlichen Museen zu Berlin* I [Leipzig, 1913] p. 47) and J. J. Clère in *Miscellanea Gregoriana* (Rome, 1941) pp. 456, 464. Schenkel considers the ideographic writing of Hathor to be characteristic of the end of Dyn. XI (*Studien*, §12). The goddess is mistress of a cult the name of which is illegible: .

30. Compare Figure 9 and the examples cited in note 47. I know of no other cases where the spaces are shortened to this degree; the closest comparison is the Eighth Dynasty false door of the Princess *Nbt*, in which they are reduced to slightly less than half the height of the offering scene (Fischer, *Coptite Nome*, p. 38).

31. See again Comment h on p. 20. In addition to the later *y*-endings, this shows the omission of the initial , which did not become at all usual until the end of the Heracleopolitan Period; see Fischer, *Dendera*, p. 131, and *Egyptian Studies* I: *Varia*, part 6.

32. For *ikr*, see Fischer, *Dendera*, p. 131, note 576, and for *mꜣꜥ ḫrw*, see Schenkel, *Studien*, §28a, to which should be added some stelae from Gebelein: Turin 13114 (*Kush* 9 [1961] p. 45 [5]) and Turin Suppl. 1270 (*Kush* 9, pl. 13 [a]).

33. Schenkel, *Studien*, §4. This criterion is evidently valid, although the group is not uncommon in the late Old Kingdom (Junker, *Gîza* VIII, fig. 34, p. 79; XI, fig. 40, p. 71; fig. 83, p. 215, etc.) and a late Sixth Dynasty stela shows (Fischer, *Coptite Nome*, no. 4). The one Eleventh Dynasty example of cited by Schenkel (the coffin of *Mrw*, *LD* II, pl. 148d) may be even later than the forty-sixth year of *Nb-ḥpt-Rꜥ* Mentuhotep, since the stela that provides this date evidently does not belong to the tomb (*Bibliotheca Orientalis* 23 [1966] p. 30).

34. See Fischer, *Coptite Nome*, p. 40; Fischer, *Dendera*, p. 226; one of the latest examples known to me—perhaps not much earlier than the Reunification—is to be found on a small representation of a false door at the bottom of Louvre stela C 15 (A. Gayet, *Musée du Louvre: Stèles de la XIIᵉ Dynastie* [Paris, 1886] pl. 54).

35. Compare *Sš sḏꜣwt-nṯr m ḥwt Ptḥ* "scribe of the god's treasure in the mansion of Ptah," discussed in *JARCE* 3 (1964) p. 26.

36. The name is usually written emblematically in the Old Kingdom and later; the phonetic writing presumably derives from the circumlocutions of Saqqara funerary texts such as Pyr. 182, 220. This writing also indicates that the name of the nome is not *ꜥnḏt*, as has generally been assumed (*Wb.* I, p. 207 [10]; Gardiner, *Ancient Egyptian Onomastica* II, p. 179*), but is *ꜥnḏty*, the god shown in the nome emblem, "he of the *ꜥnḏt*-waterway," as maintained by P. Montet (*Géographie de l'Égypte Ancienne* I: *Basse Égypte* [Paris, 1957] p. 97) and W. Helck (*Die altägyptischen Gaue* [Wiesbaden, 1974] p. 174).

37. The preposition *m* evidently introduces the nome and not the city, and such cases therefore probably do not show graphic transposition (a possibility considered in *JARCE* 10 [1973] pp. 6–7). It is instructive to compare the following late Old Kingdom epithets on the south pillar of an unpublished rock-cut tomb at Saqqara, located between the Djoser enclosure and the Unis Causeway

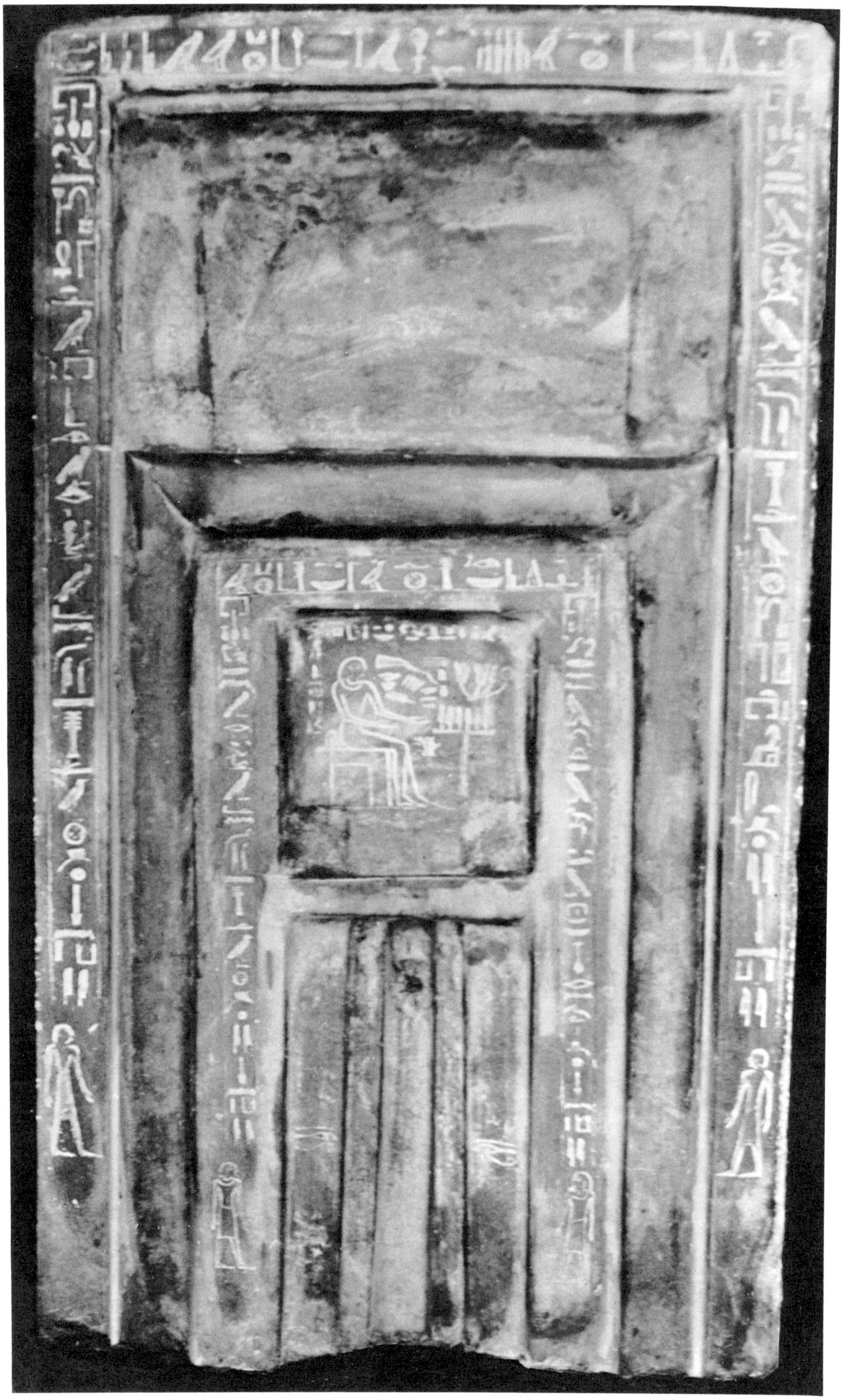

FIGURE 3
Eleventh Dynasty false door from Kom el Akhdar. (photo: courtesy Labib Habachi)

FIGURE 4
Eleventh Dynasty false door from Kom el Akhdar

FIGURE 5
Eleventh Dynasty offering slab from Kom el Akhdar. (photo: courtesy Labib Habachi)

FIGURE 6
Eleventh Dynasty offering slab from Kom el Akhdar

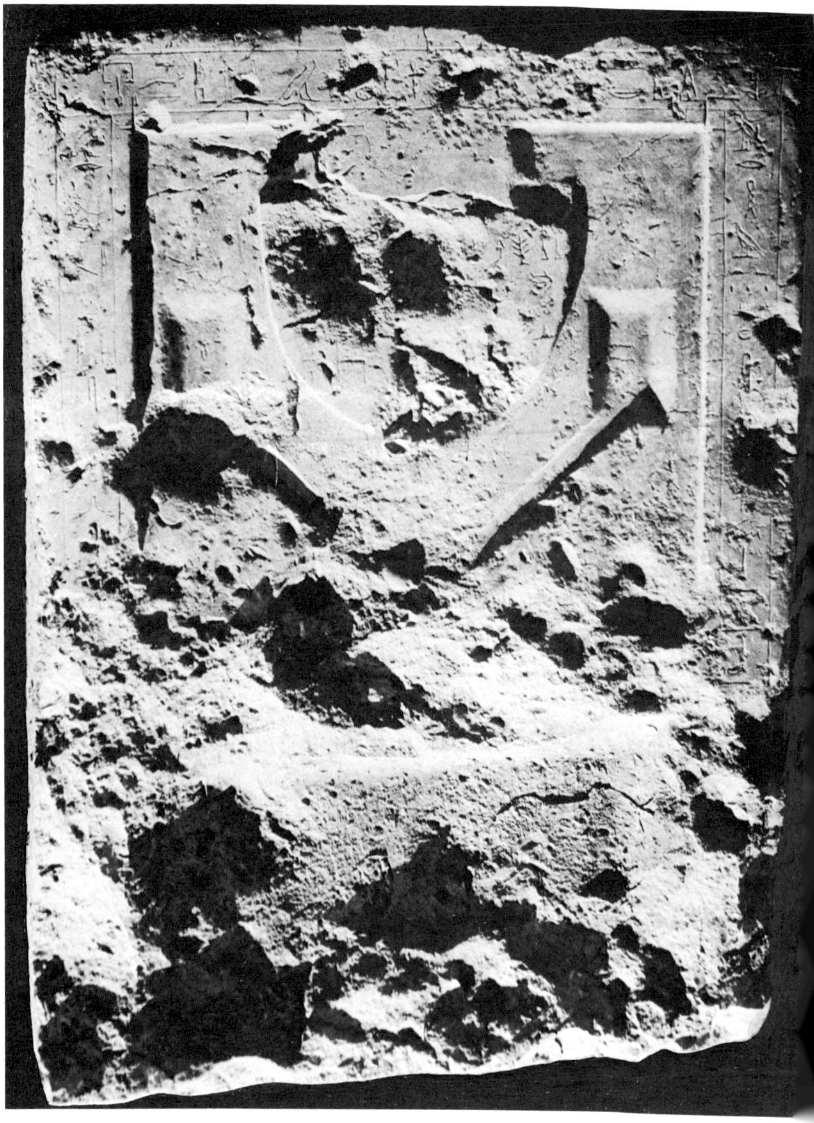

vered *Šn-kꜣy*.[38] (3) that invocation offerings go forth to the Overseer of the Army in (the Nome of) *ʿndty* (more specifically) Busiris, the Scribe of the Noble Mansion of the God, the Revered *Šn-kꜣy*.

and belonging to a certain :

"revered with Osiris Lord of Busiris in (the Nome)) *ʿndty*"; "revered with Osiris in (the Nome) *ʿndty* (more specifically) Busiris." The same construction occurs repeatedly in the Old Kingdom; see Edel, *Altäg. Gramm.*, §314, where should be prefixed to his examples from *Urk*. I, pp. 118 (14), 101 (13), and 280 (17). Although I do not know of examples in Old Kingdom titles, some Middle Kingdom titles may be compared:

(1) (Cairo CG 20105)
(2) (Cairo CG 20514)

(1) "overseer of regulations in the Panopolite Nome—*Ḥnmt-Mnw*" (see Fischer, *Coptite Nome*, p. 110); (2) "great *wʿb*-priest in the Thinite Nome—Abydos." Note, however, that the preposition *m* may precede either a nome emblem or the name of a town if these occur alone in a title, without further specification: thus (Cairo CG 20091) "steward in the Cynopolite Nome"; (Petrie et al., *Lahun* [London, 1923] pl. 64 [224]) "greatest of seers in Heliopolis." Similarly in offering formulae Osiris is (Cairo CG 20729) but also (CG 20421).

38. Not listed in *PN*.

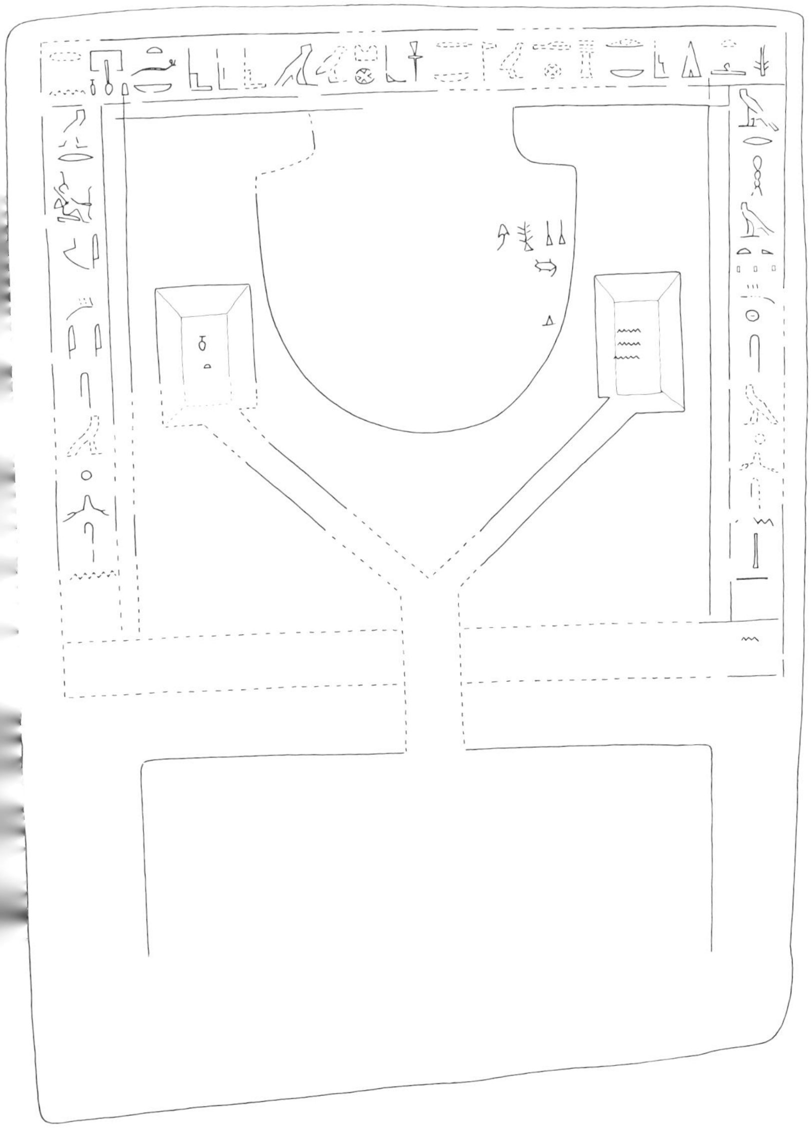

FIGURE 7

Eleventh Dynasty offering slab in Karlsruhe. From a photograph

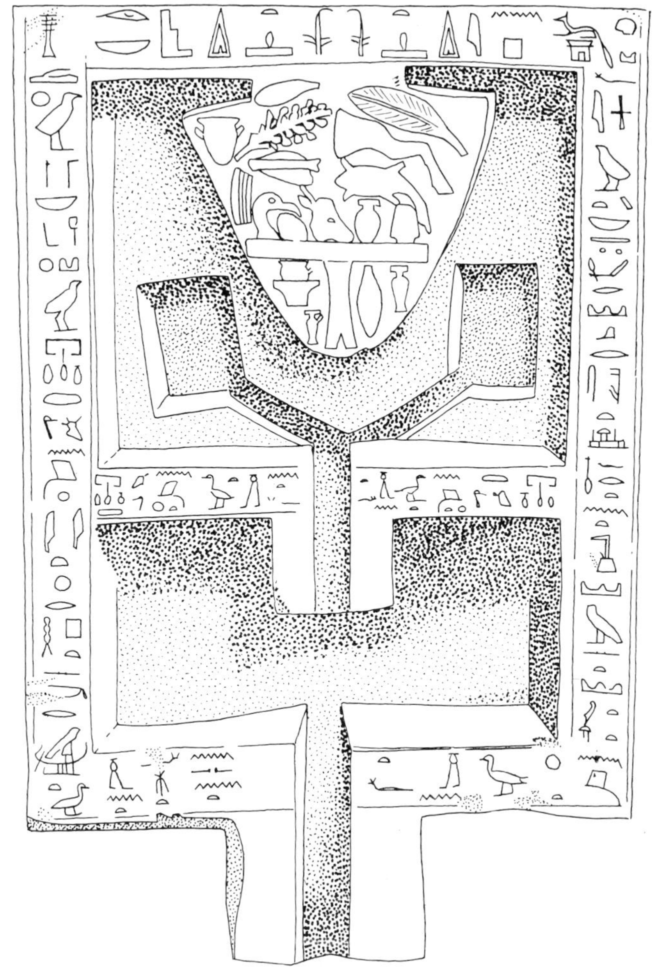

Inner frame: (1) An offering that the king gives, and Osiris, Lord of Busiris, the Great God, Lord of Abydos (2) that invocation offerings go forth to the Overseer of the Army in (the Nome of) *ꜥnḏty* (more specifically) Busiris, the Revered *Śn-kꜣy.* (3) that invocation offerings go forth to him on the *Wꜣg*-feast, on the feast of Thoth and on every good feast of a spirit,[39] the Revered *Śn-kꜣy.*

Offering scene: A thousand of bread and beer, alabaster (vessels) and clothing, oxen and fowl and everything goodly and pure to the *kꜣ*[40] of the Revered *Śn-kꜣy*, justified.

The fragmentary limestone offering slab (Figure 5) measures 50 × 67 × 35 cm. As may be seen in the schematic drawing (Figure 6), it has a pair of small basins that are linked to a larger one by narrow channels. This feature appears in some offering slabs from Saqqara

39. This phrase is to be added to those discussed by W. Barta, *Aufbau und Bedeutung der altägyptischen Opferformel* (*Ägyptologische Forschungen* 24 [Glückstadt, 1968]) p. 51 (and pp. 68, 79, 104, etc.).

40. Not significant for the date; see my comments in R. Caminos and H. Fischer, *Ancient Egyptian Epigraphy and Palaeography* (New York, 1976) p. 39 and note 41.

that may be as early as Dynasty X,[41] and the most comparable example, of unknown provenance, is probably not much later than this (Figure 7).[42] The present example more clearly belongs to the Middle Kingdom—the end of Dynasty XI or the early Twelfth Dynasty—as indicated by its more finished workmanship and the style of the inscription.[43] The presence of inscriptions at the bottom of the small basins is an unusual feature; the one on the right contains the word "water" and the one on the left is evidently to be read *ḥnḳt* "beer."[44]

The slab is inscribed for a certain *Śmḫ.śn* who is an "Overseer of the Army," like the *Śn-kȝy* whose false door has just been described, and is also "Overseer of Fields."

THE FITZWILLIAM MUSEUM FALSE DOOR

In its present state the false door in Cambridge (Figures 8, 9) has a maximum height of 82.5 cm. and maximum width of 63.5 cm.; the stone is somewhat more than 8 cm. thick. If two horizontal lines of inscription and a modest cavetto cornice are restored at the top, as shown in Figure 10, the original height is seen to be at least 131 cm. Some traces of red are visible, suggesting that the stone was painted to imitate wood or granite, as was often done at the Memphite cemeteries.[45]

As in many of the false doors of this period, the offering scene is in raised relief while the inscriptions and other representations are incised,[46] and the recesses flanking the offering scene do not extend to the top, although they are less reduced than in the case of the Eleventh Dynasty false doors described earlier.[47] The iconography and style are evidently a rather provincial version of Old Kingdom Memphite tradition, somewhat more crudely executed than the Busirite architrave of *Ḫnmw-nḏm(w)* or the false door of *Nni* at Mendes,[48] which is the only other Delta site that has yielded comparable material. The false door from Mendes may be slightly earlier in date, and so too, perhaps, a fragmentary false door of rather different style which was excavated at the same place.[49]

The representations at the top of the false door show the owner, a woman named *Ḥmi-Rʿ* or *Ḥmi*, wearing a long dress with shoulder straps, a broad collar, and a short wig bound with a fillet.[50] The representations at the bottom are much more unusual. They seem to show the owner as a girl and as an old woman, in much the same way that older and younger representations of men are contrasted on the jambs of contemporary false doors.[51] On the inner jambs she wears no discernible

41. J. E. Quibell, *Excavations at Saqqara 1905–6* (Cairo, 1907), pl. 18 (1, 2).

42. Karlsruhe Museum H416: Wiedemann, *Proceedings of the Society of Biblical Archaeology* 8 (1886) pp. 98–99 and 33 (1911), pl. 39 (15). The dimensions are 27 × 40 cm.

43. Compare two early Twelfth Dynasty examples: Alexandria Museum 460, inscribed for Amenemhet I (von Beckerath, *ÄZ* 92 [1965] p. 4 and pl. 3); MMA 22.1.21, the offering slab of *Nfrt*, presumed to be his mother (Mace, *BMMA* 17 [Dec. 1922, pt. 2] p. 12, fig. 11). Other more or less comparable examples: Cairo CG 23029 (A. B. Kamal, *Tables d'offrandes* [*Catalogue général . . . Musée du Caire*, Cairo, 1909] pl. 13); J. Gautier and G. Jéquier, *Fouilles de Licht* (*MIFAO* 6 [Cairo, 1902]) fig. 63, p. 59; MMA 32.1.213 (W. C. Hayes, *Scepter of Egypt* I [New York, 1953] fig. 69 and p. 117, where the Old Kingdom date should be corrected).

44. Compare the labels beside the two basins of the Old Kingdom offering table shown in Hassan, *Gîza* V, fig. 33, p. 185.

45. It is not possible to say whether the hieroglyphs were yellow on a red ground, imitating wood (exemplified by Junker, *Gîza* VII, pp. 241–242; XI p. 54), or green on red, imitating granite (exemplified by M. A. Murray, *Saqqara Mastabas* I [London, 1905] p. 26; Davies, *Deir el Gebrâwi* II, pl. 11).

46. This feature is discussed by Pierre Lacau in *Revue d'Égyptologie* 19 (1967) pp. 39–50.

47. As exemplified by BM 212 (James, *Hieroglyphic Texts* I^2, pl. 38), 1663 (same, pl. 42); Hassan, *Gîza* I, fig. 125, p. 69; V, p. 160 and fig. 22, p. 159; VI, pt. 3, figs. 219–220, pp. 222–223; Junker, *Gîza* VII, fig. 8, p. 25; figs. 104–107, pp. 247–252; XI, fig. 40, p. 70; Firth and Gunn, *Teti Pyramid Cemeteries*, pls. 71 (1), 73 (2); G. Jéquier, *Mastabat Faraoun* (Cairo, 1928) figs. 24–25, p. 29; Jéquier, *Monument funéraire de Pepi II* III, figs. 21–23, p. 37; fig. 60, p. 59; figs. 62–64, p. 61; fig. 70, p. 69; Jéquier, *Tombeaux de particuliers*, fig. 36, p. 34; fig. 98, p. 87; fig. 104, p. 91; fig. 138, p. 121; Cairo J. 59158 (*ÄZ* 90 [1963] pl. 6). Compare Vandier, *Manuel d'archéologie* II, pt. 1 (Paris, 1954) p. 428.

48. D. Hansen, *JARCE* 4 (1965) pl. 19 (7).

49. D. Hansen and Christine Soghor, *JARCE* 6 (1967) fig. 9 facing p. 28, and pls. 17 (32) and 18 (33).

50. There is no evidence of streamers behind the fillet. Ultraviolet examination revealed no trace of plaster in this area, but it is possible that the surface has been scraped, removing this detail.

51. In Firth and Gunn, *Teti Pyramid Cemeteries*, pl. 71 (1–2), a man is similarly shown as a naked youth on one of the inner jambs of each of his two false doors. The false doors of men contrast the normal type of representation with a more portly figure wearing a long kilt: Cairo CG 1397, 1455, 1565, 57122; BM 1191 (James, *Hieroglyphic Texts* I^2, pl. 35); Junker, *Gîza* VIII, fig. 88, p. 169; Jéquier, *Tombeaux de particuliers*, fig. 111, p. 97. As a rule the older rep-

garment, and a long pigtail projects from the back of her head, terminating in a disk.[52] On the outer jambs she wears a simple long dress and long hair; the body seems thicker and the breasts are pendulous. The last feature is emphasized by showing both breasts frontally—a mode of representation that is exceedingly rare in Egyptian art and is confined to servants in the rare instances when it occurs elsewhere. The only Old Kingdom example that is at all comparable (Figure 11) shows a woman grinding grain.[53] Representations of elderly women are still rarer; the sole examples known to me from the Old Kingdom again show servants grinding.[54] All the figures, save the one in the offering scene, hold a lotus blossom in one hand, as is frequently seen on other monuments, but the figures on the jamb show the other hand fisted rather than the open hand that is more characteristic of women.[55] It is also remarkable that the older representations are standing while the younger are seated on chairs.[56]

The Text

A (missing)

B (1) An offering that the king gives by[a] Osiris, Lord of Busiris: bread, beer and everything pure that goes forth upon the libation slab of Osiris[b] in Busiris,[c] for the Revered *Ḥmi-Rꜥ* whose good name is[d] the Acquaintance of the King, the Priestess of Hathor *Ḥmi*

(2) O ye who are living upon earth, who will pass by this way,[e] who will say:[f] "It is the pure bread of Osiris —(it) is for [g] the Revered[h] *Ḥmi*!"

C (1) [An offering] that Anubis gives, Who Presides over the Divine Booth, Who is in the Place of Embalming, Lord of the Sacred Land; an invocation offering on the *Wꜣg*-feast and on the feast of Thoth, to the Revered *Ḥmi-Rꜥ* whose good name is *Ḥmi*,

(2) [One who makes] peace and attains a state of reverence;[i] praised of her father, beloved of her [mother], revered of Hathor, Mistress of Busiris;[j] (*Ḥmi-Rꜥ*, whose good name is *Ḥmi*).

D [A thousand of bread, a thousand of beer, etc . . . .][k] to the Revered *Ḥmi*

E [1) Revered with Ptah-Sokar[l]

(2) Revered with Osiris, Lord of Busiris

(3) Revered with Anubis, Lord of the Burial

(4) The Acquaintance of the King, Priestess of Hathor, *Ḥmi-Rꜥ*, whose good name is *Ḥmi*.

F (1) May she proceed upon the good ways of the necropolis as one revered by the Great God, *Ḥmi-Rꜥ*, whose good name is *Ḥmi*.

(2) As for every scribe who will pass by this tomb, who will say: "Bread and beer to the mistress of this tomb, the Revered (*Ḥmi-Rꜥ*, whose good name is *Ḥmi*)!"

G (1) I am one who gives bread to him who is hungry and clothing to him who is naked, one praised of her husband, *Ḥmi-Rꜥ*

(2) As for all pe[ople] who will say: "Bread to *Ḥmi* in this her tomb!" I am a potent spirit[m] and will not allow it to go ill with them.[n]

Comments

a. This variation of the *ḥtp-di-nśwt* formula is unusual, but was employed a number of times toward the end of the Sixth Dynasty and later. Examples are cited by Barta, *Aufbau und Bedeutung der altägyptischen Opferformel*, pp. 24, 37, and more abundantly by Wilson, *JNES* 13 (1954), pp. 259–263. In view of the number of these examples, it seems doubtful that 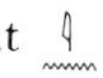 can be viewed as a

resentations occupy the inner jambs, but the opposite arrangement is found in CG 1565; in CG 1455 the figures alternate: old, young, old, young.

52. E. Staehelin discusses this detail ("der Kugelzopf") in *Untersuchungen zur ägyptischen Tracht im Alten Reich* (*MÄS* 8 [1966]) p. 181. The most familiar example is the princess *'Idwt:* R. Macramallah, *Mastaba d'Idout* (Cairo, 1935) passim.

53. From Cairo CG 1534; a line drawing is in M. Mogensen, *Le Mastaba Egyptien de la Glyptothèque Ny Carlsberg* (Copenhagen, 1921) fig. 29, p. 32, and H. Schäfer, *Von ägyptischer Kunst*, 4th ed. (Wiesbaden, 1963) fig. 207, p. 212. A similar view of a younger woman is in Wm. S. Smith, *Art and Architecture in Ancient Egypt* (Baltimore, 1958) pl. 51 (A). Both examples are from Saqqara.

54. Cairo J 56994; *Artibus Asiae* 22 (1959), fig. 10, following p. 240, and fig. 11, p. 251; also A. M. Bakir, *Slavery in Pharaonic Egypt* (*ASAE* Suppl. No. 18 [Cairo, 1952]) pl. 1. In addition there are, of course, feminine examples of 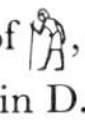, the hieroglyph representing old age, most clearly represented in D. Dunham and W. K. Simpson, *The Mastaba of Queen Mersyankh III* (Boston 1974) pl. 20 (b), and Cairo CG 1414.

55. Compare Firth and Gunn, *Teti Pyramid Cemeteries*, pls. 68, 70

56. Compare the seated figures on the inner jambs of two false doors of men, BM 212, BM 1663, both cited in note 47. Similarly Hassan, *Gîza* I, fig. 125, p. 69.

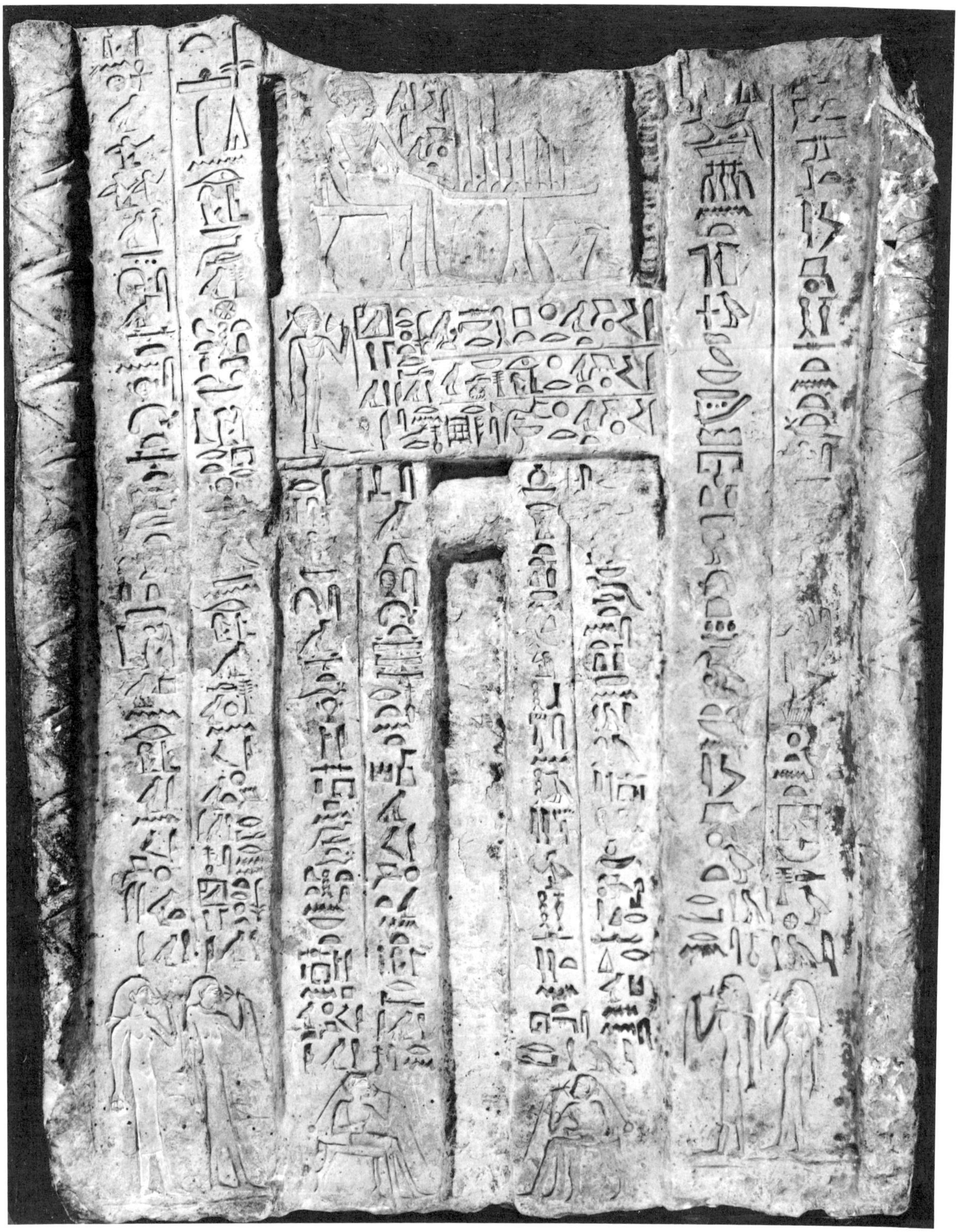

FIGURES 8, 9
False door in the Fitzwilliam Museum, Cambridge. (photo: courtesy of the Syndics of the Fitzwilliam Museum)

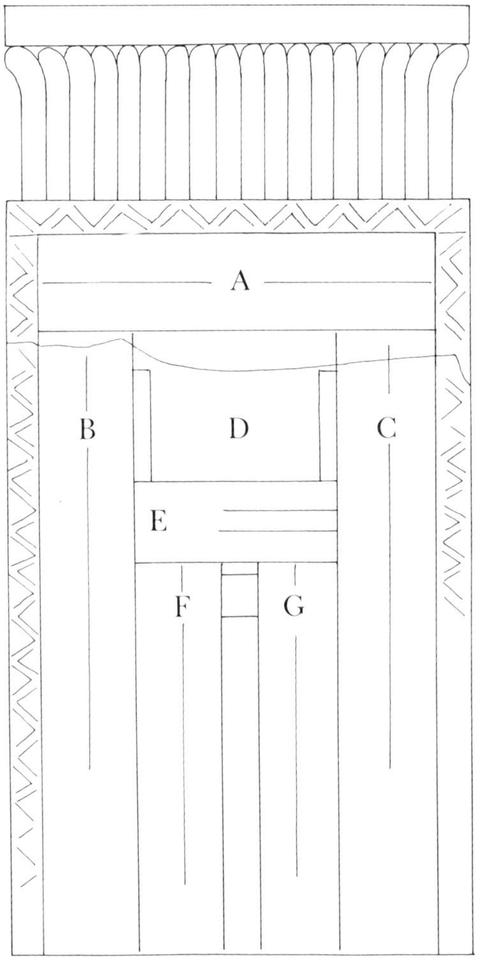

FIGURE 10

Diagram of the Fitzwilliam Museum false door

writing of dative *n*, as Barta concludes (p. 265), rather than agential *in*.[57]

b. *Wb.* III, 423 (11) gives no other meaning than "Erdboden" for *s3ṯ* in this phrase, but an early Middle Kingdom stela invokes offerings (*ḥtpt*) "which come forth upon the pure libation slab" (W. M. F. Petrie, *Tombs of the Courtiers and Oxyrhynkhos* [London, 1925], pl. 24), and it seems certain, in the present case, that *s3ṯ Wsir* is the "libation slab of Osiris." This term for "libation slab" (*Wb.* III 423 [5–6]) is known from the Sixth Dynasty biography of *Wni*, where it is written and (*Urk.* I, 99 [17], 107 [2]); in both cases it is associated with the false door, and hence, would seem to refer to the slab that was customarily placed before the offering niche. The title *ḫry s3ṯ* "libationer" (lit. "he who is over the libation slab") was occasionally given to Old Kingdom funerary attendants (Junker, *Gîza* V, fig. 58, p. 187). In one of the Sixth Dynasty tombs at Aswan an offering bearer is identified as "his sealer, he who is over the libation slab of the tomb, *Ḳri*."[58] Although arrangements for "reversion offerings" (*wdb rd*) from temples, in favor of private funerary cults, were made as early as the Fifth Dynasty,[59] the formula used here, with the verb *pri*, is evidently later. The earliest analogy known to me is and ("pure bread which comes forth from Dendera," "[bread] from the temple") on the false door of *Śn-nḏśw* (Petrie, *Dendereh*, pl. 9), which dates to the Heracleopolitan Period, but is evidently earlier than *W3ḥ-ʿnḫ 'Intf* of the Eleventh Dynasty.[60] In the course of the Eleventh Dynasty such phrases became increasingly frequent. The expression "pure bread" is well known from the Old Kingdom, however, (see Comment g below) and is probably to be regarded as a generic term, much as "bread" may mean "food" in English. Thus a listing of various offerings on the entrance architrave of *'Idw* (*BMFA* 23 [1925], 27) is followed by NN "namely pure bread of the Great God for NN"; compare von Bissing, *Gem-ni-kai* (Berlin, 1911) p. 22.

c. The unusual writing occurs in the Pyramid Texts (Pyr. 288b) where a similar writing is also used for *Ḏdwt*, Mendes.

d. Note the superfluous *n*. *Ḥmi* is known as the hypocoristicon of at least two Sixth Dynasty women named

57. Note also that Edel's sole example of as a writing of dative *n* (*Altäg. Gramm.*, §757, referring to Junker, *Gîza* III, p. 156) is subject to a different interpretation; see Comment f. But a valid example is evidently to be found on an alabaster tablet for the seven oils, MMA 11.50.1A, where the offering formula concludes with "for the Acquaintance of the King *ʿnḫ-wḏ.ś*."

58. De Morgan et al., *Catalogue des monuments et inscriptions de l'Égypte antique* I (Vienna, 1894) p. 199 (top); the transcription given at the bottom of p. 198 places the signs in the wrong sequence.

59. Berlin 15004 (*Ägyptische Inschriften* I, p. 22; A. Mariette, *Mastabas de l'Ancien Empire* [Paris, 1889]) p. 300; *Urk.* I, p. 37); for other examples of *wdb rd* see Grdseloff, *ASAE* 42 (1943) pp. 51–54. A particularly analogous Sixth Dynasty example is provided by the inscription of *Dʿw* of Abydos (*Urk.* I, p. 119 [7–8]) where the priests of the local temple are enjoined to remove offerings for him "as a reversion offering of this temple."

60. The date of his father *Mrri* is discussed in Fischer, *Dendera*, pp. 130–131; see the chronological summary on p. 187.

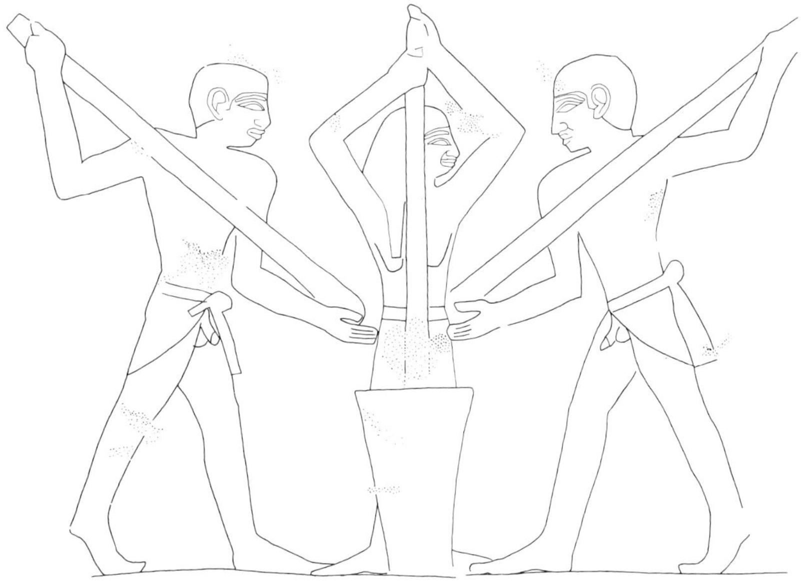

FIGURE 11
Detail of Old Kingdom relief in the Cairo Museum. From a photograph

Ḥmt-Rʿ (Davies, *Deir el Gebrâwi*, I, pl. 12; Mariette, *Mastabas*, p. 360).[61] The unusual writing of , which appears consistently on the false door under consideration, may well provide an additional relatively early example of the loss of final *t* in feminine words and, if so, this example is particularly interesting because *t* is apparently replaced by *i*. Such a replacement is altogether to be expected, but it is not attested elsewhere.[62] This interpretation of *Ḥmi-Rʿ* does not, however, offer a clue to the precise date of the false door since the loss of the final *t* in feminine names probably originated before the end of the Old Kingdom.[63] It is also possible that the longer name has been influenced by the shorter one, *Ḥmi*. But the second explanation does not preclude the first.

61. For *Ḥmt-Rʿ* see *PN* I, p. 240 (5) and for *Ḥmi* see *PN* I, p. 240 (1).

62. Schenkel, *Studien*, §22 f.

63. There is a wide diversity of opinion concerning the date of this development. Lacau (*Études d'égyptologie* I: *Phonétique* [Cairo, 1970]) thought that it happened far earlier than the Old Kingdom, while Edgerton denied its existence much before the Eighteenth Dynasty (*JNES* 6 [1947] p. 7). For Edel (*Altäg. Gramm.*, §113) the earliest probable date is Dyn. VI, and he believes it probably came about after the Old Kingdom. Schenkel puts it even later, not much before Dyn. XII (*Studien*, §22). I am inclined to believe that Clère is right in relating the loss of the final *t* to the adoption of a generic feminine for all place names (*Groupe linguistique d'études chamito-sémitiques* 3 [1939] p. 48), and in concluding that the phonetic basis for that reinterpretation was prepared in the late Old Kingdom.

e. The substitution of "way" for "tomb" is unusual; I know of no parallel.

f. The address to the living seems strangely incomplete; one misses the addition of *mrrw nśwt* (*Urk.* I, 252) or the like: "they who will say . . . are beloved of the king." See also *Urk.* I, 112, where those who invoke offerings are approved as *wnnty.śn* (*m*) *šms nṯr* "who will be in the following of the great god"; this is, as Garnot says (*L'Appel aux vivants dans les textes funéraires égyptiens* [Cairo, 1938] p. 59), the only case where the logical subject and predicate are both *śḏmty.fy* forms. In *Urk.* I, 122, *ḏdty.śn* is followed by a promise of assistance, as in G (2). But the omission of a predicate occurs again in F(2). As these two passages stand, it would seem that *ḏdty.śn* is felt to convey the sense of *ḏd.ṯn* "may ye say."

g. Compare two Sixth Dynasty examples of the same phrase, both from Saqqara:

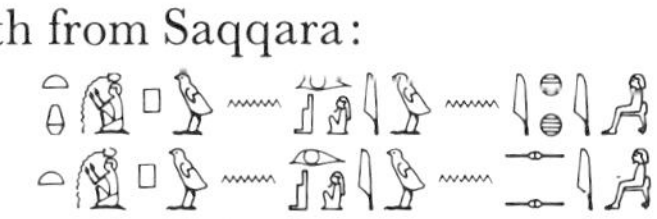

"it is the pure bread of Osiris, it is for NN." (*'Iḫḫi:* T. G. H. James and M. R. Apted, *Mastaba of Khentika* [London, 1953] pl. 31 [185] and compare pl. 32 [193]; *Ssi*: J. Capart, *Rue de tombeaux à Saqqarah* [Brussels, 1947] pl. 48). The second is quoted by A. Erman, *Reden, Rufe und Lieder auf Gräberbildern des Alten Reiches* (Berlin, 1919) p. 33, as well as a similar example of *iw* (*nn*) *n* with ellipsis of the subject: (*LD* II, 90 = Junker, *Gîza* XI, fig. 105, p. 260). A third example may be found in the tomb of *Ḳꜣr* (*BMFA* 23 [1925], p. 26): "it is for him, my father." Possibly this same interpretation is to be applied to a phrase which occurs in three tombs at Giza:

(Hassan, *Gîza* VI, pt. 3, fig. 82, p. 103, and pl. 46)
(Junker, *Gîza* III, fig. 21, p. 153)
(Ibid., fig. 48, p. 233)

Edel (*Altäg. Gramm.*, § 757) regards the second example of as a writing of dative *n*, as does Junker (*Gîza* III, p. 156). But in dealing with the third example (p. 235), Junker is inclined to regard both his examples of *in* as a peculiar use of the introductory particle that occurs in the construction *in* + noun + participle: "it is (this) which is for the *kꜣ*." A simpler and more plausible solution is to regard the initial *i* as *i*(*w*) and to explain the last example as an elliptical writing of *i*(*w*) *n*(*n*) *n kꜣ* (*n*) *mry*(*i*) "this is for the *kꜣ* of the beloved." Compare, for example, the fuller writing of "this is for the *kꜣ* of my father" (*LD Ergänzungsband*, pl. 16).

h. Elsewhere on the false door this epithet is consistently written *imꜣḫwt*, which is the usual Old Kingdom form. The curious variant with the ending is evidently to be interpreted as *-wt*>*-yt*, and possibly shows the influence of the writing *imꜣḫy*, the first dated occurrence of which belongs to the Heracleopolitan Period in the reign of Merykare (Siut tomb IV: Schenkel, *Studien*, §16b). But the replacement of final *w* by *y* is well attested in the Old Kingdom,[64] and two unpublished texts, from Giza and Saqqara respectively, show writings like the one that is under consideration. The first, from Reisner's G 7753a, has "I am one who is revered."[65] The second occurs on the wooden sarcophagus of the Hereditary Prince, Count, etc. *Nb*(.*i*)-*ib*(.*i*) (), who has the epithet "praised of his father."[66] Neither of these examples of the ending *-wy* can be dated with any accuracy, but there is no reason to think that they are later than the Sixth Dynasty.

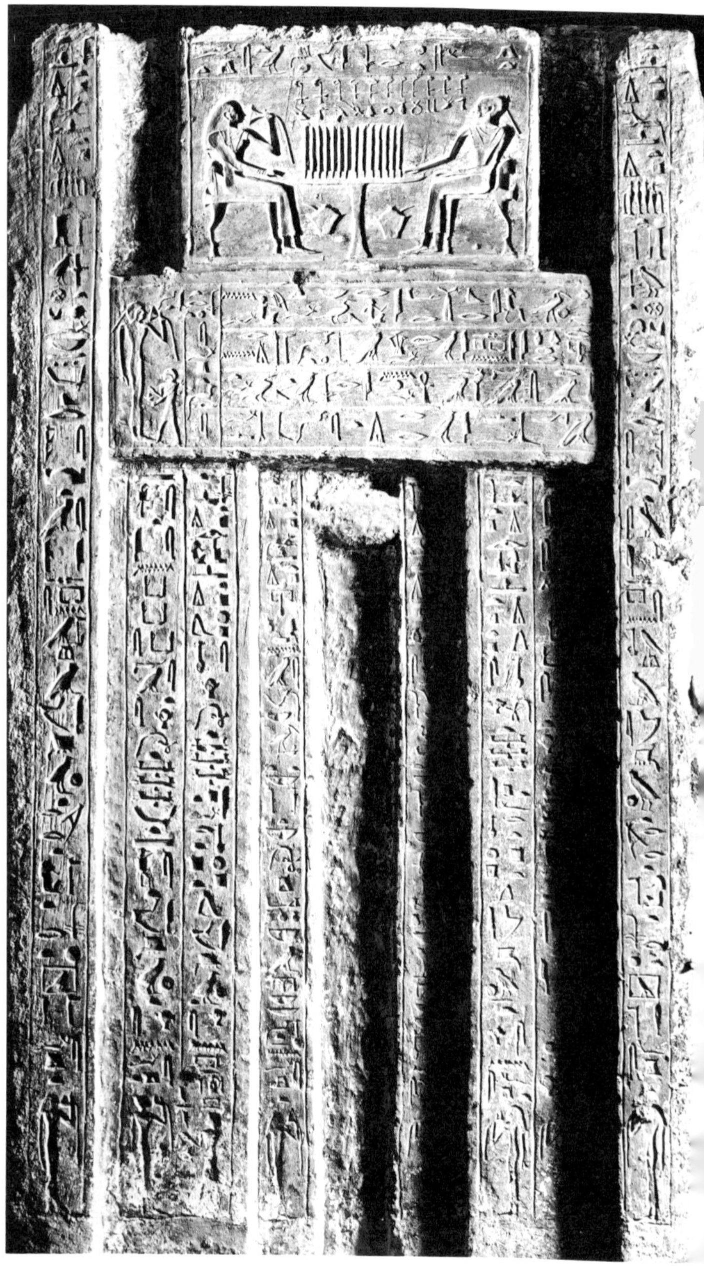

FIGURE 12

Old Kingdom false door from Saqqara. (photo: courtesy Egyptian Department of Antiquities)

64. Edel, *Altäg. Gramm.*, §146; his examples involve the complete substitution of *y* in place of *w*, rather than composite writings.

65. From his field records at the Museum of Fine Arts, Boston. This inscription seems to show a decided predilection for the ending *-w* 〉 *-y* or *-wy*, for one of the following columns has [ ] "[as for any man who will do anything ev]il to this." If *nwy* is not particularly uncommon as a variant of *nw* (Edel, *MDIK* 13 [1944] p. 50; *Altäg. Gramm.*, § 200), it is difficult to find any parallel for the writing of *ḫt ḏwi*(*t*), which is generally written . The writing is also attested for the plural (James, *Hieroglyphic Texts* I², pl. 29 [top]; compare Edel, *Altäg. Gramm.* II, p. LIX [§146]).

66. Seen in 1956 among photographs stored at the Department of Antiquities office (Firth's house).

i. For the phrase *iri ḥtpt, sbi imꜣḫ* see Junker, *Gîza* VII, pp. 208–210, and Wilson, *JNES* 13 (1954), pp. 250–251. There does not seem to be space for at the beginning of the line (for which see Hassan, *Gîza* V, fig. 101 (a–b), p. 241 [Dyn. V]; Cairo CG 20005 [Dyn. XI]).

j. Nothing of this local cult is recorded by Schafik Allam, *Beiträge zum Hathorkult (bis zum Ende des Mittleren Reiches)* (*MÄS* 4 [Berlin, 1963]), or by Montet, *Géographie de l'Égypte Ancienne* I: *Basse Égypte*, pp. 97–102. One of the later false doors replaces *Ḏdw* by the name of some other cult-center; see note 29 above.

k. This style of offering list characteristically appears at the top of offering scenes on false doors dating to the end of the Old Kingdom and after, as in the case of most of the false doors cited in note 47; compare Junker, *Gîza* VII, p. 248.

l. The determinative of Sokar is unusual; the expected form shows the falcon on the *ḥnw*-bark ( ).

m. Evidently this sign has been filled with plaster and recut, so that it now appears to have two heads. For the phrase *ink ꜣḫ iḳr* see Edel, *MDIK* 13 (1944), pp. 19–21. Since no other feminine example has yet been recorded from the Old Kingdom, it may be useful to call attention to a false door from Saqqara (Figure 12).[67] The architrave above the niche contains the following inscription: (1) "The Acquaintance of the King *Śfgt*,[68] she says:[69] (2) I am an efficacious and equipped spirit. As for any man who shall enter after having made purification, (3) in order to make invocation offerings at this tomb, I shall be his supporter in the tribunal of the Great God, having granted (4) good in his business and provision in his life. But as for him who shall enter (5) in his impurity, I shall bring about his grief."[70] Here again the word "spirit" (*ꜣḫ*) is masculine, but a feminine occurrence is to be found in another unpublished text from Saqqara, dating to the Sixth Dynasty (Figure 13):[71] "I am an excel-

67. I am indebted to the late Zakaria Ghoneim for the photograph and for permission to publish it.

68. For the name, see Ranke, *PN* I, p. 306 (27); in his addenda, *PN* II, p. 386, Ranke refers to *Wb.* IV, p. 118 (6–8). Compare the masculine name *Śdḫ* which similarly means "hidden," *PN* I, p. 323 (15); earlier examples of the latter may be found in Jéquier, *Monument funéraire de Pepi II* III, fig. 22, p. 37; Drioton and Lauer, *ASAE* 55 (1958) p. 229.

69. The first line actually follows the others, but is to be understood in this fashion, as explained in my forthcoming *Egyptian Studies* II: *The Orientation of Hieroglyphs*, pt. 1, § 21, note 142a.

70. Some portions of these statements are comparable to those discussed by Edel, *MDIK* 13 (1944) §§8, 11, 16; for *iw.i r ḥꜣy.f m ḏꜣḏꜣt nṯr ꜥꜣi* see also Altenmüller, *Studien zur Altägyptischen Kultur* I (1974) p. 18 (k). Other phrases are totally new. The texts on the jambs contribute little of interest, and the right-hand jambs repeat the texts on the left. These formulae are discussed by Wilson in *JNES* 13 (1954) pp. 251–254, but it may be noted that the unusual phrasing of *wꜣwt iptf nfrt* "those goodly ways" also occurs in Cairo 1413 and in Boston MFA 13.4333 (Fischer, *Dendera*, pl. 30 [b]). Note also that an attendant named appears on the architrave, and that another at the bottom of the left center jamb is identified as . The first name is not otherwise known; the second is quite common (*PN* I, p. 45 [15]). The title "scribe of the house of the god's book of the Great House" is attested in Murray, *Saqqara Mastabas* I, pl. 30.

71. This is the fifth and last line of the text published by Wilson, *JNES* 13 (1954) p. 260 (VIII), and omitted in his copy (from Nims). The woman in question is a princess named *'Inti* who is an elder daughter of Pepi I (according to Nims) and an elder (grand-) daughter of Teti; see also Nims, *JAOS* 58 (1938) p. 646. I first saw a photograph of this in the office of the Department of Antiquities in Saqqara; the one shown here was located by Dr. Jaromír Málek among the records of Gunn and Firth (Gunn MSS XIV.22), and I am obliged to him for permission to use it.

FIGURE 13
Old Kingdom architrave from Saqqara. (photo: courtesy Griffith Institute, Oxford)

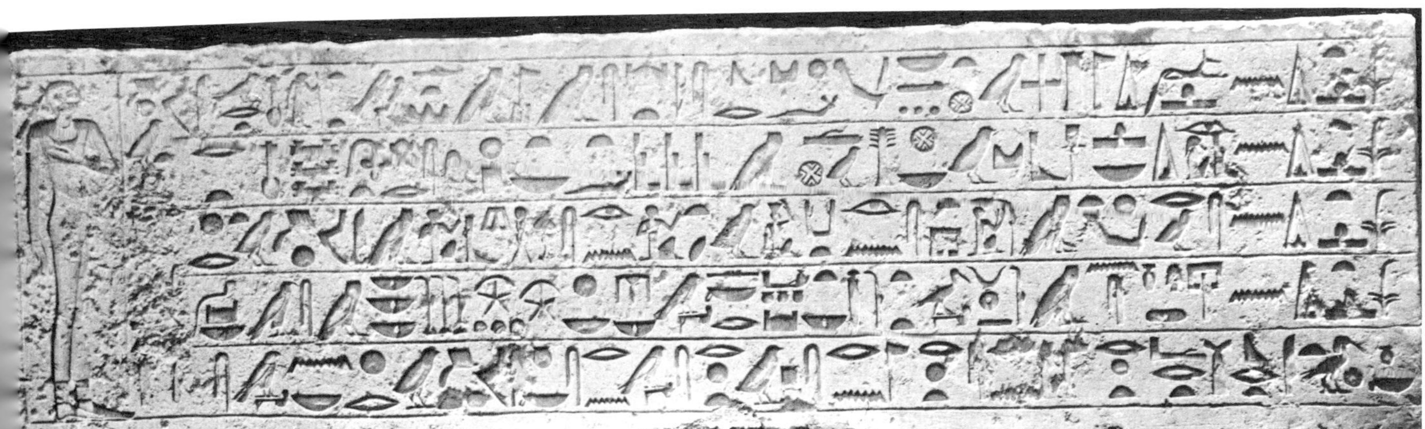

lent and equipped spirit, one whose name the god knows, one whose very name the god knows, one whose name her god knows;[72] I am one who is revered with her lord."

n. For the ellipse of the subject after adjectival verbs see Edel, *Altäg. Gramm.*, § 995, where this same passage is quoted; he discusses the future *n rdi(.i)* in *MDIK* 13 (1944), p. 15 (§15). The reversal of this phrase is probably a meaningless reversion to the dominant rightward orientation. This may be compared with late Old Kingdom false doors that show rightward orientation on some or all of the right jambs, instead of the usual symmetrical disposition of the texts.[73] The inappropriate retention of rightward orientation also occurs in the captions of figures on the architrave of *Ḫnmw-nḏm(w)*, as noted earlier.

The Date

There are very few palaeographic or epigraphic indications. Little can be concluded from the abnormal form of [hieroglyph] as the determinative of Sokar (Comment l) or the reversal of orientation at the bottom of the right inner jamb (Comment n). The sign [hieroglyph] shows the older form, but this did not begin to be replaced by other forms before the Twelfth Dynasty.[74] Similarly it was not until the Twelfth Dynasty that plural strokes were commonly added to the suffix [hieroglyph]. The form of [hieroglyph] ([hieroglyph]) shows the influence of Old Kingdom hieratic,[75] as does a similar example on a Naga ed-Deir stela that is probably not much later than Dynasty VI.[76] The form [hieroglyph] (one occurrence only) might be expected of the Heracleopolitan Period, but this also occurred as early as the Sixth Dynasty.[77] More conclusive indications of later date are the writing of [hieroglyph][78] and the phrase "everything that goes forth upon the libation slab" (Comment b).

In general, the style, phrasing, orthography, and grammar continue late Old Kingdom tradition, and one may note in particular the use of future *n sḏm.f* (Comment n). On the other hand, the false door is evidently later than the oldest of the unpublished monuments found by Ali El Manzalawy in 1928, which is probably to be dated to the very end of the Sixth Dynasty, or slightly later. And much more obviously, it is earlier than a group of three late Eleventh Dynasty false doors and an offering table that come from the same excavations. In view of these comparisons and the internal evidence, it seems very likely that the false door in the Fitzwilliam Museum belongs to the Heracleopolitan Period, and most probably the Tenth Dynasty.

CONCLUSIONS

The material assembled here is far too meager to permit many generalizations, and it must be kept in mind that these few monuments are scattered over a fairly long period—probably as much as two centuries. One is struck, however, by the degree to which they resemble those from other sites at Memphis and in Upper Egypt, and by the absence of discernible "localisms" even in the case of the false door that has been assigned to the Tenth Dynasty. There are, of course, a few unusual features such as the use of [hieroglyph] "his/her son" on the Old Kingdom architrave (Figures 1, 2), the frontal view of the woman's breasts on the Tenth Dynasty false door (Figures 8, 9), or the phrase "every good feast of the spirit" on the false door that has been dated to the late

72. The various writings of the word *nṯr* "god" are evidently to be regarded as graphic dissimilation; the writing [hieroglyph] is known from the title *ḥry sštꜣ n mdw-nṯr* ([hieroglyph]) "privy to the secret of the god's words" (Firth and Gunn, *Teti Pyramid Cemeteries*, pp. 106 [24], 132, note 3); also in the common Old Kingdom writing of *ḫrt nṯr* "necropolis" as [hieroglyph] (*Urk.* I, pp. 9 [5], 13 [13], 165 [16], 173 [18], etc.). For the misplaced *ś* in *nṯr.ś* compare *ir n.ś* in line 3.

73. Exemplified by Junker, *Gîza* VI, fig. 83, p. 215; Hassan, *Gîza* III, fig. 15, p. 16. In both cases only the inner jambs retain the rightward orientation.

74. See Schenkel, *Studien*, §2.

75. Paule Posener-Kriéger and J. L. de Cenival, *Hieratic Papyri in the British Museum* V: *The Abu Sir Papyri* (London, 1968) Pal. Pl. iii.

76. Cairo J 88884; a woman named *'Int-kmwt* ([hieroglyph]). This seems to belong to the group assembled by Vandier; see note 26 above. I have seen other examples of this hieratic form in post-Sixth Dynasty inscriptions at Aswan: *Ḫwnś* and the later tomb of *Ḥḳꜣ-ib* (a secondary inscription).

77. See Fischer, *Dendera*, pp. 78–79 and note 331.

78. Same, p. 84, and Schenkel, *Studien*, §11; the examples of *Mni* and *Ṯꜣwti/Rśi* are also later than the Sixth Dynasty (Fischer, *Dendera*, pp. 85–91).

Eleventh Dynasty (Figures 3, 4). It is difficult to say whether any of these are to be expected on other monuments of this same site or area. On the other hand, the relatively late appearance of the pair of *wḏꜣt*-eyes on the interior jambs of false doors may possibly be a regional peculiarity.

It is perhaps only coincidental that the Old Kingdom architrave provides the earliest evidence for the personal name *ꜥꜣm* "Asiatic," and that another name on the same monument seems to refer to a country called *Rtnnw* (i.e. *Rṯnw*?), which is "broken." But the later monuments add two more "overseers of the army" to the two who are already known from the Sixth Dynasty at Mendes and Horbeit,[79] and these sparse indications, combined with evidence such as *Wni*'s account of his campaigns against the Bedouin,[80] contribute to our picture of the eastern Delta as an area that was constantly exposed to raids and infiltration from the Asiatic side

The earlier monuments, like those at the nearby site of Mendes, refer exclusively to Osiris Lord of Busiris in the offering formula and in the epithet "revered with Osiris"; Abydos is mentioned only on the later ones dating to the end of the Eleventh Dynasty.[81] Busiris is also named as the locality of a cult center of Hathor, although a different cult center is assigned to this goddess on one of the late Eleventh Dynasty stelae.

More specific reference is made to the cult of Osiris on the false door of the Heracleopolitan Period, which speaks of "bread which goes forth on the libation table of Osiris in Djedu," and on the late Eleventh Dynasty false door of the general *Śn-kꜣy* who is "scribe of the god's treasure in the house of Osiris" and "scribe of the noble temple." This monument also confirms the fact that the name of the province is identical to that of the divinity who was originally present, and whose image appears on the nome emblem.

SOURCES ABBREVIATED

ARCE—American Research Center in Egypt, Cairo and Princeton, N.J.

ASAE—*Annales du Service des Antiquités de l'Égypte.*

ÄZ—*Zeitschrift für ägyptische Sprache und Altertumskunde* (Leipzig and Berlin).

BM—British Museum.

BMFA—*Bulletin of the Museum of Fine Arts* (Boston).

BMMA—*Bulletin of The Metropolitan Museum of Art.*

CG + number—Monuments in the Egyptian Museum, Cairo, numbers referring to *Catalogue général des antiquités égyptiennes du Musée du Caire:*

- CG 1295–1808: Ludwig Borchardt, *Denkmäler des Alten Reiches* I–II (Berlin, 1937–64);
- CG 20001–20780: H. O. Lange and H. Schäfer, *Grab- und Denksteine des Mittleren Reichs* I–IV (Berlin, 1902–25).

Edel, *Altäg. Gramm.*—E. Edel, *Altägyptische Grammatik* I–II (*Analecta Orientalia* 34/39) (Rome, 1955/64).

Firth and Gunn, *Teti Pyramid Cemeteries*—C. M. Firth and B. Gunn, *Excavations at Saqqara: Teti Pyramid Cemeteries* (Cairo, 1926).

Fischer, *Coptite Nome*—H. G. Fischer, *Inscriptions from the Coptite Nome, Dynasties VI–XI, Analecta Orientalia* 40 (Rome, 1964).

Fischer, *Dendera*—H. G. Fischer, *Dendera in the Third Millennium B.C. Down to the Theban Domination of Upper Egypt* (Locust Valley, N.Y., 1968).

Hassan, *Gîza*—Selim Hassan, *Excavations at Gîza* I–X (Oxford-Cairo, 1932–60).

J + number—*Journal d'entrée*, Egyptian Museum (Cairo).

JAOS—*Journal of the American Oriental Society* (Baltimore).

JARCE—*Journal of the American Research Center in Egypt* (Princeton).

79. For the general who was buried in the vicinity of Horbeit see Daressy, *Recueil de travaux* 24 (1902) p. 163; for the one from Mendes see Chaban, *ASAE* 10 (1910) p. 28 (a red granite statuette from the same tomb is in the Cairo Museum, J 38915). Note also the military character of a group of Fifth Dynasty titles pertaining to the Heliopolitan Nome East (Junker, *Gîza* III, pp. 172, 174 and Fischer, *Dendera*, p. 10, note 47); this district evidently extended northward to include Bubastis (Fischer, *JNES* 18 (1959) pp. 133–134).

80. *Urk.* I, pp. 101–105.

81. The same is true of the late Old Kingdom inscription from the eastern Delta cited in notes 9, 48, 79. This fact is hardly surprising, however, since references to Osiris Lord of Abydos are rare even in the more abundant inscriptions of the Memphite cemeteries (two cases in Junker, *Gîza* VI, fig. 93, p. 229; Hassan, *Gîza* VI, pt. 3, fig. 207, p. 209) and so too Khentiamentiu Lord of Abydos (an example published by Wilson, *JNES* 13, pl. 18A). The Sixth Dynasty stelae of Dendera and Naqada, south of Abydos, also refer repeatedly to Osiris Lord of Busiris, and the first mention of Abydos that is known there (as the cult center of Khentiamentiu) occurs on a stela of *Śnni*, dating to the Eighth Dynasty (Fischer, *Dendera*, pl. 16[a]). This evidence corroborates the view taken in note 1, that Osiris came to Abydos secondarily, by association with Khentiamentiu, and that his cult originated at Busiris.

JEA—*Journal of Egyptian Archaeology* (London).
JNES—*Journal of Near Eastern Studies* (Chicago).
Junker, *Gîza*—H. Junker, *Gîza* (*Akademie der Wissenschaften in Wien. Philosophisch-historische Klasse. Denkschriften* I–XII [Vienna, 1929–55]).
LD—C. R. Lepsius, ed., *Denkmäler aus Ägypten und Äthiopien*, I–XII (Berlin, 1849–59).
LD Ergänzungsband—C. R. Lepsius, ed., *Denkmäler aus Ägypten und Äthiopien: Ergänzungsband*, ed. and rev. by E. Naville, L. Borchardt, and K. Sethe (Leipzig, 1913).
MÄS—*Münchner Ägyptologische Studien, Münchener Universitäts-Schriften Philosophische Fakultät* (Berlin).
MDIK—*Mitteilungen des Deutschen Archäologischen Instituts Abteilung Kairo* (Wiesbaden).
MIFAO—*Mémoires publiés par les membres de l'Institut français d'Archéologie orientale* (Cairo).
MMA—Metropolitan Museum of Art.
PN—H. Ranke, *Die Ägyptischen Personennamen* I–II (Glückstadt, 1935/52).
Pyr.—Pyramid Text reference, in terms of Sethe's arrangement in *Die altägyptischen Pyramidentexte* (Leipzig, 1908–22).
Schenkel, *Studien*—W. Schenkel, *Frühmittelägyptische Studien* (Bonn, 1962).
Urk. I—K. Sethe, *Urkunden des alten Reichs* I, 2nd ed. (Leipzig, 1933).
Wb.—A. Erman and H. Grapow, eds., *Wörterbuch der ägyptischen Sprache* I–V (Leipzig, 1926–31).

NOTES

More Emblematic Uses from Ancient Egypt

HENRY G. FISCHER

Lila Acheson Wallace Curator in Egyptology, The Metropolitan Museum of Art

In my article "Some Emblematic Uses of Hieroglyphs" (*Metropolitan Museum Journal* 5 [1972], p. 22) I have described a fragmentary statue of the mid-Eighteenth Dynasty that shows a large ☥-pendant suspended from a cord around the neck. The sign 𓊵 is incised immediately below this, and it seemed likely that the whole represented the owner's name: *ꜥnḫ-ḥtp*. An apparent parallel (Figure 1)[1] is to be found on a Twelfth Dynasty coffin that, like many funerary monuments of the same period, adds an ☥-sign to the customary pair of *wḏꜣt*-eyes,[2] and more exceptionally appends the sign 𓊵 as well. In this case the pair of signs definitely alludes to the name of the deceased, "the Mistress of the House *Ḥtp* (𓊵𓏏𓊪)."[3]

The Middle Kingdom analogy might suggest that the emblems on the New Kingdom statue similarly refer to an individual named *Ḥtp*, who is in this case a man. As my footnote 69 warns, however, the principal inscription of the statue is lost, and it is therefore possible that both signs simply represent a "motto."

That alternative is confirmed by a second occurrence of the same emblems on a statue of similar date, which I noticed during a recent visit to the British Museum (Figure 2).[4] Since, in this case, the name is known to be *Tti*/*Ttity*, it is clear that the emblems can only be a motto, presumably meaning "life and peace!" or "may he live and be at peace!"[5] Labib Habachi, who has discussed the other aspects of the statue in some detail, suggests that it was placed in one of the temples at Deir el Bahri,[6] and that view is supported by the first example, which was excavated there. I do not, however, know of any other evidence from Deir el Bahri.[7]

1. From R. Engelbach and others, *Riqqeh and Memphis* VI (London, 1915) pl. 26.

2. See H. G. Fischer, "An Eleventh Dynasty Couple Holding the Sign of Life," *Zeitschrift für Ägyptische Sprache* 100 (1973) p. 24, note 36.

3. Compare Margaret Murray, *Riqqeh*, p. 28, who interprets the group as "may Hetep live"; at the same time *ꜥnḫ-ḥtp* may simultaneously be understood as a motto, as discussed below.

4. BM 888. I am indebted to T. G. H. James for this photograph and for the detail shown in Figure 3. The inscriptions are published in *Hieroglyphic Texts . . . in the British Museum* V (London, 1914) pl. 25, and have been translated and discussed by Labib Habachi in "The First Two Viceroys of Kush and their Family," *Kush* 7 (1959) pp. 45–47. This occurrence of the *ḥtp*-sign is noted by Habachi on p. 55 but the other emblems are not described or pictured here or elsewhere.

5. Taking *ꜥnḫ(w) ḥtp(w)* as old perfectives on the analogy of 𓋹𓍑𓋴 "may he live, be prosperous and be healthy!"; see Sir Alan Gardiner, *Egyptian Grammar* (London, 1957) §313.

6. *Kush* 7 (1959) p. 55.

7. I have inquired about two other block-statues in particular: E. Naville, *The XIth Dynasty Temple at Deir el-Bahari*, pt. III (London, 1913) pl. 4 (3) (Oriental Institute, University of Chicago, 8635) and pl. 5 (1) (Oriental Institute 8636). David Silverman has kindly examined both and reports that, although both statues are headless and the surface is destroyed in front of the neck, the horizontal area surrounding this point is sufficiently preserved to show that neither ☥ nor 𓊵 are present. Mr. Edward Brovarski has kindly called my attention to two somewhat later representations of ☥ over 𓊵 as an amulet, both belonging to *Ḥꜥ-m-wꜣst*, the son of Ramesses II: one is a relief in Santa Barbara, California, the other a shawabti-figurine (Mariette, *Le Sérapéum de Memphis* [Paris, 1857] pl. 13). Mr. Brovarski notes that the same combination of signs repeatedly follows the titles and name of this crown prince as an epithet on a statue of his, Cairo CG 42147 (cf. Farouk Gomaà, *Chaemwese* [Wiesbaden, 1973] fig. 24, p. 124). Here the sequence is regularly 𓊵 over ☥ or 𓊵𓏏𓊪☥ so that, in this case at least, one must understand it as "at peace and living" or *ḥtp (m) ꜥnḫ* "having gone to rest in life" (*Wb.* III, p. 191 [20–26]).

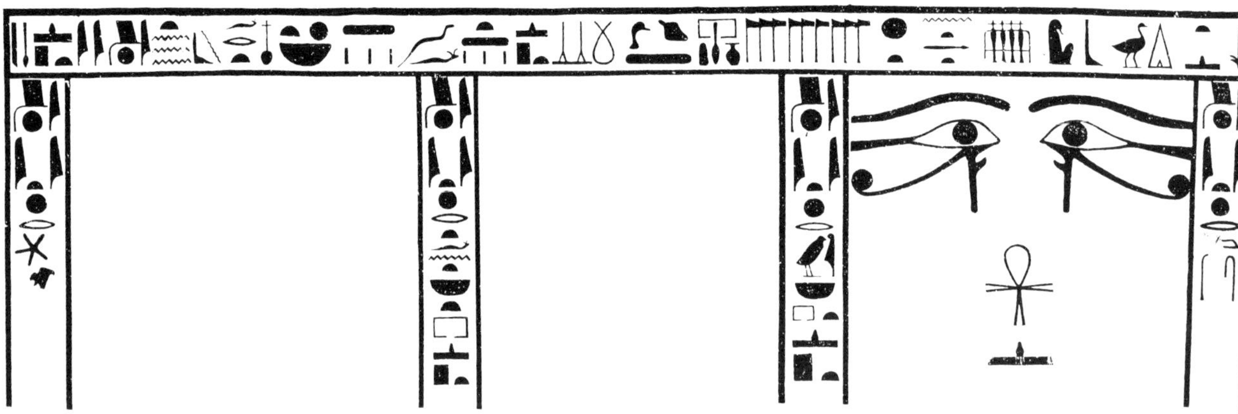

FIGURE 1

Front of coffin of *Ḥtp*. After Engelbach

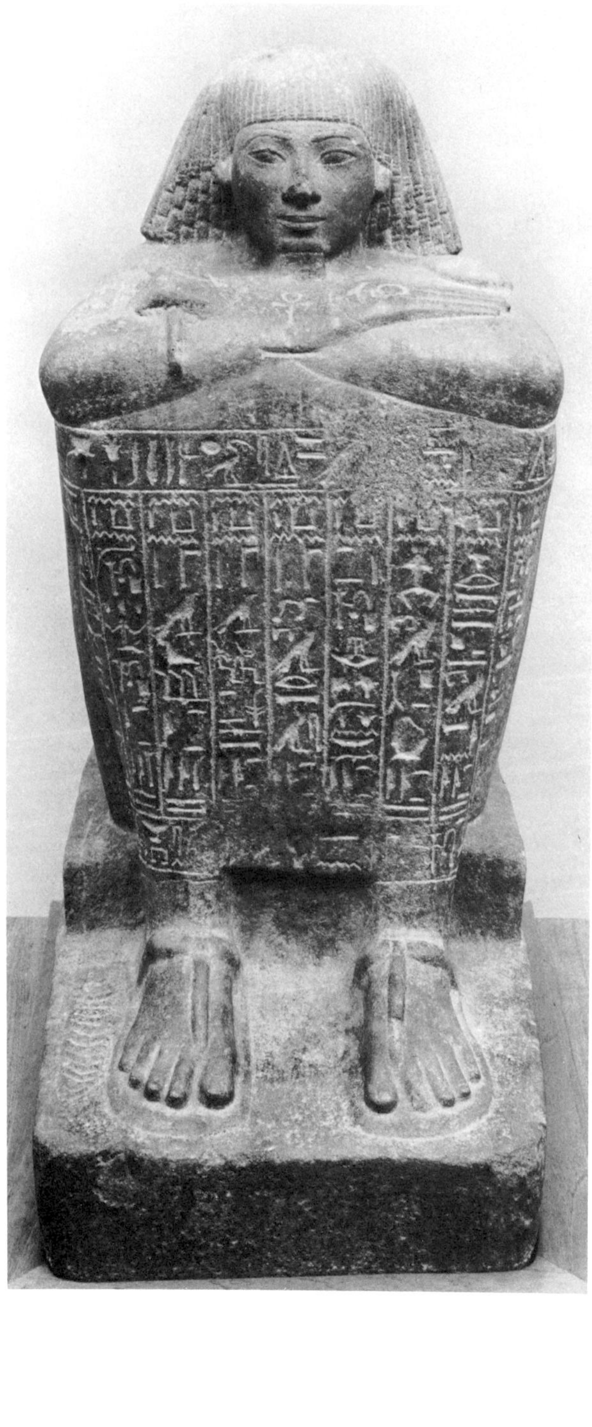

FIGURE 2

Statue of *Tti/Ttìty*, BM 888. Courtesy British Museum

The British Museum statue also displays the cartouche of Tuthmosis III on the upper part of the proper right arm—a feature that is first known from the reign of that king. In addition, the back of each hand bears a most curious pair of devices (Figure 3): on the spectator's left (in this case the statue's proper left hand, since the arms are crossed), the crescent moon is combined with the crown of Lower Egypt ([hieroglyphs]); on the right the sun is combined with the crown of Upper Egypt, to which the uraeus cobra is attached so that it appears to link both elements ([hieroglyphs]). All of this is doubtless meant to express the universal circuit in much the same way that the emblem [hieroglyph] does, placed between a pair of *wḏꜣt*-eyes of Horus at the top of funerary monuments. The eye of Horus is, in fact, equated with the crown of Upper Egypt and with the sun in hymns of the late Middle Kingdom; its counterpart is, more indirectly, equated with the crown of Lower Egypt and the moon.[8] Moreover, an inscription of Tuthmosis III reinforces the idea of an all-embracing realm as "all these things [hieroglyphs] which the moon illuminates and that which the sun-disk encompasses

8. A. Erman, *Hymnen an das Diadem der Pharaonen* (*Abhandlungen der Königl. Preuss. Akademie der Wissenschaften, Phil.-hist. Kl.* 1911, no. 1 [Berlin, 1911]). The associations with the sun and moon are discussed on pp. 12–14.

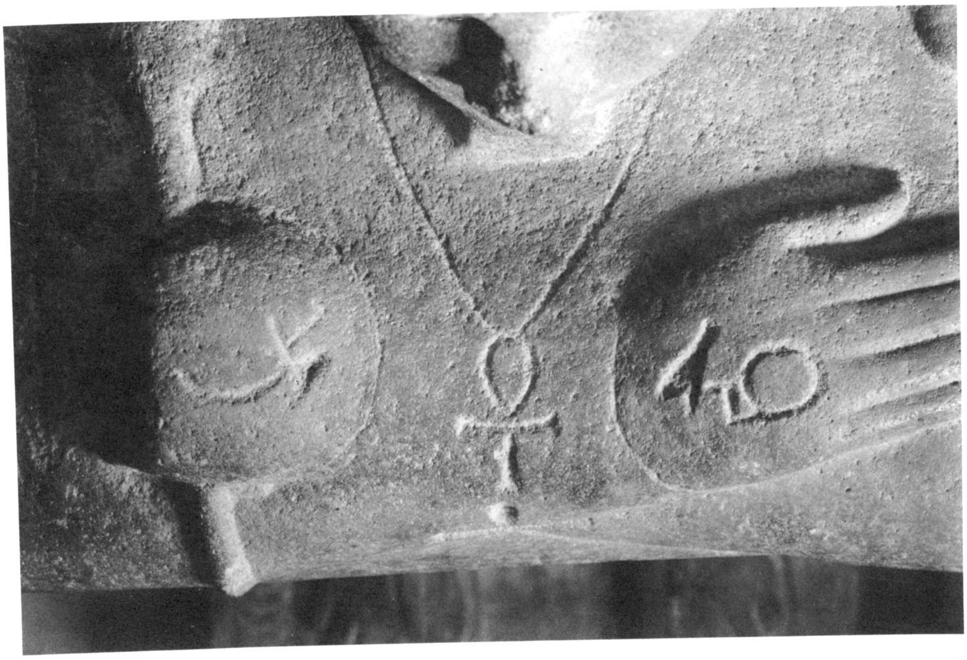

FIGURE 3
Detail of BM 888. Courtesy British Museum

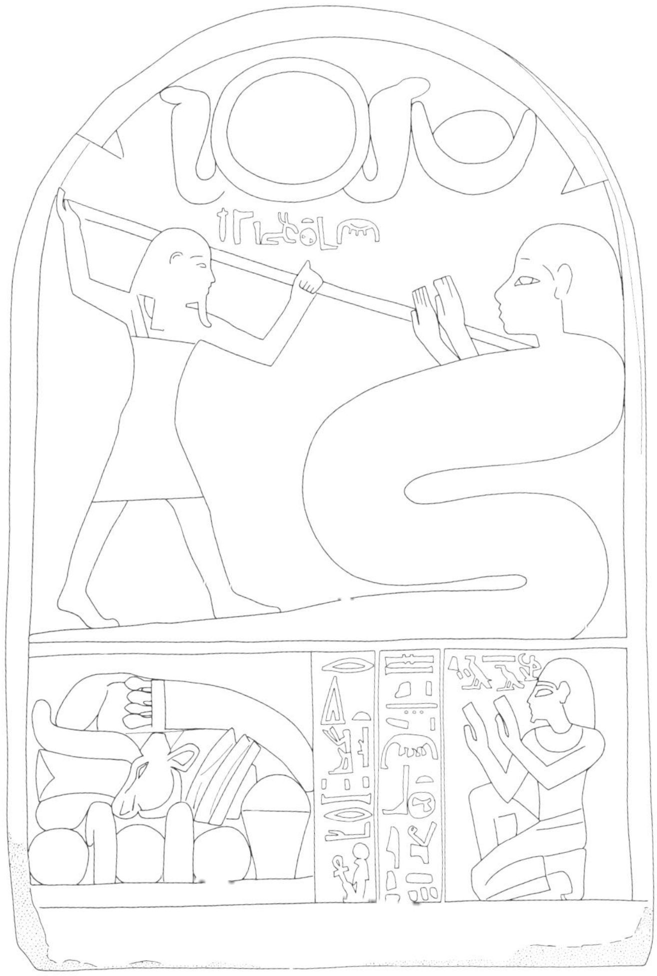

FIGURE 4
Stela of *Tḳn*, Leiden V 62

when it rises."[9] In much later inscriptions the group has an equally all-embracing meaning, but in a temporal sense, as a writing of *rꜥ nb* "every day" (*Wb.* II, p. 402 [5]).

Despite these literary associations, the sun and moon are rarely paired in ancient Egyptian iconography. The only further example known to me is a later new Kingdom stela in Leiden that shows the god Seth vanquishing the Apophis-serpent (Figure 4).[10] It will be observed that the sun is on the spectator's left, as is the victorious god, that side being normally reserved for the principal subject of any scene. And stelae of the New Kingdom and earlier regularly place emblems of Upper Egypt on

9. K. Sethe, *Urkunden der 18. Dynastie*, (Leipzig, 1907) p. 808, cited, along with kindred material, by H. Grapow, *Die bildlichen Ausdrücke des Aegyptischen* (Leipzig, 1924) p. 34. See also Ricardo Caminos, *The New-Kingdom Temples of Buhen* I (London, 1974) pl. 62 (9) and p. 49.

10. Drawn from a photograph in P. A. A. Boeser, *Beschrijving van de Egyptische Verzameling in het Rijksmuseum van Oudheden te Leiden* VI (The Hague, 1913) pl. 6 (no. 25).

the spectator's left, since the southern part of the country has priority as the "front," while Lower Egypt, the "rear," is on the right.[11] It therefore seems likely that, in the case of the statue, the sun and moon are reversed so that the greater luminary is on the back of the right hand, the lesser on the left. It is true that such an explanation cannot be applied to a statue of Queen Isis, the mother of Tuthmosis III, which has a pair of cobras on the forehead, one wearing the crown of Upper Egypt, the other the crown of Lower Egypt.[12] Here again it is the Lower Egyptian crown that is on the proper right. But this example evidently represents an exception; all the regalia of Tutankhamun regularly show the vulture of Upper Egypt on the proper right, while the cobra representing Lower Egypt is on the proper left.[13] And the crowned cobras on the statue of a Nineteenth Dynasty queen are oriented in the same manner.[14] Finally it may be recalled that New Kingdom dyads representing a man and his wife regularly locate the man on the spectator's left. Thus we may conclude—so far as the New Kingdom is concerned, at any rate—that the dominant or primary element of the composition is normally on the spectator's left (which is the monument's proper right), regardless of whether the composition is two- or three-dimensional. In both cases, the orientation is ultimately explained by right-handedness, but that of two-dimensional compositions is more immediately related to the orientation of hieroglyphic writing,[15] while that of statuary may be attributed to a New Kingdom emphasis on the right hand as such.[16]

ABBREVIATIONS

BM—British Museum

CG + number—Monuments in the Egyptian Museum, Cairo, with numbers referring to *Catalogue général des antiquités égyptiennes du Musée du Caire:*

- CG 1–1294: Ludwig Borchardt, *Statuen und Statuetten von Königen und Privatleuten* I–IV (Berlin, 1911–34);
- CG 20001–20780: H. O. Lange and H. Schäfer, *Grab- und Denksteine des Mittleren Reichs* I–IV, (Berlin, 1902–25);
- CG 34001–34189: Pierre Lacau, *Stèles du Nouvel Empire* (Cairo, 1909–26);
- CG 42001–42250: Georges Legrain, *Statues et statuettes des rois et des particuliers* I–III (Cairo, 1906–14).

Wb.—A. Erman and H. Grapow, eds., *Wörterbuch der Ägyptischen Sprache* I–V (Leipzig, 1926–31).

11. New Kingdom: CG 34026, 34099, 34183; Florence 2565 (S. Bosticco, *Le Stele egiziane del Nuovo Regno* [Rome, 1965]). CG 34025 exceptionally reverses the orientation. Middle Kingdom: CG 459, 20392, 20557.

12. CG 42072.

13. H. Carter, *The Tomb of Tut-ankh-Amen* II (London, 1923–33) pls. 69, 71, 73, 75; III, pl. 54.

14. CG 600.

15. H. Fischer, *Egyptian Studies II, The Orientation of Hieroglyphs; Part 1: Reversals* (forthcoming) §4.

16. R. Engelbach, "Some Remarks on *Ka*-statues of Abnormal Men in the Old Kingdom," *Annales du Service des Antiquités de l'Égypte* 38 (1938) p. 295.

ADDENDA (all by H. G. FISCHER)

pp. 31–33. Yitzhak Margowsky has suggested to me that the schist hands (both of them right) illustrated by E. Amélineau in *Les nouvelles fouilles d'Abydos* (Paris, 1899) pl. 28, may have belonged to dishes like the one in the Metropolitan Museum. Some degree of similarity seems likely, but the better preserved fragment (also shown in Amélineau's figure 48, p. 211) shows protuberances below the palm and beyond the fingers, so that—in this case, at least—the form cannot have been identical.

p. 34. Another schist cosmetic palette displaying is illustrated by Z. Y. Saad, *Excavations at Helwan* (Norman, Oklahoma, 1969) pl. 75; and in this case the sign , flanked by and appears between the hands, so that they present "dominion, life and duration"; the preceding drawing is made from his plate.

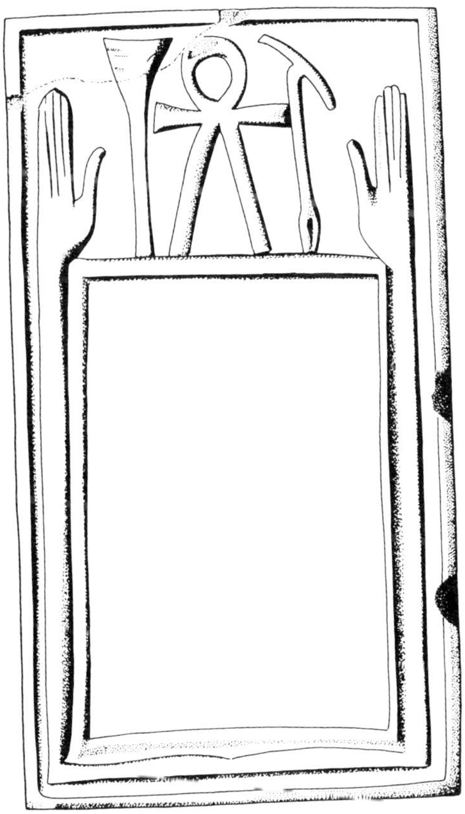

p. 37. The subject of composite hieroglyphs is explored more thoroughly in *MMJ* 12 (1977).

p. 37, n. 24. Further interpretations of the Horus name have been suggested by Edmund Meltzer, who takes *dn* to mean "cut" or "sever," as attested from the Middle Kingdom onward (*JNES* 31 [1972] pp. 338–339), and by Klaus Baer (*ibid.*, n. 1), who, like Kaplony (*Orientalia Suecana* 7 [1958] pp. 54–69), reads *dwn*, but with the meaning "Harpooner" rather than "One Who Deploys the Wings."

p. 45. Among the earlier examples of emblematic representations, mention might also have been made of Junker, *Gîza* VI, fig. 33 (detail shown below). Although this representation is appropriate to any son who invokes offerings for his father, regardless of his name

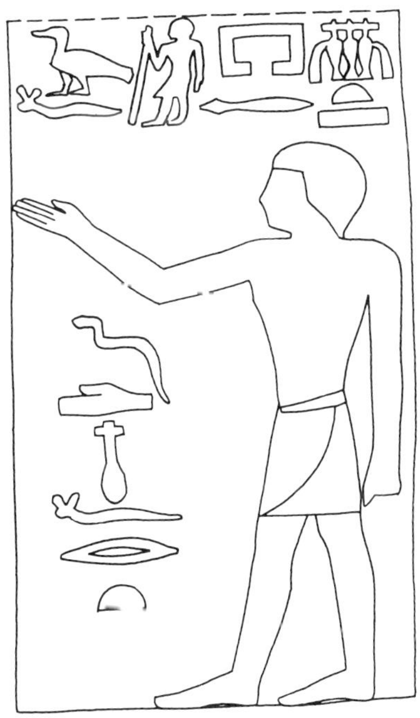

(cf., for example, *op. cit.* III, fig. 22), the way the name is displayed suggests that the gesture of invocation was felt to be emblematic in this case, since the name describes the action of "one who says what is good."

p. 45 (and Figure 26). Cf. also the sign ☥ which is inscribed to the right of the entrance of the tomb-chapel of [hieroglyphs] (A. Fakhry, *Sept tombeaux à l'est de la Grande Pyramide de Guizeh* [Cairo, 1935] p. 4); but Fakhry does not indicate how large this was, nor is it certain that it is not a later addition.

p. 48, n. 65. For Berlin 2293 see also Sauneron and Yoyotte in *Revue d'Égyptologie* 7 (1950) pp. 9–10.

p. 49 and Figure 32. For Boston MFA 1971.403 see now Wm. K. Simpson, *Chronique d'Égypte* 47 (1972) pp. 45–50, and H. Goedicke, *Göttinger Miszellen* 17 (1975) pp. 27–30, who questions the authenticity of the inscription. There are, in fact, many problematic features, as well as some that are difficult to credit to the imagination of a forger; possibly it is a modern copy of an ancient text. However this may be, it is of interest to note that another Middle Kingdom inscription in the British Museum, BM 565 (*Hieroglyphic Texts* II, pl. 10) shows a similar variation of the sign for *iry* in lines 3 and 4. T. G. H. James, in response to an inquiry, has kindly supplied the following copies:

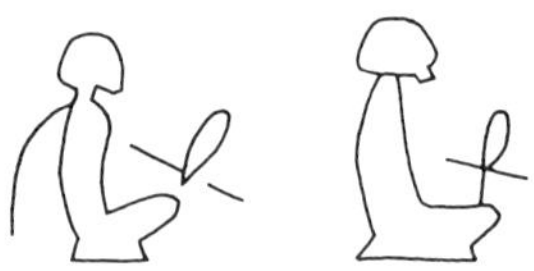

pp. 51–52 and Figure 3. B. J. Kemp (*Göttinger Miszellen* 8 [1973] pp. 23–25) notes that the Old Kingdom dating of this seal confirms the relatively late date of the Khentiamentiu temple, which he had already suggested in *Mitteilungen Deutschen Archäologischen Instituts Abteilung Kairo* 23 (1968) pp. 138–155.

p. 58. A fragmentary tête-bêche seal, probably dating to the Old Kingdom, has been found at Giza, providing a second example made of wood; it was pierced with a wide flaring hole throughout its length: Karl Kromer, *Österreichische Ausgrabungen in Giseh, Sitzungsberichte der Österreichischen Akademie der Wissenschaften*, Phil.-hist.

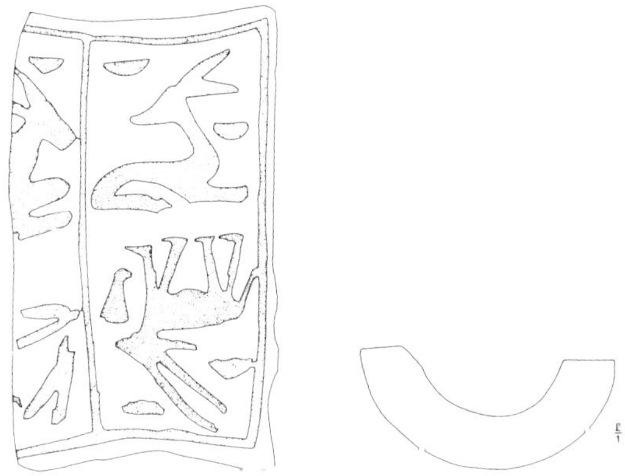

Kl., 279. Bd., 5. Abh. (Wien, 1972) fig. 7 (4, as shown above), pp. 27, 34. This is also illustrated in *Antike Welt* 4/3 (1973) p. 33.

pp. 59–60. For *ḏꜣw* "stores" read *wḏꜣ*, for which see *Wb.* I, 402, and to the Old Kingdom references add *Urk.* I, 254 (9).

pp. 59–61. Like the pair of cylinder seals found by Junker (p. 59, figs. 19–20) a limestone example in the Ashmolean Museum, Oxford, no. 1933.89, is again only incompletely perforated, as Mrs. J. Crowfoot Payne has kindly informed me. But like several of the other Old Kingdom seals that are made of limestone it bears the lowly title of "sealer"; the inscription is otherwise unintelligible except for the names *Wnš* and *Ḏnf* (cf. *PN* I, p. 80 [4, 5] and 407 [2]). The provenance is Elephantine (Sayce, *PSBA* 22 [1900], plate facing p. 278 [B4]).

p. 61, n. 37. For Cairo J. E. 44200 see P. Kaplony, "Die Siegelabdrücke" in *Das Sonnenheiligtum des Königs Userkaf* II (*Beiträge zur ägyptischen Bauforschung und Altertumskunde* 8 [Cairo, 1969]), p. 84 and note 5.

p. 64. Another Vth Dynasty example from Saqqara, like nos. 1–4, with the sunshade held over a standing person, is to be found in *The Tomb of Nefer and Ka-hay* by Ahmed Moussa and Hartwig Altenmüller (Mainz am Rhein, 1971) pl. 18. This resembles example 3, but the flap is completely vertical and makes a right angle with the main part of the shade.

p. 67. For the term *ḥry šbꜣ* "sunshade carrier" see also Fischer, "Notes, Mostly Textual, on Davies' *Deir el*

Gebrâwi," *JARCE* 13 (1976) fig. 2, p. 10. I suspect that yet another occurrence of [*ḫry*] *šbꜣ* is to be recognized in the traces above the sunshade carriers in Petrie's *Deshasheh* (London, 1898) pl. 24; the sign ★ is certain, and the trace above it is probably the heel of the foot in the group [𓏤] 𓃀.

p. 87 (24). The addition of 𓎟 after the woman's name might also be compared with the masculine 𓂓 after the name of a man named *Nfri* in Abu Bakr, *Giza*, p. 59, fig. 39; the name *Nfri* is attested for both men and women in the Old Kingdom (*PN* I, p. 203 [11]).

p. 88. With the use of the det. 𓁐 after women's names in the context of their husbands' tombs one may perhaps compare the use, on a Second Intermediate Period stela from Edfu, of 𓀀 after the masc. sing. suffix in two cases where the suffix follows a feminine substantive (𓎟𓁐𓆑𓀀 "his wife"; 𓅭𓁐𓏏𓆑𓀀 "his daughter"), while it is omitted after 𓅭𓀀𓆑 "his son" (Jerzy Halicki, *Meander* III/5–6 [1948] pp. 279–283).

p. 114 and Figure 1. The correction in Meḥu's tomb chapel is now shown in color by Altenmüller in C. Vandersleyen, *Das alte Ägypten* (*Propyläen Kunstgeschichte*, Vol. 15 [Berlin, 1975]) pl. XXIII.

p. 114, n. 7. For the erasure discussed by Drioton, see now Selim Hassan, *Excavations at Saqqara 1937–1938* (Cairo, 1975) II, pp. 8–9 and fig. 4, where, however, the accompanying inscription is published less completely.

p. 115, and n. 16. For the ritual breaking of staves see now Ali Hassan, *Stöcke und Stäbe im Pharaonischen Ägypten* (Munich, 1976) pp. 122–127. An additional note on the subject will appear in "Some Notes on Sticks and Staves," §10, *MMJ* 13 (1978).

pp. 116–117, and Figure 4. B. van de Walle informs me that he has heard—probably on the authority of Jean Capart—that Alexandre Barsanti was responsible for writing the name Alexander in the tomb of Sen-nufer. It should be added, however, that this attribution was unknown to P. Virey when he described the tomb in *Recueil de travaux relatifs à la philologie et à l'archéologie égyptiennes et assyriennes* 22 (1900) p. 85.

pp. 118–119, and Figure 7. In his *Excavations at Saqqara 1937–1938* (Cairo, 1975), Vol. III, p. 80 and pl. 57A, Selim Hassan shows another deletion of a jackal. On a tablet listing the seven oils, and designed for the burial chamber, the group 𓃢 has been erased in the offering formula and replaced by 𓇓𓊵𓏏𓇳 "an offering that Anubis gives."

p. 120, and n. 42. The nose of the aged Amenhotpe, son of Hapu, Cairo CG 42127, was evidently broken and recarved in antiquity so that it became, as Legrain says, "camard" (*Statues et statuettes* I, p. 80) but I doubt that this restoration had the effect of "depressing the cheeks on either side," as Winlock says in *JEA* 10 (1924) p. 1.

p. 121. T. G. H. James has called my attention to another case where an ancient statue bears a modern inscription: BM 1229, dating to the Twenty-seventh Dynasty. Cf. H. R. Hall, *JEA* 16 (1930) pp. 167 f. and fig. 1.

Although it was—and is—not my intention to cite more than one or two examples of various types of alterations, it may also be useful to note a reworked statue bearing modern inscriptions that name Piankhy and Shepenwepet. This is illustrated in the Sotheby *Catalogue of the MacGregor Collection of Egyptian Antiquities* (London, June 26–July 6, 1922) pl. 46 (1626), and has been acquired by the Metropolitan Museum with the collection of Albert Gallatin; it has not been given an accession number.

p. 125, n. 65. See also Henri Wild, "Une statue de la XIIe dynastie utilisée par le roi hermopolitain Thotem-het de la XXIIIe," *Revue d'Égyptologie* 24 (1972) pp. 209–215; although, as the author is careful to observe in his initial footnote, there is no evidence of any erasure on the surviving fragment.

p. 128, and Figures 25–27. The reworked fragment University College 14346 is published anew by Anthea Page, *Egyptian Sculpture—Archaic to Saite—From the Petrie Collection* (Warminster, 1976) pp. 49–50.

p. 133, n. 83. Another Old Kingdom example of "in his name, in his dignity, in his rank": T. G. H James and M. R. Apted, *The Mastaba of Khentika* (London, 1953) pl. 6 (C[10]).

p. 135, n. 97 and Figure 40. The pair of statues in the Pushkin Museum are described and discussed in greater detail by E. S. Bogoslovsky in *Études et Travaux* VII (*Travaux du Centre d'Archéologie Méditerranéenne de l'Académie Polonaise des Sciences* 14, Warsaw, 1973) pp. 22–40. He notes that the inscriptions were evidently added later, replacing those of another couple of not much earlier date than those who are named.

pp. 148–50. For and , the cloth partly and completely folded, compare the cloth that is held by the tomb owner in W. K. Simpson, *The Mastabas of Qar and Idu* (Boston, 1976) figs. 23 and 25, as shown in the following drawing.

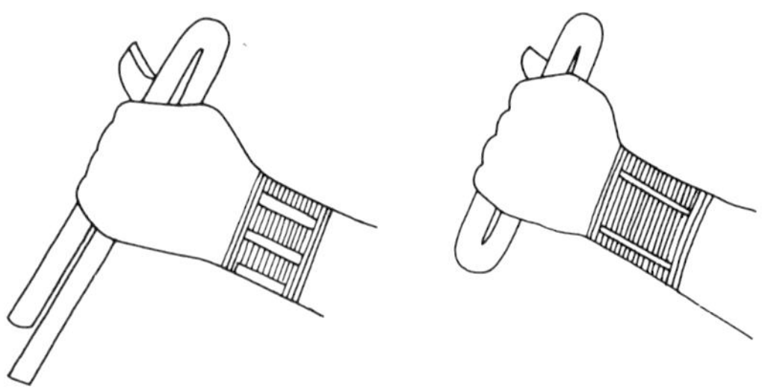

p. 150, n. 48, and Figures 12–14 on pp. 152–153. Dr. Ungar has informed me that the reliefs from Mariette's B4 are now on permanent loan at the Rietberg Museum für außereuropäische Kunst, Zurich.

p. 154, n. 55. One of the unpublished examples cited here may now be found in Selim Hassan, *Excavations at Saqqara 1937–1938* III, figs. 40–41, p. 78.

p. 161, n. 29. In connection with the three examples of *ḥmt* for *ḥmt-nṯr*, it is perhaps worth noting that a King Khety of the Tenth Dynasty is called *ḥm Ḥryšf*, probably meaning "priest of Arsaphes," on an alabaster vase, Cairo JE 38955 (Daressy, *ASAE* 11 [1911] p. 47).

pp. 165–166. Another offering slab of the type discussed here is illustrated in Jéquier, *Tombeaux de particuliers contemporains de Pepi II* (Cairo, 1929) fig. 97, p. 86. It seems unlikely that this example is appreciably earlier than the others that have been cited; the inscriptions are symmetrically oriented, whereas those that appear on Old Kingdom offering slabs usually face rightward throughout (cf. Fischer, *Egyptian Studies* II: *The Orientation of Hieroglyphs*, Part I: *Reversals*, §7).

p. 170, comment b. A Sixth Dynasty example of the formula with *pri* is known from Saqqara: 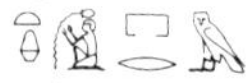 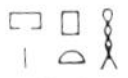 "pure bread that comes forth from the house of Ptah," Selim Hassan, *Excavations at Saqqara 1937–1938* I, fig. 4, p. 19. The Saqqara parallel diminishes the force of this particular indication for the post-Old Kingdom date of the false door from Busiris (cf. p. 174), although it remains true that the use of *pri* became much more frequent after the Sixth Dynasty.

p. 172, comment g. The phrase from the tomb of *Ḳ3r* may be found in W. K. Simpson, *The Mastabas of Qar and Idu* (Boston, 1976) fig. 25. On p. 7 Simpson translates *iw n ft.f* "(it) is for salving him," but gives no evidence for *ft*. My translation assumes that the officiants are sons of the deceased, as the first of them certainly is.

p. 172, comment h. The writing 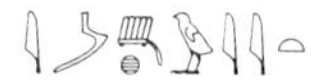 also occurs on early Middle Kingdom coffins from Asyut (Chassinat-Palanque, *Fouilles dans la nécropole d'Assiout* [Cairo, 1911] pp. 167–168, 176–177), as does masculine 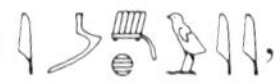, pp. 165–166, 178–179, 190.

INDEX

EDNA R. RUSSMANN

Assistant Curator, The Metropolitan Museum of Art

1. General Index (including transcribed personal and place names)

2. Objects Cited by Museum Numbers

3. Selected Personal Names in Transliteration

4. Royal Names in Transliteration

5. Divine Names in Transliteration

6. Place Names in Transliteration

7. Titles and Epithets in Transliteration

(*Those given entirely in brackets are written in hieroglyphs in the text.*)

8. Words, Phrases, Grammatical Elements in Transliteration

9. Forms of Signs

The initial letter and number refer to Gardiner's Sign List

10. Groups of Signs